B.R. Ambedkar
The Quest for Justice

Editorial Advisory Board

Anand Teltumbde
Annapurna Waughray
G. Haragopal
Kalpana Kannabiran
Laurence R. Simon
Meena Dhanda
Moses Seenarine
Rochana Bajpai
S. Japhet
Sukhadeo Thorat
Suraj Yengde
Valerian Rodrigues

B.R. Ambedkar

The Quest for Justice

VOLUME V
Religious and Cultural Justice

Edited by
Aakash Singh Rathore

Oxford University Press is a department of the University of Oxford.
It furthers the University's objective of excellence in research, scholarship,
and education by publishing worldwide. Oxford is a registered trademark of
Oxford University Press in the UK and in certain other countries.

Published in India by
Oxford University Press
22 Workspace, 2nd Floor, 1/22 Asaf Ali Road, New Delhi 110002, India

© Oxford University Press, 2021

The moral rights of the authors have been asserted.

First Edition published in 2021

All rights reserved. No part of this publication may be reproduced, stored in
a retrieval system, or transmitted, in any form or by any means, without the
prior permission in writing of Oxford University Press, or as expressly permitted
by law, by licence, or under terms agreed with the appropriate reprographics
rights organization. Enquiries concerning reproduction outside the scope of the
above should be sent to the Rights Department, Oxford University Press, at the
address above.

You must not circulate this work in any other form
and you must impose this same condition on any acquirer.

ISBN-13 (print edition): 978-0-19-012789-3
ISBN-10 (print edition): 0-19-012789-9

ISBN-13 (eBook): 978-0-19-099199-9
ISBN-10 (eBook): 0-19-099199-2

Typeset in Trump Mediaeval LT Std 10/13
by Tranistics Data Technologies, Kolkata 700 091
Printed in India by Rakmo Press, New Delhi 110 020

Contents

Foreword by Kancha Ilaiah Shepherd   vii

Preface by S. Japhet   ix

List of Abbreviations   xvii

Introduction by Aakash Singh Rathore   xix

PART ONE: RELIGIOUS JUSTICE

1. Searching for a Theology of Liberation in India   3
   LAURENCE R. SIMON

2. Ambedkar's Critical Hermeneutics of Religion   33
   KANCHANA MAHADEVAN

3. Civil Religion, Uncivil Society: A Reflection on Baba Sahib Dr B.R. Ambedkar's Conception of a 'Religion for Civil Society'   52
   DEBORA SPINI

4. The Gaze on Justice: A Genealogy from Anagarika Dharmapala to B.R. Ambedkar   67
   PRIYANKA JHA

5. B.R. Ambedkar's Philosophy of Religion   91
   BANSIDHAR DEEP

6. Two Concepts of Conversion at Meenakshipuram: Seeing through Ambedkar's Buddhism and Being Seen in EVR's Islam   112
   MATTHEW H. BAXTER

PART TWO: CULTURAL JUSTICE

7. Marginality, Suffering, Justice: Questions of Dalit
   Dignity in Cultural Texts　　　　　　　　　　　　　151
   PRAMOD K. NAYAR

8. Asura: Myth into Cultural Reality　　　　　　　　170
   Y. SRINIVASA RAO

9. Cultural Rights in the Context of Ambedkarite
   Social Justice　　　　　　　　　　　　　　　　　　202
   JOHN CLAMMER

10. Education in a Hierarchical Culture　　　　　　　218
    RAJU SAKTHIVEL

11. Ambedkar in/and Academic Space　　　　　　　256
    JADUMANI MAHANAND

Index　　　　　　　　　　　　　　　　　　　　　　271

Editor and Contributors　　　　　　　　　　　　　285

Foreword

This volume, *Religious and Cultural Justice*, is an important addition to the existing literature on religion and culture in India. Religions in India suffer from two main cultural problems that religions in other countries do not. They are injustices related to caste and untouchability. Though caste and untouchability are constructions of Hinduism, these two anti-God institutional practices have spread into every religion operating on Indian soil. Hinduism does not allow even the richest Shudra to become a priest in a Hindu temple, leave alone Dalits and Adivasis.

Because of Ambedkar's carefully drafted Constitution, all political rights, including the right to become the president or the prime minister of India, are achievable by people of all castes and religions, both men and women. However, the right to become a priest in the temple of Tirupathi or Jagannath is unthinkable for any Hindu Shudra, Dalit, or Adivasi. As of now, A. Ramnath Kovind, a Dalit, is the president of India; Venkaiah Naidu, a Shudra, is vice-president; and Narendra Damodardas Modi, an OBC, is the prime minister. They are all strong Hindus trained in the Rashtriya Swayamsevak Sangh (RSS), which is a proponent of the idea of a Hindu Rashtra. However, neither of them have the right to become a priest, even by undergoing the required training, in any temple of Hinduism. This is among the greatest spiritual injustices in human history. Without the right to priesthood to all members of a given religion, the attainment of moksha or Swarga is unthinkable. In other words, the Shudras, Dalits, and Adivasis who are claimed to be Hindus get no basic spiritual justice in Hinduism. In other religions such as Islam and Christianity, men of all caste have the right to be a mullah or a pastor, but no woman has this right. The women in these religions, world over, do not have a way to equally realize moksha or heaven.

All religions must grant their members all religious rights without taking cognizance of their gender, caste, or race. In India, Muslim women, more than the women of any other religion, are denied the right to dress as they like and to have the control of their own body. We must oppose such practices in all religions.

The right to religion, to have the freedom to embrace any religion that one wants, has come under threat since the Bharatiya Janata Party (BJP) came to power at the Centre and in many other states. The anti-conversion laws pose a major threat to the right to religion of millions. These laws must be repealed in all states forthwith. Another sad development is the growing attack on some communities' food culture in the name of the protection of cows. This takes away the right to life itself. This is a problem created by the Hindu right, with an unusual spiritual definition of food culture: that vegetarianism is spiritually valid, and meatarianism and pescatarianism are not. Such a definition of food centred on caste and racial purity is a dangerous spiritual principle. This link between food and spiritual purity (or impurity) must be opposed very firmly. Food preference must be left as an individual's personal matter.

I hope this volume serves a positive purpose in educating people on all these issues.

Kancha Ilaiah Shepherd
Former Director, Centre for the Study of Social Exclusion
and Inclusive Policy,
Maulana Azad National Urdu University,
Gachibowli, Hyderabad, India

Preface

This book forms part of a five-volume publication entitled *B.R. Ambedkar: The Quest for Justice*, an ambitious project that originated during the B.R. Ambedkar International Conference, 'Quest for Equity', held at Bengaluru, India, in July 2017, with some 350 speakers and thousands of participants. The conference took place keeping in view that the values of social, political, and economic justice that were so vigorously championed by Dr Ambedkar are now under attack at several levels: constitutional norms and public institutions created to fight against dominance and subservience have proved inadequate or have been subverted; norms and policy often merely pay lip service to egalitarian considerations; and the rise of social intolerance and exclusion tends to effectively whittle down and even sabotage an inclusive conception of polity and citizenship. The complexity of the social, political, and economic environment in which the value of social justice has to be envisaged too has undergone significant changes: we understand social inequality and diversity to be layered and multidimensional; and the State has to reckon with several competing centres of religious, communal, and cultural allegiances. Despite these serious challenges, new sites for social and political assertions have re-emerged, renewing the call for justice. These five volumes are very much part of that engagement.

Social activism in India today is inspired by Dr B.R. Ambedkar's insightful lifework analysing complex social and political challenges and proposing daring and radical policy measures in response. His approach to critical intellectual and policy challenges may inspire similar interventions elsewhere in the world, particularly throughout the Global South. Thus, in the light of the conference, this five-volume collection emerged as an invitation to scholars and policymakers to substantially rethink current political, social, legal, economic, gender, racial, religious, and cultural paradigms motivated by Dr B.R. Ambedkar's imaginative and creative work.

The project has succeeded in encouraging a wide interdisciplinary engagement among academics, scholars, activists, and policymakers on each of these themes, which are treated across the five volumes. This is apparent from a review of their tables of contents:

B.R. Ambedkar: The Quest for Justice

(in five volumes)

Volume I: *Political Justice*

1. Bhikhu Parekh *The Intellectual and Political Legacy of B.R. Ambedkar*
2. Cosimo Zene *B.R. Ambedkar and Antonio Gramsci: Justice for the Excluded, Education for Democracy*
3. Anand Teltumbde *Ambedkar and Democracy: Critical Reflections*
4. Neera Chandhoke *Repairing Complex Historical Injustice*
5. Pradeep Gokhale *Dr Ambedkar and the Trio of Principles: Liberty, Equality, and Fraternity*
6. Vidhu Verma *Discrimination, Colonial Injustice, and the Good Society*
7. Scott Stroud *Communication, Justice, and Reconstruction: Ambedkar as an Indian Pragmatist*
8. J. Daniel Elam *Of Castes and Crowds: B.R. Ambedkar's Anticolonial Endosmosis*
9. Pushparaj Deshpande *A Constellation of Ideas: Revisiting Ambedkar and Gandhi*
10. Shaunna Rodrigues *Self-Respect as a Primary Political Ideal: Ambedkar's Challenge to Political Theory*

Volume II: Social Justice

1. Martin Fuchs *Ambedkar's Theory of the Social: The Universal Condition of Recognition*
2. James Manor *B.R. Ambedkar: Visionary and Realist*
3. G.C. Pal *Caste and Delivery of Social Justice: Revisiting Ambedkar*
4. Meena Dhanda *'Made to Think and Forced to Feel': The Power of Counter-Ritual*
5. David N. Gellner, Krishna P. Adhikari, and Arjun Bahadur B.K. *Dalits in Search of Inclusion: Comparing Nepal with India*
6. Navyug Gill *Ambedkar, Labour, and the Political Economy of Dalit Conversion in Colonial Panjab*
7. Shailaja Menon *The Fractured Society of the Republic*
8. Karen Gabriel and Prem Kumar Vijayan *Whose State Is It Anyway? Reservation, Representation, Caste, and Power*
9. Jagannatham Begari *Reclaiming Social Justice and Deepening Democracy*
10. Suraj Yengde *Ambedkar's Internationalization of Social Justice*
11. Karthik Raja Karuppusamy *Foregrounding Social Justice in Indian Historiography: Interrogating the Poona Pact*
12. Ajay Verma *Ambedkar and the Metaphysics of Social Justice*

Volume III: Legal and Economic Justice

Part One: Legal Justice

1. Upendra Baxi *Lawless Law, Living Death, and the Insurgent Moral Reason of Babasaheb Ambedkar*
2. R. Sudarshan *B.R. Ambedkar's Exemplary Adherence to Constitutional Morality*
3. Arvind Narrain *Radical Constitutionalism: Towards an Ambedkarite Jurisprudence*
4. Antje Linkenbach *B.R. Ambedkar's Imaginations of Justice*
5. Umakant *The Significance of Rights and Rule of Law under the Indian Constitutional Framework*
6. Anupama Rao *B.R. Ambedkar and Indian Democracy*

Part Two: Economic Justice

7. Vijay Gudavarthy *Development through Informalization and Circulation of Labour: The Emerging Anatomy of an Uncivil Society*
8. Joseph Tharamangalam *India's Paradox of 'Hunger Amidst Plenty' Has a Name: Caste-Based Discrimination and Exclusion*
9. Aseem Prakash *Dalits Enter the Indian Markets as Owners of Capital: Adverse Inclusion, Social Networks, and Civil Society*
10. Pritam Singh *Ambedkar's Economic Methodology for Social Justice: The Centrality of Dalits*
11. Jawed Alam Khan *Economic Justice: Policy and Public Investment for Pasmanda Muslims*

Volume IV: *Gender and Racial Justice*

Part One: Gender Justice

1. Sanghmitra S. Acharya *Double Disadvantage of Sanitation Workers and Government Responses*
2. Mushtaq Ahmad Malla *The Shame of India: Stigma and Shame among Dalit Women in Rural Agricultural Relations*
3. Rajesh Raushan *Gender Equality and Women's Empowerment: Ambedkar in Contemporary Context*
4. Sunaina Arya *Ambedkar as a Feminist Philosopher*
5. Mala Mukherjee *Ambedkar on Women's Empowerment and the Status of Dalit Women in Karnataka*
6. Komal Rajak and N. Sukumar *Constructing a New Female Subjectivity: Ambedkar's Perspective*

Part Two: Racial Justice

7. Moses Seenarine *Organic Resistance: The Relevance of Ambedkar, Du Bois, and Garvey to Diaspora, Caste, Race, and Women's Liberation*
8. Goolam Vahed and Ashwin Desai *Racelessness and Ambedkar's Idea of Annihilation: Post-apartheid South Africa*

9. Kevin Brown and Lalit Khandare *Common Struggles? Why There Has Not Been More Cooperation between African-Americans and Dalits*
10. Goolam Vahed *Can Ambedkar Speak to Africa? Colour, Caste and Class Struggles in Contemporary South Africa*

Volume V: *Religious and Cultural Justice*

Part One: Religious Justice

1. Laurence R. Simon *Searching for a Theology of Liberation in India*
2. Kanchana Mahadevan *Ambedkar's Critical Hermeneutics of Religion*
3. Debora Spini *Civil Religion, Uncivil Society: A Reflection on Baba Sahib Dr B.R. Ambedkar's Conception of a 'Religion for Civil Society'*
4. Priyanka Jha *The Gaze on Justice: A Genealogy from Anagarika Dharmapala to B.R. Ambedkar*
5. Bansidhar Deep *B.R. Ambedkar's Philosophy of Religion*
6. Matthew H. Baxter *Two Concepts of Conversion at Meenakshipuram: Seeing through Ambedkar's Buddhism and Being Seen in EVR's Islam*

Part Two: Cultural Justice

7. Pramod K. Nayar *Marginality, Suffering, Justice: Questions of Dalit Dignity in Cultural Texts*
8. Y. Srinivasa Rao *Asura: Myth into Cultural Reality*
9. John Clammer *Cultural Rights in the Context of Ambedkarite Social Justice*
10. Raju Sakthivel *Education in a Hierarchical Culture*
11. Jadumani Mahanand *Ambedkar in/and Academic Space*

Despite the wide range of themes spread across these five volumes, the collection as a whole is oriented towards articulable specific aims and objectives. These aims and objectives are inspired by and fully consistent with the life and legacy of Dr Ambedkar, a man who was, on the one hand, a scholar of indubitable genius, and on the other hand, a dynamic agent of social and political action.

1. *B.R. Ambedkar: The Quest for Justice* seeks to explore the multifaceted idea of justice in dialogue with Ambedkar's *opus* for a society that encompasses manifold social inequalities, deep diversities, exclusion, and marginality.
2. In dialogue with Ambedkar's writings, the contributions to the collection aim in an overall way to suggest constitutional, institutional, and policy responses to the concerns of justice, and to reformulate the conceptual and policy linkages between social justice and other related norms and concerns.
3. Through high-level scholarship, this collection aims to help identify modes of thought and agency and social and political practices inimical to the pursuit of justice, and to delineate social and political agency and modes of action conducive to the furtherance of justice in line with Dr Ambedkar's own writings and mission.

Thus, in sum, Dr Ambedkar's conception of justice and his life's work shaping the idea of India offer this collection the vantage points for sustained reflection on concerns of justice and its relation to other human values. This is particularly relevant, indeed urgent, in our day, not only in India but also throughout the world.

As convener of the organizing committee of the Dr B.R. Ambedkar International Conference, 'Quest for Equity', held at Bengaluru, India, in July 2017, where many of the chapters included in this volume were originally presented, I would like to gratefully acknowledge the people and institutions that made the conference a success and helped to make these volumes possible.

First and foremost, I must acknowledge the Government of Karnataka with Chief Minister Siddaramaiah at the helm, which hosted and funded the conference. Many put in extraordinary time and effort: Dr H.C. Mahadevappa, convenor and hon'ble minister for Public Works Department (PWD); H. Anjaneya, hon'ble minister for Social Welfare Department; Dr G. Parameshwara, hon'ble minister for home affairs; Sri T.B. Jayachandra, hon'ble minister for law and minor irrigation; Sri R. Roshan Baig, hon'ble minister for infrastructure development and information; Sri Basavaraj Rayareddy, hon'ble minister for higher education; Shrimati Umashree, hon'ble minister for women and child welfare development; Priyank M. Kharge, publicity convener and hon'ble minister for information technology and biotechnology; Krishna Byre Gowda, logistics convener and hon'ble minister for agriculture; and Captain

Manivannan, secretary, Social Welfare Department. Thanks also to Dr M.C. Srinivasa, joint director, Social Welfare Department, and Dr H. Nataraj, secretary, State Safai Karmachari Commission, both nodal officers attached to Captain Manivannan, for taking care of the logistics of the conference organization. I would also like to thank Dr Nagalakshmi and Mehroz Khan, who were coordinators for the conference; Shri Srinivasulu, managing director, Ambedkar Development Corporation, attached to Krishna Byre Gowda; and Dr Nandan Kumar, officer on special duty to Priyank Kharge. I must also thank Luthfulla Ateeq, principal secretary to the chief minister; Shri Venkataiah, special advisor to Social Welfare Department; M.V. Savithri, commissioner, Social Welfare Department; and numerous other officials and staff of the Social Welfare Department who worked so diligently.

Special thanks are due to the Scheduled Castes Department team of the All India Congress Committee: Shri. K. Raju, head of the Congress President's Office, for his ideation and immense political support, and Pushparaj Deshpande, in-charge of the Quest for Equity website and other logistical support. I cannot fail to mention Oum, Navil, Deepika, and the rest of the Phase I team, who worked tirelessly.

I would like to express my profound thanks to the members of the various committees, especially members of the academic committee: Professors Sukhadeo Thorat, Valerian Rodrigues, G. Haragopal, Aakash Singh Rathore, Rochana Bajpai, Sudhir Krishnaswamy, S.G. Siddaramaiah, K. Marulasiddappa, Siddalingaiah, L. Hanumanthaiah, Mallika Ganti, and K.B. Siddaiah. Special thanks are also due to the editorial advisory board for their invaluable advice and assistance throughout, including those members from the academic committee mentioned earlier, as well as Dr Suraj Yengde and Professors Anand Teltumbde, Kalpana Kannabiran, Lawrence R. Simon, and Meena Dhanda. My heartful thanks to Professor Aakash Singh Rathore for taking the responsibility of editing these volumes.

Of course, I cannot fail to mention the support of Shabin John and Chandrashekar for their office and logistics support and Dr Ramkhok Raikhan for research assistance to the editor.

S. Japhet
Professor and Vice Chancellor,
Bengaluru Central University, India

Abbreviations

AIBSF	All India Backward Students Forum
AIIMS	All India Institute of Medical Sciences
BJP	Bharatiya Janata Party
BSP	Bahujan Samaj Party
CABE	Central Advisory Board of Education
DU	University of Delhi
FIR	first information report
GCPI	General Committee for Public Instruction
GDP	gross domestic product
GNP	gross national product
HAF	Hindu American Foundation
HCU	Hyderabad Central University
IIDS	Indian Institute of Dalit Studies
ILO	International Labour Organization
ISKCON	International Society for Krishna Consciousness
IT	information technology
JNU	Jawaharlal Nehru University
LGBTQ	lesbian, gay, bisexual, transgender, and queer
LSE	London School of Economics
NCERT	National Council of Educational Research and Training
OBC	Other Backward Classes
PROBE	Public Report on Basic Education
RGNF	Rajiv Gandhi National Fellowship
RSS	Rashtriya Swayamsevak Sangh
SC	Scheduled Caste
ST	Scheduled Tribe

TPDK	Thanthai Periyar Dravidar Kazhagam (Elder Periyar Dravidian Group)
TTB	top twice born
UDHR	Universal Declaration of Human Rights
UNDP	United Nations Development Programme
UNESCO	United Nations Educational, Scientific, and Cultural Organization
UNO	United Nations Organization

Introduction

AAKASH SINGH RATHORE

Like the previous two volumes in this collection, this volume includes two themes—religious justice and cultural justice. They are treated in two different parts of the book.

Religious Justice

The first part, religious justice, covers terrain that was dear to Dr Ambedkar throughout the entire length of his life. This terrain is not uncontested; indeed, much of it is controversial in various respects. During the final decade of his life, Ambedkar was hard at work on a book manuscript that would eventually prove to be one of his most controversial publications, *Riddles in Hinduism*. Although critics often take this work as nothing more than a motivated attack on Hinduism, what they fail to understand is that Ambedkar turned his razor-sharp rationalism to Buddhism just as much as he did to Hinduism. Ambedkar's monumental *Buddha and His Dhamma* stands testament to his relentless demand that religion be rational.

Beginning around 1948, Ambedkar had decidedly turned to Buddhism as his personal faith as well as an ideology that offered an alternative to Hinduism. On 14 October 1956, he formally converted to Buddhism, alongside hundreds of thousands of his followers. In doing so, he finally fulfilled his vow that he had made publicly at Yeola, Maharashtra, in 1935, that although he was born a Hindu, he would not die a Hindu. To the Navayana, or new Buddhists, now numbering in the millions, Ambedkar was nothing less than a Bodhisatta, leading all on the path to liberation.

Sometime around 1935, Ambedkar had written about 30 pages of an unfinished autobiography, now known by the title *Waiting for a Visa*. It consists of a series of brief stories about the profound discrimination and humiliation that he was forced to suffer throughout his childhood and early years. Several of these motifs (for example, inability to find drinking water, exclusion from school) would eventually transform into major issues that the mature Ambedkar would address structurally and nationally. But *Waiting for a Visa* is not the only autobiographical writing of Ambedkar's that we have.

The other main autobiographical work of Ambedkar's that is extant is the Preface to *Buddha and His Dhamma*. Ambedkar's autobiographical narration in the Preface explains how he came to prefer Buddhism over all of the other world religions that he had been studying, as he states, 'for the last 35 years'. Since the Preface is dated April 1956, it suggests that Ambedkar began the study of religion assiduously in 1921, dating back to his goal of learning Sanskrit at the University of Bonn, Germany. The origin of his interest in Buddhism is described by Ambedkar in a detailed account of his sceptical and rationalistic reading of Hindu works (specifically the Mahabharata and the Ramayana). However, the important point here is not his sceptical attitude against Hindu writings (for example, his deep aversion to Rama's treatment of Sita, which he refers to as 'beastly behavior'), but that he carries precisely that same attitude where Buddhist writings are concerned. Ambedkar subjects Buddhist scripture to the identical sceptical inquiry that he had subjected Hindu scripture to. The rejection of the four noble truths is precisely a result of this scepticism. The four 'Aryan' truths, as he opted to call them, just as the Brahmanical rendition of *kamma* and rebirth, failed Ambedkar's hermeneutic test regarding religious doctrine consistent with human reason. Ambedkar describes this test in *Buddha and His Dhamma*.

> As the Buddha was nothing if not rational, if not logical, anything, therefore, which is rational or logical, other things being equal, may be taken to be the word of Buddha. The second test is that the Buddha never cared to enter into a discussion which was not profitable for man's welfare. Therefore anything attributed to the Buddha which did not relate to man's welfare cannot be accepted to be the

word of the Buddha. There is also a third test. This is that the Buddha divided all matter into two classes, viz. about which he was certain and about which he was not certain. On matters which fell into the first category he had stated his views definitely and conclusively; and on matters which fell into the second category, he had expressed his views that they are only tentative views. (Ambedkar 2011, xxxi)

Beyond Ambedkar's position on conversion, his exposé of the riddles of Hinduism, and his similar analysis and solution to numerous riddles in Buddhism (that is, debrahmanizing Buddhism), other controversies also abounded with respect to Dr Ambedkar's thought and practices on pressing issues of religious justice. The entire episode of the Hindu Code Bill is another of many such examples. But it is not only controversy that abounds; it is also inspiration and hope, feelings of empowerment and liberation. It is especially these latter aspects that are canvassed in the chapters of part one of this volume. A perfect example is the opening chapter by **Laurence R. Simon** ('Searching for a Theology of Liberation in India'). Simon compares Ambedkar's mission with others who have inspired movements against a social pathology that breeds endemic and acute poverty rooted in social injustice. Evoking the words of such social visionaries as Fr Gustavo Gutierrez, W.E.B. DuBois, James Baldwin, and Paulo Freire, the author places the work of Ambedkar in a global context and shows the epoch-changing potential of his rejection of a psychological state of mind that trapped Dalits in the delusion of birth-based hierarchy. Ambedkar, like Moses, the author contends, did not reach the Promised Land, for they both died in the wilderness. However, concepts of justice and human dignity prevailed and are evident in the new-found assertiveness of the oppressed.

The next chapter by **Kanchana Mahadevan** ('Ambedkar's Critical Hermeneutics of Religion') explores Ambedkar's reading of the Gita as a practice of critical hermeneutics. Mahadevan attempts to situate Ambedkar's interpretation of the Gita within the hermeneutic tradition by comparing it to Juergen Habermas's project of critical hermeneutics. The author argues that Ambedkar develops his own perspective to the Gita by scrutinizing interpretations that were politically nationalist (such as Tilak's) and psychological (such as Gandhi's). Ambedkar critiques both interpretations as rooted in the violence of varna. The latter can be critiqued and transcended only through a socially and historically responsible interpretation. Moreover, for Ambedkar, readings of texts are often intertextual, whereby an egalitarian reading of the Gita becomes possible through its relation to Buddhism.

Debora Spini ('Civil Religion, Uncivil Society: A Reflection on Baba Sahib Dr B.R. Ambedkar's Conception of a "Religion for Civil Society"') next hones in on a particular idea mentioned by Mahadevan, and pursues a reflection upon it in the fourth chapter: That is, her chapter critically reconsiders some aspects of Ambedkar's thoughts on religion—specifically, whether only the form of religion such as that which Ambedkar espoused, which is more concerned with creating social bonds than with a quest for a transcendental God, can be fully compatible with a democratic public sphere. Spini elucidates the reasons for discarding the transcendental hypothesis while appreciating Ambedkar's legacy in the contemporary debate on religion's role in political conflict.

In the fourth chapter, **Priyanka Jha** ('The Gaze on Justice: A Genealogy from Anagarika Dharmapala to B.R. Ambedkar') traces a genealogy of innovative and unorthodox reinterpretations of Buddhism. Jha takes up four thinkers—Anagarika Dharmapala, Dharmanand Kosambi, Ananda K. Coomaraswamy, and Rahul Sankrityayan—who dynamically drew from Buddhism in the late nineteenth and early twentieth centuries. These forerunners initiated discourses of dignity and self-worth based on the life and teachings of the Buddha. In this respect, they can be seen as sources of foundation or inspiration for the unique approach of Ambedkar in Navayana Buddhism.

Next, **Bansidhar Deep** ('B.R. Ambedkar's Philosophy of Religion') discusses how Ambedkar engaged religions from the perspective of philosophy. According to Deep, this approach was necessary to unshackle the dogmas of the Hindu social order, responsible for oppression, domination, and discrimination of the 'lower castes' and women. According to the author, Ambedkar delved into epistemology in an effort to replace Hindu dogma with an alternative knowledge system. For Ambedkar, philosophy was meant to reconstruct the world, not just to explain it. Just as for Buddha, for Ambedkar too religion is meant to bring happiness to the world, but not to explain its origins. Ambedkar's philosophy changes the narrative of religion, evolving from dogmatism to a rationalistic conception of religion that thus paves the way for equality.

In the final chapter of Part One on religious justice, **Matthew H. Baxter** ('Two Concepts of Conversion at Meenakshipuram: Seeing through Ambedkar's Buddhism and Being Seen in EVR's Islam') insightfully adds texture to the question of conversion. Baxter uncovers, he argues, two different concepts for understanding the relationship between mass conversion and democracy. Taking issue with the standard assumption that Ambedkar's notion of conversion is as a psychic process of changing ones principles in order to see the world differently, Baxter proposes that the historic 1981 conversion at Meenakshipuram is better framed with reference to E.V. Ramasami's (EVR's) notion of conversion as an exterior somatic process of changing appearances, so as to be seen differently in the world. These two concepts of conversion—seeing differently versus being seen differently—raise alternative ways of engaging with issues of text, force, foreignness, time, and Marxism.

These latter aspects of Baxter's impressive work take us from religious justice to cultural justice, or the second main part of this volume.

Cultural Justice

Part Two of the present volume turns to cultural justice, about which Dr Ambedkar was often puzzled and concerned. Ambedkar was aware that culture was a double-edged sword. On the one hand, culture nurtures the individual and provides the environment for the exercise of liberating human agency. But on the other hand, culture can also undermine human agency and sustain subservience and marginality. Thus, culture is yet another sphere within which we must be ever-attuned to the dictates of justice.

Earlier in this Introduction we looked at autobiographical expression in relation to Ambedkar's particular experiences and aspects related to religious justice, such as conversion. There is also a great deal in these writings that bears an impact upon cultural justice, which is explored here. In particular, we should draw attention to the idea of dignity, because this is a concept that several essays in Part Two, on cultural justice, focus upon. In Ambedkar's own story we find the intertwining of dignity and self-respect with the cultural dimensions of caste. This would prove in later years to become a recurring theme throughout Dalit autobiography as a genre of its own, and Dalit literature more broadly.

There is no doubt, for example, that self-respect is one of the most recurring motifs in Eknath Awad's powerful autobiography,

Strike a Blow to Change the World (Awad 2018), which is heavily infused with reflections on the cultural logic of caste, especially in terms of the psychology of violence. Worth recalling here is Frantz Fanon's masterpiece, *The Wretched of the Earth* (Fanon [1961] 2004), on the necessity of violence for decolonization, as it seems to resonate well with Eknath Awad's own experiences. According to Fanon, violence righteously exercised by the oppressed has an emancipatory and cathartic power that allows a colonized (read caste-oppressed) subject to physically and psychologically liberate herself. It allows her to recreate herself with a new, positive identity grounded in essential equality, ultimately laying the ground of self-respect.

Awad's book, right along these same lines, is peppered with episodes of sacrifices that had to be made toward the crucial end of self-respect. For example:

> When the Dalit begins to discover selfhood and self-respect, she begins to speak out. When she speaks out, there's always a backlash and atrocities happen. … For four wounds inflicted, only one may be returned, but even this change is very significant. (Awad 2018, 209)

Or:

> At every festival or village event, the Mangs would play the *haalki* [a simple percussion instrument] and *shehnai* [a double-reed Indic oboe]. … The Mangs were not paid for their Mangbaajaa. … And so, the bonfire of [a] village's musical instruments was set alight. When those beautiful *shehnais* were burning, I felt bad but it was the self-respect that I could see generated in the Mangs through these flames that was of prime importance. (Awad 2018, 182–3)

In a certain sense, Awad's autobiography functions as a guide for achieving self-respect. The term itself appears dozens of times throughout the book, and always within the most poignant of events—for example, in passages describing families suffering from hunger but refusing to eat carrion; in numerous descriptions of the coerced shaving of the heads of institutionalized religious Mang beggars (the *potraj*); and whenever the question of education arises.

Indeed, Awad even saw his long years of development work and social activism as geared ultimately toward helping Dalits to attain this immaterial, but priceless value.

> It is not possible to solve the problem of untouchability by providing the Dalit with food and building a few cement houses for them. It is much more important to awaken their sense of self-respect. (Awad 2018, 118)

Another early and famous autobiography—entitled *Baluta*—by the activist, poet, and writer Daya Pawar, confirms precisely all of these same motifs. Pawar records how Ambedkarites would go from village to village 'urging the Mahars ... to refuse demeaning labour, to live with self-respect' (Pawar 2015, 95). Interestingly, throughout Pawar's book, Dr Ambedkar himself is represented as the perfect incarnation of self-respect.

> As long as Babasaheb was alive, he was a vital force in politics. ... 'Maharki is slavery. We won't do this work!' was the slogan of self-respect that resounded in our world. We now had the power and the courage to bring down mountains. (Pawar 2015, 213)

Part of this was because, as Pawar points out, Dalits everywhere were inspired by the Mahad agitation that Ambedkar had led—the great Dalit revolt for dignity and self-respect. Another big component was, of course, his role in shaping the egalitarian Constitution of India (Pawar 2015, 133).

We find that a parallel cultural logic unfolds in another explosively powerful work of Dalit literature, Baburao Bagul's *Jevha Mi Jaat Chorli Hoti* (When I Hid My Caste). Unlike *Baluta*, Bagul's book is not an autobiography, but a collection of short stories, each of which is eruptive, disruptive, and cathartically poignant. Originally published in 1963 when Bagul was a feisty 32-year-old (that is, a decade before the launch of the revolutionary Dalit Panthers, in which he played an inspirational role), *Jevha Mi Jaat Chorli Hoti* shocked the Marathi literary community, which had been dominated by the formalist style of 'high-caste' authors. It shocked because of the explicit, anti-romantic representation of violence, penury, rape, and caste humiliation, and because its protagonists consisted of a motley cast of pimps, prostitutes, gangsters, and outcastes. Decades on, all of these are the hackneyed staples of contemporary fiction, but Baburao Bagul's work continues to move the reader in other, even more reflective ways.

One such way is the light that Bagul's fiction throws upon our cultures of systemic exploitation—whether it be in terms of the reliance of 'upper-caste' people living in the centre of villages upon the crucial, multifaceted services of destitute residents of the Maharwadas, the reliance of townships upon the dehumanizing sanitation system imposed on Methars and Bhangis, or the stifling patriarchal system, a pillar of which rests upon Dalit prostitutes. Several of the chapters on cultural justice in this volume will make mention of these very phenomena.

Many of Bagul's characters are engaged in defying the social roles thrust upon them, and some of them are triumphant (the story 'Bohada'—about 'the village Mahar' who irrepressibly asserts himself and ends up dominating a village festival, to the awe and astonishment of everyone—is probably the best example). But, for the most part, such revolutions end tragically ('Revolt'—about a brilliant boy forced to give up his studies to inherit his father's job of cleaning dry toilets with his bare hands, may be the most agonizing example). Bagul's stories thereby dramatize the lesson of all reform movements: it takes more than a solitary individual, no matter how gifted, to overturn a hydra-headed system of oppression. It is within this backdrop that the chapters in Part Two explore cultural justice.

While Ambedkar eschews violence, there is no question that Eknath Awad and Ambedkar meet with one voice on the crucial importance of awakening self-respect, an idea confirmed by numerous Dalit activists and authors, such as Daya Pawar and Baburao Bagul. Ambedkar summed up this conception of dignity and self-respect beautifully in an essay condemning the patronizing attitude that leaders of the nationalist movement had with regards to Dalits. In it, Ambedkar points out that the impoverishment of Dalits, which they have been forced to endure for centuries, is of less consequence than the 'insult and indignity' that it has been their misfortune to bear.

> I have no doubt that what [Dalits] expect to happen in a sovereign and free India is a complete destruction of Brahmanism as a philosophy of life and as a social order. If I may say so, the servile classes do not care for social amelioration. The want and poverty which has been their lot is nothing to them as compared to the insult and indignity which they have to bear as a result of the vicious social order. Not bread but honour is what they want. (Ambedkar 1991, 212–13)

In Part Two of the present volume, each of the contributors, often in dialogue with the writings of Ambedkar, take up issues of central relevance to explore the nature and destiny of cultural justice, either as such or specifically in terms of their interpretation of Dr Ambedkar's own position. In the first chapter of Part Two, **Pramod K. Nayar** ('Marginality, Suffering, Justice: Questions of Dalit Dignity in Cultural Texts') turns to the question of dignity. According to Nayar, Dalit dignity is organized around caste-determined labour that fits them into hierarchies of social dignity but which, in savage irony, renders them undignified as humans through social death. He also argues as a corollary, however, that the self-conscious, agential narrative enactment of life-as-death and the performance of death enables the Dalit text to establish the dignity of the Dalit body.

Y. Srinivasa Rao ('Asura: Myth into Cultural Reality') then takes the reader into the fascinating landscape of culture and counterculture. He concentrates on the cultural construction of subalternity, and the resistance of this process by counter-narratives. According to Rao, Ambedkar, Periyar, and Phule created counter-narratives, but in order to sustain counter-narratives subalterns have to also popularize the hegemonic narratives of their ideological masters. Rao speaks of this and related processes as demythicalization. The author's burden is to begin to historicize and demythicalize the mythical *asura* [demigod], in order to support the spreading and longevity of counter-narratives such as Ambedkar's.

In the next chapter, **John Clammer** ('Cultural Rights in the Context of Ambedkarite Social Justice') addresses cultural rights. In particular, he tries to reframe the question of cultural rights in relation to human rights, which he then broadens out to questions of social justice, and then places that, in turn, within questions of peace and sustainability. The author introduces these topics at a theoretical level, after which he roots them in the context of Indian culture, and in the nature of Ambedkar's thought. As such, Clammer attempts to justify the concept of cultural rights and argue for an expansive notion of social justice that includes cultural rights and which provokes new thinking about policies designed to alleviate the situation of marginalized and disadvantaged groups.

Raju Sakthivel ('Education in a Hierarchical Culture') then changes the orientation towards the interface of pedagogy and culture. The author argues that the postcolonial state in India is itself embedded into the culture of caste-grid values of Hinduism, and thus the State has failed in its role to ensure human dignity.

Relying on Ambedkar's own position on the issue, and supplementing this by documentary evidence, Sakthivel critiques the contradictory nature of the Indian state, which has invested more in 'silicon valleys' than in slates, the symbolic expression for universal primary education.

The final chapter of the volume also addresses issues of pedagogy and culture, but not pedagogy at the level of primary education; rather, that of academia. **Jadumani Mahanand** ('Ambedkar in/and Academic Space') takes up the issue of Ambedkar's radically egalitarian ethos and thought and how it is included and/or excluded from the university curriculum in order to problematize our idea of academic space. Mahanand asks: Why is Ambedkar's work not as visible as compared to other figures such as Gandhi, Nehru, Patel, or Tagore? The author suggests that Ambedkar's political thought becomes reduced to a form of identity politics, and, in the process, becoming a zone of contestation in university spaces, whether inside or outside the classroom (for example, in student politics, seminar presentations, discussions in library canteens, and so forth). This reduction serves to protect the interests of certain social strata that dominate academia. Indeed, the author suggests that exclusion of Ambedkar's political thought protects privileged knowledge systems in the university setting. Mahanand links this privileging of certain social strata and knowledge systems that support their dominance to the current crisis of higher education in India as well as the phenomenon of student suicides.

With Mahanand's chapter, volume five comes to a close.

Where, then, do we go from here? Action is required, beyond only study and scholarship, if we are to effect change. Thankfully, we are not left without guidance and knowledge about what it is exactly that we each ought to be doing. That work was perfectly well captured in the Conclusion of the Bengaluru Declaration (2017). Citing that text would seem to be a fitting way to bring to a close this Introduction to the final volume of this five-volume collection.

> India's founders consciously chose to create a society where each individual—irrespective of caste, gender, ethnicity, region, religion, income capacities or ideological inclination—was to be recognised, by both the State and by every other citizen, as possessor of equal value and inalienable dignity. They sought to ensure that every

person had equal access to the promise of this nation. In the last 70 years the leaders of modern India have strived to ensure that every citizen—especially SCs, STs, OBCs, Women and Minorities—enjoyed equal rights and that no one gets left, or held behind.

Regressive social and political forces have consistently resisted and tried to undermine both the constitutional idea of India and the efforts of the State in the last 70 years. These forces also seek to homogenise India and restore the principles of hierarchy, patriarchy and fundamentalism that Babasaheb Ambedkar, Jawaharlal Nehru, Jagjivan Ram, Vallabhai Patel, Maulana Azad and other founders rejected at the birth of the nation. Now that they enjoy State power, they are systematically dismantling the institutions that are the foundations of our society, by undermining India's holistic welfare and affirmative action architecture and by destroying the pluralistic fabric of our nation. This poses a grave threat to the idea of India espoused by the freedom movement and spelt out in the Constitution.

We need to address these concerns urgently, and resist these attacks boldly. India needs to return to its noblest ideals, the spirit of its Constitution. It is time for the Indian people to recognise the constitutional path we chose 70 years ago and dedicate ourselves to protect and enhance this legacy. In this quest, the Bengaluru Declaration hopes that all progressive forces, collectively and across party lines, will adopt and implement these recommendations to fulfil Babasaheb Ambedkar's dream of an equitable, just and egalitarian society.

References

Ambedkar, B.R. 1991. 'What Congress and Gandhi Have Done to the Untouchables'. In Dr. *Babasaheb Ambedkar: Writings and Speeches*, vol. 9, edited by Vasant Moon. Mumbai: Government of Maharashtra.
———. 2011. *The Buddha and His Dhamma: A Critical Edition*, edited by Aakash Singh Rathore and Ajay Verma. Delhi: Oxford University Press.
Awad, Eknath. 2018. *Strike a Blow to Change the World*, translated by Jerry Pinto. New Delhi: Speaking Tiger.
Fanon, Frantz. 2004 [1961]. *The Wretched of the Earth*, translated from French by Richard Philcox, Preface by Jean-Paul Sartre, Foreword by Homi K. Bhabha. New York: Grove Press.
Pawar, Daya. 2015. *Baluta*, translated by Jerry Pinto. New Delhi: Speaking Tiger.

Part One

Religious Justice

1

Searching for a Theology of Liberation in India

LAURENCE R. SIMON

A caste system is an ancient form of social distinction among hereditary classes with some inheriting exclusive privileges sanctioned by law, custom, or religion. While belief in the purity of lineage may be a source of pride in a cultural heritage, it may also lead to illusions of superiority, or even to genocide, as in the Holocaust that befell the Jews of Europe at the hands of the 'Master Race'. The indigenous peoples of the Americas were subjected to such concepts of purity of race and suffered genocide at the hands of European settlers. The English word 'caste' derives from the Latin *castus* meaning being cut off or separated, and the Portuguese *casta* carried that further into purity of lineage, race, or breed, thus separating the colonial Portuguese from the indigenous and mixed races. This concept of purity can evolve into rigid social hierarchies of privilege and pseudospeciation, a term first used by the American psychologist Eric Ericson to describe marginalized groups considered so inferior that they have become distinct and subpar species in the eyes of the oppressors. They become the 'other'. The Rohingyas of Myanmar have lived under threat of expulsion. Blacks in apartheid states of Africa lived as a pseudospecies providing cheap labour, forced off arable lands. The Jews of Imperial Russia were confined to the Pale of Settlement, where most lived in the poverty of their little towns known as *shtetls*, subjected to routinized violence and limited to Jewish quotas for education. The Roman

Catholic Church turned a blind eye or worse to the persecution of Jews even during the Holocaust. Resurgent communal violence against Muslims in Sri Lanka, as in Myanmar, is today led by radical Buddhist clergy and laypeople. The Roma people of Europe and the African Americans may live in multi-faith democracies, but racism against them persists. These are all caste-like social oppressions often based in the origin myths of diverse peoples and faiths.

Among Savarna Hindus, a birth-based hierarchy has survived millennia into the modern world. It hinders the lives of millions of Dalits in India and South Asia and even into far-flung diaspora communities. It remains a leading cause of horrendous acts of violence including gang rape and lynching often for the smallest transgression from rigid norms of conduct. And while caste is more muted in urban spaces, discrimination in some of India's finest universities continues to torment low-caste students. Despite reformist movements and affirmative action policies, the stigma of untouchability exists. Despite being outlawed in the Constitution of India, caste discrimination is deeply embedded in culture derived from ancient scripture. Poverty in India disproportionately affects low-caste and tribal peoples.[1]

In countries with caste-bound poverty and inequality, social movements with religious leaders in the forefront have been an essential part of societal change for inclusive development. The Anglican Archbishop Desmond Tutu may have been the most recognizable and beloved figure internationally, yet many members

---

[1] India has one in three of the world's poor population, with 30 per cent of its people living below the international USD 1.90 per day poverty line. Incomes of the poorest are growing slower than average in India (World Bank 2016b). Poverty in India affects not only material well-being but also rights of the poor. Educational access has expanded dramatically for primary and secondary education and across castes and income groups (Marmolejo and Beteille 2017). Yet, tertiary education as well as effective job training absorb a relatively small percentage of the 270 million Indians who are poor by World Bank standards. Twenty-seven per cent are poor in India's small villages, which also have the highest percentage of poverty in the country. While only 28 per cent of Indians belong to Scheduled Castes and Scheduled Tribes (that is, those recognized by the government), they represent 43 per cent of the nation's poor. Forty-five per cent of India's poor are illiterate (World Bank 2016a). India's poverty profile is dismal, especially in caste-bound rural areas.

of the South African clergy risked their lives to oppose apartheid. Rabbi Ben Isaacson was a modern-day prophet who, as an early anti-apartheid leader, lived under death threat, police harassment, and then a long but vocal exile in Zimbabwe. For others, such opposition came slowly out of fear of retribution or in the case of the Dutch Reformed Church (the major church of the Afrikaner population), it required a soul-searching overhaul of their beliefs.

> Some of the major Christian churches gave their blessing to the system of apartheid. And many of its early proponents prided themselves in being Christians. Indeed, the system of apartheid was regarded as stemming from the mission of the church. ... Religious communities also suffered under apartheid, their activities were disrupted, their leaders persecuted, their land taken away. Churches, mosques, synagogues and temples—often divided amongst themselves—spawned many of apartheid's strongest foes, motivated by values and norms coming from their particular faith traditions. (Truth and Reconciliation Commission 1998: vol. 4, 59)

Rev. Martin Luther King Jr, marched and went to jail with Christian and non-Christian faith leaders of the United States of America (USA). He carried in his pocket *The Prophets*, a book written by Rabbi Abraham Joshua Heschel. Clergy and theologians have been among the leadership of almost all social movements for equality in the USA: from the abolitionists against slavery in the mid-1800s, to the anti-poverty Moral Revival Movement today led by the charismatic Rev. William J. Barber II and Rev. Liz Theoharis. This author witnessed first-hand the rise of the most sweeping social justice movement in Latin American history, that of Liberation Theology, involving thousands of Roman Catholic priests, sisters, and lay leaders working with village-based Base Christian communities in the study of the Bible. Across many nations, often illiterate peasants and workers sat together to reflect on the social gospel of Jesus in the context of their inter-generational poverty, increasing landlessness and oppression, and in contrast to the hereditary privilege of landed elites.

This chapter raises the author's concerns for an apparent dearth of religious leadership against caste in India that would be necessary for a theology of liberation to address the causal relationship between caste and poverty.

We begin then with the creation of the essential metaphor underpinning theologies of liberation and that has been carried through the ages and across cultures—from Moses of the Old Testament to the American slave spiritual 'Go Down Moses, Way Down in Egypt land, Tell old Pharaoh to Let my people go'. For centuries, the Exodus story has been recited in Jewish homes for the annual Seder dinner commemorating Passover:

> This is the bread of affliction
> which our ancestors ate in the land of Mitzrayim.
> All who are hungry, let them enter and eat.
> All who are in need, let them come celebrate Pesach.
> ... Now we are enslaved. Next year we will be free. (Rabinowicz 1982, 31)

Identification with the Oppressed: The Prophetic Tradition

The story of Exodus of the Israelites from slavery in Egypt to the Promised Land was a defining moment in the development of Western political history and thought.[2] Given the rule of oligarchy in the history of Latin America, the Argentine theologian Severino Croatto said, 'If we take the Exodus as our theme, we do so because in it Latin American theology finds a focal point ... and an inexhaustible light' (Croatto 1981, iv). That light emanated from the covenant of Exodus and continued through Christianity, 'drawing its meaning and logic from the history of a two-stage alliance: the first between God and Israel, and the second between God and mankind at large' (Lessay 2007, 243). Political implications of covenantal theology seeded not only the Protestant Reformation but the erosion of feudalism itself. It seeded the stirrings of discontent among peoples indoctrinated to accept their fated lowly place. It shown a light on a path that, though haltingly, led Moses to climb the mountain and to bring a higher purpose to his people.

The story has taken on such life for it is more than an escape from slavery. It is a story of being lost far deeper than the boundaries of a desert. It is a story of a people without a guide, without a vision

---

[2] There is an extensive scholarship on the influence of Exodus and covenantal theology to political thought as well as social movements. For a few, see Boyarin (1992), Brett (2018), Coffey (2013), Berman (2008), Winnett (1949), Walzer (1985), and Lessay (2007).

of authentic freedom that can only be achieved by the breaking of the shackles of the mind. It is a story of a journey from dissolution to peoplehood, connected by the eternal values of obligation and responsibility—not in a graded hierarchy but in radical equality. This was the story very much in mind when Bhimrao Ramji Ambedkar likened his own journey to that of Moses.

In the story of Exodus, God did not deliver the people to the Promised Land, for it is said they wandered the desert for 40 years. They engaged in a long and arduous march; a march far longer than reason dictates, into a wilderness far beyond physical geography. God gave them an opportunity for freedom and self-affirmation. Yet, deliverance meant struggle, doubt, and despair. Before they could enter the land of Israel, they had to shed the conditioning of slavery, overcome the confines of oppression, and find within themselves the possibility of a new kind of community. That community was based on a code of conduct, commandments that discarded the master–slave dialectic of the pharaohs, and one that ushered into history a society based on mutual obligations superior to the laws of man and beast.

Moses began his own life journey unaware of his humble origins as a baby hidden from the pharaoh's genocide of all new-born Hebrew males. Found in a basket floating in the reeds of the Nile, the daughter of the pharaoh named him Moses, meaning one drawn from the water, and though she must have known he was a Hebrew, brought him up in the splendour of wealth and privilege. For many, that would have blinded them to the injustice inflicted on slaves. Yet Moses felt compassion for their misfortune.[3] Perhaps it was at the beginning nothing more than pity but the story attributes a growing consciousness to Moses, for over time he identified with these people thoroughly and bonded with their longing, as yet unformed but palpable in their anguish.

Freud, in *Moses and Monotheism*, contrasts the birth story of Moses with prior myths of the birth of heroes. 'Following Rank[4] we

---

[3] The biblical account in the Torah, the Jewish Bible, is that the Pharoah's daughter unbeknownst hires the boy's mother to nurse the child and that she cares for him at home for three months with his sister and brother. The implication is that they maintained some contact with Moses into adulthood.

[4] See Rank (2004). As one of Freud's closest disciples, Otto Rank, original name Otto Rosenfeld, was an Austrian who extended psychoanalytic theory to the study of legend.

reconstruct ... an "average myth" that makes prominent the essential features of all these tales, and we get this formula. "The hero is the son of parents of the highest station, most often the son of a king." During his mother's pregnancy or earlier an oracle or a dream warns the father of the child's birth as containing grave danger for his safety' (1939, 16). The father 'orders the child to be killed or exposed to extreme danger; in most cases the babe is placed in a casket and delivered to the waves' only to be saved by animals or people of humble birth (Freud 1939, 16). These origin stories end with the son rediscovering his noble parents and, by taking vengeance on his father, attaining greatness.

> It is very different in the case of Moses. Here the first family—usually so distinguished—is modest enough. He is the child of Jewish Levites. But the second family—the humble one in which as a rule heroes are brought up—is replaced by the Royal house of Egypt; the princess brings him up as her son. This divergence from the usual type has struck many research workers as strange. (Freud 1939, 20)

Freud presents the case that the original form of the myth adhered to the usual pattern. Moses was an Egyptian whose father, the Pharaoh, indeed was told his infant son would someday lead the Jews to rebel against him. He was put adrift in the Nile and taken in by the Jewish people and brought up as their own. He argues that the myth could not have originated with the Egyptians for they surely had no reason to glorify Moses. But why would the Jews glorify their leader as an Egyptian? The birth story of Moses was flipped over time. 'What good is a legend to a people that makes their hero into an alien' (Freud 1939, 21).

Either way then, the first triumph of the Exodus story is not the plagues inflicted upon the Egyptians, nor even the fantastic parting of the Red Sea. The triumph was compassion and love for the stranger. For if Moses was an Egyptian brought up by Hebrews, the triumph of the Exodus was an affirmation of Jewish compassion and love for a discarded child. If Moses was a Hebrew brought up in Pharaoh's home, the triumph was that of a mind shedding the adornments and baggage of his upbringing to act upon the oppression of another.

The story of Exodus ultimately is about the covenant. More than a contract with God, it is a covenant among God's people to expect justice, to give justice, and to live by that code of conduct in all relations within the community. The story of Exodus begins with the denial of justice and reaches its apex with the giving of the law. Thereafter, the story of liberation for the Jewish people becomes one for all humanity. We call that *tikkun olam*—to heal creation, to heal the world. This is done through acts of *mitzvah*—usually translated as charity; but it has a deeper meaning—to be close to God, not because you are commanded to do *mitzvah* but because its real meaning is to emulate God's goodness in everyday acts on earth.

Dr B.R. Ambedkar and the Search for a Religion of Liberation

The story of Exodus was not foreign to B.R. Ambedkar.[5]

> The story of the Jews told in the Old Testament is a moving tale. It has few parallels. ... The pathos inherent in the subjugation and ultimate emancipation of the Jews cannot, but affect the emotions of those who are as depressed as the Jews were in Egypt in the days of Pharaoh [sic]. But the heart of everyone who is working for emancipation of a depressed people is bound to go to Moses, the man who brought about the emancipation of the Jews. ... I confess that if anything sustains me in my efforts to emancipate the Depressed Classes, it is the story of Moses undertaking the thankless but noble task of leading Jews out of their captivity. (Ambedkar 2014: vol. 17, part 1, 342, 344)

---

[5] While a student at Columbia University in New York, Ambedkar studied with Jews and others who were deeply influenced by Judeo-Christian ideas of religion and social justice. In addition to John Dewey, Ambedkar studied with Edwin R.A. Seligman, the progressive economist whose German–Jewish family encountered anti-Semitism in the USA; James Shotwell of Quaker parents, whose 1913 book *The Religious Revolution of Today* spoke of the secularization of religion as the keynote of modern development and who was one of Ambedkar's mentors; James Harvey Robinson, the influential proponent of a new history incorporating perspectives on culture and social reform; the cultural anthropologist Alexander Goldenweiser, who became fascinated with Ambedkar's paper 'Castes in India: Their Mechanism, Genesis and Development' and arranged for its publication in *Indian Antiquary* (published as Ambedkar 1917).

On 14 August 1931, Ambedkar had his first meeting with Mahatma Gandhi. After speaking frankly about the Congress Party's insensitivity to the problem of untouchability, he said: 'Gandhiji, I have no homeland' (Ambedkar 2014: vol. 17, part 1, 53). Gandhi mildly rebukes him and says 'you have a homeland. ... I know you to be a patriot of sterling worth' (Ambedkar 2014: vol. 17, part 1, 53). And like Moses, Ambedkar pleads the case of his people: 'How can I call this land my homeland and this religion my own wherein we are treated worse than cats and dogs, wherein we cannot get water to drink? No self-respecting Untouchable worth the name will be proud of this land' (Ambedkar 2014: vol. 17, part 1, 53).

For Moses, the promised land could only be found through an awakening to a covenantal community. Ambedkar had a similar task to bring his people out from the subalternity of submissive consciousness to awareness of their full humanity. Only then would they know a homeland. The story of Exodus and the Laws of Moses stand in stark contrast to the laws of Manu and to the ages that followed and justified the social divisions of caste as a recurring reality in a cosmic scheme of birth and rebirth that only allows a corruption of justice as life-long punishment or reward.

Many religions in their histories have been both the oppressor and the oppressed. The early Christians were fed to the lions in Rome. Roman Catholic priests rode into South America with the Conquistadors that unleased centuries of genocide and slavery. And today Israeli Jewish settlers appropriate Palestinian land in a quasi-religious fervour. There are terrorists who kill in the name of Allah. Buddhist monks in Sri Lanka and Myanmar lead violent attacks on Muslims in the name of Buddha. There are Hindus in India who still enforce untouchability despite constitutional safeguards and laws against caste-based atrocities.

In Latin America, the hierarchy of a conservative, calcified Church reinforced the privileges of a feudal system of separation of classes in an ever-deepening divide between the powerful and the poor. With few exceptions and not until the early twentieth century did the Latin American Church begin a deep reflection on its own teachings.

These were reinforced by the series of Papal Encyclicals on poverty and human dignity. Pope John XXIII issued the *Pacem in Terris* in 1963. The encyclical opens with 'Peace on Earth—which man throughout the ages has so longed for and sought after—can never be established, never guaranteed, except by the diligent observance of the divinely established order' (John XXIII 1963). Yet the divinely established order of the encyclical is not the division of men and women into qualities that determine their rights and obligations. In contrast, Pope John XXIII gives guidance to the faithful on safeguarding the personal freedom, dignity, and potential of all people on earth. He speaks of the inadequacy of institutions and customs and calls for the integration of faith and action based on love of all people.

This teaching continues today. In *Caritas in Veritate* of 2009, Pope Benedict XVI expounds on the obligations of charity and truth on which all Christians should base their social interactions.

> A Christianity of charity without truth would be more or less interchangeable with a pool of good sentiments, helpful for social cohesion, but of little relevance. In other words, there would no longer be any real place for God in the world. Without truth, charity is confined to a narrow field devoid of relations. It is excluded from the plans and processes of promoting human development of universal range, in dialogue between knowledge and praxis. (Benedict XVI 2009, Para. 4)

For Pope Benedict XVI, truth is not relative to one's culture or upbringing. It is the careful application of God's love in the receiving of grace which enables us to judge man's actions, and our own, against the common good for the covenantal community, a community based on universal good without exception.

Francis, the first Pope from Latin America and deeply steeped in the liberation theology of his continent, continues the teaching on love and truth in social relations. In 2013, Pope Francis issued the *Lumen Fidei*.

> [Paragraph] 27. The truth we seek, the truth that gives meaning to our journey through life, enlightens us whenever we are touched by love. One who loves realizes that love is an experience of truth, that it opens our eyes to see reality in a new way, in union with the beloved. In this sense, Saint Gregory the Great could write that '*amor ipse notitia est*', love is itself a kind of knowledge possessed of its own logic (*Homiliae in Evangelia*, II, 27, 4: PL 76, 1207.) It is a relational way of viewing the world, which then becomes a form of shared knowledge, vision through the eyes of another and a shared vision of all that exists.

... [Paragraph] 46. Similarly important is the link between faith and the Decalogue. Faith, as we have said, takes the form of a journey, a path to be followed, which begins with an encounter with the living God. It is in the light of faith, of complete entrustment to the God who saves, that the Ten Commandments take on their deepest truth, as seen in the words which introduce them: 'I am the Lord your God, who brought you out of the land of Egypt' (*Ex* 20:2). The Decalogue is not a set of negative commands, but concrete directions for emerging from the desert of the selfish and self-enclosed ego in order to enter into dialogue with God, to be embraced by his mercy and then to bring that mercy to others. (Francis 2013)

The encyclicals throughout the ages show an evolution of thought on theological and social issues. They were opportunities for the Church to remain relevant, to warn society when it moved in directions contrary to the core teachings, and to persuade and at times cajole recalcitrant Cardinals and give guidance all the way down to parish priests, nuns, and monks.

Even before the 1968 Medellin Conference of Bishops issued the revolutionary break between the Latin American Church and the landed oligarchs, a movement of priests and sisters bolstered by Latin American theologians called for solidarity with the outcastes of their societies (CELAM 1973, 29).

They sought to bring the social gospel of Jesus back into the Church and to confront the stark poverty and injustice sustained by oppression of the masses. They sought to counter the dispossession of the *campesino* from their lands and sought to empower rural leadership for social change. Some of the many thousands of these Base Christian Communities in Latin America preferred a low profile by meeting in village homes to study the social gospel. Others were more assertive. Figure 1.1 shows the church in Dominican Republic in the 1970s of Father Lou Quinn of the Scarboro Fathers from Canada who painted murals on the facade identifying Jesus with the quest for liberation of his impoverished parishioners. One of the murals proclaims:

So Jesus was born
Like this poor Dominican
Child from the countryside
To teach us
To free us from misery

The Catholic theologians of social liberation had a different challenge than the reformers of Hinduism. First, they believed

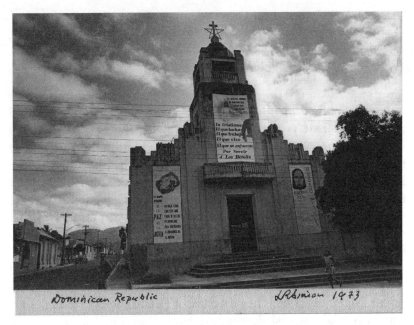

Figure 1.1 The Iglesia Nuestra Señora De La Altagracia, in San José de Ocoa, Dominican Republic, 1973.

Source: Author.

fervently that the teachings of Jesus were consistent with the values of Exodus and the teachings of the Torah, the Jewish Bible. There were several versions of the Old Testament at the time of Jesus and an oral tradition that recited the scriptures. Liberation theologians believed that Jesus followed in the tradition of Jewish prophets with compassion for the poor and the hungry and righteous disdain for an uncaring rich.

Second, Jesus' own words were definitive about human obligation. He spoke to his disciples at the Last Supper saying:

> For I was an hungred, and ye gave me meat: I was thirsty, and ye gave me drink: I was a stranger, and ye took me in: Naked, and ye clothed me: I was sick, and ye visited me: I was in prison, and ye came unto me. (Bible 1853, Matthew 25: 34–40)

Then the disciples answered,

> Lord, when saw we thee an hungred, and fed thee? or thirsty, and gave thee drink? When saw we thee a stranger, and took thee in? or

naked, and clothed thee? Or when saw we thee sick, or in prison, and came unto thee? And the King shall answer and say unto them, Verily I say unto you, Inasmuch as ye have done it unto one of the least of these my brethren, ye have done it unto me. (Bible 1853, Matthew 25: 34–40)

For a theology of liberation, this is the authentic meaning of the Eucharist. It is more than a ritual for the everyday person who comes to take the sacrament of bread and wine to embrace the presence of Jesus. For Jesus called the bread he lifted at the Last Supper the bread of affliction harking back knowingly to the Exodus when the slaves hurriedly baked unleavened bread for their journey to liberation. The sacrament is a reminder of sacrifice and social justice. *As you did it for the least of these my brethren you did to me.*

Hindu reformers have had a harder challenge. The foundational scriptures that shaped Hindu culture and society remain an impediment. Manu described the structure of Hindu society through four varnas (social classes) descending from Brahmin (as priests and academics), Kshatriya (as warriors and administrators), Vaishya (as merchants and landowners), and Sudra (as commoners, peasants, and servants). The very bottom of the social pyramid, below the lowest caste, were Untouchables who traditionally performed occupations such as removal of carcasses, as in Figure 1.2, or manual scavenging. Thousands of years into the twenty-first century and despite being outlawed under the Prohibition of Employment as Manual Scavengers and Their Rehabilitation Act, 2013, the practice still exists.

> Manual scavenging has been called the worst surviving symbol of untouchability. The International Labour Organisation defines it as the removal of human excreta from public streets and dry latrines, and cleaning septic tanks, sewers and gutters. ... The people engaged in carrying out this act are usually from the lower castes: namely, the Dalits. The Supreme Court found in 2014 that there were over 9.6 million dry latrines in India which required manual emptying. ... Deaths arising from manual scavenging are commonplace in India, and there has been press attention turned to the scavengers' dangerous conditions of work in the National Capital. (Tripathi 2017)

Notable efforts at reforms within Indian history have inspired some to believe in their possibility today. Yet Mark Juergensmeyer

Figure 1.2 *Untouchable with Dead Cow-II* by Savi Sawarkar, depicting the responsibility assigned to Untouchables to clear away animal carcasses.

Source: Used by the permission of the artist.

cautions us for the difficulties ahead that need to be considered. He writes of the complexity of religious identity in India seen even among the Punjabi sweepers in Delhi.

> As one might expect, they felt that their poverty was to blame for their limitations—that and the social stigma of untouchability that linger still, despite the government's concerted efforts at reform. But then, with a surprising vehemence, they turned to religion. Because the concept of untouchability is a religious one, they explained, a

change in religious concepts would have to accompany economic and social progress. 'Besides,' they continued, 'Hinduism is not ours. It is the religion of the rich people and the upper castes.' (Juergensmeyer 2009, 1)

Asking what their own religion was, a cacophony of responses included other religions, caste names, occupations, and family involvement in the Ad Dharm religious movement of the Punjab. Juergensmeyer tested his Western notion against the lived experience of the people and found that religious identity and cultural affiliations are more complex in the Indian context (Juergensmeyer 2009, 2).

This complexity is compounded by the overwhelming dominance of a religious culture derived from Hinduism. As the street sweepers tried, one can remove oneself from Hinduism, but the age-old attitudes of caste still affect one's life. Even in a Western nation, cultural legacies are hard to change. Even after 250 years of slavery in the USA, a constitutional amendment, another 100 years of discriminatory laws in many southern states, federal civil rights acts, and Supreme Court decisions overturning laws of separation of races, racism exists still.

Complicating reform in India, Louis Dumont notes, 'Hygiene is often invoked to justify ideas about impurity. In reality, even though the notion may be found to contain hygienic associations, these cannot account for it, as it is a religious notion' (Dumont 1980, 47).

Attempting to reform religious notions gets at the heart of the difficulty faced by Hindu social reformers. We turn our attention briefly to a few reforms that could be described as early formulations of liberation theology. However, despite being brave and inspired, they have not transformed the larger culture.

Jainism broke away from Hinduism's structure of caste and Brahmin priesthood. Jainism dates back well before the mid-sixth century BCE when Prince Vardhamana of the Kshatriya caste left his palace for ascetic life. Upon attaining enlightenment, he was called Mahavira (great hero); he codified for his age the ancient vows of Jainism. The highest of these was *ahimsa,* a creed of nonviolence that for the Jain extended toward all the world's living beings. Jainism is today small with somewhat over four million in India.

The Ad Dharm in the Punjab of the 1920s was an early Dalit assertion movement to create a religious identity independent of

Hinduism. The movement aimed to nurture a new consciousness as a people seeking to free themselves from social domination through cultural transformation, spiritual regeneration, and political assertion (Ram 2004, 329–49).

Jyotiba Phule, from a low-caste background, felt the injustice of caste discrimination in 1848 when he was accused by his friend's parents of crossing caste boundaries to attend his friend's wedding. His hurt brought into focus his determination to reform religious cultural attitudes. Phule permitted Untouchables to use bath tanks and drink water from his wells and is remembered today for leading a movement for empowerment of low castes and schooling for girls. When the fear of retribution gripped local teachers, Phule's own wife became the first female teacher in India. Their compassion extended to upper-caste widows and opened a school for them to counter the dismal custom of widows living alone and descending into poverty.

Earlier, Guru Nanak founded the Sikh faith towards the end of the fifteenth century, distinct from Hinduism, that believed in the worship of one creator, equality of all people, and life-long striving for social justice. Though Guru Gobind Singh, in 1699, abolished caste inequality in the community of faith, debate over caste still surfaces. One view is that castes exist but all castes are equal, while a second view is that caste should not exist at all. Despite this, marriages are often arranged between members of the same caste grouping with mobility mostly within sub-castes. Inter-caste marriages, particularly within the middle castes, are increasingly occurring among higher-educated and professional Sikhs.

The Sikh worship service concludes with the sharing of the *karah prasad*, a warm sweet dough, which, among many interpretations, demonstrates equality of all and the rejection of caste. People of all faiths and classes are welcome to enter the 'gurdwara', a Punjabi word meaning the residence of the Guru. Free food is served here, kept purposefully simple and vegetarian so that people of all social classes and dietary customs share together. The four doors to the gurdwara are said to represent peace, livelihood, learning, and grace, and symbolically welcome people from the four corners of the earth and from the four varnas.

Of interest too is the founding of the Lingayat faith in twelfth-century Karnataka by social reformer Basavanna. Lingayat emerged within the Bhakti movements that 'swept across South India from the eighth century CE onwards. The Bhakti tradition was a social reform movement that developed around Hindu gods and goddesses but split away from the Hindu fold by offering a path to spirituality regardless of their caste and creed' (Roychowdhury 2018). Today, Lingayats continue to protest against Hindu notions of caste.

In the vast landscape of Indian spiritual movements, one that drew this author's attention in the late 1960s was that of Sri Aurobindo. Born in Kolkata in 1872 and educated at Cambridge, he was imprisoned by the British for a year after he started the 'Go Home British' movement. His vision evolved to the need for a spiritual awakening of India. He developed the method of Integral Yoga to enable the human mind to achieve a higher consciousness and an integration into the unfolding of a universal spirituality that otherwise would take many births to achieve. A French admirer of his, Mirra Alfassa, took his philosophy to create Auroville in 1968, a utopian community near Pondicherry where the community would be free of government, religion, and social distinctions including caste. Like nineteenth-century utopian communities in the USA, Auroville could not sustain its vision as a place of spiritual growth unimpeded by the exigencies of the larger society. At one time the most famed countercultural experiment in the world, Auroville remains more a remnant of its ambition than a burgeoning spiritual hub for a new India and a new world.

These are but a few efforts at reforming and envisioning a more egalitarian India. However inspiring they may be, no religious or spiritual awakening has occurred on the scale necessary to finally rid India of its original sin. Ambedkar's social movement in the first half of the twentieth century remains the most enduring of these efforts. His movement was benefited by and contributed to the emerging norms of human rights throughout the world and their articulation in high-level political forums such as the United Nations General Assembly's adoption of the Universal Declaration of Human Rights in 1948. Nevertheless, his work was met with the resistance of an entrenched culture; and while the movement he led hoped beyond hope for a reformation of Hinduism, he called for its demise. Ambedkar used the tactics of radical social movements to challenge political and Hindu leaders to annihilate the very concept of caste as India approached independence and democracy. And there is no figure in modern Indian history who did more to create a covenantal community among the oppressed.

For Dr Ambedkar, a transformation was needed within the Hindu worldview, or Hinduism risked alienation from modern society. Yet it remains the dominant culture of India and has morphed into a political ideology. To tame it in the name of freedom requires a personal and social transformation of Wagnerian proportions, affecting not only the oppressed but the oppressor in a quest for a common humanity. Both Ambedkar and the Latin American theologians of liberation believed that their societies exhibited a social pathology. That pathology was found not only in the obscene attitudes of the oppressor but was also seen among the poor in whom the weight of oppression had created a veil of piousness. The phase of the anti-caste movement today called Dalit assertion is a dramatic result of Ambedkar's mission, for it challenges the piousness and humility forced upon and conditioned by the overwhelming pressure of subaltern dependency within a dominant culture that dehumanizes and subjugates.

Secondly, they believed that religions must confront their past in order to heal society. Peruvian theologian Fr Gustavo Gutierrez, O.P., often called the father of liberation theology, said: 'The denunciation of injustice implies the rejection of the use of Christianity to legitimize the established order' (Gutiérrez 1973, 69).

> But the poor person does not exist as an inescapable fact of destiny. His or her existence is not politically neutral, and it is not ethically innocent. The poor are a by-product of the system in which we live and for which we are responsible. They are marginalized by our social and cultural world. They are the oppressed, exploited proletariat, robbed of the fruit of their labor and despoiled of their humanity. Hence the poverty of the poor is not a call to generous relief action, but a demand that we go and build a different social order. (Gutiérrez 1983, 44)

The Dutch Reformed Church of South Africa, the major church of the Afrikaner people, taught for many years the biblical justification of racial apartheid. As the anti-apartheid movement gained strength, it prompted their religious leaders to look inward, to search their souls and their understanding of their God—and they issued a deeply reflective apology and embraced the liberation of all South Africans.

Pope John Paul II, as the leader of Roman Catholics, asked forgiveness for the sins and crimes committed in the name of his faith with special reference to 'the persecutions of Protestants, for the crimes of the Crusaders; he has asked forgiveness for the abuses of Europe's colonial-era proselytizing around the world; he has voiced regret at the church's repression of Galileo' (Bohlen 1997). The Pope was the first to visit a synagogue and the Catholic bishops of Germany, Poland, Hungary, and France have apologized for the failure of their churches to oppose the Holocaust (Bohlen 1997).

To find the basis for a theology of liberation within the scriptural foundations and subsequent evolution of Hinduism, a respected leadership would have to emerge to speak directly to the destructive nature of caste and varna. Hinduism is highly decentralized and there is no forum analogous to the Roman Catholic Vatican Councils or the regional Conference of Bishops. Yet the movement for liberation theology in Latin America began with scholars and activist priests and sisters and the nurturing of many thousands of Base Christian Communities to study the social gospel of Jesus. Reform in the training of Hindu priests, monks, and other religious vocations would be needed to engage high- and low-caste communities in a similar effort of reflection and spiritual awakening to authentic social justice.

Ambedkar did not believe it would ever happen. Shortly before he died, he converted to Buddhism. Years before, Gandhi was deeply troubled by Ambedkar's talk of conversion, but he poses for us the dilemma faced in India even today. In articles in *Harijan*[6] Gandhi himself voiced the essential challenge to Hindu belief.

> No Hindu who prizes his faith above life itself can afford to underrate the importance of this indictment. Dr. Ambedkar is not alone in his disgust. He is the most uncompromising exponent and one of the ablest among them. He is certainly the most irreconcilable among them. Thank God, in the front rank of the leaders, he is singularly alone and as yet but a representative of a very small minority. But what he says is voiced with more or less vehemence by many leaders belonging to the depressed classes. Only the latter, for instance, Rao Bahadur, M.C. Rajah and Dewan Bahadur Srinivasan, not only do not threaten to give up Hinduism but find enough warmth in it to

---

[6] *Harijan* (children of God) is the name Gandhi gave to the Untouchables. He changed the name of his newspaper from *Young India* to *Harijan* to emphasize the importance of reducing the stigma attached to untouchability. Many Untouchables rejected the name as a superficial gesture.

compensate for the shameful persecution to which the vast mass of Harijans [see Figure 1.2] are exposed. (Gandhi 1936, 82)

Gandhi expresses his objection to caste oppression but makes a distinction between caste and varna. The concept of varna comes first from a hymn in the Rig Veda, the oldest of the known Hindu sacred books. The four social classes were presented in this hymn.

'Caste has nothing to do with religion,' Gandhi asserted. 'It is custom whose origin I do not know for the satisfaction of my spiritual hunger. But I do know that it is harmful both to spiritual and national growth.' Varna and Ashrama (the four stages of life from student to householder, and from retired to renunciate)

> are institutions which have nothing to do with castes. The law of Varna teaches us that we have each one of us to earn our bread by following the ancestral calling. It defines not our rights but our duties. It necessarily has reference to calling that are conducive to the welfare of humanity and to no other. It also follows that there is no calling too low and none too high. All are good, lawful and absolutely equal in status. (Gandhi 1936, 83)

In words that seem to impair more universal notions of democratic ideals, Gandhi puts a gloss on varna that today alienates those in pursuit of social justice.

> The callings of a Brahmin—spiritual leader—and a scavenger are equal, and their due performance carries equal merit before God and at one time seems to have carried identical reward before man. Both were entitled to their livelihood and no more. Indeed one traces even now in the villages the faint lines of this healthy operation of the law. Living in Segaon with its population of 600, I do not find disparity between the earnings of different tradesmen including Brahmins. ... Arrogation of a superior status by and of the Varna over another is a denial of the law. And there is nothing in the law of Varna to warrant a belief in untouchability. (Gandhi 1936, 83)

A noisy debate still exists about the origin and evolution of caste in Hindu philosophy and belief. The prevailing view of many Dalit activists is that caste was from its origins a rigid and unjust social division. If so, this makes the possibility of reformation enormously harder. This is unlike the Protestant Reformation in Europe which rebelled against perceived corruption in the teachings of the Catholic Church but where Martin Luther held fast to the origins of Christianity. Other views of caste in antiquity are scorned partly for the peril that they may give a measure of legitimacy to a hated system of discrimination in modern times. Yet is it possible for common cause to be found with those who believe that caste originally was not birth-based but merely occupational vocations handed down from one generation to another and that caste as birth-based reflections of *sanchita karma*, the sum of all good and bad works in prior lives, came into Hinduism later.

One such proponent of this view is the International Society for Krishna Consciousness (ISKCON), well known in America as the Hare Krishna movement whose adherents, many of them non-Indian, are often seen chanting in parks and airports. ISKCON is an outgrowth of a monotheistic tradition within Hindu culture and is representative of the older Bhakti tradition of devotion to a personal deity. In a statement on caste-based discrimination,[7] ISKCON condemns a birth-based caste system and its concomitant discrimination. Referring to ISKCON's founder, His Divine Grace A.C. Bhaktivedanta Swami Prabhupada, the statement presents their opposition.

> In speaking out against caste, Prabhupada followed a venerable tradition, within the Vaishnava fold, of opposing caste-based discrimination. Prabhupada's own guru, Srila Bhaktisiddhanta Saraswati Thakura, challenged prominent Hindus of that day who claimed that the scriptures supported such caste-based discrimination. Bhaktisiddhanta Saraswati argued against this spurious view in public debates (for which his life was later threatened). He also demonstrated his practical opposition to such discrimination by offering the ceremonial sacred thread and the opportunity to become a Brahmin priest to anyone, regardless of caste. Prior to Bhaktisiddhanta Saraswati and Prabhupada, other Vaishnava teachers and saints had similarly opposed a birth-based caste system. These include, for instance, the poets Kabir and Mirbai, and such renowned scholars as Sripada Ramunuja and Sripada Madhvacharya. (HAF n.d.)

Yet, like Gandhi's 'ancestral calling', ISKCON defends varna as the social divisions of society based on inner qualities that classify a person's aptitude and hence occupations. In an interview

---

[7] Oddly, this statement appears only on the Hindu American Foundation website and not on any of the ISKCON's own websites when this chapter was written.

with *Bhavan's Journal* in 1976, Prabhupada answers the question whether the fundamental values of the Hindu religion would be in any way affected by the eradication of the caste system?

> Srila Prabhupada: The Vedic system of religion we have been describing—the *varnashrama* system created by Krishna—is not to be confused with the present-day caste system—determination of social divisions by birth. But as to eradication of all social divisions, it cannot be done. ... But the difficulty is that this so-called caste system has come in, on account of the false notion that in order to be a Brahmin, one must be the son of a Brahmin. That is the caste system. But Krishna does not say that. He says 'according to quality and work'. He never says 'according to birth'. So this so-called caste system in India is a false notion of *catur-varnyam*, the system of four social divisions. The real system of *catur-varnyam* means *guna-karma-vibhagasah*, determination of the four social divisions according to quality and work. One must be qualified.
>
> So people who want to become Brahmins must be educated to acquire these qualities. It is not enough simply to abolish the caste system, which is contaminated by the false conception of qualification by birthright. Certainly, this wrong caste system should be abolished. Also, educational centers should be opened for teaching all people how to become genuine Brahmins and Kshatriyas. (HAF n.d.)

One can see the difficulty of incorporating ISKCON into a broader mobilization of religious leadership against caste. But could they still be a willing ally in a broad enough anti-caste movement?

> Following the example set by his predecessors, Srila Prabhupada was unfaltering in his belief that no one should be denied opportunity on the basis of birth or caste. At the same time, Prabhupada was also critical of some efforts to eradicate caste-based discrimination through political slogans and shallow calls for equality, or by attempting to expunge the Hindu tradition of any mention of *varna*. He rejected such efforts, well intentioned as they might be, as superficial remedies that failed to address the underlying disparity of educational opportunities that lay at the heart of the issue. (HAF n.d.)

The ambiguities inherent in this view are daunting and would make for uncomfortable coalition against caste.[8]

---

[8] ISKCON is the prime mover in the Akshaya Patra Foundation which feeds millions of school children in India. An independent evaluation of Akshaya Patra's mid-day meal programme in Lucknow in 2018, conducted

The most formidable intellectual and historian of Hinduism, and perhaps the most disappointing, was Dr Sarvepalli Radhakrishnan, a Brahmin historian of Indian philosophy and India's first vice president and later president. That Hinduism has survived longer than other cults and creeds, and therefore should be preserved, according to Radhakrishnan, is no solace to Ambedkar. In his reply to Radhakrishnan, Ambedkar offers the moral argument that the question is not whether a community lives or dies but on what plane it lives: 'the gulf between merely living and living worthily' (Ambedkar 2014: vol. 17, part 2, 19).

In his lectures of 1942, published under the title 'Religion and Society', Radhakrishnan defends the importance of world religions. 'Every civilisation is the expression of a religion, for religion signifies faith in absolute values and a way of life to realise them' (Radhakrishnan 1947, 21).

In a hopeful passage, he said: 'The subject I have chosen is social reconstruction in the light of religious ideals' (Radhakrishnan 1947, 9).

> Human roots go deeper than the fibres of race and nationality. ... We all have the same mental processes, the same emotional reactions, the same basic impulses and the same longings and aspirations. ... One of the recognized tests of an advance in civilization is the gradual extension of the boundaries of the group. Darwin would marvel at the talk of racial purity, the exaltation of one breed of men as the chosen favourites of the gods. (Radhakrishnan 1947, 13–14)
>
> We should not do to others what will be offensive to us. This is dharma in essence; other behaviour is selfish desire. The Hindu dharma gives us a programme of rules and regulations and permits their constant change. The rules of dharma are the mortal flesh of immortal ideas, and so are mutable. (Radhakrishnan 1947, 108)

It is this mutability that is the essence of the debate around ancient Hindu social structures and their friction with norms of human rights and democracy. In his classic two-volume study *Indian Philosophy*, Radhakrishnan presents caste as having mutated over the ages from its origins as a form of racial coexistence.

> The Purusa Sukta has the first reference to the division of Hindu society into the four classes. To understand the natural way in which

---

by this author's Center for Global Development and Sustainability, observed no discrimination in the provision of meals.

this institution arose, we must remember that the Aryan conquerors were divided by differences of blood and racial ancestry from the conquered tribes of India. The original Aryans all belonged to one class, every one being priest and soldier, trader and tiller of the soil. There was no privileged order of priests. (Radhakrishnan 1929, 111)

'In the period of the hymns, professions were not restricted to particular castes. Referring to the diversity of men's tastes, one verse says: "I am a poet, my father is a doctor, my mother a grinder of corn"' (Radhakrishnan 1929, 112). And again the following view is presented:

> The system of caste is in reality neither Aryan nor Dravidian, but was introduced to meet the needs of the time when the different racial types had to live together in amity. It was then the salvation of the country, whatever its present tendency may be. The only way of conserving the culture of a race which ran the great risk of being absorbed by the superstitions of the large numbers of native inhabitants was to pin down rigidly by iron bonds the existing differences of culture and race. Unfortunately this device to prevent the social organisation from decay and death ultimately prevented it even from growing. The barriers did not show any signs of weakening when the tide of progress demanded it. While they contributed to the preservation of the social order they did not help the advancement of the nation as a whole, but this gives us no right to condemn the institution of caste as it was originally introduced. Only caste made it possible for a number of races to live together side by side without fighting each other. India solved peaceably the inter-racial problem which other people did by a decree of death. (Radhakrishnan 1929, 112–13)

Radhakrishnan was influenced by the work of Thomas William Rhys Davids on the hardening of classes into castes.

> It is most probable that this momentous step followed upon and was chiefly due to the previous establishment of a similar hard and fast line preventing any one belonging to the non-Aryan tribes from intermarrying with an Aryan family or being incorporated into the Aryan race. It was the hereditary disability the Aryans had succeeded in imposing upon the races they despised, which, reacting within their own circle and strengthened by the very intolerance that gave it birth, has borne such bitter fruit through many centuries. (Davids 1881, 23)

Davids was a British scholar of the Pali language and a civil servant posted in Ceylon (now Sri Lanka). In his Hibbert Lectures of

1881, he continues the narrative that there is no mention of caste in the oldest hymns of the Vedas.

> But the bitter contempt of the Aryans for foreign tribes, their domineering and intolerant spirit, their strong antipathies of race and of religion, are in harmony with the special features of caste as afterwards established. ... It is accordingly only in some of the latest Vedic hymns that we find the first mention of those four classes ... to which all the later castes have been subsequently traced back. ... It seems certain that when the Brahmanas were first composed the barrier between all the higher classes had become impassable, or, in other words, that these classes had been hardened into castes. (Davids 1881, 22–3)

Despite his view of the origins of caste, Radhakrishnan grapples with the balance of continuity and change. 'Nothing is more subversive to society as a blind adherence to outworn forms and obsolete habits which survive by mere inertia' (Radhakrishnan 1947, 113).

Writing in 1947 amidst monumental changes occurring in India—the partition that created Pakistan, the appointment of a drafting committee for a new constitution, Dalit agitation for human rights, and within sight of independence from colonial rule—Radhakrishnan reflects on the promise and challenges of the new India to be a democratic and secular State.

> If we are wedded overmuch to the rules of the past, if the living faith of the dead becomes the dead faith of the living, the civilisation will die. We must make rational changes. If an organism loses the strength to excrete its own waste, it perishes. ... We cannot restore the practices of the Vedic period, for that would be to deny the dialectic of history. ... In the history of every community a time comes when radical changes in the social order are obligatory, if the community is to exist as a living force, and continue to progress. ... We must purge society of man-made inequalities and injustices and provide, for all, equality of opportunity for personal well-being and development. Today we will be acting in the spirit of the Hindu tradition if those well-versed in our culture (bahusrutah), and keen on preserving its spirit, bring about radical changes in our social organisation. In India we cannot wipe the slate clean, and write a new gospel on a virgin surface. ... We have changed so often in the past that a mere change does not disturb the spirit of the religion. Some of our institutions have become formidable

obstacles to social justice and economic well-being, and we must strive to remove these obstacles, fight the forces which maintain superstition, and transform the mind of the people. (Radhakrishnan 1947, 118–20)

Perry Anderson takes a dim view of Indian high-caste intellectuals who, despite philosophical opposition to caste, do not walk the muddy path to change Hindu culture. The failure he says lies 'in the tension of the relationship of so many Indian intellectuals to the traditional faith surrounding them. ... On the whole, only *dalit* activists have broken ranks' (Anderson 2013, 172).[9]

Yet, I am surprised. I read Radhakrishnan when I was a young philosophy student and imagined him in the vanguard of Hindu reformation. However, his legacy is deeply marred by his standing on the sidelines of social agitation. Christopher Queen writes that Braj Rajan Mani enjoys mentioning that in 1927, while Ambedkar and his followers were being beaten by police for attempting to sip water at the public tank in Mahad, Professor Radhakrishnan was 'waxing eloquent on the Hindu view of life, vindicating and glorifying the caste system at Oxford' (Mani 2005, 356). I remember from those days reading the almost off-hand remark made by Karl Marx and Frederick Engels in critique of Ludwig Feuerbach: 'The philosophers have only *interpreted* the world differently, the point is, to *change* it' (Marx 1947, 199).

Of the reformers of Brahmanism, Buddhism is seen today as the most promising for a theology of liberation for India. Yet, the chances of a massive revival of Buddhism in India seem fanciful. Ambedkar was prescient in creating a new space outside Hinduism for the future anti-caste leaders. Within Hinduism they would remain Untouchable by the larger culture. By conversion to Buddhism, and with 200,000 Untouchables taking the vows with him in a public square, Ambedkar was most visibly the Moses of his people. In the space of 22 vows echoed

---

[9] E.V. Ramasamy (known as Periyar), the 'great Tamil iconoclast', was an exception to Anderson. A rationalist, and someone against religion, Periyar maintained a militant stand against caste throughout his life, led protests, left the Congress party to join the Justice Party in Tamil Nadu, and started the Self-Respect Movement. Earlier he had quarreled with Gandhi over separate dining for Brahmin and non-Brahmin students at Gurukkulam, a Congress-sponsored school.

by his people, he created that covenantal community as their spiritual homeland.[10]

Born in the sixth century BCE at what is today the frontier of India and Nepal, Buddha may not have led an overt social movement. Yet, his teachings implicitly created the potential for a new social landscape. As we have seen, he was not alone in admitting those of all caste backgrounds into a religious order.

> If any one speaks of a democratic element in Buddhism, he must bear in mind that the conception of any reformation of an ideal earthly kingdom, of a religious Utopia, was quite foreign to this fraternity. There was nothing resembling a social upheaval in India. ... Caste has no value for him, for everything earthly has ceased to affect his interests. (Oldenbert 1882, 153–4)

Nevertheless, renunciation of man's social order and an affirmation of an ascetic brotherhood that transcended the taboos of society would in itself have been a stunning psychological liberation for the postulants, especially as most of the early adherents were from high castes. Moreover,

> The exact extent of the Buddhist protest may be a matter of debate but it would be running counter to the entire historical perspective if the protestant character of the Buddhistic reformation movement is sought to be denied by interpreting Buddha as a democratizer of Upanisadic idealism. It is true that Buddha did not organize a crusade for the liquidation of the iniquities of the caste oppression and slavery but there can be no denial of the fact that he prepared the foundations of a more liberal and critical approach in matters of

---

[10] Doniger gives the figure at 5 million Dalits who converted with Ambedkar in 1956. Another 50,000 converted to Buddhism in 2001. In 2006, on the 50th anniversary of Ambedkar's conversion, large numbers of Dalits began converting again. 'As a result, the Hindu Nationalist Party reclassified Buddhism and Jainism as branches of the Hindu religion, to prevent the mass conversions of the Dalits from eroding the political fabric, and several states ... introduced laws' requiring State permission for conversion. Thousands of protesters burned the new laws and in November of 2006 the government banned a mass conversion rally in Nagpur that aimed to convert one million Dalits. 'Despite the ban and the barricades, thousands of Dalits from across India gathered at the Ambedkar Bhawan' (Doniger 2009, 634–5).

metaphysics and sociology. ... In the context of Indian society with its deep roots in hoary tradition his words of social wisdom did have momentous value. (Varma 1973, 355)

Buddha was confronted with the problem of caste in both social and religious dimensions and 'condemns the traditional *Varna* system ... and controverts the claims of Brahamanical superiority' (Varma 1973, 356).

Dr Ambedkar wrote in the Prologue of *Annihilation of Caste* that 'it is not possible to break Caste without annihilating the religious notions on which it, the Caste system, is founded' (Ambedkar 2014: vol. 1, 27). I have reviewed but a few of the varieties of religious experience in India that have attempted to modify or reject early Hindu notions of caste and varnas and have drawn a stark contrast with the religiously inspired grassroots movement in Latin America that brought Christian teachings back to its origins. The caste system continues to corrode the most sacred endeavour of all—the humanization of all facets of modern society and economy and of all people without distinction. This was the core belief in the revolutionary pedagogy of Paulo Freire (1970) to raise a consciousness among the oppressed to reject a state of mind that God created the never-ending poverty of their lives.

For Ambedkar, humanization was an act of conversion to Buddhism and for his followers to reject a state of mind. Ambedkar stands between Buddha and Moses, in this author's view. One represents the teachings of the Metta Sutta, the Buddhist practice of radiating kindness to all sentient beings without distinction; the other represents the giving of the law for a new and just social order. Ambedkar, like Moses, did not reach the promised land. Yet, the values of the Exodus are alive in the Ambedkarite movement, insisting on the humanization of the oppressed, and through the building of a new form of a covenantal and Buddhist community in a secular and democratic India.

References

Ambedkar, B.R. 1917. 'Castes in India: Their Mechanism, Genesis and Development'. *Indian Antiquary* 41(May): 81–95.
———. 2014. *Dr. Babasaheb Ambedkar: Writings and Speeches*. 17 Volumes. New Delhi: Dr. Ambedkar Foundation.
Anderson, Perry. 2013. *The Indian Ideology*. London: Verso.

Benedict XVI (Pope). 2009. *Caritas in Veritate.* Rome: Libreria Editrice Vaticana.
Berman, Joshua A. 2008. *Created Equal: How the Bible Broke with Ancient Political Thought.* Oxford: Oxford University Press.
Bible (King James Version). 1853. New York: American Bible Society.
Bohlen, Celestine. 1997. 'Apology and the Holocaust; The Pope's in a Confessional, And Jews Are Listening'. *The New York Times,* 30 November. Available at https://www.nytimes.com/1997/11/30/weekinreview/apology-and-the-holocaust-the-pope-s-in-a-confessional-and-jews-are-listening.html. Last accessed on 2 June 2018.
Boyarin, Jonathan. 1992. 'Reading Exodus into History'. *New Literary History* 23, no. 3: 523–54. doi: 10.2307/469219.
Brett, Mark G. 2018. 'Exodus Politics and Colonial Contestation'. *Journal of New Zealand Literature (JNZL)* 36, no. 2: 131–46. doi:10.2307/26565642.
CELAM (The Second General Conference of Latin American Bishops). 1973. *The Church in the Present-Day Transformation of Latin America in Light of the Council* (II Conclusions). Washington, D.C.: United States Catholic Conference
Coffey, John. 2013. *Exodus and Liberation: Deliverance Politics from John Calvin to Martin Luther King Jr.* Oxford: Oxford University Press.
Croatto, J. Serverino. 1981. *Exodus: A Hermeneutics of Freedom.* Maryknoll, N.Y.: Orbis.
Davids, T.W. Rhys. 1881. *Origin and Growth of Religion as Illustrated by Some Points in the History of Indian Buddhism.* In the series of Hibbert Lectures. London: Williams and Norgate.
Doniger, Wendy. 2009. *The Hindus: An Alternative History.* New York: Penguin.
Dumont, Louis. 1980. *Homo Hierarchicus: The Caste System and Its Implication.* Revised edition, Chicago: The University of Chicago Press.
Francis (Pope). 2013. *Lumen Fidei.* Rome: Libreria Editrice Vaticana.
Freire, Paulo. 1970. *Pedagogy of the Oppressed.* New York: Continuum.
Freud, Sigmund. 1939. *Moses and Monotheism.* London: The Hogarth Press and the Institute of Psycho-Analysis.
Gandhi, M.K. 1936. 'A Vindication of Caste'. *Harijan,* 11 July. A reprint of his article is in *Dr. Babasaheb Ambedkar: Writings and Speeches.* New Delhi: Dr. Ambedkar Foundation.
Goldenweiser, Alexander. 1933. *History, Psychology and Culture.* Oxford, England: Knopf.
Gutiérrez, Gustavo. 1973. *A Theology of Liberation: History, Politics and Salvation.* Maryknoll, N.Y.: Orbis Books.
———. 1983. *The Power of the Poor in History.* Maryknoll, N.Y.: Orbis Books.

HAF (Hindu American Foundation). n.d. 'Statement against Caste-based Discrimination: The International Society for Krishna Consciousness (ISKCON)'. Available at https://www.hafsite.org/media/pr/caste-statement-iskcon-communications. Last accessed on 21 June 2018.

Heschel, Abraham Joshua. 1962. *The Prophets*. New York: Harper Collins Publishers.

John XXIII (Pope). 1963. *Pacem in Terris: Encyclical of Pope John XXIII on Establishing Universal Peace in Truth, Justice, Charity, and Liberty*. Rome: Libreria Editrice Vaticana.

Juergensmeyer, Mark. 2009. *Religious Rebels in the Punjab: The Ad Dharm Challenge to Caste*. Revised edition, New Delhi: Navayana Publishing.

Lessay, Franck. 2007. 'Hobbes's Covenant Theology and Its Political Implications'. In *The Cambridge Companion to Hobbes's Leviathan*, edited by P. Springborg, 243–70. Cambridge: Cambridge University Press.

Mani, Braj Ranjan. 2005. *Debrahmanising History: Dominance and Resistance in Indian Society*. New Delhi: Manohar Publishers.

Marmolejo, Francisco, and Tara Beteille. 2017. 'India: Is a College Degree Worth It?' Washington, D.C.: World Bank. Available at http://blogs.worldbank.org/education/india-college-degree-worth-it. Last accessed on 15 May 2018.

Marx, Karl. 1947. 'Appendix' from 'Theses on Feuerbach in Marx and Frederick Engels'. In *The German Ideology*. New York: International Publishers.

Oldenbert, Hermann. 1882. *Buddha: His Life, His Doctrine, His Order*. London: Williams and Norgate.

Rabinowicz, Rachel Anne, ed. 1982. *Passover Haggadah: The Feast of Freedom*. Second edition, New York: The Rabbinical Assembly.

Radhakrishnan, S. 1929. *Indian Philosophy*. Revised edition, London: George Allen and Unwin, Ltd.

———. 1947. *Religion and Society*. London: George Allen and Unwin Ltd.

Ram, Ronki. 2004. 'Untouchability, Dalit Consciousness, and the Ad Dharm Movement in Punjab'. *Contributions to Indian Sociology* 38(3): 323–49.

Rank, Otto. 2004. *The Myth of the Birth of the Hero: A Psychological Exploration of Myth*. Baltimore: The Johns Hopkins University Press.

Robinson, James Harvey. 1912. *The New History: Essays Illustrating the Modern Historical Outlook*. Springfield, Massachusetts: Walden.

———. 1921. *The Mind in the Making: The Relation of Intelligence to Social Reform*. New York: Harper.

Roychowdhury, Adrija. 2018. 'The Lingayat Sect: Why Hindu and Why Not Hindu?' *The Indian Express*, 21 March. Available at http://

indianexpress.com/article/research/lingayat-karnataka-hinduism-basava-veerashaivism-4982608/. Last accessed on 6 April 2020.

Seligman, Edwin Robert Anderson. 1949. *The Economic Interpretation of History*, second edition. New York: Columbia University Press.

Shotwell, James T. 1913. *The Religious Revolution of Today*. Boston: Houghton Mifflin Co.

Tripathi, Swapnil. 2017. 'The Dignity and Rights of Manual Scavengers in India', *Oxford Human Rights* (blog), 14 October. Available at http://ohrh.law.ox.ac.uk/the-dignity-and-rights-of-manual-scavengers-in-india. Last accessed on 31 May 2018.

Truth and Reconciliation Commission. 1998. *Truth and Reconciliation Commission of South Africa Report*. Pretoria: Government of South Africa.

Varma, Vishwanath Prasad. 1973. *Early Buddhism and Its Origins*. New Delhi: Munshiram Manoharlal Publishers.

Walzer, Michael. 1985. *Exodus and Revolution*. New York: Basic Books.

Winnett, F.V. 1949. *The Mosaic Tradition*. Toronto: University of Toronto Press.

World Bank. 2016a. 'India's Poverty Profile', 27 May. Available at http://www.worldbank.org/en/news/infographic/2016/05/27/india-s-poverty-profile. Last accessed on 15 May 2018.

———. 2016b. 'Poverty and Shared Prosperity Report'. Available at http://www.worldbank.org/en/publication/poverty-and-shared-prosperity. Last accessed on 15 May 2018.

2

Ambedkar's Critical Hermeneutics of Religion

KANCHANA MAHADEVAN

> For if it is true to say that Gita is saturated with Sankhya philosophy it is far more true to say that the Gita is full of Buddhist ideas.
> —Ambedkar (2014f, 369)

Ambedkar's account of religion as *dhamma* or ethics emerged through a critical and comparative reading of traditional texts such as the Gita and Dhammapada. Although he turned to tradition and its texts for his reflections on religion, he did not regard interpretation as a seamless continuous whole with such traditions as Hans-Georg Gadamer did. Rather his hermeneutic practice's critique of tradition resonates with Habermas's critical interpretation. For Ambedkar, an understanding of tradition was possible through a break with tradition. Moreover, it also involved a dialogical model of reason that engaged with competing interpretations of the same text.

This chapter explores Ambedkar's reading of the Gita as a critical hermeneutic exercise. It argues that for Ambedkar interpretations that are politically nationalist (such as Tilak's) and internally psychological (such as Gandhi's) are both rooted in the violence of *varna*.[1] The latter can be unravelled and critiqued only through

---

[1] Ambedkar questioned Gandhi's distinction between *varna* and *jati* (caste), where the former is a four-tiered system (*chaturvarna*) based on an individual's potential/ability and the latter on birth (1979a, 86–96). He

socially and historically responsible interpretation. Moreover, for Ambedkar, readings of texts are intertextual, whereby an egalitarian reading of the Gita becomes possible through its relation to Buddhism. Such intertextual readings open prospects for peace and tolerance. They also offer ways of thinking about culture and civilization that go beyond the beaten track of Eurocentrism. For Ambedkar's reading of religious tradition and text is also non-Orientalist; rather than emphasize a spiritual otherworldly mysticism, he thinks of religion as ethical and social. Consequently, religion is infused with freedom and equality as well as social responsibility. It is from this point of view that Buddhism, which was guided by the same ideals as the French Revolution, impacted Ambedkar's critical assessment of the Gita and the Dhammapada.

Mindful Conversion

Ambedkar's conversion from Hinduism to Buddhism in Nagpur on 14 October 1956, along with over 3,00,000 followers from underprivileged castes, marked the renewal of Buddhist practice in India after over a dozen centuries (Lal 2018). It also led to the possibility of rethinking the notion of conversion—both as a philosophical concept and in terms of its relationship to interpretation of texts. Religious conversion to Buddhism (and Christianity) has become a routine practice in India by people from underprivileged castes struggling for dignity (Lal 2018).² Yet, conversion is a contentious issue in the Indian context that is dominated by caste Hinduism.³

---

argues that Gandhi did not consider *varna* to be a stigma because he overlooks how caste is not merely inegalitarian, it is rather 'graded inequality' (1979b, 167). However, Ambedkar argues that the division of labour into four inexorable categories inevitably leads to their segregation and compartmentalization from each other. Further, it is structurally based on exploitation of those who are situated in the lower tiers. Hence, for Ambedkar, the inherent violence of inequality renders distinction between *varna* and *jati* untenable.

² Also see Schmepp (2007).

³ See Heredia (2004) for an account of a range of hostile responses. As Heredia notes, even Gandhi had an ambivalent attitude to religious conversion (4547–8).

Indeed, several states in India have even passed anti-conversion laws. Moreover, it has not received adequate attention from the academic community. Ambedkar's critics apart, even scholars who are sympathetic towards his egalitarian mission tend to underplay the complex theory–practice connect in his conversion. Thus, Barlingay engages with Ambedkar and also appreciates his quest for dignity against hierarchical Hinduism. But his remarks on conversion reveal the tendency of scholars to dismiss it as a superficial matter of 'religious formalities' that tries to bring out psychological change from within via the externality of rituals (1974, 153). Barlingay is sympathetic to Ambedkar's project of transforming society to an egalitarian community in which each individual has dignity. However, he is critical of the method of conversion, which he regards as intellectually inadequate. Thus, for Barlingay, Ambedkar's focus on conversion to bring about caste equality is an attempt to influence human psychology through rituals. He is apprehensive about Ambedkar's stress on the psychological dimension of change from within through Buddhism, although he was well aware of the materiality of the problem of caste hierarchy.

Barlingay's response to conversion, however, misses Ambedkar's resolution to change his religion (and that of the underprivileged castes) from Hinduism to a more humane point of view in the light of the material, political, cultural, and religious oppressiveness of the hierarchical concept and lived reality of caste. Conversion was a fulfilment of his resolve in 1935 (13 October) to renounce Hinduism and his reflective choice of Buddha over Christ, Krishna, or Mohammed (2014b). Barlingay overlooks the fact that Ambedkar's reflective resolve was based on a critical and comparative hermeneutics of religion, although he does acknowledge that Ambedkar's momentous conversion to Buddhism in 1956 shifts from the framework of reforming Hinduism to an alternative world view of Buddhism. Ambedkar's conversion both constituted and affirmed a new social solidarity; it was not a ritual conversion to an already existing hierarchical community. With his conversion, Ambedkar aimed at discarding the identity of both the individual and the community constituted through oppressive religious practices. He instead attempted to forge an alternate community that valued freedom, equality, and dignity. Thus, with conversion he moved towards what Habermas regards as both individuation and social solidarity (Habermas 2003, 81).[4] With conversion, Ambedkar integrated a socio-cultural critique and also introduced a non-dogmatic socio-religious dimension grounded in the freedom to choose a religion. He brought together a theoretical engagement with critique and free choice with a practical realization of solidarity between individuals. Indeed, such a conversion to Buddhism was for Ambedkar what Heredia terms as 'process and not an event' (Heredia 2004, 4549).[5] Rather than a goal, it was the starting point of a process of interrogation and critique of both the former and new religions of the convert.

Ambedkar's turn to Buddhism is not simply governed by what Barlingay discerns to be an unstinting commitment to reason as science.[6] Although Ambedkar does uphold reason as a criterion for critique, social change, and political transformation, he does not subscribe to a scientistic view of reason. He does not commit himself to a deductive or inductive materialist method oriented towards a singular notion of truth, as his contemporary Indologist

---

[4] For Habermas the project of critical hermeneutics brings together the individual and society by resisting social pathologies and individual isolationism (2003, 81). This chapter argues that Habermas's project resonates with Ambedkar, who also tries to balance the individual and the society in a hermeneutics that critiques the alienated individual and a pathological society.

[5] Heredia observes that the phenomenon of conversion has four theoretical dimensions (2004, 4543–6). These include individual sociocultural and socio-religious identity, in addition to the economic and political aspect. This chapter follows Heredia in adopting his theoretical framework to comprehend Ambedkar's conversion (2004, 4546–7). However, it also extends it to the practical context as Ambedkar's theoretical reflection emerges from experience of the practice of untouchability and also aims at transforming society. Moreover, this paper moves beyond Heredia in using his theoretical framework as a philosophical approach to conversion with a broad focus on its sociocultural and socio-religious dimensions. It assumes that the individual is the other side of the social for Ambedkar since his focus has been on conversion as a public act. Besides, this chapter merely hints at the political–economic and theoretical–practical aspect of conversion. Also see Viswanathan (1998) for an account of conversion as a critical process.

[6] He cites Carvaka philosophy as an example of the use of reason.

Kosambi does, for example.⁷ Rather, reason entails an insightful, critical, and creative reading of texts as well as a capacity to engage in dialogue with one another. Hence, Ambedkar did not endorse closing off textual readings with singular meanings. As his own reading of Bhagwad Gita reveals, it is possible to discern both violence and compassion within the same text. Ambedkar's interpretations can be viewed as exercises in creative and critical faith. For instead of seeking tangible scientific evidence, Ambedkar turns to religious stories and symbols to critique them and also reconstruct them in egalitarian ways. Thus, Ambedkar's conversion signifies a break with doctrinal conversion as a movement towards cultivating a critical mindset without dogmas. It marks a consciousness change whereby the social disparity of Hinduism can be addressed through the egalitarianism of a Buddhism that has also been subject to critical scrutiny. Such consciousness change is, for Ambedkar, in tune with the spirit of the democratic ideals of the Indian nation that emerged through an interface with modern Western philosophical ideas.

Barlingay attempts to make a case for a material transformation to an egalitarian society without caste. He argues that Ambedkar was well aware of a large section of underprivileged castes being denied access to property; moreover, for Ambedkar property ownership stood in the way of freedom of thought. Barlingay notes that Ambedkar was a critic of liberal individualism since he saw the human being in more social ways than the social contract theorists. Hence, in Barlingay's view, Ambedkar should have stressed on the material dimension of equality, which is in fact the pressing problem confronting caste. In a society where knowledge and intellect are instrumentalized and commercialized, the problem is material. For Barlingay it is 'strange' (1974, 153) as to how a conversion to a Buddhist Sangha can resolve such a material problem. Such an outward ritual, he maintains, may not bring about the required change from within. Barlingay believes that it can do

---

[7] See Kosambi (1998) and Pollock (2008, 53–5). Kosambi discerns its attempt to balance its contradictions as the Gita's 'peculiar fundamental defect' and 'doublethink' (1998, 17). His own interpretation is an application of modern science to society, where science is 'logical deduction from planned experiment' (Kosambi 1998, 37). Chattopadhyaya also subscribes to such a scientific notion of reason (1959).

so to an extent through the psychological perspective on a 'majority' scale. Thus, to an extent, the outward trappings of conversion might fuel an internal change, which is the end of both law and religion, by providing a psychological motivation. Ambedkar was critical of such a focus on an exclusive material mode of social change as it did not nurture social solidarity (2014c). He notes that although the Russian revolution ushered equality, it did so at the cost of freedom. In the context of communism he notes that their disavowal of religion neglects the human quest for something more than mere material well-being in religion and spirituality. It is in the light of such a quest that freedom of religion and tolerance acquire meaning. Indeed, for Ambedkar, religion is not a personal or mysterious relationship between an individual and a supernatural being (2014a, 409). Anticipating Habermas's claim that one needs to go beyond the positive to seek solidarity in religion (Habermas and Ratzinger 2005, 40–7), Ambedkar regards religion as a force of solidarity akin to language. This is precisely why it needs to be reformed and reconstructed.

Barlingay's critique sidesteps the fact that Buddhist conversion is not a mere external ritual for Ambedkar but is based on a careful sociological study of conversion to other religions such as Christianity (2014e). Ambedkar notes that Christians were hardly referenced by the anti-colonial movement because their numbers were small, and they were isolated and fragmented. Hence, for conversion to matter, the number of converts should be large enough to make a difference and establish social solidarity. In the context of a stratified Hindu social order, the very act of conversion offers the possibility of mobility and symbolizes the notion of free choice in adopting religious practices. Besides, the ethics underlying conversion is one of freedom and equality. Further, conversion questions the logic of caste, namely that of being fixed with an essential identity at birth. It introduces the possibility of human beings making their own identity—which is pivotal to challenging the fixity of violent caste-based identity. Indeed, as an activity, conversion is not a sudden spontaneous outburst, but is the outcome of a reflection—a long drawn one on culture and its texts. Thus, the hermeneutics of reading texts—such as those of Hinduism and Buddhism critically motivates Ambedkar's conversion. It is through a critical hermeneutic study of texts such as the Gita and Dhammapada that Ambedkar engages in a comparative study of religion.

Ambedkar read texts such as the Gita and Buddhist Suttas. He did not read them in a vacuum, but did so in the context of what other thinkers have said about them. He contested their claims as well. Through dialogues with religious-cultural texts, ranging from the hegemonic Brahmanical ones to those that were not at the centre of cultural discussions in India, Ambedkar demonstrated that there were multiple and contestatory ways of understanding society through traditional cultural resources in India.[8] There was a Brahmanical hierarchical way of dealing with Indian social order and a non-Brahmanical and egalitarian way as well. In his *Buddha and His Dhamma*, Ambedkar narrates the story of Buddhism in India through Gotama Sakyamuni, who responded to the ritualism in Aryan/Brahmanical society through renunciation and commitment to the ethical (1957). The Buddha's teaching became a 'religious revolution' (against ritualism and the infallibility of the Vedas) that in turn gave way to political and social revolution—where equality and inclusion of women and the former Untouchables in the community mattered. Thus, the lack of shared space between Brahmanism and Buddhism was for Ambedkar symptomatic of the lack of a community or kinship between them; it also revealed the heterogeneity of ancient Indian society—which cannot be reduced to the Vedic/Upanishadic mode. Within his moral critiques of Indian culture and insights (Blackburn 1993, 3), Ambedkar distinguished between conflicting Brahmanical and indigenous cultural spaces. His critique of the Brahmanical interpretation serves as the basis for founding an alternative social order.

Ambedkar's conversion is a capacity to transform human beings mentally, from within. This transformation is the foundation of a community of equals, a community that is yet to come. It is a philosophical rather than just an external legal change. Perhaps such a philosophical change from within is a necessary condition for changing the world from without. For it is a transcendental condition for the law.

Thus, a critical hermeneutics of culture was central to Ambedkar's theoretical interventions, which in turn motivated the praxis of conversion. Ambedkar was not quite filled with the desire to clutter ordinary lives with mindless ritual practices. However, he did envisage alternative modes of rituals, such as conversion,

---

[8] Blackburn draws upon R.S. Khare for this point.

which brought people together in a kinship mode. Thus, rituals themselves are not dismissed as Barlingay does. Further, Ambedkar did not seek a separate way of communicating with the masses via conversion. This would lead to an uncritical/unphilosophical mindset, which was against Ambedkar's spirit. The latter would only reinforce the caste system through a dichotomy between the masses and the classes!

This vision which is a part of the Buddhist goal is for Ambedkar a deeply reflective philosophical exercise of cultural criticism. It compelled him to pursue the path of conversion. A critical reading of religion, especially in a colonial Orientalist context ridden with the desire for spirituality, compelled Ambedkar to uphold conversion as a practical mode of action to resist the caste system, which was so endemic to the mainstream religion of Hinduism. As Blackburn (1993, 3) notes, Ambedkar linked 'Buddhism, religion, kinship and nationalism as a related set of terms with social and political implications'. This led to his vision of community that transcended the domains of nation towards a cosmopolitan reach.

Reading the Gita, Reading Suttas—albeit, Critically

One discerns a subtle and in-depth hermeneutical approach which is combined with the hermeneutics of suspicion in Ambedkar's readings of both the Gita and Buddhist texts.[9] He goes beyond the surface level to unravel unexpected aspects of texts through readings that go against the grain. This is because for Ambedkar, texts are sedimented with prior interpretations or 'preunderstanding'

---

[9] Shah attributes to Ambedkar an economic–political perspective without any concern for religion or spirituality in contrast to Gandhi (1978, 102). He also considers Ambedkar to be indifferent to Hindus from privileged castes with his emphasis on social conflict rather than consensus (yet again in contrast to Gandhi). Shah's account of Ambedkar has clearly not taken his large body of work on religion (2014c, 2014f) and conversion (2014a, 2014d) into account. In keeping with this, Shah does not offer any textual evidence for these sweeping claims. Moreover, by assuming that caste hierarchy is only a problem for underprivileged castes, Shah fails to discern its roots in Brahmanical hierarchy. As Ambedkar argues, the root of 'untouchability' lies in caste Hinduism (2014g).

(Habermas 2003, 73)[10] with which the reader approaches the text. The text itself is never outside its multifarious reception of interpretative history. Ambedkar acknowledges this, but also believes that this is precisely why one needs to engage in dialogue with the text.[11] Yet in this dialogue, one is ready to read even texts that go against the ideals of democracy to comprehend and interrogate their position in the larger cultural landscape of interpretations. Thus, Ambedkar engages with what Habermas terms as 'the methodologically pertinent question of the validity of competing interpretations' (2003, 73).[12]

Textual history for Ambedkar had to come from the space of those who were most oppressed by Hindu caste society, as Orientalism and nationalism overlooked caste. Ambedkar himself, in the course of critiquing Tilak's interpretation of the Gita as political swaraj, did not engage with Gandhi who saw it as a text of non-violence.[13] For Kumar (2013), Ambedkar made Gandhi an Untouchable in not mentioning his perspective on the Gita. After all, the psychological interpretation of the Gita offered by Gandhi ignores its implication in caste violence and, thus, tacitly endorses it. But even though he does not name Gandhi, his interpretation of the Gita as a terrifying text in inaugurating the karmic law which banishes the Untouchable castes to oblivion, exploitation, and drudgery is a critique of Gandhi. Thus, rather than treat Gandhi as an Untouchable following Kumar, Ambedkar regards Gandhi's psychological interpretation of the Gita as the unconscious psychology of the sociology and politics of caste. Ambedkar's reading of the Gita (2014e) is, at one level, critical. For him the Gita is neither philosophy nor religion, it is a philosophical defence of the religious and social dogma of caste hierarchy that is supported by

---

[10] Habermas makes this claim with reference to Gadamer; see Gadamer (1989, 307–79) for an account of his hermeneutics as universal dialogue that fuses the horizons of the interpreter with text.

[11] Ambedkar does not subscribe to a positivist reading of texts like Kosambi. But then he also differs from Gadamerian non-positivist hermeneutics for which interpretation is simply a matter of acknowledging the universality and continuity of tradition. For an account of Gadamer, see Habermas (2003, 73).

[12] Habermas refers to Apel in this context.

[13] Kosambi does reference Tilak's and Gandhi's interpretations of the Gita despite his own positivistic approach.

the quietist mindset of devotion or bhakti.[14] Composed during the Gupta King Baladitya's time (AD 467),[15] the Gita is a defence of the counter-revolution of Brahmanism against the Buddhist revolution. Its rituals, excesses, warfare, and the caste system have been pivotal in advocating an antiethical point of view. These aspects are, therefore, antithetical to the moral perspective of Buddhism. Hence, against Radhakrishnan and Tilak, Ambedkar argues that Buddhism is not an offshoot of the Gita or Hinduism.[16]

However, Ambedkar does not dismiss the Gita as a closed text; there is an aspect of the Gita, namely its ethical dimension, which he takes into account (2014e). For Ambedkar, it is from this point of view that the Gita reflects the influence of Buddhism, which it endeavours to deny at another level. He notes that chapter VII (verses 13–20) of the Gita lists the qualities of a devotee for Krishna, namely that of *maître* (loving kindness), *karuna* (compassion), *mudita* (sympathizing joy), and *upeksha* (unconcernedness). According to Ambedkar, this is a repetition of the Bhavanas or the mental attitude that are necessary for training the mind/heart spelled out by Buddha in the *Mahapadana Sutta*, and *Tevijja Sutta*, which focus on non-possessiveness, selflessness, and compassion. Ambedkar gives two other illustrations of such literal overlap between the Gita and the Suttas. Indeed, he even notes a structural similarity between the form of Gita and the Suttas: they are both in dialogue form, they both endeavour to reach out across barriers and both espouse the leader as a boundless unity.[17]

---

[14] Kosambi believes that it was through bhakti or devotion that caste hierarchy was primarily preserved as a 'basic need' by the Gita during the feudal period (1998, 31–3).

[15] Kosambi also dates the Gita similarly as a 'logical performance of the early Gupta period' (1998, 29).

[16] Heredia poses a significant question about such assimilationism: Since Buddhism is subsumed under Hinduism (along with Jainism and Sikhism) in the Indian Constitution, the question of conversion is erased (Heredia 2004, 4546–7). For a conversion to Buddhism is not really a conversion!

[17] In his layered and critical reading of Kosambi, Lele notes that the Gita is not merely a text championing caste (1988). One can also find in it traces of agency and critique by underprivileged castes and other socially vulnerable groups. Lele's reading differs from Nanda (2016) who attributes

The emergence of Buddhism in India is often attributed to the Orientalist project of Western colonization mastering and homogenizing Indian knowledge systems to suit its interests. Thus, Batchelor claims that in the eighteenth century the rise of Enlightenment, the weakening of religious authority, and the hold of colonialism enabled a modern version of Buddhism to take shape.[18] Yet, as King notes, the Orientalist (colonial Western) pursuit of Buddhist Studies tended to homogenize Buddhism and treat the Buddha as a mystical personality. Further it came to India at a very late stage of its development—Buddhology—and as a result there was a tendency to see Buddhism as an offshoot of the large banyan tree called Hinduism. As Blackburn notes, Ambedkar did refer to Orientalist approaches to Buddhism, but then he also ruptured them.

Ambedkar's reading of Buddhist Suttas offered an alternative to colonial and nationalist readings. For the colonialists Buddhism was mystical, for the nationalists it was an offshoot of Hinduism. Ambedkar published his views on Buddhism in the *Maha Bodhi* magazine for English-speaking Buddhists in 1950 (2014b). It was the official organ of the Maha Bodhi Society founded by Anagarika Dharmapala in 1892. The president of the society was a Brahmin and anathema to Ambedkar. Yet this publication in English aimed at reaching out to a large number of readers globally about the relevance of Buddhism in a modern democratic context—as a religion and as spirituality. In this essay he distinguishes Buddha from other religious figures, compares Buddhism with Hinduism, expresses faith in the revival of Buddhism in India, compares Buddhism to other Indian religions (non-Hindu), and outlines ways in which Buddhism can be spread around the globe.

Ambedkar's reading of the Gita similarly questions its Orientalist and nationalist readings that were common during the colonial period. Moreover, he also explicitly turns to interpretation, in a critical way, to contest expert cultures that controlled the process of interpretation and offered an essentialist notion of Indianness.

---

to Ambedkar a scientisitc perspective on the Gita as a casteist text. However, though Ambedkar does critique casteist hierarchy in the Gita, he does see it as offering egalitarian possibilities as well (2014f). In this respect, Lele's reading comes closer to Ambedkar than Nanda's.

[18] Stephen Batchelor quoted in King (2001, 143).

Thus, in Ambedkar's reading, the Gita is not a quintessential Indian text. Depending upon what it means to be an Indian, Buddhist texts too could find a place in the Indian landscape. Ambedkar's dialectical reading of the Gita reveals how an intertextual reading of the Gita—that overlaps and is the outcome of Buddhist ethical principles—enables one to recover the figure of Krishna not as a nationalistic militant (Aurobindo's reading) or a psychological force (Gandhi) but rather as an ethical figure akin to the Buddha.

Revisiting Ambedkar's Hermeneutic Project

Thus, against Barlingay, 'Ambedkar converts to Navayana Buddhism precisely as an act of the greatest responsibility. Here, there is not only a criticism of religion (most of all, Hinduism, but also prior traditions of Buddhism), but also of secularism, and that criticism is articulated moreover as a religion' (Skaria 2015, 451). Ambedkar's act of conversion/transformation is not random but is rooted in a critical interrogation of traditional texts—both Hindu and Buddhist. His labour of critical hermeneutics examines the hidden assumptions on which texts depend. Hence, Ambedkar's is a critique in a very academic sense (despite which his work does not get classified as Indian philosophy).

Inaugurating a non-hegemonic approach to Indian philosophy, Chattopadhyaya (1959) suggests doing it as a materialist enterprise. He observes that contemporary Indian philosophies are neither homogeneous, nor ready-made givens discovered through a so-called objective lens. He argues that contemporary efforts to define Indian philosophy are what K.C. Bhattacharyya terms as constructive interpretation(s) (1983, 5). This entails reading ancient texts in creative ways, adding to the knowledge of the various schools of philosophy, exploring their hitherto unexplored potential. Moreover, interpretation as an act of reading the text is also a form of labour. It is not a mode of thought performed in isolation from practice. Rather, the interpreter or the reader has to engage with a diverse range of alternate readings of the text to consolidate his or her own reading. The context and material conditions of the reader—Chattopadhyaya focuses on class—are crucial to interpretation, which has an inevitable subjective dimension. Thus, in writing a philosophical point of view, one also critically reads and interprets. One can discern in Ambedkar's writings parallel endeavours to read the Indian philosophical tradition on a critical and discursive note. Ambedkar has meticulously read the Indian philosophical tradition to explore its potential via critique. He has introduced caste and gender as analytical categories that emerge from the material context of the reader. His 'Revolution and Counter-Revolution' (2014e), 'Buddha or Karl Marx' (2014c), and 'The Buddha and His Dhamma' (1957) are critical readings of the ancient Indian philosophical tradition. He analyses the persistence of caste in mainstream Indian philosophy and also argues for alternate reflective narratives of Sankhya and Buddhism. He argues against the Orientalist view that Indian society is equal to that of the Hindus; moreover, he also demonstrates that it is not a static entity, but evolving and changing. Thus, Bhattacharyya's constructive interpretation is also a part of Ambedkar's philosophical project. He innovated an approach to writing Indian philosophy through responsible practices of reading.

Ambedkar engages with the textual history of the Gita (2014a, 357–80), it is for him in Kumar's words a 'non-text' (2013, 138) as unlike the Bible, Koran, or Dhammapada it does not have a consistent meaning. It is plagued with an internal inconsistency. Hence, one cannot approach it in the manner of Tilak—as a linear Hindu text with a singular message about the law that can be decoded through participation in nationalist politics. Yet, one needs to engage with it and the textual tradition of Hinduism to dismantle it, to explore its intertextual resonance and discern alternative traditions such as that of Buddhism.[19] Besides ahimsa, Buddhism is committed to social, economic, and political freedom. It is a socially responsible religion unlike Hinduism. Thus, for Ambedkar, it provides a model of religion without aura, one that views human beings as socially interdependent; this makes morality necessary. Religion's capacity to forge unities and create new communities of equality at the social level becomes the condition for a political community of institutions. It is characterized by the need to be ethical and live in a community of equals. The establishment of a Bhikshu Sangha is meant to guide the masses, serve humanity, and spread the word. This, for Ambedkar, is in keeping with the spirit of the Buddha

---

[19] Kosambi also notes the Buddhist influence on Gita via the karma theory and its celebration of detachment in verses 55–72 of its second chapter (Kosambi 1998, 16; Mascaro 2003).

to constantly rekindle interest in Buddhism: 'To provide a model of the ideal society, to create an intellectual elite, and to create a society whose members were free to render service to the people' (Sangharakshita 1986). Ambedkar's social–ethical religion is also one of care for others. Sangharakshita (1950), in a discussion of 'The Buddha and the Future of His Religion', mentions that Ambedkar himself did not meditate in a formal way. But then the notion of both mindfulness and spirituality are embodied in his dedication to the life of the mind (in his engagement with philosophical texts) and his concern for the well-being of others. One might extend this to imply that Ambedkar could articulate a desacralized ethical religion based on care as practice of service to others because of his critical engagement with Hindu texts.

Ambedkar's critical hermeneutics struggled with the received interpretations of the text, especially those of his contemporaries. This was particularly so with regard to the Gita. He did not read the Gita like Gandhi: with a spiritual experience of its supposed truth with a sense of authority as an insider (Godrej 2009, 145).[20] This is simply because he was forced to approach the Gita as an outsider: tradition did not allow him access as Untouchables such as Ambedkar were prohibited from reading Sanskrit. Thus, Ambedkar approached the Gita through his own specific existential facticity of caste to reconstruct it in more culturally open ways.[21] Yet, he was also an insider because Hinduism maintained itself through the exploitation of underprivileged castes and the ideology of bhakti.[22] Through critical interpretation, Ambedkar introduced caste struggle in antiquity. The distance between Untouchable castes and the text, considering their lack of access to education, that they are not

---

[20] All references to Ambedkar's perspective on the Gita in this discussion are derived from Ambedkar (2014a, 357–80) unless explicitly mentioned otherwise. Citing Parekh, Godrej suggests that the authority of Gandhi's interpretation of the Gita—despite his not being a Sanskrit scholar—emerged from his moral–spiritual experience of seeking the truth through endless experimentation (145–6). But this is not unique to Gandhi as Ambedkar too approaches the Gita via the experimental perspective grounded in his experience of the oppressiveness of the caste system.

[21] The possibility of an existential engagement with texts which are reconstructed is derived from Godrej's account of interpretation (2009).

[22] Following Lele one could alternatively consider bhakti as social criticism by the masses of audience who imbibed the Gita (1988).

named in texts that nevertheless depend upon them, creates the space for critique. Distance is not isolation but an opportunity for communication (Swartz and Cilliers 2003, 17). This communication is not a quest for interpretive consensus or a dialogue with the text in the spirit of friendship following Gadamer. Further, communication with the Gita is also not in continuity with tradition where there is 'fusion of horizons' (Gadamer 1989, 306–7). Instead, Ambedkar's communication with the Gita, his critical interpretation, names tradition's rupture with Untouchable communities. Ambedkar's point was precisely that the Gita's karmic law legitimizes/institutionalizes the prevailing violence against and erasure of underprivileged castes. Hence, as a member of this caste, Ambedkar does not experience the entitlement to dialogue. He rather confronts a silence, where the conditions of dialogue are non-existent. The Gita is silent on underprivileged castes producing surplus labour so that Krishna and Arjuna can dialogue. Its brazen defence of the caste order produces a distance with individuals such as Ambedkar (predicated on its distance from underprivileged communities). Hence, Ambedkar focuses on the repressed dimension of the Gita: Gandhi's privileged caste interpretation as non-violence, the absent figure of the Untouchables underlying Krishna's and Arjuna's dialogue. Confronting the repressed dimension of caste reveals that the Gita does not have one determinate meaning—even on a temporary fallible note (as Gadamer envisages). There is instead a 'surplus' (Derrida 1982, 210–11) of conflicting meanings.[23] Hence, there cannot be a final outcome of interpretation in terms of determinate meaning. Instead, conflictual meaning emerges in historically specific situations that open up finite possibilities and where there is exclusion (as the Habermasian model of hermeneutics conveys). Texts are embedded in ideological and sociological layers of violence, by naming and acknowledging it the power structures within and without a text have to be confronted.[24]

[23] See Swartz and Cilliers for their diverse perspectives (2003). However, although Habermas is not mentioned in this essay, he can be added along with Derrida as someone who defended the possibility of excess meaning in interpretation. For Derrida such excess is apprehended via deconstruction, while for Habermas dialogue apprehends excess. Ambedkar's interpretative strategies have greater affinities with Habermas rather than Derrida, given his project of social criticism.

[24] Ambedkar resonates with Habermas on this as well.

Ambedkar discerns a bond between Buddhism and the Gita (2014a, 369–71) that was lost in the course of binary readings. This bond, prior to the violence of the dharmic law in which Krishna commands a fratricidal war and a caste system, invokes hope for social/consciousness change. Thus, in reading the Gita and naming its violence, Ambedkar breaks away from Tilak's modern-day politics of vendetta and Gandhian stoic inwardness. Both readings isolated the Gita from Buddhism and alienated the erstwhile Untouchables and assumed the value of hierarchy. In contrast, Ambedkar aimed at ending the isolationism by evoking a kinship between the Gita and Buddhist texts. He worked towards a community of equals who are also interdependent. To quote from his essay:

> From the point of view of the group, kinship calls for a feeling that one is first and foremost a member of the group and not merely an individual. From the point of view of the individual, the advantages of his kinship with the group are no less and no different than those which accrue to a member of a family. ... Kinship makes the community take responsibility for vindicating the wrong done to a member ... it is kinship which generates generosity and invokes moral indignation which is necessary to address a wrong. ... Kinship with another community in best insurance which the untouchable can effect against Hindu tyranny and Hindu oppression. (Ambedkar 2014a, 414)

To establish kinship, the members of the community should have come from one ancestor and share the same blood. Ambedkar's reading of the Gita enunciates the possibility of heterogeneous textual traditions, which are nevertheless implicated in power. His view that texts are both open and closed is relevant in the contemporary context of decolonizing thought and particularly Indian philosophy. It is from this perspective that Ambedkar has a global/'cosmopolitan' relevance against those such as Pollock who localize him.[25] Pollock makes a passing mention of Ambedkar in a larger discussion whose focus is Kosambi's contribution to Indology (2008). He claims that Marxism–Leninism universalism is on the decline, while 'located doctrines' such as Ambedkarianism are ascendant (2008, 58). Pollock clearly overlooks the universalism implicit in Ambedkar's struggle

---

[25] Godrej identifies a third hermeneutic moment as cosmopolitan (2009, 155–60).

for conversion to an egalitarian world view through Indology as a comparative study of religions. Ambedkar himself noted that his would be 'the first case in history of genuine conversion' (2014a, 405) through an examination of religions on a comparative note. In this spirit, Ambedkar focused on a comparative evaluation of Hinduism and Buddhism. Moreover, Pollock also does not heed Ambedkar's being 'located' in the entanglement of theory and practice, similar to Marx. Ambedkar does not merely offer the possibility of opening non-Western perspectives to counter the dominance of Western thought in the mode of external decolonization. Instead, Ambedkar suggests that decolonization is also a process of immanent criticism of the violence within each cultural framework. Ambedkar's critical interpretations are not instances of fusing horizons and enlarging contexts on a Gadamerian note. For Ambedkar these are exercises in extending violence even further. In contrast, Ambedkar's reading of the Gita and Buddhism suggests that accepted contexts need to be ruptured to discern the discontinuities in their horizons. Ambedkar represents the possibility of interpretation by disrupting the mainstream conversation that has become a habit.[26] This will allow for new contexts and new meanings to emerge from texts, which in turn opens up the possibility of egalitarian meanings (which too are not stable). As Ambedkar's critique of caste reminds us, resisting such violence is also a willingness to be open to the porousness of cultural horizons and identities.

References

Ambedkar, B.R. 1957. *The Buddha and His Dhamma*. Siddharth Publications: Bombay.

———. 1979a. 'On Caste'. In *Dr. Babasaheb Ambedkar, Writings and Speeches*, vol. 1, 3–96. New Delhi: Dr. Ambedkar Foundation.

———. 1979b. 'On the Problems of Linguistic States'. In *Dr. Babasaheb Ambedkar, Writings and Speeches*, vol. 1, 165–70. New Delhi: Dr. Ambedkar Foundation.

———. 2014a [1989]. 'Away from the Hindus'. *Dr. Babasaheb Ambedkar, Writings and Speeches*, vol. 5, 403–21. New Delhi: Dr. Ambedkar Foundation.

---

[26] Shwartz and Cilliers make this point with reference to Derrida (2003, 17).

———. 2014b [2003]. 'Buddha and the Future of His Religion'. *Dr. Babasaheb Ambedkar, Writings and Speeches*, vol. 17, part 2, 97–108. New Delhi: Dr. Ambedkar Foundation.
———. 2014c [1987]. 'Buddha or Karl Marx'. *Dr. Babasaheb Ambedkar, Writings and Speeches*, vol. 3, 441–62. New Delhi: Dr. Ambedkar Foundation.
———. 2014d [1989]. 'Caste and Conversion'. *Dr. Babasaheb Ambedkar, Writings and Speeches*, vol. 5, 422–5. New Delhi: Dr. Ambedkar Foundation.
———. 2014e [1989]. 'The Condition of the Convert'. *Dr. Babasaheb Ambedkar, Writings and Speeches*, vol. 5, 445–76. New Delhi: Dr. Ambedkar Foundation.
———. 2014f [1987]. 'Revolution and Counterrevolution'. *Dr. Babasaheb Ambedkar, Writings and Speeches*, vol. 3, 151–437. New Delhi: Dr. Ambedkar Foundation.
———. 2014g [1989]. 'Untouchability—Its Source'. *Dr. Babasaheb Ambedkar, Writings and Speeches*, vol. 5, 3–5. New Delhi: Dr. Ambedkar Foundation.
Barlingay, S.W. 1974. 'Dr. Ambedkar and Conversion to Buddhism'. *Indian Philosophical Quarterly* 1, no. 2: 144–53.
Bhattacharyya, K.C. 1983 [1958]. 'Studies in Vedantism'. In *Studies in Philosophy*, edited by Gopinath Bhattacharya, 1–90. Delhi, Varanasi, Pune: Motilal Banarasidass.
Blackburn, Anne M. 1993. 'Religion, Kinship and Buddhism: Ambedkar's Vision of a Moral Community'. *The Journal of the International Association of Buddhist Studies* 16, no. 1: 1–23.
Chattopadhyaya, Debiprasad. 1959. *Lokayata: A Study in Ancient Indian Materialism*. People's Publishing House: New Delhi.
Derrida, Jacques. 1982. *Margins of Philosophy*. Chicago: The University of Chicago Press.
Gadamer, Hans-Georg. 1989 [1975]. *Truth and Method*. Crossroad: New York.
Godrej, Farah. 2009. 'Towards a Cosmopolitan Political Thought: The Hermeneutics of Interpreting the Other'. *Polity* 41, no. 2: 135–65.
Habermas, Jürgen. 2003. *Truth and Justification*. Polity Press: Cambridge.
Habermas, Jürgen, and Joseph Ratzinger. 2005. *The Dialectics of Secularization: On Reason and Religion*. Ignatius Press: San Francisco.
Heredia, Rudolf C. 2004. 'No Entry, No Exit: Savarna Aversion towards Dalit Conversion'. *Economic and Political Weekly* 39, no. 41: 4543–55.
King, Richard. 2001 [1999]. *Orientalism and Religion: Postcolonial Theory, India and the Mystic East*. London and New York: Routledge.

Kumar, Aiswarya. 2013. 'Ambedkar's Inheritances'. In *Political Thought in Action: The Bhagavad Gita and Modern India*, edited by Shruti Kapadia and Faisal Devji, 127–54. Cambridge: Cambridge University Press.

Kosambi, Damoder Dharmanand. 1998. *Myth and Reality*. Mumbai: Popular Prakashan.

Lakshman, P.P. 1992. 'Ambedkar and Gita'. *Economic and Political Weekly* 27, no. 33 (15 August): 1702.

Lal, Amrith. 2018. 'Why Buddhism Invites Dalits'. *Indian Express* (1 May).

Lele, Jayant. 1988. 'On Regaining the Meaning of the "Bhagavad Gita"'. *Journal of South Asian Literature* 23, no. 2: 150–67.

Mascaro, Juan, trans. 2003. *The Bhagavad Gita*. Penguin Books: London.

Nanda, Meera. 2016. 'Ambedkar and Gita'. *Economic and Political Weekly* 51, no. 49: 38–45.

Pandit, Nalini. 1992. 'Ambedkar and the "Bhagwat Gita"'. *Economic and Political Weekly* 27 (20/21): 1063–5.

Pollock, Sheldon. 2008. 'Towards a Political Philology: D.D. Kosambi and Sanskrit'. *Economic and Political Weekly* 43, no. 30 (26 July–1 August): 52–9.

Sangharakshita. 1950. 'Questions and Answers on "Buddha and the Future of His Religion" by Dr. B.R. Ambedkar'. *Maha Bodhi Journal* (April/May). Available at https://www.freebuddhistaudio.com/texts/. Last accessed on 22 July 2016.

———. 1986. *Ambedkar and Buddhism*. Windhorse Publications.

Schempp, Bellwinkel Maren. 2007. 'From Bhakti to Buddhism: Ravidas and Ambedkar'. *Economic and Political Weekly* 42, no. 23: 2177–83.

Shah, K.J. 1978. 'Consensus and Conflict: Some Considerations'. *Indian Philosophical Quarterly* 6, no. 1: 101–8.

Skaria, Ajay. 2015. 'Ambedkar Marx and the Buddhist Question'. *Journal of South Asian Studies* 38, no. 3: 450–65.

Swartz, Chantélle, and Paul Cilliers. 2003. 'Dialogue Disrupted: Derrida, Gadamer and the Ethics of Discussion'. *South African Journal of Philosophy* 22, no. 1: 1–18.

Viswanathan, Gauri. 1998. *Outside the Fold: Conversion, Modernity and Belief*. Princeton: Princeton University Press.

3

Civil Religion, Uncivil Society

A Reflection on Baba Sahib Dr B.R. Ambedkar's Conception of a 'Religion for Civil Society'

DEBORA SPINI

This chapter will move from Ambedkar's vision of a 'religion for civil society', and will consider if and how his vision may be applied to the current debates on the role of religion in political conflict. The chapter will debate if only a religion such as Ambedkar wished for—a religion that should be secular, humanist, and rational—has the potential to be integrated into a democratic public sphere, and if his model of religion, more concerned with creating warm social bonds rather than with a quest for a transcendental God, is the only one that a does not trigger violent conflict.

Ambedkar's views on religion are a very well-explored topic; with no ambition whatsoever to compete with existing scholarship, I shall provide a few comments on how his views resonate in light of the current debates on the crisis of modernity and on the transformation of the paradigm of secularization. Evidently, all the reflections exposed hereafter are profoundly influenced by the climate of the European province out of which they originated; which raises doubts about the legitimacy of using Ambedkar out of his geographical and historical framework. Rodrigues, among others, provides the answer: Ambedkar can and must be considered as a full-fledged political theorist (Rodrigues 2002), and thus as a point of reference valid beyond its original context.

The question that underlies these pages is whether Ambedkar's solutions apply to the current scenario. The chapter will argue that the evident crisis that characterizes the present condition of late modernity calls for a thorough reconsideration of Ambedkar's thought on religion and politics, so profoundly shaped by his confidence in the progressive and rationalizing power of modernization processes. This work of re-assessment will necessarily require us to discard some of the more evident features of his thought, which at a first glance seem to be easier to export out of his geographical and historical context. Yet, the question whether Ambedkar's thought on religion should be altogether discarded will receive an equally negative answer. This chapter will conclude by highlighting how the vital legacy of Ambedkar's thought is not to be found in his attempt to reconcile religion with immanence as much as in his framing religious identity as a conscious choice, conducive to individual moral autonomy and fully fledged political agency.

A Religion for Civil Society

Although Ambedkar's vision of 'a religion for civil society' has been widely debated, it may not be entirely superfluous to recall some problematic points in view of the questions debated in the second part of the chapter. The very term 'civil society' is far from being neutral; and in fact a rich literature has questioned whether the category in its various versions—from Hegel and Marx to Habermas—is applicable and relevant in a postcolonial context (Chandoke 2002; Barghava and Reifield 2005). By 'civil society', Ambedkar means a civilized society: a democratic, tolerant, egalitarian public sphere where individuals can flourish and exercise their autonomy, a space informed by equality and brotherhood. His interpretation of Buddha's Dhamma testifies of a vibrant passion for equality and justice as the only possible basis for any social bond that does not stifle the quest for individuality, and that, on the contrary, cherishes and cultivates the value of each human being, of each and every project of life.

Evidently, Ambedkar's civil society is a political project rather than a pre-existing set of social interactions, a normative perspective rather than a social space. To be completed, this project needs political instruments, primarily the structure of rights enshrined in the Constitution. Correctly, Gopal Guru highlights Ambedkar's confidence in the role of the State and his corresponding scepticism on the capacity of a Hindu public sphere 'marked as it was with a consciousness that fed on itself on the denial of equality to others' to promote genuine equality. Given civil society as it actually is, the most effective weapons for constructing a civil society as it should be are political and constitutional reforms (Barghava and Reifield 2005, 263; Chatterjee 2014, 14–15).

In this framework, 'religion for civil society' means a religion that fosters equality and brotherhood by providing the moral bond necessary to implement the political project of inclusive citizenship, identified in a revisited form of Buddhism. As Ambedkar's Buddhism has been—and still is—the object of a wide scholarly debate (Blackburne, 1993; Singh 2016), for this reflection it is more important to focus on his quite specific definition of religion. In Buddhism—'his' Buddhism—Ambedkar sees something very different from what is commonly defined as religion, either as a way to salvation or as a series of rules. In *Buddha and His Dhamma* he affirms: 'All prophets have promised salvation. The Buddha is the one teacher who did not make any such promise. He made a sharp distinction between a moksha data and a marga data, one who gives salvation and one who only shows the way. He was only a marga data. Salvation must be sought by each for himself by his own effort' (Ambedkar 1992, 218; Fuchs 2001). *Annihilation of Caste* describes religion as a set of principles, spiritual and universal in opposition to a mere series of rules (Ambedkar 2014, 160–1) and as 'an associated mode of living' (Ambedkar 2014, 137).

Ambedkar's conception of religion, in line with his pragmatist background,[1] evidently gives little or no place to a transcendent God, and concentrates on the sphere of immanence, assigning priority to the social function. The divine is not a transcendental being, and inter-subjectivity itself—the common world of human beings—becomes the focus of religious sentiments. Religion thus acquires an essentially inter-subjective, 'public' nature, which should not be 'personal' but 'social [...], fundamentally and essentially so': a nature that he finds fully realised in Buddhism (Ambedkar 2011, 168). The Dhamma does not pre-exist social interaction, but

---

[1] Aishwary Kumar highlights the importance of Bergson and Durkheim, along with Dewey and James, in the genesis of Ambedkar's religious thought (Kumar 2015).

becomes necessary whenever social interaction occurs. If Dhamma exists only within society, 'society cannot do without Dhamma' (Ambedkar 1992, 316); in this perspective, Ambedkar describes it as an instrument of government, although surely not in the sense of Machiavelli's *instrumentum regni*, but as a point of equilibrium between anarchy and dictatorship. The Dhamma can be defined as a religion essentially because its is a form of morality fully realized in social interactions. 'Dhamma at one and the same time is seen as a moral code, for both the individual's conduct of life and social interaction, and as a constitutional necessity for society' (Fuchs 2001, 315). The Dhamma is not religion insofar as religion is not morality. When religion is conceptualized as the worship of transcendence, the inquiry about God and the finite and the infinite, morality is but peripheral; but, in Dhamma, morality takes the place of God although there is no God in Dhamma. Echoing Dewey's interpretation of God as a community of ends, in the *Buddha and His Dhamma*, Ambedkar explains 'the centre of religion lay not in the relation of man to god. It lays in the relation between man and man'. Consequently, the central question on religion is whether it has a role to play in our public life and if so, what is the nature of such religion?' (Rodrigues 2017, 104), the answer being that 'the purpose of religion is to teach man how he should behave towards other men so that all men may be happy'; religion is morality and the essence of morality is fraternity 'against the bitterness of nature' (Ambedkar 1992, 254).

The public character of religion implies that it may, rather it should, be submitted to some kind of critique and assessment, as it is not enough to adopt 'the placid look of the anthropologist' (Ambedkar 2014, 164). Religious beliefs are not entirely subjective (in his own words they are not 'simply a matter of likes and dislikes'). Both *Annihilation of Caste* and *The Buddha or Karl Marx* stress the importance of the spiritual dimension in human agency. In line with his pragmatist background, Ambedkar affirms that religious convictions must be assessed for the kind of morality and of social interactions they promote, and for their potential for social transformation (Ambedkar 2014, 150–2). An important corollary is the affirmation that any social transformation and reform should be prepared by some kind of religious change as demonstrated by the case of the Mauryan dynasty (Roy 2014, 124; Ambedkar 2014, 161). As religions should be assessed in light of their social outcomes,

Hindus too 'must examine their religion and their morality in terms of their survival value' (Ambedkar 2014, 164) and in so doing they will call upon themselves their final judgement, as any social or political reform that takes religion into consideration would end up necessarily in destroying the authority of the Vedas (Ambedkar 2014, 153).

Ambedkar trusted science and Enlightenment (meant as the progress of reason) (Singh 2016; Chatterjee 2014), and believed them to be the forces that could promote his goals of equality, humanity, and justice. Such a faith did not bring him towards atheism or strict secularism, exactly because his conception of religion was capable of adapting to modernity, and did not clash with rationalisation and scientific spirit. Having identified one specific faith as the source of most of India's social evils, Ambedkar engaged in the quest for a religion that would not be in contrast with science and rationality and that would foster 'public spirit and public charity'. He found it in Dhamma, the only religion capable of providing a foundation for equality and fraternity, so necessary for the construction of democracy.

Dissonances

The faith in the progressive character of modernity provided the framework of reference for Ambedkar's theory of religion; as has been already mentioned, Ambedkar saw in a gradual rationalization of religion—in other words, in its capacity to negotiate with modernity—the key for its insertion into civil society. In the better tradition of pragmatism, he expected religion to lose its truculent attachment with transcendence to become a gentle, warm bond of moral obligation among citizens. This more 'humanistic' and less 'theological' religion was to be the best guarantee of the flourishing of civil society. The contours of this framework have drastically changed, thus posing new set of challenges. The first of them is by the evident incapacity, or at least extreme difficulty, of modernity in maintaining its promises of progress and enlightenment, which makes it quite hard to share Ambedkar's confidence in the chances of transforming religion into an exquisitely human bond devoid of all references to a divine transcendence. Horkheimer and Adorno (2007) highlighted the dialectic tensions that innerve the project of enlightenment, whilst Marcuse

(2002) warned against the dangerous inclination of contemporary *homo democraticus* to adjust to a comfortable and tolerant un-freedom. But most of all, the contradictions of modernity are becoming manifest in their most tragic magnitude in the whole history of the twentieth century. The rise of totalitarian regimes with all their frightening baggage of organized mass violence is not a parenthesis or a temporary slowdown in modernity's progress, but an integral part of its itinerary. That these tragic occurrences cannot be considered simply a relic of the past, but a tile in the wider mosaic of the in-bred dialectic of modernity is demonstrated also by more recent but equally terrifying events, such as the long string of wars and massacres in former Yugoslavia. European history teaches a very hard lesson, as it demonstrates that the passage of religion into modernity is not necessarily the guarantee against all evil. Christian Europe did not find salvation from a form of religion reconciled with modernity, because modernity itself has not been the barrier against the horrors of totalitarianism; actually, totalitarianism is the monstrous brainchild of modernity. Not surprisingly, Nazism and the Shoah mark the utter failure of liberal Protestantism, the Protestantism that wanted to reconcile Christian theology with reason and enlightenment to make it more acceptable to a modern world. This enlightened, rationalistic, humanistic theology of liberal Protestantism, so intellectually and spiritually close to the religious conceptions of Ambedkar's great mentors did not prevent the spiritual collapse of Germany or of European Christianity in general. The response to total evil came from the rediscovery of a totally other God such as that witnessed by the Confessing church, by the 'religionless Christianity' of Dietrich Bonhöffer, and by the dialectic theology of Karl Barth.[2] It came from a theological perspective that did not

---

[2] The Confessing Church (*Bekennende Kirche* in German) was a minority section of the Lutheran Church in Germany, opposing Hitler's attempt to establish full control over German Christianity. The faith of the Confessing Church is summarized by the Barmen Declaration of 1934. Among its outstanding leaders was the Lutheran theologian Dietrich Bonhöffer, executed in 1944 in the concentration camp of Flossenburg. In his letters from prison, Bohöffer spoke of a 'religionless Christianity', opposing the authenticity of faith to the social construction of religion. Karl Barth (1886–1968), a Swiss Reformed theologian, was also involved in the drafting of the Barmen Declaration. Author of a seminal commentary

even try to humanize religion, but emphasized, on the contrary, the unbridgeable gap between a transcendent God and the dimension of human affairs.

The morphology of contemporary politics is marked by profound contradictions. At the beginning of the twenty-first century, modernity is not only omnivorous (Heller 2002) but self-devouring; the crisis is so deep as to make a diagnosis of the end of modernity a possible scenario. Modernity has been taken up in the grip of a boomerang effect, as its productive forces become forces of destruction, part of the problem rather than the solution. The current ecological crisis is more than a bump in the road of progress; on the contrary, it reveals how science and technology are utterly failing in their ambition of dominating the world, as they are in the first place incapable of governing the unforeseen turn taken by their own developments. Such is the case, most notably, of climate change, the substantial irreversibility of which leaves open only second-best options such as adaptation or mitigation. The backfiring of modern scientific rationality does not only impose adopting reflexivity as a sort of default frame of mind (Beck 1997, 11–19; Carleheden and Jacobsen 2017), but also a deep reconsideration of many underlying assumptions of modern politics. In the age of the anthropocene, humanity can no longer look at the future as a scenario of progress and 'growth', as the planet's resources are in fact reaching the point of exhaustion. The need to find limits to 'growth' gives rise of a series of questions of justice and redistribution between 'developed' and 'underdeveloped' countries 'North' and 'South' of the globe, whose magnitude can hardly be exaggerated. In this framework, the expectation of a full completion of the project of modernity, with its aura of progress and enlightenment, does not provide an adequate answer to the challenges of the present time.

As the overall framework has drastically changed, so has the role of many crucial actors of modern politics, to begin with, by the State and the form of democracy that flourished, in which Ambedkar vested such hope for the realization of justice and equity. Globalization, the ultimate form of economic capitalist rationality,

---

The Epistle to the Romans, Barth opened the way for dialectic theology, a theological approach that focuses on God's transcendence rather than on accommodating Revelation and human reason.

is eroding the capacity of States to exercise substantial political control over their borders, and the crisis of sovereignty thus caused necessarily entails also a crisis of democracy and of the legitimacy of its foundations. Within this scenario, modern politics has lost the capacity to provide a horizon of meaning for human action, whilst on the contrary religious actors and ideologies re-occupy the stage of the public sphere.

Evidently, on a global scale the advance of modernity did not correspond to a withdrawing of religion, as in the forecast of most social theorists from Weber onwards. The wager of modernity—replacing transcendence with transcendental reason (Seligman 2000)—does not look anymore as a very safe bet. As is well known, Habermas was among the first to elaborate on the possibility of a post-secular paradigm. But whilst Habermas' approach to post-secular society aimed at a sort of division of labour between *glauben* (faith) and *wissen* (knowledge), others have interpreted this shift of paradigm as a crisis of secularization and the advent of a post-secular age characterized by a belligerent re-occupation of the public sphere by religious actors. In many cases, the return of religion appears as a downright revenge (Kepel 1994), as religious groups are not becoming more enlightened or more inclined to practising the virtue of tolerance and humanity that Ambedkar considered so essential for civil society. On the contrary, violent conflicts are often motivated with religious vocabulary and symbolism. The instrumental nature of the use of religion in political violence is evident; nonetheless, the sheer fact that religion does perform a motivating function, that it may constitute a *Weltbild* (world view) that mobilizes in view of political conflict, is in itself a major source of concern. Religions seem to be back from their 'Westphalian exile' (Petito and Hatzopoulos 2004), and in many cases in the form of radicalism, whilst 'secular' political forces, actors, themes, and arguments appear to be on the retreat. The appeal of religious radicalism is amplified by the evident exhaustion of politics as a source of meaning. Peter Sloterdijk formulates its diagnosis on the crisis of modern politics in terms of an opposition between a 'horizontal' (adaptive) and a 'vertical' and radically agonistic attitude towards the world, where religion may claim to be the only 'vertical' alternative to the status quo of neoliberalism, the only collection point of passions otherwise left to evaporate (Sloterdijk 2013). Only religious actors seem to be capable of that form of 'radical' politics, meant as the capacity of articulating drastically alternative visions and perspectives for transformation, that was the propellant force of modern politics. Meanwhile, political actors and paradigms seem to be capable only of sailing along the coast. In most Western societies, a growing disaffection and anesthetization towards public issues (what Richard Sennett [1977] famously defined as the decline of the public man) is the order of the day. This cooling off of political passions does not necessarily promote more tolerant, inclusive, and participatory democracies. Although disaffection and depoliticization are its marking features, the Western world is not untouched by the phenomenon of politicization of religion. On the contrary, indifference is a fertile ground for breeding cruelty. Political disaffection may very well go hand in hand with processes of weaponization of religion. Religious beliefs are an important component in the discourse of right-wing populist sovereignism in Europe as they represent an apparently inexhaustible reservoir of symbols and vocabulary for tribalist and non-inclusive forms of collective identity. Such is the mechanism that allows European citizens to remain untouched by the tragedy of the death sentence declared for all the desperate human beings trying to save themselves from war, persecution, or simply from hunger or poverty.

Resonances

The current situation, if interpreted in terms of crisis of modernity and resurgence of religion, resonates with some central features of Ambedkar's thought, and seems to confer fresh relevance to his reflection. Most notably, the debates on the polemogenous character of religion—and of *some* religions in particular—seem to harmonize quite well with the theses defended in *Buddha and His Dhamma*. That religions may fuel conflicts is almost a commonplace. A long and illustrious genealogy of thinkers, from Hume to Bertrand Russell, has identified a specific relation between monotheism and violence. Abrahamic religions have been accused of being inclined to violence because of their specific conception of Truth, which they enshrine, with varying degrees of rigidity, in one revealed book, which would make them intrinsically intolerant. The hypothesis of a special link between monotheism and violence is still quite alive in the contemporary debate. A host of contemporary authors are working along Hume and Russell's thread, most notably Sloterdijk himself, who identify in the worship of a God at the same time the transcendent and personal origin of the psychological type of the zealous servant, dominated by 'extremism of the will to obedience' (Sloterdijk 2009, 86) and consequently most prone to intolerance.

However, the most immediate and evident resonances between Ambedkar's religious thought and the contemporary situation are not necessarily the more promising paths to explore. This affirmation may sound less cheeky when confronted with the actual political scenario.

The political situation unfolding daily in front of our eyes demonstrates that it is not one confession or another that is more inclined towards radical and violent forms of conflict. Everyday chronicles provide sufficient evidence to refute Radhakrishan's (2009) view of Hinduism as a universal religion and, therefore, as the only one to be intrinsically tolerant and alien from violence. Nor can the direct link with transcendence be identified as the violence-generating factor. Contemporary European politics provide ample evidence that religion may ignite violent conflicts even when reinterpreted purely in terms of a social bond and when the umbilical cord with a transcendent God has been severed. Extreme right populist forces make extensive use of the reference to religion to justify policies aiming at political exclusion and discrimination, as well as to fuel anti-refugee hysteria. These nationalist and xenophobic parties and movements use the reference to Christianity as an identity marker, to enact processes of racialization of religion which foster an 'us versus them' mentality (where the target is obviously Islam) (Marzouki, McDonnell, and Roy 2016; Zuquete 2017).

Religion is narrated essentially in cultural terms, as a 'way of life' rather than as a faith. Whereas 'culture' becomes a destiny, Christianity is presented as the only religion capable of providing the ground for 'a civil society', the only tolerant, liberal, open-minded religion; further, Christianity is presented as the only religion that is compatible with secularism, a self-representation that easily becomes a weapon for ethnocentric and exclusionary politics. Evidently, severing the link with transcendence is not the key to avoid the weaponization of religion and to promote peaceful coexistence, tolerance, and inclusive public spaces, nor is the rationalization of religious belief the necessary ingredient to repel violence. The relevance of Ambedkar's thought for our late modern condition cannot therefore be identified with his attempt to reformulate religion as an immanent, human bond, emancipated from transcendence and thus reconciled with rationality and scientific spirit.

The reality of the late modern world is more complex than that encapsulated in the simple slogan the 'return of religion' may convey. The narrative of modernity as a radial and unrestrainable expansion from a centre to a periphery does not account for the uncanny complexity of the contemporary scenario, just as the dynamic of secularization and post-secularization must be explained according to a richer paradigm than that of the 'return' of religion. Modernity must be conceived in the plural, as a polycentric space of multiple modernities; correspondingly, secularization does not simply 'advance' or 'retrocede'. The presence of religion in the contemporary public sphere can be understood solely within the framework of modernity itself. The two phenomena sketched in the preceding paragraphs—resurgence of religion as a fuel for political conflicts and spreading of disaffection and anesthetisation towards politics—re in fact two sides of the same coin. Religious radicalisms, which should be more appropriately defined as forms of radical politics motivated by religion, are not a leftover of modernity, doomed to disappear with its full deployment. On the contrary, these movements, actors, and ideologies are intrinsically modern as, in spite of their reference to transcendental principles, they follow a typically and uniquely modern scheme of radical, 'jacobine' political agency (Eisenstadt 1999). Adopting a richer definition of 'secularization' that does not coincide with the withering away of religion helps to clarify the modern character of religious radicalism. For Charles Taylor, 'secularization' indicates a condition where the whole of natural and social phenomena may be explained within a frame of immanence, without resorting to a transcendental order of explanation. Secularization, therefore, does not erase religion but reformulates it in the terms of a voluntary, autonomous, and reflexive choice. As mentioned earlier, framing religion as a choice may assume a radical character, which may even lead to 'vertical' forms of conflict; however, it is also the channel for autonomous, empowering agency (Taylor 2007).

This change of perspective permits to capture the undeniable relevance of many aspects of Ambedkar's legacy, as manifested not only in his scholarly work, but also in his intellectual biography. The completion of his reflection on religion as well as of his life's journey materialized in the open and public choice of embracing Buddhism. Ambedkar's conversion calls for a thorough reformulation of his relationship with modernity, which moves the focus from his faith in rationality and progress to the quest for individual autonomy, a reformulation which may thus cross paths with all these analysis of secularization and modernity which look beyond a sharp zero-sum scheme, such as that previously evoked by Taylor. Gauri Viswanathan has highlighted the political significance of his conversion of Buddhism by remarking how it constituted 'less a rejection of political solutions than a rewriting of religious and cultural change into a form of political intervention' as it created 'a new mythology around which the political identity of dalits could be mobilized' (Viswanathan 1998, 212). These comments highlight how deeply Ambedkar's conversion is embedded in his quest for justice and liberation, and its meaning as an act of resistance against structures of domination that work at an even deeper level then economic and political injustices. Ambedkar's *Annihilation of Caste* provides an illuminating definition of 'slavery': 'For slavery does not merely mean a legalised form of subjection. It means a state of society in which some men are forced to accept from others the purposes, which control their conduct. This condition obtains even where there is no slavery in the legal sense' (Ambedkar 2014, 144). Choosing Buddhism, therefore, constituted a forceful re-affirmation of autonomy through the re-appropriation of the values and principles that constitute individual as well as collective identities. Disentangling Ambedkar's position on religion from any hasty identification with a mechanical ('colonial') modernism, Mishra and Hodges remark how it constituted 'a performative act that underlined the importance of the religious act as a mode of postcolonial intervention. The incomplete project of modernity is therefore not simply a matter of working within emancipatory protocols (legislative, juridical, economic, and so on) but also an intentional return to the felt-life forms of the subject as constituted by premodern modes of belief' (Mishra and Hodges 2005, 394).

Ambedkar's public conversion still has a great political meaning as it illustrates the possibility of conceiving of religion as a choice rather than as a destiny, and thus as a channel towards fuller political agency: a reminder that is of extreme importance in numerous and diverse contexts, and that resonates with particular vibrancy in the context of the debates aiming at constructing a genuinely inclusive public sphere in Western democracies. Thus reframed, Ambedkar's engagement with the project of modernity cannot be dismissed as a simple assimilation into a naive trust in an enlightened progress or in a mainstream Westphalian framework. Rather, it gains relevance in light of another, and much more normatively valid, promise of modernity, that of individual autonomy.

Ambedkar's conversion reminds us that identity is a project and it is not a destiny: however, this affirmation of the value of moral autonomy does not enforce a naive view of moral normativity, nor does it constitute an endorsement of mainstream individualism—the model of individual that, to cut a long story short, was perfectly compatible with capitalism in Ambedkar's time and that continues, today, to be perfectly fit to live and consume in the neoliberal world. His lesson is today all the more important, as an affirmation of individuality coming from the point of view of the oppressed among the oppressed.

References

Ambedkar, Bhimrao Ramji. 1992. 'The Buddha and His Dhamma'. In *Writings and Speeches*, vol. 11, edited by V. Moon. Bombay: Education Department, Government of Maharashtra.

———. 2011. 'The Buddha and His Dhamma'. In *The Buddha and His Dhamma: A Critical Edition*, edited by A. Singh Rathore and V. Verma. New Delhi: Oxford University Press.

———. 2014 [1936]. *Annihilation of Caste*, edited by S. Anand. London: Verso.

Barghava, Rajeev, and Helmut Reifeld. 2005. *Civil Society, Public Sphere and Citizenship: Dialogues and Perceptions*. New Delhi: Sage Publications.

Beck, Ulrich. 1997. *The Reinvention of Politics: Rethinking Modernity in the Global Social Order*. Cambridge: Polity.

Blackburne, A.M. 1993. 'Religion, Kinship and Buddhism: Ambedkar's Vision of a Moral Community'. *The Journal of the International Association of Buddhist Studies* 16: 1–24.

Carleheden, Mikael, and Michael Hviid Jacobsen, eds. 2017. *The Transformation of Modernity: Aspects of the Past, Present and Future of an Era*. London: Routledge.

Casanova, José. 2013. 'Exploring the Postsecular: Three Meanings of "the Secular" and Their Possible Transcendence'. In *Habermas and Religion*, edited by C. Calhoun, E. Mendieta, and J. VanAntwerpen. Cambridge: Polity Press.

Chandoke, Neera. 2002. *The Conceits of Civil Society*. New Delhi: Oxford University Press.

Chatterjee, Partha. 2014. *The Politics of the Governed: Reflections on Popular Politics in Most of the World*. New York: Columbia University Press.

Eisenstadt, Shmuel. 1999. *Fundamentalism, Sectarianism, and Revolution: The Jacobin Dimension of Modernity*. Cambridge: Cambridge University Press.

Fuchs, Martin. 2001. 'A Religion for Civil Society? Ambedkar's Buddhism, the Dalit Issue and the Imagination of Emergent Possibilities'. In *Charisma and Canon. Essays on the Religious History of the Indian Subcontinent*, edited by V. Dalmia, A. Malinar, and C. Martin. New Delhi: Oxford University Press.

Guha, Ramachandra. 2010. 'Gandhi's Ambedkar'. In *Indian Political Thought*, edited by A. Singh and S. Mohapatra. London-New York: Routledge.

Heller, Ágnes. 2002. 'Omnivorous Modernity'. In *Culture, Modernity and Revolution: Essays in Honour of Zygmunt Bauman*, edited by R. Kilminster and I. Varcoe. London-New York: Routledge.

Horkheimer, Max, and Theodor W. Adorno. 2007. *Dialectic of Enlightenment*. Stanford: Stanford University Press.

Kepel, Gilles. 1994. *The Revenge of God. The Resurgence of Islam, Christianity, and Judaism in the Modern World*. Cambridge: Polity Press.

Kumar, Aishwary. 2015. *Radical Equality: Ambedkar, Gandhi, and the Risk of Democracy*. Stanford: Stanford University Press.

Marcuse, Herbert. 2002. *One-Dimensional Man*. London, New York: Routledge.

Marzouki, Nadia, Duncan McDonnell, and Olivier Roy, eds. 2016. *Saving the People. How Populists Hijack Religion*. London: Hurst.

Mishra, V., and B. Hodges. 2005. 'What Was Post Colonialism?' *New Literary History* 36, no. 3: 375–402.

Petito, Fabio, and Pavlos Hatzopoulos. 2004. *Religion in International Relations. The Return from Exile*. New York: Palgrave-McMillan.

Radhakrishnan, Sarvepalli. 2009. *The Reign of Religion in Contemporary Philosophy*. Charleston: Bibliobazaar.

Rodrigues, Valerian, ed. 2002. *The Essential Writings of B.R. Ambedkar*. New Delhi: Oxford University Press.

———. 2017. 'Ambedkar as a Political Philosopher'. *Economic and Political Weekly* 52, no. 15: 100–7.

Roy, Arundhati. 2014. 'The Doctor and the Saint'. In Bhimrao Ramji Ambedkar's *Annihilation of Caste*, edited by S. Anand. London: Verso.
Seligman, Adam. 2000. *Modernity's Wager: Authority, the Self, and Transcendence*. Princeton: Princeton University Press.
Sennet, Richard. 1977. The *Fall of Public Man*. New York: Alfred A. Knopf.
Singh, Aakash. 2016. The Political Theology of Navayana Buddhism. In *The Future of Political Theology, Religious and Theological Perspectives*, edited by P. Losonczy, M. Luhoma-Aho, and A. Singh. London-New York: Routledge.
Skaria, Ajai. 2015. 'Ambedkar, Marx and the Buddhist Question'. *South Asia: Journal of South Asian Studies* 38, no. 3: 450–65.
Sloterdijk, Peter. 2009. *God's Zeal, the Battle of the Three Monotheisms*. Cambridge: Polity Press.
———. 2013. *You Must Change Your Life: On Anthropotechnics*. Cambridge: Polity Press.
Strout, Scott R. 2017. 'Pragmatism, Persuasion, and Force in Bhimrao Ambedkar's Reconstruction of Buddhism'. *Journal of Religion* 97, no. 2: 214–43.
Taylor, Charles. 2007. *The Secular Age*. Cambridge, MA: Harvard University Press.
Vidhu, Verma. 2010. 'Reinterpreting Buddhism: Ambedkar on the Politics of Social Action'. *Economic and Political Weekly* 45, no. 49: 56–65.
Viswanathan, Gauri. 1998. *Outside the Fold. Conversion, Modernity and Belief*. Princeton: Princeton University Press.
Zuquete, José Pedro. 2017. Populism and Religion. In *The Oxford Handbook of Populism*, edited by C. Rovira Kaltwasser, P. Taggart, P. Ochoha Espejo, and P. Ostiguy, 445–66. Oxford: Oxford University Press.

4

The Gaze on Justice
A Genealogy from Anagarika Dharmapala to B.R. Ambedkar

PRIYANKA JHA

The manner in which we, the people of India, think of our lives and the world we inhabit has been deprived of a rich tradition of thought which has contributed to our sense of who we are for over several thousand years. This chapter attempts to highlight one aspect of this rich tradition, namely Buddhism. It argues that the invisibilization of this tradition is an injustice.

The point of reference for the nation on many occasions was constructed from 'outward sources'. This was manifest in the Constituent Assembly debates. It led to the marginalization of the Indian traditions of thought. This was on account of particular constructions of these traditions as being from the Orient (Rathore and Mohapatra 2017, 264–71), on the one hand, and being a subsidiary of the nation and state,[1] on the other. This prepared the ground for a disproportionate constitutionalism in our lives. For instance, key ideas and values such as those of compassion, Buddhahood, forgiveness, and self-improvement were superseded.

---

[1] Subsidiary relates to the manner of construction of Buddhism as relational to Hinduism, denying autonomous and independent existence. Buddhism along with other traditions have been classified as part of the extension of Hindu system.

In the past decades, debates have shifted on account of the search for internal sources for the creation of the self. They are present in non-hegemonic, non-dominant discourses, in the rebelling and critical traditions, and in the little and small selves found in the vernaculars and the colloquial. This chapter attempts to locate Buddhism in this universe to lay the ground for a political discourse that is drawn from the richness of diverse epistemes.

The categories selected for political discourse of the nation need not necessarily be derived from outside.

Dr B.R. Ambedkar, as chairman of the drafting committee of the Constitution, positioned his interpretation of Buddhism within the European Enlightenment frame. This lexicon of enlightened modernity privileged a particular construction of a rational being by constructing the 'other' as an un-progressive, traditional, and retrogressive being. This was fundamentally significant, especially for an India that had cross-cutting hierarchies and divisions caused by social formations erected by caste. His reading of Buddhism was constructed with a selection of precepts and concepts from the colossal body of Buddhism and Buddhahood.

Navayana Buddhism: The expression of this Buddhism was invoked as a radical philosophy. This was a socially and politically engaged Buddhism and its radicalness was manifested in the mass conversions that took place post Ambedkar's conversion in 1956. As a new religion for the Dalits, this reading became a traditional religion for some, a way of life for many, and a means of radical selfhood for many more on the map of new India. The act of mass conversion under the leader was a big act of legitimation of this religion in its own independent existence, distinguishing it from the so-called Hindu fold. This act was social, political, and historical as it revived an important line of thought/religion/way of life which had almost disappeared or got eclipsed in the nineteenth century in the very land of its birth, the very source of its emergence. It was seen as that corpus which was to provide the new nation its symbols and ideas of righteousness and ethics in public life.

However, this reading of Buddhism was also an invisibilization, as it privileged one reading of Buddhism at the expense of the other. It is, perhaps, necessary to find out to what extent the marginalization that ensued was an act of violence on the discourses of earlier Buddhism, rendering the other readings of the life and philosophy of the Buddha as obsolete and antiquated. It can be argued that this act sought to create a singular grand and meta understanding of the Buddha. A closer look at this phenomenon shows a 'subtle invisibilization'.[2]

Against this background, this chapter argues that the act of justice is to overcome the injustice of invisibilization by making available adequate space and time to be heard.

In the discussions of justice as a value and a moral lynchpin for humans, there have been umpteen theories that have been enumerated and explained in political theorization, such as retributive, distributive, Marxian, social, procedural, capability-based, and end-state theories of justice.[3] This chapter draws upon the feminist theorization of invisibilization and the subtle injustices that were and are being perpetrated. This includes shrinking, denying, and destroying social spaces. This feminist perspective does not solely look at the frames of patriarchy but at larger epistemological frames of truth, knowledge, and justice. The discourse of invisibilization draws on rationality. This has been articulated in *Ethical Loneliness: The Injustice of Not Being Heard* (Stauffer 2015). This text draws our attention to the suffocation and the trauma caused from not being heard. These are the parameters for determining the notions of justice. In the context of this chapter, the violence that has emerged from the imposition of singularities as the frame of reference can be seen in the dispensation of the State: its imposition on its citizens of the necessity to work with a singular constitutional frame of references.

The thinkers discussed in this chapter are positioned in the larger colossal knowledge of the Buddha and Buddhahood where there is no one singular but multiple and multi-layered understandings. The political and social values that this nation cherishes has

---

[2] Subtle invisibilization is distinct from gross invisibilization. In the previous category, the act is covert while it is overt in the latter, which is manifested in racism, casteism, and homophobia. Gross invisibilization is challenged and addressed; it cannot disappear from the public eye. However, the subtle goes unnoticed on many occasions. The manner in which the American and European scholars have given their interpretation of the 'revival' shows that there is discernible subtle invisibilization.

[3] Some of the key texts are Rawls' *A Theory of Justice*, *Justice as Fairness: A Restatement* and *Political Liberalism*; Nozick's *Anarchy, State and Utopia*; Sandel's *Liberalism and the Limits of Justice*; Pateman's *The Sexual Contract*; Nussbaum's *Frontiers of Justice*; Young's *Justice and the Politics of Difference*; Philips's *The Politics of Presence*; and Okin's *Justice, Gender and the Family*.

a long genealogy. In this act of tracing it, one realizes that looking inward is necessary 'to be fully present' and in order to confront the challenges of the contemporary world.

The idea of justice in the works of thinkers such as Anagarika Dharmapala (1873–1933), Dharmanand Kosambi (1876–1947), Ananda K. Coomaraswamy (1877–1947), and Rahul Sankrityayan (1893–1963) dynamically draws from Buddhism in the late nineteenth and early twentieth centuries. Their scholarship mapped the nation and its values using tropes of Buddhism which not only allows us a perusal of the Buddha himself but also to the cultures of criticality that Buddhism was espousing. Some of the questions that this chapter attempts to address are: How was 'the other' constructed in the works of the four thinkers? How was 'the other' constructed in the colossal world of the Buddha? How does the notion of otherness get constructed in the notion of justice?

The Genealogical Outline

The four thinkers invoked here—Dharmapala, Kosambi, Coomaraswamy, and Sankrityayan—have produced dynamic readings of the life and precepts of the Buddha. As disseminators and founders of organizations, each helped in the survival of a system of episteme and were instrumental in shaping readings of Buddhism as a thought that gave resilience, hope, and strength to those pushed to the margins. It was the contributions of these thinkers that made the field germane, to be later ploughed by the likes of Dr B.R. Ambedkar, who then seeded a very emancipatory Buddhism as a source of self for the new nation. The genealogical method attempts to map the kinship between the ideas of these four thinkers. What appears to be the pattern is that each of the thinkers selects certain precepts and propositions of the colossal Buddhist tradition and frames it with the categories of the colonial discourse of the times. The first thinker, Dharmapala, uses his understanding of Buddhism as a counterpoint. Kosmabi has an emancipatory reading of socialism, while Coomaraswamy positions his reading as a system of aesthetics and Sankrityayan does so by treating it as a perspective. These positions draw upon a certain notion of otherness of colonizers as well as that of the Buddha. In the narrative that follows, an attempt is made to describe the salient features of each of these positions and delineate the otherness of colonizers.

Anagarika Dharmapala's Quest for Identity

Anagarika Dharmapala[4] (1863–1933) was not born as 'Anagarika' but as David Don Hewavitharana in an elite Sri Lankan family in 1863 in Colombo, Sri Lanka. Dharmapala in his initial years received formal education in an English convent school. However, his transformation occurred upon his travel to India in 1885, which he undertook on the advice of the Theosophists;[5] he visited Bodh Gaya in 1891. It was at this juncture that he abandoned worldly life and took on the name and role of Anagarika Dharmapala.

His life can be read in three broad phases. The first phase, 1870–1900, is associated with his early attempts at creating a global Buddhist consciousness through his travels to various parts of the world, lecturing and writing on the cause of Buddhism. This phase was informed by two important events: establishment of the Maha Bodhi Society in 1891 and Dharmapala's representation of Buddhism at the World Congress of Religions at Chicago in 1893 where he delivered his famous lecture 'The World's Debt to Buddha'. The second phase was during the years 1900–15, when Dharmapala was instrumental in rallying the cause of nationalism and Sinhala patriotism, establishing the Sinhala identity on the lines of the sons of the soil theory. The third and last phase, 1915–33, of his life were dedicated to the cause of creating a pan-Buddhist outlook, as he systemically worked towards the creation of Buddhist spaces in India in the form of temples and *viharas* (monasteries), reinforcing the line of reasoning of distinct space and existence of Buddhism

---

[4] The biographical details of Dharmapala have been drawn from Guruge (1965). This is an interesting text as it was the government of Sri Lanka that commissioned it for disseminating Dharmapala's message to the masses. This act is seen as one of the first steps undertaken by the government to invoke and erect Dharmapala as the Father of Modern Lanka. This text is also seen as Dharmapala's autobiography.

[5] The Theosophical Society came to Sri Lanka in 1880 at the request of the Buddhist priests Sumangala and Gunanda, who were actively involved in the revivalism of Buddhism in Sri Lanka. Madame Blavatsky was instrumental in convincing Dharmapala to learn Pali and assess the condition of Buddhism in India. As mentioned by Dharmapala in his autobiography, Edwin Arnold's *Light of Asia* moved him extremely to visit Bodh Gaya and the sight of the decadence was the moment of his transformation.

in the lifeworld of Indian epistemes and philosophies. It is fascinating that it was only in 1933 that Dharmapala was ordained as a monk in Sarnath right before his death. He undertook the task of reinvigorating Buddhism and its dissemination throughout his life without any religious commitment.

Anagarika Dharmapala translates as 'homeless defender of the faith', a role that he had assumed on himself for the restoration of Buddhism in India, where it was dying a slow death. This may sound melodramatic, but not so for him; he was operating in times when Buddhism was on the verge of passing into oblivion. This was caused largely by the attempts to appropriate Buddhism into Hinduism, stating it to be an extension of the larger Hindu fold, with the Buddha as the ninth avatar or reincarnation of Vishnu. In a manner of denying any independence or distinction, Buddhism was understood by the general public as a sister extension of the Hindu way of life. This was challenged and critiqued by Dharmapala who articulated the massive distinctions between the two.

According to him, as recorded in *Return to Righteousness* (Guruge 1965),[6] these attempts were being undertaken in covert as well as overt manners, with Buddhist temples and sites of reverence held under the custodianship of Hindu priests and *mahants* (chief priests) being the most glaring instances. Dharmapala started his journey in India with the Bodh Gaya temple and the struggle to bring it back to Buddhist custodianship.[7] For this very cause, Dharmapala established the Maha Bodhi Society in the year 1891, and its mouthpiece the *Maha Bodhi Journal* in 1893, which played a crucial role in reviving Buddhism by the means of preservation and restoration of Buddhism in India. Over a period of time, this society became instrumental in bringing Buddhism back into the public sphere. It revived Buddhism as one of the most important sources of Indian episteme. It was the Maha Bodhi Society that

---

[6] This text is the primary text for Anagarika Dharmapala as it is the compilation of writings by Dharmapala. It consists of the writings that were published in entirety, as entries in the *Maha Bodhi Journal*, and speeches and lectures given by him at various events.

[7] Dharmapala fought the famous Bodh Gaya Case against Hemant Giri who was accused of worshipping the image of the Buddha as the ninth avatar of Vishnu. The case has been discussed extensively in Trevithick (2006).

funded the many visits that Kosambi and Sankrityayan would take to Buddhist lands such as Nepal, Tibet, and Sri Lanka to bring back home the lost Buddhist texts, scriptures, and canons. It was a huge contribution because in the absence of this organization, Buddhism would have definitely lost its place and position in the universe of epistemologies.

Dharmapala, through his writings, vociferously defended and argued the responsibility of India in preserving Buddhism as it was the very land where it all started. He envisioned the idea of Buddhist pilgrimage, with Bodh Gaya as the Buddhist Jerusalem. According to him,

> It was in Kusinagra, under the sal trees attending his disciple Ananada, Buddha said, Ananda, there are four places where the Bhikkus, Bhikkunis, Upasakas and Upasikas should visit. By seeing them they will rejoice and with gladdened heart they will say: this is the place where the tathagata was born; this is the place where he attained supreme knowledge; this is the place where he promulgated the niravanic law; this is the place where he attained Nibbana. These places are Kapailavastu, Buddh Gaya, Isipatana in Benaras and Kusinagra. (Guruge 1965, 561)

Of all the four sites, Bodh Gaya[8] was the most important for Dharmapala as this was where stood the same Bo tree under which the Buddha had attained enlightenment and the very tree from which Ashoka had sent some leaves along with a small sapling to Sri Lanka with Mahinda and Sanghmitta. The sapling was planted there, ushering the regime of righteousness by establishing Buddhism in Ceylon. He wrote,

> What Benaras is to Savities, Vishnupad at Gaya to Vaishnavities, Mecca is to Muhammadens and Jerusalem for the Christians, it is Bodh Gaya for the Buddhist as it is the Holiest shrine. (Guruge 1965, 561)

---

[8] Bodh Gaya was a very important space in Dharmapala's life. It was key to his idea of Buddhism as it was under the Bo tree in Gaya that the Buddha had attained enlightenment. It was much later, after a long struggle, that Bodh Gaya was transferred to the custodianship of Buddhists. It is presently seen as one of the most sacred sites of reverence for Buddhists worldwide.

This needs to be contextualized in the present times when the Government of India has been actively involved in the idea of Buddhist circuits and tourism, selling India as the holy land of Buddhism and attracting large numbers of Buddhist followers from across south-east Asia. The identification of the sites and their preservation need to be credited to Dharmapala along with the archaeological excavations undertaken by Alexander Cunnigham. It is fascinating that both the founder of Buddhism as a distinctive religion and the preserver were foreigners. Over a period of time, Dharmapala established viharas in Sarnath (Mulagandha Kuti) and Calcutta (Dharmarajika Chaitya), which became the beacons for the Buddhist dispensation.

Dharamapala lived a dual life, one of a restorationist in India and the other of the progenitor of the 'Sinhala' in Sri Lanka. He believed that India had to preserve Buddhism as it was the land where it originated and Sri Lanka had to salvage itself from colonial powers and other aliens as it was the promised land of Buddhism. He was central to the Sinhalese Sri Lankan imagination to the extent that he has the stature of being the 'Father of Modern Lanka'. His newspaper *Sinhala Bauddhaya* played a crucial role in creating a certain kind of nationalist consciousness that made Sinhala the key identity of Sri Lanka, placing it over other ethnic and religious identities. Buddhist monks of the likes of Gunanada and Sumangala shaped the ideas of the nation, which hinged on the critique of British colonialism as unrighteous and immoral. The promised land of the Buddha was converted into a den of arrack-drinking, beef-eating, and Bible-holding *kala suddha*s (brown sahibs). Dharmapala's contribution to this idea was huge as he created the two categories of foreigners and aliens: the first were the colonizers along with the missionaries; and the second were the pariahs, Tamils, Malayalis, and moors who were brought with the colonial master. He took the route of *Maha Kosha* tradition, invoking the history of the nation using the three historical texts *Mahavamsa*, *Cullavamsa*, and *Dipavamsa* to educate the Sinhalese of their great blood and race. His articulations divided the society between the sons of the soil and the others. Buddhism was invoked in an identarian manner that did lead to fractures and fissures which were worsened by future governments. However, his contributions in creating the space for Buddhism were substantial.

Dhramanand Damodar Kosambi's Concern for Equality

Dharamanand Damodar Kosambi[9] (1876–1947) was born in a Gaud Saraswat Brahmin Family in Goa, India, in 1876. Kosambi's journey of truth and knowledge started from Pune and the initial years (1880–1910) of his life were marked by endless travels to various parts of the country and outside. He started his quest by learning Sanskrit, which made him travel to Ujjain, Kashi, Indore, and Gwalior; his travels culminated in Sri Lanka, where he came in touch with Buddhism. It was at the Vidodaya Parivena, a Buddhist school set up by the Sri Lankan Buddhist priest Sumangala, that Kosambi received his formal training in Buddhism. He was trained for three years in Buddhist epistemology and Pali. Kosmabi was ordained as a Buddhist monk in Sri Lanka. Post his ordination, he travelled to Burma, where he undertook comparative study of Buddhist texts in the Burmese language. It was after seven years that Kosambi returned to India. It was during this phase (1910–late 1920s) that Kosambi was instrumental in setting up departments of Pali in Calcutta and Poona. This phase also witnessed some of the key texts on Buddhism being written by Kosambi. He also translated Buddhaghosha's *Visuddhimagga* upon the request of Professor James Haugton Woods for the Harvard Oriental Series. In the last phase of his life, 1930–40, we can see Kosambi's Gandhian overtures and his involvement with the nationalist struggle for Independence.

Making Pali a medium of instruction was a significant move that was needed for the democratization of Buddhism. The need was felt to draw Buddhist philosophy out from the cannons and texts. It was the very language in which the texts and inscriptions were written. Kosambi felt that an authentic reading of and scholarship on Buddhism necessitated taking it out of the hold

---

[9] Kosambi's autobiography, *Nivedan*, was published in Marathi. Meera Kosambi (his granddaughter) in 2011 translated the same (Kosambi 2011). In 2013, Meera Kosambi authored *Dharmanand Kosmabi: The Essential Writings*, which was a collection of some of the important essays that Kosambi had written in his lifetime. These were translated from Marathi to English by her. The biographical details are drawn from these sources and also from some of his writings which were translated to Hindi.

of the Oriental scholarship of his time, and he worked towards indigenizing the same. Kosambi felt this need very strongly and as a result worked towards setting up Departments of Pali in the Universities of Poona and Calcutta. These were among the first departments that trained scholars in Pali. At the same time, he translated key Buddhist texts into vernaculars such as Marathi and Gujarati. This was an important act, scholars would argue, as through this he was making the teachings of the Buddha available for the common masses. Before this, they had heard about Bhagvan Buddha, but for first time it was possible for them to engage directly with the Buddha's philosophy themselves.

Many scholars[10] would argue that Kosambi was instrumental in bringing the Buddha into the land of Maharashtra, which had seen some of the greatest critical Warkari and Bhakti traditions. But the land was given the Buddha for the first time by Kosambi. Through his writings, he also introduced Marx and Hegel, and the Marxian and socialist ideologies. It would be fascinating to trace if Kosambi was instrumental in shaping the line of thought that Ambedkar eventually picked. Gail Omvedt argued that Kosambi's *Bhagvan Buddha*[11] was inspirational in Ambedkar's choice of Buddhism over other religious and rational dispensations (Omvedt 2003, 235).

Kosambi read socialism in the Buddhist epistemology and drew parallels between the two dispensations, working towards negotiating the possibilities of leading a humane life in colonial conditions. The idea of 'equanimity' was the link that he drew between socialism and Buddhism. Kosambi was involved in the national movement and was influenced by Gandhi's non-violence. The reason he was moved by the idea of non-violence was precisely because he felt that the defining values of the Indian civilization were non-violence

---

[10] Suthankar, Omvedt, and M. Kosambi have argued on these lines.

[11] Kosambi's *Bhagvan Buddha* was the magnum opus written on the Buddha and Buddhism in 1940 in Marathi. However, the Sahitya Parishad took up the task of its translation into eight Indian languages, including Hindi. Kosambi wrote many other texts on the theme, which included *Buddha, Dharma ani Sangha* (1910); *Buddha-lila-sara-sangraha* (1914), also translated to Gujarati as *Buddha-lila, Baudhha Sanghacha Parichay* (1926); *Hindi Sanskriti ani Ahinsa* (1935), translated to Hindi as *Bhartiya Sanskriti our Ahinsa* (Meera Kosambi translated the same into English as *Indian Civilisation and Non Violence*). The list is endless. For more works, refer to M. Kosambi (2011, 414–17).

and truth. In his text *Hindi Sanskriti ani ahinsa*,[12] Kosambi traced the genealogy of non-violence. He argued that the defining feature of almost each and every epoch was the value of *karuna* that imbibed the principle of living a non-violent life. His reading of Buddhism was through the lens of socialism. He led the life of a disseminator and activist who worked rigorously towards the upliftment of the weak; he established the Bahujan Vihara, which was the centre of activities for the same cause.

Ananda Kentish Coomaraswamy's Construction of the 'Civilizational'

Ananda Kentish Coomaraswamy[13] (1877–1947) was born in Ceylon in 1877 but spent his life in the distant land of England. Coomaraswamy's re-entry into Ceylon was necessitated by his doctoral research (1902–6) in 1902 and this was with a different vantage point, as that of a geologist and mineralogist. During this period, he was also the director of the Ceylon Mineralogical Survey and it was during this stint that he had his encounter with colonialism. In the course of his travels and visits to the countryside, he realized that the culture and traditions of Ceylon were dying. His writings of this phase were marked with a particular understanding of colonialism as the harbinger of destruction, depredation, and appropriation. Moved by these conditions, he set up the Ceylon Social Reform Society, which was instrumental in initiating an anti-colonial discourse with regard to art and culture.[14] The second phase of his life and writings

---

[12] This work uses the Hindi translation of the text available as *Bharatiya Sanskriti aur Ahinsa* (1926) and its English translation *Civilization and Non Violence* (1935) in M. Kosambi (2013, 327–57).

[13] The biographical details of Coomaraswamy have been drawn from the authoritative three-volume series written by Roger Lipsey (1977). Moni Bagchee's *Ananda Coomaraswamy: A Study* (1977) and S. Durai Raja Singham's *Ananda Commaraswamy: Remembering and Remembering Again and Again* (1974) have been helpful.

[14] It was in this phase of life that Coomaraswamy posed some of his strongest attacks on the colonial regime on the grounds of cultural depredation and aesthetics. Some of his writings of this phase include *Art and Swadeshi* (1912), *Essays in National Idealism* (1909), *Message of the East* (1923), and *The Bugbear of Literacy* (1947).

(1913–30) centred around the question of the place of art forms in the nation and its imaginations. This was also informed by his professional position as the curator of the Boston Art Museum. As a result, this phase witnessed voluminous scholarship on the themes of art, its representation, typologies, kinds, and modes of understanding them.

Writing on the theme of differentiated totalities, he also took to deconstructing and challenging the Western understandings and assessment of Indian art forms, questioning the homogenous category that was used to understand them without substance. It was his authorship and scholarship on every fine detail in the world of Indian art that helped him in cataloguing and writing extensive bibliographies on Indian art forms.[15] He published a large corpus of material on Indian art in the *MFA Bulletin*.[16] This phase also witnessed some of the key arguments that Coomaraswamy brought in with regard to cultural roots of art forms and the necessity of understanding the cultural locations. As a result of this, he wrote on the differences and peculiarities of art forms of the East and the non-Eastern.

His most creditworthy act as an art historian was his defence of Indian art forms as being original and proving that many art forms, such as the Buddha image, as being of Indian origin. These arguments were carried forward in the third phase, 1930s–40s, of his writings within the frames of what he referred to as Philosphia Perennis, which was the understanding of the philosophies of religion to understand the human condition. He wrote extensively on Buddhism and the Buddha.

Coomaraswamy's works form a large corpus. In his lifetime, he wrote extensively on a variety of issues and concerns; hence, there is a difficulty in typifying and establishing him within a certain

---

[15] Some of the works in this capacity were the *Catalogue of Indian Collections in the Museum of Fine Arts* (*Part I: General Introduction, Part II: Sculpture, Part III: Buddhist Art, Part IV: Jaina Paintings and Manuscripts, Part V: Rajput painting* and *Part VI: Mughal Painting*). All these catalogues were published by the Boston Museum of Fine Arts. Apart from these volumes, he published *Bibliographies of Indian Art* and *Portfolio of Indian Art: Objects Selected from the Collection of the Museum*.

[16] *MFA Bulletin*, Bulletin of the Museum of Fine Arts, Boston.

kind of scholarship. Coomaraswamy has usually been regarded as an art historian by a large number of scholars writing on art and history of art. However, it would be a partial and incorrect assessment of his scholarship to judge him solely as an art historian. There is a need to take him out of this mould which has led to a restricted understanding of his work. His scholarship and writings need to be treated as that of a thinker's who proposed a body of ideas for the reconstitution of public life. Coomaraswamy wrote extensively on culture, civilization, religion, art and representation, nation, nationalism, and philosophy.

While writing on various themes and ideas, Buddhism was central in his scheme for reinventing and creating a new kind of inventory for the Indian nation and civilization. Coomaraswamy's inventory was distinct from that of other thinkers invoking Buddhism, as he explored the life and meaning of the Buddha through the various manifestations and representations in art forms. This act was undertaken very rigorously and vociferously as he attacked and critiqued the Western scholarship on Eastern and especially Indian art forms, which according to him were misinterpretations and distortions to the extent that their real meaning and essence were lost. Imploring the category of cultural subjectivity, he argued that the writings were incorrect assessments of the true meaning of what the art forms represented.

He undertook the daunting task of pluralizing and diversifying the various art forms, salvaging them from the homogenous category of Indian art forms. He ventured into art terrains that were never explored as he went on to bring out the nuances of art forms, articulating the lines of distinction between Mughal and Rajput paintings, and the lines of distinctions within the monolithic Pahari art, articulating the distinction of Kangra art from Jammu and to Chamba art. This was significant as he pushed the idea of why there was a need to understand the fine lines of distinction. According to him, art and art forms are the passions of races, through which they chose to represent themselves in a certain way, and they are the memories of civilizations; any attempt to homogenize and typecast all in one mould was a huge injustice to the way cultures thought of and represented themselves.

Coomaraswamy used his writings to pitch in a significant aspect of being, that is, culture. In the context of the nationalist struggle, whereby the focus of the movement was political, social, and economic, Coomaraswamy invoked the 'Question of Culture', articulating the incompleteness of the normative in nation-building if the base of culture is not invoked. According to him, more than any other historical moment, the moment of dealing with the cultural being was the most significant.

Through his writings on Buddhist art forms and iconography, Coomaraswamy invoked the Buddha as the exemplar and ascertained that it was only the Buddha who had the capacity to be an exemplar. The manner in which the image of the Buddha[17] travelled extensively to distant lands and cultures, where this image was localized and absorbed in the specific cultural milieus, speaks volumes on the life and philosophy of this *margadarshak* (guide and preceptor). He argued that one has to understand the transition of his representation from early symbols such as the lotus and *paduka* (footprints) to the anthropomorphic form, whereby the Buddha is given a human form (as in the Gandhara and Mathura schools), as giving a physical shape to the exemplar was fascinating. He explained the reasons for the spread of the Buddha image. It garnered the kind of followership it did because of the way the Buddha spoke about the human condition. According to Coomaraswamy, the Buddha was an exemplar as well as the biggest artistic, cultural, and civilizational icon.

He distinguished between Eastern and other civilizations:[18] the latter manifested itself as the 'modern', 'mechanical', and 'industrial', which in the name of human progress converted the creative, skilful self to an alien and mechanical self. However, the Eastern civilizations were distinct and this civilizational matrix emerged from the strength of philosophies, traditions, and religions of which Buddhism was an integral part—Buddhism was shared and lived by various cultures within the 'Eastern' matrix. He argued vehemently that Indian nationalism should be strengthened by this kind of civilizational strength which is spiritual in nature. He defines the civilizational project as a philosophical one with Buddhism as its authentic foundation and the Buddha as an exemplar, creating a new understanding of India as a civilization and nation. For the

---

[17] Coomaraswamy articulated these ideas in two important tracts: *The Origin of the Buddha Image* (1927) and *The Elements of Buddhist Iconography* (1935).

[18] 'The other' in this chapter refers to the European and American.

new nation to create a future, it was of great importance to know its glorious past, a past that saw great traditions coexisting in harmony and standing as systems of wisdom, knowledge, values, and, above all, spiritualism.

According to Coomaraswamy,

> Every Race contributes something essential to the world's civilization in the centre of its own self- expression and self-realization. The character built up in solving its own problems, in the experience of its misfortunes is itself a gift which it offers to the world. The essential contribution of India, is simply her Indianness: her great humiliation would be to substitute or to have substituted for this own character (Svabava) a cosmopolitan veneer, for them indeed she must come before the world empty handed. (Coomaraswamy 1952, 21)

Rahul Sanskrityayan's Dialectics of Engaged Buddhism

Invoked as Mahapandit, Rahul Sanskrityayan[19] (1893–1963) is remembered in the national memory as the first travelogue writer and polygot who, through his writings, explained the distinction between travelling and exploring. Sanskrityayan was born as Kedarnath Pandit in Azamgarh, India, in 1893 and later took the name of Rahul Sanskrityayan post his conversion to Buddhism. His life navigated through various ideological transitions. His early life was influenced by Dayanand Saraswati, at which time he took up the role of an Arya Samajist. It was during this time of his life that he started travelling across the nation. He felt rather incomplete in his search, which took him to Sri Lanka; it was there that he undertook the extensive study of Buddhism and later converted to a Buddhist Bhikshu.

During this phase of his life he made journeys to Nepal, Ladakh, and Tibet in search of lost Buddhist manuscripts and texts. Some of the Buddhist Pali and Sanskrit texts were part of libraries of the Buddhist universities of Vikramshila and Nalanda. Apart from the texts, Sanskrityayan was attributed to have found lost treasures in the

---

[19] Sanskrityayan's autobiography, *Meri Jivan Yatra* (1944), along with *Volga se Ganga* (1943), *Dharshan Digghadarshan* (2018) were read for the biographical details. Alaka Atreya Chudal (2016) was used for other details.

form of artefacts, sculptures, and *tankha*s (painting on cotton, silk appliqué, usually depicting a Buddhist deity, scene, or mandala), which he brought back to India after undertaking umpteen arduous visits. His autobiography, *Meri Jeevan Yatra*, and books such as *Volga Se Ganga* and *Darshan Digghadarshan* provide interesting insights into the various transitions that Sankrityayan's life went through.

Over a period of time, he transitioned into the Marxian fold as he was involved with the agrarian question in the nationalist struggle. He was critical of colonial rule and as a result of his active role in the *kisaan andolan* (farmers' movements), he was arrested twice. It was during one of his stays in jail that Rahul wrote *Baisvinsadi* (Sankrityayan 2017), which was his ideal picture of utopia. He gave a blueprint of the society he imagined, which was a fusion of Buddhist–Marxian utopia, a commune on the lines of Nalanda. The Buddhist logic was to be the foundational principle on which the commune would exist devoid of any sense of ego, greed, or desire and with complete annihilation of private property. This would be a self-sufficient society/village with just and ethical beings. In the last phase of his life, he was an ardent Marxian nationalist. In all the avatars of Rahul Sankrityayan, the common link was that of being an explorer, a Ghummakad Shastri, that is, the composer of the *Ghummakad Shastra*). This work is important in understanding him as a Buddhist monk who read Marxism and Buddhism as parallels.

According to Sankrityayan, Buddhism was one of his first serious engagements with organized religions as it thwarted many of the big claims and ideas that they represented. The Buddha was the first 'explorer' for him, who explored the terrains of human subjectivity and provided the meaning of being human. For Sankrityayan, the Buddha placed primacy on knowledge and truth, which one had to arrive at by oneself in the absence of any mediation. This was based on the edifice of anti-superstition and anti-blind faith. The manner in which religion came to the people was problematic as the focus shifted from the human and became god-centric, which not only brought the burden of rituals and faith on humans but also converted them into blind followers. Religion, according to him, was a liberating experience that was meant to give agency but instead put the individual in shackles. For Sankrityayan, the emergence and spread of Buddhism was one of the most defining moments of human history. In *Bauddha Darshan*, the key text that

Sankrityayan wrote, he articulated his *dharmic vichar* (righteous views) on the basis of Buddhism. In this he brought forth two important themes: first, the exposition of the life and meaning of the Buddha and second, the reason for the spread of Buddhism. He went to the extent of referring to Buddhism as Annishawarvad, meaning anti-god thesis.

The dialectics of Buddhism and the deployment of its philosophy, values, and principles for sociological, economic, political, and environmental concerns can be discerned in his work *Buddhist Dialectics*. Writing from a Marxian perspective,[20] he argued that the big category of analysis of Buddhist philosophy was *dukkha* (misery) and its annihilation. For him *dukkha* was not solely an individual category but a social one and the *nidaan* (solution/annihilation) of the same had to be social. He links it to the economic category of private property ownership and, as a true Marxian, would also link it to the question of equality and justice. He articulated that till private property exists there are little or no chances for society to be just and egalitarian. This was a realization he came to when he was involved in the peasants' agitation in Bihar and on the question of land reform.

According to Sankrityayan,

> For Buddha the origin of monarchy did not lie in any divine source but kingship was the product of the growth of private property. Private property led to inequality or class division among the people, who started quarrelling among themselves (overtly and covertly) started snatching each other's property, and selected one from among them as their judge, who by accumulating power for selfish ends developed into a king. (Sankrityayan 1970, 2)

---

[20] The Buddhist–Marxian praxis in Sankrityayan's writings is clearly articulated in 'Buddhist Dialectics' in *New Age: Political Monthly of Communist Party* (1956, 42–8), which was later republished as the essay 'Buddhism: The Marxist Approach' in a four-essay collective in Sankrityayan (1970). However, he wrote on the themes of Buddhism and Marxism separately in many of his other works. His exposition of Buddhism is included in some of his works: *Bauddha Darshan* (1944), *Darshan Digghadarshan*, *Baisvinsadi*, *Tibbetmein Bauddha Dharma* (1948), *Divodass*, *Kinnardeshmein*, and *Ghummkad Shastra*. On the theme of Marxism, his works include the biographies of Marx and Mao titled *Karl Marx*, *Mao Che Tung*, and *Samyavaad Hi Kyun*.

He further writes,

> Buddha lived in the 6th–5th century BC (death 483 BC). At that time too economic and social discrimination was very sharp. For the eradication of economic and social discrimination was very sharp. For the eradication of economic inequality Buddha confined his efforts to the monastic communes alone, but the abolition of social inequality he attempted on a universal scale. His voice raised against casteism had its effect but the basic foundation of casteism lay in the high caste 'haves' and the low caste 'have nots'. Without removing the one the other could not be done away with. All the same Buddha's communes granted equal rights in the monastic order to the lowest castes. Buddhism fervently advocated the brotherhood of man without any distinction of race, country or caste. The principle of coexistence embodied in the panchshila was put into practice by Buddhism. (Sankritayan 1970, 2–3)

He read an advanced social and political theory in Buddhism. He wrote that at the time of the Buddha too, Buddhism was invoked as the social, political, and moral theory of how kingdoms should work. If one picks up Marxian ideas on dialectical materialism, one finds resonance with Sankrityayan's writings on private property and annihilation of *dukkha*.

Sankrityayan, in his pursuit of finding the true sources of Buddhism—in the form of texts, canons, and scriptures—travelled across the length and breadth of the Buddhist centres which resulted in a number of visits to Nepal, Tibet, and Burma. At the time of his writing and exposition, Sankrityayan found that many of the key Buddhist sources had disappeared from India. He undertook the task of travelling to hostile and difficult terrains to get them back. Many of these scripts were in Sanskrit and were translated to Tibetan. Sankrityayan not only undertook the daunting task of retrieval but also of translating them to Devanagari. This is an important contribution, like the legacy of Kosambi—democratizing the canons, making the texts available to the masses for them to understand for themselves the true meaning and essence of Buddhism. Interestingly, Sankrityayan also brought back with him rare artefacts and *thanka*s from Tibet as it was also reeling under the pressure of the cultural revolution of mainland China. These are now housed in the Sankrityayan collection at the Patna Museum, Bihar, India. Sankrityayan's contribution in the mapping of Buddhism is immense at two levels: first, in the restoration of lost Buddhist sources and texts and second, in radicalizing the reading of Buddhism.

The Sakhya and Navayana readings of Buddhism undertaken by Pandit Iyothee Thass and B.R. Ambedkar have been mostly invoked as emancipatory readings of Buddhism, emphasizing the ideals of self-respect, equality, and human dignity in Indian life. However, this chapter argues that this kind of radical reading was made much earlier, in the invocations of Kosambi, Dharamapala, Coomaraswamy, and Sankrityayan. The next section will look at the categories of justice from their understanding of the Buddha.

The Buddha as 'the Other'

In the reading of Buddhist philosophy in all the four scholars we have discussed, the Buddha is invoked as an 'exemplar'. The Buddha is the master for these students. Can we then know about the master's discursive formation through the various readings of these students?

The agency is in humans themselves and not outside. The capacity of and possibility for each to transform one's life and being is upheld by the Buddha. The doing away with the middlemen or mediators is clear in the exposition of the thinkers insofar as they value *atmagyan* or self-transformation in the Buddha. The radicalization which eventually became central in the Navayana mapping was articulated in each of the readings. This becomes comprehensible in Dharamapala's *Return to Righteousness* and Sanskrityayan's *Buddha Darshan* and their categories of identity and dialectics. The idea of justice is social, whether in the equality that Kosambi invokes in *Bhagvan Buddha* or in civilization that Coomaraswamy invokes in *The Origin of the Buddha Image, Hinduism and Buddhism,* and *Elements of Buddhist Iconography.*

Otherness and Notions of Justice

It can be argued that the construction of the notion of justice varies with the way otherness is constructed. Dharmapala invokes otherness in the sense of a counterpoint to the creation of identity. Kosambi's understanding of emancipatory Buddhism was foregrounded in the value of equality in Buddhism and took it closer to socialism.

Coomaraswamy positions his reading as a system of aesthetics in the realization of civilization, while Sankrityayan's perspective emanates from the Marxian–Buddhist dialectics. These positions draw upon a certain notion of otherness of colonizers as well as that of the Buddha.

In the works of the four thinkers, the Buddha's precepts and propositions have been positioned within the frames of liberty, equality, and fraternity. These come together as notions of righteousness. The notion of justice embedded in righteousness is 'discursive justice'. Dharmapala uses these precepts as counterpoints to discuss identity. Kosambi used the precepts to argue for equality. This was the basis for his emancipatory reading of socialism. Coomaraswamy uses them to delineate systems of aesthetics. Sankrityayan uses these precepts to develop a dialectical perspective.

The notion of Buddhahood that was invisibilized is the one based on the 'emptiness of objective existence'.[21] From this emerge three fundamental ideas for the dispensation of justice, which are *karuna*, *kshama*, and *atma gyan* which can be translated as compassion, forgiveness, and self-reconstruction. Here, the otherness of the Buddha is an inspiration for the perfectibility of human beings.

The idea of justice is central to the life of the Buddha. The reasons for the emergence of the Buddha as the exemplar can be understood from his philosophy, as it is also a political theorization of man/woman and his/her world. The construction of the Buddha in the works of thinkers brings out clear codes of how humans are to live and how the political/social state must function. In their readings, the Buddha is available to everyone from the smallest beings to the largest tribe. Justice is available not only at the centre but also at the peripheries. They would go to the extent of articulating that the Buddha's envisioning, in fact, emanates from the peripheries and margins. There are no relegations, divisions, and differentiations in the life world for the Buddha; in fact, this impinged on the critique of the Brahmanical social order. The real values for the society were lived in the Buddha and realized in the texts which prescribed the annihilation of *dukkha*, which can be read as the attainment of self-perfection. Another important argument reiterated by almost all the thinkers was that the life of the Buddha was a text in

---

[21] This idea has been discussed in the works of Nalanda masters.

itself, and in order to know about the values and principles that the Buddha espoused, understanding his life was enough. One really did not have to read Buddhist texts to do so.

Another dynamic understanding of the category of justice can be found in the idea of one having to salvage oneself from 'the other', who could be the source of trials, tribulations, and injustices. This emanates from the very manner in which 'the other' is constructed and invoked, which has always been posed as 'the adversarial other'. As a result, the self has to be constructed as antithetical to 'the other'; the self has to be pitted against it, in contradistinction to it; the self has to be distinct from it. During the course of the nationalist struggle for independence in colonial societies, many of the responses were informed by this notion of 'the colonial other'. As a result, the colonizers were constructed as 'the other' from whom the nationalist self was to be preserved, saved, and salvaged. The focus was on the preservation of distinctiveness. In the processes of creation of identity, whether nationalist, religious, or ethnic, there is always this other that one needs to be very distinct from. However, this chapter has attempted to understand the category of 'the other' in a different manner.

In this case 'the other' then could be a creator, interactor, or facilitator. 'The other' is not adversarial but a *margadarshak*, the exemplar and the ideal from whom one has to learn the lexicon of righteousness and good being. The 'other' with which there is a fusion of one's self is referred to as the authoritative horizon, the exemplar paradigm. This is the one who informs us about the larger possibilities of what being human means. There is a constant process of evolution as the self is in interaction with and learns from 'the other', who helps in learning and unlearning at the same time. The Buddha is invoked as 'the other' in each of the thinkers that this chapter considers as the makers of modern India. The search which is inward then attempts to create an understanding of justice, distant from other notions of justice which are anchored in the language of law, order, rules, and punitions.

* * *

According the Hegel, the 'Oriental Spirit' is the

> [r]espect for reality within reality and ornamentation of the imagination. The orientals have firmly determined personalities. As they

are once, they change no more. They do not stray from the direction of the path once taken. What is beyond their path does not exist for [Oriental spirit]. But what disturbs them on the path is hostile for them. Their once firmly determined character cannot let go of itself, it cannot integrate or propitiate what is against it. One becomes dominant, the other is dominated. (Rathore and Mohapatra 2017, 264–5)

Based on this work, questions need to be posed to the Hegelian construction of the 'Orient spirit' which is foundational to the subsequent construction of east and southeast Asia as the Orient. The otherness of the Buddha as read and invoked by Dharmapala, Kosambi, Coomaraswamy, and Sankrityayan is antithetical to the construction of the Orient. *Karuna, kshama,* and *atmagyan,* as grounded in the emptiness of objective existence, present a completely different rendition of the so-called Oriental spirit. And this spirit, more than anything else, was closer to reflectivity, assessment, revisability, and, most importantly, perfectibility of the self. The tall *margadarshak*s such as the Buddha, the Jain Trithankaras, Bhakti and Sufi saints, and the gurus of Sikhism gave primacy to this kind of self, which informs us of the falsified, incorrect, and untrue construction of the Oriental spirit and the caution one has to take before venturing into their romanticization.

Within the Oriental and nationalist discourses, the convergence is on the 'revival' of Buddhism. However, in the civilizational/discursive discourse the concern is about the 'return'. There is a need to clearly demarcate the categories of reference, that is, revival and return. The thinkers invoked in this chapter have been constructed as revivalist by both colonial and post-colonial thought. This chapter tries to argue that this is the injustice of not being heard, and if heard, then in a way that distorts their voice. Based on the glimpse of their readings of Buddhism, we find that it is possible to look deeper into the question of the 'return'.

References

Ambedkar, B.R. 2006. *The Buddha and His Dhamma*. Delhi: Siddharth Books.

Chatterjee, Margaret. 2011. *Modalities of Otherness: A Serpentining Tale of Enemies, Strangers, Neighbours, Mortality, Hospitality, and Cognate Matters*. New Delhi and Chicago: Bibliophile South Asia.

Chatterjee, Partha. 1986. *Nationalist Thought and the Colonial World: A Derivative Discourse.* London: Zed Books.

Chudal, Atreya Alaka. 2016. *A Free Thinking Culturalist: Life History of Rahul Sankrityayan.* Oxford: Oxford University Press.

Coomaraswamy, Ananda Kentish. 1909. *The Message of the East.* Madras: Ganesh.

———. 1912. *Art and Swadeshi.* Madras: Ganesh.

———. 1927. 'The Origin of the Buddha Image'. *Art Bulletin*: 287–329.

———. 1943. 'Eastern Wisdom and Western Knowledge'. *Isis* 34, no. 4: 359–63.

———. 1952. *The Dance of Shiva: Fourteen Indian Essays.* Bombay: Asia Publishing House.

———. 1956. *Buddha and the Gospel of Buddhism.* Bombay: Asia Publishing House.

———. 1975. *Hinduism and Buddhism.* New Delhi: Munshiram Manoharlal.

Gombrich, Richard, and Obeyesekre Gananath. 1990. *Buddhism Transformed: Religious Change in Sri Lanka.* Delhi: Motilal Banarsidass.

Gombrich, Richard. 2006. *Theravada Buddhism: A Social History from Ancient Benares to Modern Colombo*, Second Edition. London: Routledge.

Guruge, Ananda. 1965. *Return to Righteousness: A Collection of Speeches, Essays and Letters of the Anagarika Dharmapala.* Ceylon: The Government Press.

Kosambi, Meera. 2011. *Nivedan: The Autobiography of Dharmanand Kosmabi.* Ranikhet: Permanent Black.

———. 2013. *Dharmanand Kosambi: The Essential Writings.* Ranikhet: Permanent Black.

Kymlica, Will. 2002. *Liberalism, Community and Culture.* New York: Oxford University Press.

Lipsey, Roger. 1977a. *Coomaraswamy, Part 1: Selected Papers, Traditional Art and Symbolism.* Bollingen Series, Princeton: Princeton University Press.

———. 1977b. *Coomaraswamy, Part 2: Selected Papers, Metaphysics.* Bollingen Series, Princeton: Princeton University Press.

———. 1977c. *Coomaraswamy, Part 3: His Life and Work.* Bollingen Series, Princeton: Princeton University Press.

Malagoda, K. 1976. *Buddhism in Sinhalese Society: 1750–1931.* Berkeley, California: University of California Press.

Narasu, P. Lakshmi. 1993. *The Essence of Buddhism.* Reprint, New Delhi: Asian Educational Services 1993, originally published in Colombo, 1907.

Nussbaum, Martha. 2007. *Frontiers of Justice: Disability, Nationality. Species Membership.* Harvard: Harvard University Press.

Omvedt, Gail. 2003. *Buddhism in India: Challenging Brahmanism and Caste*. New Delhi: Sage Publications.
Rathore, Aakash Singh, and Rimina Mohapatra. 2017. *Hegel's India: A Reinterpretation, with Texts*. Oxford: Oxford University Press.
Rodrigues, Valerian, ed. 2002. *The Essential Writings of B.R. Ambedkar*. Oxford: Oxford University Press.
———. 2006. 'Dalit-Bahujan Discourse in Modern India'. In *Political Ideas in Modern India: Thematic Explorations*, edited by V.R Mehta and Thomas Pantham, Vol. X, Part 7. New Delhi: Sage Publications.
Sankrityayan, Rahul. 1970. 'Buddhism: A Marxist Approach'. New Delhi: People Publishing House.
———. 2017. *Baisvinsadi*. Allahabad: Kitab Mahal. Originally Published in 1923.
Stauffer, Jill. 2015. *Ethical Loneliness: The Injustice of Not Being Heard*. New York: Columbia University Press.
Taylor, Charles. 1989. *Sources of the Self: The Making of the Modern Identity*. Harvard University Press.
Trevithick, Alan. 2006. *The Revival of Buddhist Pilgrimage at Bodh Gaya (1811–1949): Anagarika Dharmapala and the Mahabodhi Temple*. Delhi: Motilal Banarasidass.

5

B.R. Ambedkar's Philosophy of Religion

BANSIDHAR DEEP

Ambedkar was never given enough attention in the academia,[1] but these days we find some literature about his thoughts on sociology, political science, social exclusion and discrimination, and so on. Therefore, we find very little literature on Ambedkar which are genuinely written on him and his philosophy. Even what is available is political and written with personal motivations.[2] The emergence of the Dalit Panther movement in Maharashtra in the early 1970s had induced some writings which reflected the lived experiences of and ground realities for Dalit-Bahujans; later many Dalit-Bahujans also started writing on Ambedkar. The space for

---

[1] For details, see Aakash Singh Rathore's article in the *Huffington Post* titled 'Indian Academia's Shunning of Ambedkar the Philosopher Reeks of Social Exclusion' (Rathore 2018). In this article he has broadly focused on how Ambedkar was excluded from the syllabi of philosophy departments in India but we can also argue here that the Indian academia has in fact treated Ambedkar as an Untouchable by keeping his writings out of academic curriculums.

[2] These days, many scholars and researchers, including upper-caste academicians, are writing on Ambedkar. This trend of writing on Ambedkar by upper castes may be interpreted by some as being motivated by political and commercial purposes as Dalit writings and issues have started to increasingly gain acceptance in the global academic world.

Ambedkarite literature to emerge has been created through the rise and articulation of the Ambedkarite discourse across India through the Dalit Panther movement, the Republican Party of India, the Bahujan Samaj Party, and the Mandal Commission. One finds that there is still a dearth of literature on Ambedkar's ideas on religion and philosophy. This chapter attempts to address this lacuna in the literature by looking at the concept of religion and philosophy from the perspective of Ambedkar.

I would argue that Ambedkar dealt with religion very rationally/pragmatically and philosophically rather than merely sociologically. Many philosophers in the West were critical about religion such as Plato, Rene Descartes, Immanuel Kant, G.W.F. Hegel, and so on. Likewise, in India, many have critically engaged with religion, starting from Charvaka, Buddha, Nagarjuna in the ancient time, up to Kabir during the Bhakti movement to Jotirao Phule, Periyar Ramaswamy, and Ambedkar in the modern era. However, they did not reject the essentiality of religion in human society. Ambedkar as a philosopher (Gokhale 2008a, 3–11) was very critical of religions; nevertheless he did not reject religion in its totality but accepted it in a pragmatic and normative sense. But, Ambedkar's ideas on religion remain relatively unexplored in academia and, therefore, needs our attention.

Ambedkar being a staunch critic of religions scrutinized the dominant religions in the world such as Hinduism, Christianity, Islam, Sikhism, and Buddhism. I will discuss the issues/questions regarding Ambedkar's notion of religion and philosophy in sections in this chapter. In the first section I have discussed how Ambedkar encountered and countered religious and caste-based experiences in his life, from his school days to his professional life. In the second section I have tried to explore the idea of the essentiality of religion in Ambedkar's philosophy of human life/society: How is his conception of religion different from others? Why did he convert to Buddhism and not to any other religion? In the third section I have explained how Ambedkar dealt with religion very rationally/pragmatically and philosophically as well, rather than merely sociologically. In the fourth section I have explored how Ambedkar has dealt with philosophy and particularly the philosophy of religion. In other words, how did Ambedkar engage with philosophy of religion in particular and religion in general? In the last/fifth section I have discussed the multiple ontological realities of religion in Ambedkar's thought.

Encountering and Countering Religiosity and Caste-Based Experiences in Ambedkar's Life

When one talks about the philosophy of religions, it is perceived as a critical estimation of the existing religions to evaluate the teachings and doctrines of each religion, whether it be Hinduism, Islam, Christianity, Sikhism, Buddhism, or any other. This is what has been done by Ambedkar. He was very critical of Hindu religious practices, worship, values, norms, beliefs, rituals, ceremonies, prayers, sacrifices, and so on; this was also true of his outlook towards other religions.

Ambedkar's interest in the study of religion and theology probably arose from the deep experiences of inequality that he experienced in his own society. He extensively studied theology and religions of the world (Ambedkar 1987, 5–6), consequently producing a large body of literature on the subject. He also had the first hand experiences of being discriminated against and isolated; this was the discrimination which was the result of particularly orthodox Hindu religious belief. For instance, he served as a military secretary of the king of Baroda and stayed in a Parsi Dharamshala, but when it became known that he was an Untouchable Hindu, he was thrown out, for no other reasons but for belonging to an Untouchable caste. In his desperate condition 'No Hindu, no Muslim gave him shelter in the city of Baroda' (Keer 2012, 34). Untouchables like him were seen as polluted beings and were not allowed access to public places such as barber shops, wells, places of worship, modes for conveyance, schools, and so on. At Satara school, where he studied, he was isolated from other students and made to sit outside the class room on a piece of gunny mat which he had to carry to the school. The feeling of isolation and discrimination got worse when some teachers refused to touch his notebooks for fear of being polluted (Narain and Ahir 2010, 1–2). All these unequal treatments and discriminations, as Ambedkar believed, are primarily the consequence of the deeply rooted Hindu religious doctrines of inequality and purity. These various experiences led him to not accept any religion at face value and critically examine religious beliefs and practices. He accepted that in all religions there is caste discrimination at different levels but the castes among non-Hindus (Mohammedans, Sikhs, and Christians) are fundamentally different from castes among Hindus (Ambedkar 2007, 33). Caste is essential in the case of a Hindu and his/her religion, whereas it is not so in the case of non-Hindus.

'Among the non-Hindus, caste is a practice, not a sacred institution. They did not originate it. With them it is only a survival. They do not regard caste as a religious dogma' (Ambedkar 2007, 34). The caste system of Hindus percolated into other religions or non-Hindus, and non-Hindus do not have their own castes. But in practice caste is prevalent in non-Hindus too in India. Other religions are no exception to Ambedkar's critique:, he questioned the deep-rooted metaphysical conception of God in Islam and Christianity and the associated supernatural practices in these religions, which he claimed subordinated human beings and undermined their significance in the world (Ambedkar 2003a, 97–108). His critique equally extended to practices and institutions in Buddhism too, where he raised certain questions about the Bhikkhu Sangha and their practices in contemporary time (Ambedkar 2003a, 106–7). According to him, Bhikkhus are not performing the social role properly, not spreading Dhamma among common people nor enlightening them on the matters of morality and religion. Nevertheless, according to Ambedkar Hinduism is the most exploitative religion and inequality is the official gospel of Hinduism. This was the reason why he burnt the *Manusmriti* in public on 25 December 1927 (Ambedkar 2007).

Thus, for Ambedkar, religiosity is not so much about the transcendental aspects of bliss and purity but rather it is about the human conditions of equality and fraternity. The aspect of religion which reflects equality and fraternity can be seen through a philosophical lens. Ambedkar himself drew close to Buddhism, which basically dwells on human suffering and the way out of it. As he believed, in Buddhism there is a possibility to transcend the caste system and Brahmanism because the Buddha had revolted against Brahmanism. With this hope in Buddhism, he gave up Hinduism and converted to Buddhism in 1956 along with more than 500,000 people at Nagpur.

Ambedkar on Religion and Its Necessity to Human Society

One may wonder whether Ambedkar rejects religion in totality and considers it detrimental to social equality. As we can see from many of his writings, he did not reject religion and its practices per se, but what he does is to break away from those aspects of religion which breed inequality in society. Through his philosophical elaboration of Buddhism he tries to explore the true nature of religion, which according to him is to propagate humanity. Once Ambedkar reacted in his characteristic way and said—'some people think that religion is not essential to society. I don't hold this view. I consider the foundations of religion to be essential to life and practices of society' (Keer 2012). Religion is essential only when we understand the true nature of religion. As Ambedkar said:

> I tell you, religion is for man and not man for religion. If you want to organize, be successful in this world, change this religion. The religion which does not recognize you as human beings, or give you water to drink, or allow in to enter the temples is not worthy to be called a religion. The religion which forbids you to receive education and comes in the way of your material advance is not worthy of the appellation religion. The religion which does not teach its followers to show humanity in dealing with its co-religionists is nothing but a display of force. The religion that asks its adherents to suffer the touch of animals but not the touch of human beings is not religion but mockery. That religion which precludes some classes from education, forbids them to accumulate wealth and to bear arms is not religion but a mockery. The religion which compels the ignorant to be ignorant and the poor to be poor is not a religion but visitation. (Keer 2012)

We can see from his philosophical illustration of religion that for him Hinduism is nothing but a 'mockery'. According to him, religion should be founded on the principles of liberty, equality, fraternity, and justice in all fields such as society, economics, politics, and education. Only in this way can religion propagate equality among humanity. Sadly, Ambedkar did not see much of this principle in many religions, and it was totally absent in Hinduism. Ambedkar did a thorough study of religious concepts (Ambedkar 1997, 227–351) of Hinduism. He examined Indian philosophy extensively to compare and contrast it with Buddha's philosophy. According to Ambedkar, the six orthodox systems of Indian philosophy, namely Mimamsa, Vedanta, Samkhya, Yoga, Vaiseshika, and Nyaya, are founded upon blindly accepting the primacy of the Vedas unlike the Sramanik (Buddhist, Jain, and so forth) and Lokayata modes of thought (Rodrigues 2017, 107). This is why he rejected all six systems of orthodox Indian philosophy.

According to Ambedkar, the caste system has been originated from and sanctified by Hindu religion (Ambedkar 2007, 34). So one cannot and should not understand Hinduism and the caste system separately because caste is an irrevocable part of Hindu society (Ambedkar 2007, 34). This has been justified by Hinduism morally and philosophically.[3] These justifications can be found in Hindu mythological texts such as the Vedas, Puranas, Manusmriti, Bhagavat Gita, Ramayana and Mahabharata, and so on. For example, in Ramayana, we find the story of Sambuka, a Shudra risi (ascetic), who was murdered by Rama (the Hindu god). Sambuka was murdered because he performed *tapasya* (ascetic exercise), which is against *Dharma* (sacred law) for a Shudra. According to Dharma, tapasya should be performed by the twice-born (Brahmins) alone and the Shudra should be in the service of the twice born (Ambedkar 2014, 332). In the Mahabharata, before the battle of Kurukshetra, Krishna (a Hindu god) advises Arjuna on his duty by saying that since Arjuna belonged to the Kshatriya varna it was his duty to fight and kill his enemies (Ambedkar 1987, 377). Here, as per Krishna, one's birth determines the ontology of one's caste and duties. Therefore, Ambedkar exposes the problems in Hindu scriptures and argues that there is no scope to evolve a positive, non-violent, egalitarian religion based on these texts. In *Annihilation of Caste* he says emphatically:

> You must not forget that if you wish to bring about a breach in the system, you have got to apply the dynamite to the *Vedas* and the *Shastras*, which deny any part to reason, to *Vedas* and *Shastras*, which deny any part to morality. You must destroy the Religion of the *Shrutis* and the *Smritis*. Nothing else will avail. (Ambedkar 2007, 44)

Hindu religion and its texts had confined the minds of the Untouchables by not allowing them access to education.[4] As a

---

[3] The moral and philosophical justification of untouchability and Brahmanism has been used by Brahmanic scholars to justify Hinduism and caste through their writings, and that is what we have witnessed historically in texts such as *Manusmriti*, *Bhagavat Gita*, and such others.

[4] Dr Babasaheb Ambedkar established 'Bahishkrit Hitkarini Sabha' on 20 July 1924, at Bombay and he appealed to all the marginalized lower castes including women that Educate, Agitate, and Organize, because it

consequence of this upper-caste domination prevailed and the lower castes blindly followed the religious injunctions without understanding what was at stake for them. This is why they were not able to overcome the dogma of caste and religion. According to Ambedkar, the way out of such shackles was to enlighten the minds of the people through education. Hence, he established many educational institutions and inclusive policies for oppressed communities, such as Milind College at Aurangabad and Siddharth College of Arts, Science and Commerce in Mumbai. He founded the People's Education Society in Bombay on 8 July 1945 to promote higher education amongst the poor middle classes in general and the Scheduled Castes in particular (Rattu 1997, 65–70). For Ambedkar education is the tool through which subjugated people can reclaim their worth; a tool which can help them overcome the dogma of caste and religion. He was very confident that understanding Buddhism will help them overcome this dogma. For him Buddhism was not necessarily a religion but it was a philosophy (Ambedkar 2003a, 98)[5] or philosophy of religion. He compared and distinguished Buddhism from Hinduism, Islam, and Christianity and to understand the meaning and nature of all these religions he raised some important points:

> That society must have either the sanction of law or the sanction of morality to hold it together. Without either, society is sure to go to pieces ... religion in the sense of morality, must therefore remain the governing principle in every society. That the religion as defined in the first proposition must be in accord with the sciences. In other

---

will enlighten the people from the dogma of caste. Both Ambedkar and Jotiba Phule say that when people will get to know that they are living in slavery they will not remain as slave. And education can help them to know this that they are living in the slavery.

[5] In the *Mahaparinirvan Sutta* the Buddha told Ananda that his religion was based on reason and experience and that his followers should not accept his teachings as correct and binding merely because they emanated from him. According to Buddha, his words are not final or absolute, thus anyone is free to modify or even abandon any of his teachings if it is found to not apply at a given time and in a given circumstance. Therefore, the philosophy of Buddha and Ambedkar gives the space for questioning and free thinking, making Buddhism itself more like a philosophy than a religion.

words, religion if it is to function must be in accordance with reason which is merely another name for science. It is not enough for a religion to consist of a moral code, but its moral code must recognize the fundamental tenets of liberty, equality and fraternity. That the religion must not sanctify or ennoble poverty. (Ambedkar 2003a, 103–5)

By putting forth these standards Ambedkar investigates all religions to check whether these requirements are fulfilled in them or not. He says it may be that some religions fulfil one requirement and some two but none of the existing religions fulfil all the requirements except Buddhism. And that is the reason why he converted into Buddhism and not to any other religion.

Religion has to be studied as a system, ideology, institution, and so on. Can we understand anything in society whether it is politics, society, economy, culture, or anything related to human beings without discussing religion? One can say religion is much closer to every aspect of our life in a pragmatic sense. This is recognized by Ambedkar very well and therefore it does not make sense to study anything related to Ambedkar without bringing in religion. It is very difficult to think of human beings in the sense of a community without a religion. It may be possible theoretically and intellectually but still one can argue that it is very hard to live without a religion in a pragmatic sense. In other words, it is very difficult to think about not having a religion from a layman's point of view. In order to understand the necessity of a religion, let us see what Ambedkar has to say:

> While I condemn a religion of rules, I must not be understood to hold the opinion that there is no necessity for a religion. On the contrary, I agree with Burke when he says that—true religion is the foundation of society, the basis on which all true civil government rests, and both their sanction. Consequently, when I urge that these ancient rules of life be annulled, I am anxious that its place shall be taken by a religion of principles which alone can lay claim to being a true religion. Indeed, I am so convinced of the necessity of religion that I feel I ought to tell you in outline what I regard as necessary items in this religious reform. (Ambedkar 2007, 46)

In India, almost everyone believes in some religion; religion has played an important role in the day to day life of people throughout history.[6] One cannot reject religion because religion defines one's humanness and everyday life, and it is not only reason that defines humanness but also spirituality and so on. Ambedkar rejected the religion of violence, intolerance, inequality, and divinity but he accepted the importance of religion/spirituality in human life as a development of sympathy, equality, and freedom in one's life. So for Ambedkar, there is a close relation between religiosity and spirituality. But when religion propagates violence, intolerance, inequality, and divinity it loses its spirituality (Ambedkar 2003b, 113–29). Therefore, religion is an inescapable human reality which is related with everyday practices, from food to marriage, clothing to sexuality, and birth to death. According to Ambedkar, in a Brahmanical and castiest society if one does not have a mechanism or platform where one can get a common sense of belonging there will be conflict and such a society will be full of injustices. According to him, religion should bring a feeling of belonging, and therefore to develop this belongingness Ambedkar chose religion as the single best platform. For example, Ambedkar's conversion to Buddhism can be seen from this point of view (Rodrigues 2017, 104). He did this because he wanted to transcend caste and Brahmanism. In Hinduism, because of caste, bringing unity among already divided castes and build a sense of belongingness and the 'we' feeling is not possible. However, in Buddhism, the core of discussion is on human beings and their development. Ambedkar rejects the virtue ethics based on gods and supernatural power. The Buddha did not impose his ideas on people and he recognized the principles of liberty, equality, fraternity, and justice as core. This is what his philosophy of morality is based on which Ambedkar did not find in other religions, normatively and in a pragmatic sense.

---

[6] According to estimates by the United Nations the world population stands at 7.6 billion as of May 2018. And about 85 per cent of the world's population believes in some form of religious beliefs. The remaining population is religiously unaffiliated and includes atheists, agnostics, and people who do not identify with any particular religion in surveys. However, many of the religiously unaffiliated have some sort of beliefs. Religious beliefs are not abstract ideas but they have a major impact both in a negative and a positive sense on individual and society throughout the world. Therefore, we can consider religion to be essential for people in their actual life-world.

Ambedkar has philosophically detailed about religions throughout his writings and speeches. But specifically in *The Riddles in Hinduism*, in the first riddle, 'the Difficulty of Knowing Why One Is Hindu', Ambedkar looks at the importance of religion in one's life. In fact, when he was trying to understand the sense of philosophy of religions he found it difficult to understand Hinduism as a religion because of polytheism, which was its core value. There were many gods, but there was no set of core principles that constituted a system of beliefs. There was nothing that anchored or bound people together. This was strange as after all the word 'religion' traces its roots back to the Latin *religare* which means to bind and to be bound by an obligation (Ambedkar 2016b, 28).

At the time of Ambedkar, he observed that all the lower castes, including Untouchables and backward castes, were suffering from Hinduism. In Jotiba Phule's language Sudra and Ati-Sudra were oppressed because of Brahmanism/Hinduism. The biggest challenge before Ambedkar was to make the oppressed people liberated from caste or Brahmanism. According to him, it was not possible within Hinduism. In fact, he tried to look and search for every possibility within Hinduism but he did not see any hope. Therefore, he had to convert to some other religion. In this context, conversion as a category (within the discourse of philosophy of religions) philosophically becomes very significant for the people. Conversion thus is a revolutionary category. Ultimately Ambedkar converted into Buddhism and chose that religion as an alternative for the oppressed people in particular and humanity in general. Ambedkar thought it very essential to have a religion for human beings[7] and recognized the importance of religion in human society, therefore appealing for a conversion:

> Whether I remain a Hindu or not it makes little difference to me. I can become a judge of the high court, a member of legislative assembly or even a minister. But it is for your emancipation and advancement that conversion appears to be very necessary to me. (Ambedkar 2004, 6)

[7] Having a religion is very essential category for Ambedkar. In *Buddha or Karl Marx*, Ambedkar raises a question, will men not need some sort of government and the same he would argue for religion. That is the reason why he did not reject religion in the complete sense from the layman point of view. But his religion is the religion of principle which he terms a true religion in the Burkean sense. For details, see Ambedkar (1987, 2003a, 2003b).

For Ambedkar, conversion is necessary for freedom, sympathy, and equality. According to him, conversion is not the path of escapism or cowardice, or child's play and is not to be treated as a subject of entertainment, rather it is a path of wisdom (Ambedkar 2004, 6). Therefore, Ambedkar's path is the one that leads him to an alternative outside Hinduism, but not necessarily outside the religious discourse.

Pragmatic and Rational Sense of Religion

Ambedkar was not against the religious or cultural matrix per se; rather he was looking for a religio-cultural space without hierarchy and inequality. He was in search of a religion where oppression is minimum if not absent (Raghuramaraju 2010, 165). Thus, Ambedkar uses the concept 'religion' very rationally[8] and pragmatically. It is not what one generally thinks religion is, that is, superstition, blind beliefs and magic, and so forth. He has clearly investigated the philosophy of religions.[9] In this context let us see what he means by religion in the rational sense:

> I take religion to mean the propounding of an ideal scheme of divine governance the aim and object of which is to make the social order in which man lives a moral order. This is what I understand by religion. (Ambedkar 2010, 6)

However, the Hindu social order is not an ordered society, rather it is divided on the basis of castes and is a disordered society. Therefore, there is little chance to make a moral[10] order in India under

---

[8] Here I have used the term 'rational' because Ambedkar took religion as rationality rather than traditional thinking. That is way at the end of this chapter I have argued that his religion is very close to modernity and its value system.

[9] Ambedkar's philosophy of religions can be investigated in his texts such as *Philosophy of Hinduism, Buddha and Future of His Religion, Buddha and His Dhamma, Riddles in Hinduism*, and *Revolution and Counter-Revolution in Ancient India*.

[10] Moral means good conduct and respect for each other to recognize liberty, equality, and fraternity as a social and moral principle. According to Ambedkar, morality means fraternity. See, for details, Ambedkar's *The Buddha and His Dhamma*.

Hinduism. In fact, he emphasizes that only moral order in terms of moral code is not enough if it does not recognize the fundamental social principles of liberty, equality, and fraternity (Ambedkar 2003b, 104). However, according to Ambedkar, the divine governance means not supernatural powers (god, soul, and world) but 'religion' in the sense of spiritual principles, truly universal, applicable to all races, to all times' (Ambedkar 2007, 45), and which are ideals or standards such as liberty, equality, and fraternity. These principles are not the issuance of the divine, rather these are human discoveries. The Buddha discovers these and propagates to establish those in society. Ambedkar was sceptical about the philosophy of Hinduism because it does not have any philosophy in it. So he differentiated between 'philosophy of Hinduism' and 'philosophy of religion' (Ambedkar 1987, 3). In fact, he says 'Hinduism is not a religion; it is a collection of castes. Hindu society is a myth. Hindu society as such does not exist' (Ambedkar 2007, 17). For Ambedkar, morality is the foundation of religion. Without it a religion becomes 'anarchy'. Hence, Ambedkar's engagement with religion has to be understood in two senses; pragmatic and theoretical or philosophical. In other words, Ambedkar's understanding of religion is philosophical, pragmatic, and epistemological.

Philosophy and Philosophy of Religion in Ambedkar

Ambedkar has said that religion and philosophy are adversaries if not antagonistic. For him religion is theology. And he uses the term 'philosophy' in its original sense which is twofold:

> It meant the teachings as it did when people spoke of the philosophy of Socrates or the philosophy of Plato.[11] In another sense it means the *critical reason* used in passing judgments upon things and events. (Ambedkar 2010, 4)

Further he says,

> proceeding on this basis, philosophy of religion is to me not a merely descriptive science. I regard it as being both descriptive

---

[11] Long ago, Plato described philosophy as the synoptic view of things. That is to say it is the attempt to see things together to keep all the main features of the world in view, and to grasp them in their relation to one another as parts of the whole.

and normative. In so far as it deals with the teachings of a religion, philosophy of religion becomes a descriptive science. In so far as it involves the use of critical reasoning for passing judgment on those teachings, philosophy of religion becomes a normative science. (Ambedkar 2010, 4)

Philosophy in general is to be able to show the students of philosophy to be insightful, show clarity, critical thinking, and make distance from dogmatic beliefs, which is fundamental to religion.[12] Philosophy tells us what is acceptable and what is not. It re-evaluates, rethinks, and continues or discontinues some thinking or practices. Philosophy of religion analyses divine attributes (god, soul, and world), questions religious beliefs and tells us how to do things well, which promote humanity. Therefore, what is preached by 'godfathers' or so-called religious messengers is unacceptable,[13] if their messages were found unjustified. Philosophy of religion lays bare the inconsistency involved in religious beliefs and helps in the development of an alternative humanist world view and a platform for dialogue between different religious beliefs, their commonalities and differences. It questions superstitions and fanatical beliefs.

Practising the philosophy of religion starts by questioning religious beliefs, the existence of god, soul, world, and eternal reality. And all these questions are metaphysical ones. Ambedkar as a philosopher of religion[14] has questioned the existing religions, gods, eternity, immortality, infallibility, souls, religious scriptures, and its related rituals. Ambedkar looked to the Buddha as a spiritual guide to question the fundamental roots of religion: gods, soul,

---

[12] Ambedkar was never fundamentalist and rigid on anything without reasoning and experience. He criticizes all religions and accepted whatever is beneficial and scientific. Philosophy provides students self-reflective control over their beliefs and develops critical thinking.

[13] In *Kalama Sutta*, Buddha tells the Kalama what to believe and what not, when and how to believe. See, for details, *The Buddha and His Dhamma*. Greek philosopher Socrates has also said that unexamined life is worthless. It is nothing but the philosophy of religion.

[14] Ambedkar is a philosopher in multiple senses: he is a socio-political philosopher, philosopher of law/legality, feminist philosopher, philosopher of history, philosopher of religion, philosopher of social sciences, philosopher of economics, and philosopher of ethics, and so forth.

Veda, eternity, rebirth, karma, immortality, infallibility, religious practices, beliefs, and so on. That is why he is also considered to be a philosopher of religion.

Ambedkar looked at religion from the point of view of philosophy because it helps to understand religions properly and systematically. Philosophy of religion guides people to understand the social world better and helps to question the religious prejudices, injustices, discrimination, exploitation, humiliation, and oppression. Ambedkar studied philosophy seriously. He studied Plato, Aristotle, Russell, Marx, Dewey, Burke, Nietzsche, J.S. Mill, Herbert Spencer, Thomas Aquinas, Rousseau, Comte, Voltaire, and many others.[15] The task of a philosopher is to generate new knowledge. And it is possible only through concepts and theories. Ambedkar as a philosopher in multiple senses has discussed a number of concepts and has provided on them proper analysis and meaning. For example, dharma (religion), dhamma, *saddhamma, prajna, maitri, karuna, karma*, rebirth, Constitution, democracy, franchise, rights, conversion, liberty, equality, fraternity, justice, ideology, nation, nationality, dignity, minority, representation, self-respect, caste, class, Hinduism, Brahmanism, and so on. He scrutinized the orthodox tradition of Indian philosophy because it does not propagate a philosophy of religion and he found the injustices in them. In this context, one can say that all the orthodox philosophies are nothing but 'protected ignorance' (Alone 2017, 140–69). In order to protect Brahmanical hegemony they use ignorance as a protective tool. Gopal Guru also emphasizes on this in different way. He says 'Brahminhood seeks to preserve itself through the process of Sanskritization' (Guru and Sarukkai 2012, 206). Brahmins or Savarna caste Hindus, in some or the other way protect the hegemonic Brahmanical tradition in their philosophies. Ambedkar understands the nature and structure of Indian society. He theorizes it properly. He also tries to give an example of an alternative epistemology or knowledge system in India. For instance, in his book *Caste in India* he has theorized the origin, genesis, and development of caste. In his works *Philosophy of Hinduism, The Buddha and His Dhamma, Buddha and Future of His Religion,* and in many of his other works he has theorized religion properly to understand the human world in general and Indian society in particular.

---

[15] For details, see Ambedkar (2008) and his other writings and speeches.

However, one thing we should not be confused about is how on the one hand Ambedkar uses the term 'religion' in a very rational sense and on the other he negates the same term and uses the Buddha's word 'Dhamma'. Now, one can argue that there is no difference between Dhamma and Dharma. However, the meaning and content are very different for these two terms. Ambedkar in his text *The Buddha and His Dhamma* clearly defined what is Dhamma and religion. What is the purpose of the Dhamma and what is the purpose of the dharma or religion? 'The purpose of religion is to explain the origin of the world and the purpose of Dhamma is to reconstruct the world' (Ambedkar 1997, 322). According to Ambedkar, the word 'religion' is an infinite word with no fixed meaning. In order to understand this proposition, he investigates the evolution of religion. In the initial phase of society, people were not able to understand most of natural phenomena such as lightning, rain, and floods and primitive man could not explain the reasons behind their occurrence. Any performance thought to control the phenomena was called 'magic'. In the second stage, religion came to be identified with beliefs, rituals, ceremonies, prayers, and sacrifices. In the third stage since man could not explain the magic, they thought that there must exist some power which was the cause of it. So, it was viewed as God's creation. Man considered that God created this world and also human beings (Ambedkar 1997, 315).

The Multiple Ontological Realities of Religion in Ambedkar's Thought

According to Ambedkar, 'religion, it is said, is personal and one must keep it to oneself. One must not let it play its part in public life' (Ambedkar 1997, 316). However, this proposition of Ambedkar is a political and constitutional one. But the original position of Ambedkar's religious doctrine might be social and holistic rather than individual and personal. That is why he criticized the liberal idea that religion is a private affair (Rodrigues 2017, 104). This proposition can also be better understood if we explain why Ambedkar makes the distinction between customary law and legal law, because religion as collective practice functions in a larger context and as we see these days it plays a very important role in politics, economy, and society. More importantly in a caste-ridden society the legal laws are not considered more powerful than customary law. For example, if we understand caste as individual fact/matter we will miss the whole point and this is same with religion. Therefore, Ambedkar's idea of religion needs to be understood beyond the political and constitutional/legal domain. For example, in *Annihilation of Caste* he writes about the political aspect of religion and that there is a clear relationship between religion and power. He argues that religion is the source of power as illustrated by the history of India 'where the priest holds a sway over the common man often greater than the magistrate and where everything, even such things as strikes and elections, so easily take a religious turn and can so easily be given a religious twist' (Ambedkar 2007, 11). This shows how religious leaders and godmen are very powerful and can easily influence politics. In India, this is completely visible in the context of Hinduism. Many Hindu sadhus exert a strong influence on politics, directly and indirectly. Interestingly, Ambedkar has pointed out the impact of religions on women and gender discrimination. He has written about the Hindu religious scriptures where women are treated as subhuman such as in *Manusmriti, Arthashastra,* Ramayana, and Mahabharata.[16] According to Hindu scriptures, women are not allowed to read the Vedas and so education is denied to them. Neither are they allowed to perform religious rituals and activities.

Religion also has an economic dimension and Ambedkar has clearly pointed it out in the *Annihilation of Caste*. He argues that the political economy of India is regulated by caste. In the political economy of caste, division of labourers based on graded inequality plays a more important role than division of labour (Ambedkar 2007, 14–15). In order to understand this relation of economy and religion one can also see Max Weber's study *The Protestant Ethic and the Spirit of Capitalism* (1992). Here he studied Hinduism, Islam, Confucianism, and Christianity and has shown that there is a clear relation between economy and religion.[17] This economic aspect of religion has been studied by Kancha Ilaiah in his book *Post-Hindu India* (2017). He argues that Indian capital is

---

[16] See, for details, Ambedkar (1987, 429–37; 2014, 323–43).

[17] See for details in Weber's the *Protestant Ethic and Spirit of Capitalism* (1992).

not mercantile capital but it is a capital conditioned in Hindu scriptures and structured in caste terms (Ilaiah 2017, 169–74). So, we see that the ontology of religion has multiple realities which Ambedkar has understood and explained throughout his writings and speeches. Ambedkar could clearly see the essentiality of religion not necessarily for merely political purposes but for human life in totality. Therefore he says that 'religion is for man and not man for religion' (Narain and Ahir 2010, 3). But if we see Hinduism, or in Ambedkar's language Brahmanism, there are no core principles in it which can uphold the philosophy of religion like other religions uphold in theory and practice. Whatever principles or rules exist in Hinduism they strengthen caste, degrade lower castes, and disrespect and underestimate others including the minority communities. Here, one example can be given in which Ambedkar writes about Jews and Brahmins. Jews are faithful to their religion under whatever circumstances (Ambedkar 2003b, 342–4). Brahmins on the other hand never believe in the core of their principles or rules; rather they consider it a matter of trade and commerce and that is why if they are in a loss-making situation, they can change their position, practices, and so on (Ambedkar 2016b, 35). This can also be understood if one understands the politics of appropriation. There exist many examples of appropriation in Indian history which Ambedkar himself mentions in his writings and speeches. At its peak when Buddhism was preaching non-violence and the middle path which is very inclusive, democratic, and egalitarian, Brahmins suddenly changed their practices and became like Buddhists and vegetarians in order to strengthen Brahmanism. Recently, when Ambedkarism is in the discourse in politics and society right wings forces are appropriating and doing the same. So this is nothing but the politics of Brahmanical hypocrisy (Ambedkar 2016b, 40–1).

Contrary to this conventional way of understanding religion, Dhamma is social righteousness, which means right relation between human beings in all spheres of life. It consists of *prajna* (wisdom) and *karuna* (compassion). So, religion in Ambedkar's sense is morality in the context of Dhamma which means right relation between human beings. This helps people to hold on to each other rather than dividing them into different groups and individuals (Ambedkar 2003a, 104). Thus, in Ambedkar's understanding of Buddhism there is a greater emphasis on morality. Religion is close to gods, soul, and eternal reality, but Dhamma is nothing but morality which has no god, no soul, and no supernatural power.

Hiriyanna interestingly put Indian philosophy into two groups: orthodox and heterodox (Hiriyanna 2005, 16). One is the orthodox school which believes in gods or the infallibility of the Vedas, and the other is the heterodox tradition which rejects the Vedas, existence of gods and infallibility or any supernatural power. The genealogy of religion and philosophy in Ambedkar can be found in the latter. In his works he had clearly mentioned about his philosophy of religion. His idea of religion can also be seen in *Annihilation of Caste* where he distinguished between the religion of rules and religion of principles and he was in favour of religion of principles (Ambedkar 2007, 32). Since he believes in the religion of principles it becomes very close to the modernist principles such as liberty, fraternity, equality, and justice. Thus, for Ambedkar, religion is morally grounded through reason and scientific temper, making it a humanistic approach and in a way modern, much as Rousseau's Civil Religion and John Dewey's pragmatist approach towards religion (Joseph 2013, 50). One of the differences with Rousseau would be that Rousseau sees religion from within the State point of view (Rousseau 2002, 245–53) whereas Ambedkar goes beyond the State. As far as the essentiality of religion in society and the pragmatic aspect of religion are concerned Dewey and Ambedkar are similar. But Dewey did not explore different ontological realities of religions as Ambedkar did. Ambedkar's idea of religion is similar to Immanuel Kant's notion of universal moral principles which are based on categorical imperative, maxim of universal law, maxim of treating humans as ends and maxim of the kingdom of ends (where everyone is a rational agent, and acts as a member of kingdom of ends) (Kant 2004, vii–xxvi). However, Ambedkar's morality is not deontological as is Kant's, in which one is to act on duties and moral maxims. Ambedkar considers liberty, equality and fraternity/sympathy as three maxims/standards in his moral and social philosophy but this does not mean that one has to be deontic, it goes beyond mere rule following.

* * *

In this chapter I have attempted to highlight Ambedkar's basic arguments of his philosophy of religions. My argument here is to show that Ambedkar being a pragmatist and a philosopher goes beyond the narrow understanding of religion and politicking of religion. As such, he critically engaged different ontological realities of religions such as social, economic, gender, and other aspects. In his attempt to bring religion back from transcendental to actual human condition he made religion deprived of metaphysical gods, soul, and supernatural power and brought it closer to modern values such as liberty, equality, fraternity, and justice which are propagated by modern philosophers such as Kant, Rousseau, and Dewey. Religion for him is not mere faith or belief but a scientific endeavour which has to be justified by reason. Thus Ambedkar's understanding of religion is philosophical, pragmatic as well as epistemological. A religion which can hold up to the test of reason, science, and humanism is essential for any society. Philosophy helps us to critique religions and lifts up the veil of ignorance to see clearly what is good for us, here on earth. In his final analysis of religions Ambedkar chose Buddhism as the religion which fulfils the test of reason, science, and humanism. Thus he embraced Buddhism and abandoned blind belief in Hinduism.

References

Alone, Y.S. 2017. 'Caste Life Narratives, Visual Representation, and Protected Ignorance'. *University of Hawai'i Press* 40, no. 1: 140–69.

Aloysius, G. 2004. *Dalit-Subaltern Emergence in Religio-Cultural Subjectivity: Iyothee Thassar and Emancipatory Buddhism*. New Delhi: Critical Quest.

Ambedkar, B.R. 1987. *Dr. Babasaheb Ambedkar: Writing and Speeches*, vol. 3. Mumbai: Higher Education Department, Government of Maharashtra.

———. 1997. *The Buddha and His Dhamma*. Nagpur: Buddha Bhoomi Publication.

———. 2003a. *Dr. Babasaheb Ambedkar: Writing and Speeches*, vol. 17, part 2. Mumbai: Higher Education Department, Government of Maharashtra.

———. 2003b. *Dr. Babasaheb Ambedkar: Writing and Speeches*, vol. 17, part 3. Mumbai: Higher Education Department, Government of Maharashtra.

———. 2004. *Conversion as Emancipation*. New Delhi: Critical Quest.

———. 2007. *Annihilation of Caste*. New Delhi: Critical Quest.

———. 2008. *Dr. Babasaheb Ambedkar: Writing and Speeches*, vol. 3. Mumbai: Higher Education Department, Government of Maharashtra.

———. 2010. *Philosophy of Hinduism*. New Delhi: Critical Quest.

———. 2013. *Caste in India*. New Delhi: Critical Quest.

———. 2014. *Dr. Babasaheb Ambedkar: Writing and Speeches*, vol. 4. New Delhi: Dr. Ambedkar Foundation, Ministry of Social Justice and Empowerment, Government of India.

———. 2016a. *Dr. Babasaheb Ambedkar: Writing and Speeches*, vol. 1. Mumbai: Higher Education Department, Government of Maharashtra.

———. 2016b. *Riddles in Hinduism: The Annotated Critical Selection. With 'The Riddle of Ambedkar': An Introduction by Kancha Ilaiah*. New Delhi: Navayana.

Dewey, John. 2013. *A Common Faith*, with an introduction by Thomas M. Alexander. New Heaven and London: Yale University Press.

Gokhale, Pradeep. 2008a. 'Dr. Ambedkar as a Philosopher: Beyond Reductionism'. In *The Philosophy of Dr. B. R. Ambedkar*, edited by P. Gokhale. Pune: Sugava Prakashan.

———. 2008b. 'Dr. Ambedkar's Interpretation of Buddhism'. In *The Philosophy of Dr. B. R. Ambedkar*, edited by P. Gokhale. Pune: Sugava Prakashan.

Guru, Gopal, and Sunder Sarukkai. 2012. *The Cracked Mirror: An Indian Debate on Experience and Theory*. New Delhi: Oxford University Press.

Hiriyanna, M. 2005. *Outlines of Indian Philosophy*. Delhi: Motilal Banarsidass Publishers Private Limited.

Ilaiah, Kancha. 2017. *Post-Hindu India: A Discourse on Dalit-Bahujan, Socio-Spiritual and Scientific Revolution*. New Delhi: Sage.

Joseph, M.T. 2013. 'Dr. B.R. Ambedkar's Views on Religion: A Sociological Analysis'. *Indian Anthropological Association* 43, no. 2: 43–54.

Kant, Immanuel. 2004. *The Metaphysics of Morals*, edited by Mary Gregor, introduction by Roger J. Sullivan. United Kingdom: Cambridge University Press.

Keer, Dhananjay. 2012. *Dr. Ambedkar: Life and Mission*. Bombay: Popular Prakashan.

Narain, A.K., and D.C. Ahir. 2010. *Dr. Ambedkar, Buddhism and Social Change*. Delhi: Buddhist World Press.

Raghuramaraju, A. 2010. 'Problematizing Lived Dalit Experience'. *Economic and Political Weekly* 45, no. 29: 162–7.

Rathore, Aakash Singh. 2018. 'Indian Academia's Shunning of Ambedkar the Philosopher Reeks of Social Exclusion'. *Huffington Post*. Available at https://www.huffingtonpost.in/aakash-singh-rathore/indian-academias-shunning-of-ambedkar-the-philosopher-reeks-of_a_22025150/. Last accessed on 17 July 2020.

Rattu, Nanak Chand. 1997. *Last Few Years of Dr. Ambedkar*. New Delhi: Amrit Publishing House.

Rodrigues, Valerian. 2017. 'Ambedkar as a Political Philosopher'. *Economic and Political Weekly* 52, no. 15: 101–7.

Rousseau, J.J. 2002. *The Social Contact and the First and Second Discourses*, edited and with an introduction by Susan Dunn. New Heaven and London: Yale University Press.

Weber, Max. 1992. *The Protestant Ethic and Spirit of Capitalism*, translated by Talcott Parsons, with an introduction by Anthony Giddens. London and New York: Routledge.

6

Two Concepts of Conversion at Meenakshipuram

Seeing through Ambedkar's Buddhism and Being Seen in EVR's Islam

MATTHEW H. BAXTER

In February 1981, roughly 180 Dalit (Untouchable) families converted to Islam in the small south Indian village of Meenakshipuram (*Sunday*, 1982). Within months, this not uncommon event on the subcontinent—where lower-castes collectively change religious affiliation to challenge everyday upper-caste abuse, often inflected by labour conflict—gained national attention. Such attention was a product of the recently legitimated Hindu right—a broad movement that had been politically marginalized until joining forces that opposed the Emergency, the secular Congress government's suspension of democracy under Indira Gandhi from 1975 to 1977. With this newfound democratic legitimacy, the Hindu right formed a political party in 1980 called the Bharatiya Janata Party (BJP, 'Indian People's Party'). The BJP seized upon Meenakshipuram as a national threat, leading to a possible Pakistan in the south fuelled by a rich post-1970s oil crisis Middle East. The BJP subsequently catapulted itself into political power by the 1990s, particularly after the December 1992 violent destruction of the Babri Masjid built on the alleged birthplace of Lord Rama in Ayodhya. In short:

Hindutva, the politics in the name of Hinduism, came up from the mid-1920s. ... India [instead] took the path of secular democracy and Hindutva remained dormant till quite recently.

In the early 1980s it started asserting itself. ... [F]rom the Meenakshipuram conversion of [D]alits to Islam, [Hindutva] went on to build itself aggressively. (Puniyani 2005, 17)[1]

The 1981 mass conversion to Islam at Meenakshipuram is not the only politically high-profile mass conversion of Untouchables out of Hinduism in twentieth-century postcolonial India. In 1956, Dr B.R. Ambedkar—a globally educated scholar and Untouchable politician from western India who was central in crafting the Republic of India's Constitution—led a mass conversion of Untouchables to Buddhism that remains foundational for contemporary Dalit politics. Scholars have subsequently framed Meenakshipuram's event with Ambedkar's thought, refracting the sociological analyses of the former's moment through the theory articulated in the latter's publications. This framing revolves around an alternative nationalism, opposing mainstream nationalism's upper-caste Hinduism by grounding modern political community in the lived experience of marginalized groups demanding democracy's fulfillment. For example, Gauri Viswanathan claims that Meenakshipuram's Islamic conversion is not the 'separatist and antinational' spectre feared by Hindutva but instead expresses 'alternative conceptions of nation and community' along the lines of Ambedkar's Buddhist conversion, a move from 'premodernity['s]' abusive hierarchy to 'modernity['s]' egalitarian rights (Viswanathan 1998, 215, 228, 231–2). For Gyan Pandey, Meenakshipuram illustrates an important minority 'fragment' of history resisting upper-caste nationalism, but it is Ambedkar's thought that articulates the 'fundamental principles' of 'liberty, equality, and fraternity' that make 'the time of dalit conversion ... the time of Indian democracy'.[2] Other scholars likewise suggest that Meenakshipuram's converts be understood

---

[1] For an earlier, broader, and subsequently canonical account, see Jaffrelot (1996, esp. 338–68).

[2] Gyanendra Pandey mentions Meenakshipuram but not Ambedkar in 'In Defence of the Fragment' and Ambedkar but not Meenakshipuram in 'Time of the Dalit Conversion'.

as 'little Ambedkars', 'product[s] of political and economic modernization' deploying individual 'rights' and communal 'plight' (Mujahid 1989, 36–7), equating Ambedkar's Buddhism with Meenakshipuram's Islam in the disadvantaged's 'desire ... for greater freedom and respect' (Dallmayr 1996, 13–14).

> In post-colonial times, mass conversions of former untouchables ... critique ... Indian identity [as] a matter of blood, or race. BR Ambedkar and his followers became Buddhists while claiming Indian citizenship, and the Muslim converts of Meenakshipuram make a similar demand. ... [T]hey reclaim religious identity as primary and in tension with any nationalist project that ... supersede[s] ... other forms of group membership. (Laine 2007, 342)

The problem with this academic equation is that, despite a clearly shared thematic terrain, such framing has little evidence. First, Ambedkar's Buddhism was dismissed in south India at the time of Meenakshipuram as politically ineffective, not only 'because Harijans [Untouchables/Dalits] became second class Buddhists ... and continued to live much as before' (Singh 1981), but because 'Buddhism is seen as a protestant branch of Hinduism' without the 'political reaction' generated by 'conversions to Islam' (Verghese 1981). For example, following similar Islamic conversion threats by Dalit labourers in November 1981 outside Chennai, a Dalit union leader noted that 'older people ... preferred conversion to Buddhism rather than Islam', whereas '[y]oungsters' rejected 'Buddhism as ... too close to Hinduism' (*Indian Express*, 1981a). And when roughly 160 regional Dalits embraced Buddhism that December with 25,000 more promised, commemorating Ambedkar's 25th death anniversary, very little reaction was noticed—locally or nationally (*Hindu* 1981).

Second, rather than Ambedkar, references to the local non-Brahmin leader E.V. Ramasami Naicker (a.k.a. Periyar or EVR) saturate investigations published not only by his own Dravidar Kalakam movement (the radical atheist non-Brahmin social reform movement EVR formed in 1944 out of his earlier Self-Respect Movement begun in the mid-1920s) (Viramani 2003, 1) but also by the Hindu right (Seshadri 1981, 16),[3] academics (Mujahid 1989, 123–5), and the secular press, with indirect references to EVR evident in

---

[3] Seshadri's claims are an uncited quote from *India Today* (1981).

government reports (*Sunday*, 1982, 17). For example, investigations repeatedly cited a variously transliterated Omar Shariff, née Durai Raj, as 'very relevant' among 'the educated Harijan youths who volunteered to take up the responsibility of mass conversions' (Khan 1983, 123), which involved years of petitioning the local south Indian Ishathul Islam Society, and whose 'leading role in the mass conversion' responded to both the discrimination he experienced working at the 'local fund audit department' and the widespread 'ill treatment of ... harijans' in Meenakshipuram (*Sunday*, 1982, 17). Building upon a background of general discrimination, this treatment arose from a complicated confluence of local events: the 1977 elopement of a lower-caste Thevar girl and an Untouchable Pallar boy; disputes since 1980 between Thevars and Pallars over revenues from cultivating local land owned by the Thiruvaduthurai Adheenam, a powerful Saivite monastery; the murder of two Thevars hired to ensure Pallar labour continued on a neighbouring estate after recent strikes; and the subsequent violent harassment of Pallars by Thevars who also happened to constitute the local police.[4] Not only did Omar Shariff quote EVR's central idiom in declaring 'Our feeling of self-respect [*cuyamariyatai*] encouraged us to convert religion!' (Pilal 1981, 21) and affirm being 'those-of-the-principle-of Periyar [*periyar kolkaikkarankal*]' as a reason to favour Islam over Hinduism (Viramani 2003, 1), he also claimed that Tamil Nadu's anti-caste 'awareness' was 'influence[d]' by EVR's insistence 'on rationalism and equality ... awaken[ing] the people' (Khan 1983, 123–5). This echoed fellow converts' claims that 'association with the Periyar [EVR] movement ... taught ... hatred against the oppressive caste system' (Mujahid 1989, 76). As one journalist writes after interviewing a man involved in one of many 'copycat' regional conversions following Meenakshipuram:

> His own conversion ... stemmed from his long association with Muslims. ... [E]ven when he was an atheist and a Dravida Kazhagam activist Islam had some fascination. ... Mr. E. V. Ramasamy Naicker ... had himself suggested once that all non-Brahmin communities should embrace Islam in order to escape from ... Brahmin oppression.

[4] These events are a synthesis of the above articles, my own conversations around Meenakshipuram June–August 2005, and *Indian Express* (1981b). See also Kalam (1990, 39–48).

> ... Again and again, this statement of EVR was mentioned by many Harijans ... as a justification of their conversion. (Gopalan 1981)

Of course, Meenakshipuram's embracing of EVR and Islam over Ambedkar and Buddhism could be relatively unimportant when compared to Ambedkar's and EVR's shared emphasis on mass religious conversion of 'Untouchables' outside the fold of Hinduism to secure democratic promise against Brahmanical caste hierarchy. After all, Ambedkar and EVR are often positioned as commensurable figures in the assertion of lower-caste politics, despite Tamil-speaking south India's general focus on EVR to Ambedkar's exclusion and EVR's relative opacity to north India's caste politics alongside periodic invocation.[5]

However, I argue that Meenakshipuram serves as a rubric for reading the work of Ambedkar and EVR that provides contrasting accounts of just how religious mass conversion realizes democracy's fulfillment in liberty, equality, and fraternity. In short, Meenakshipuram draws attention to two concepts of conversion, a variant on the distinction between 'conversion of the heart ... unseen, inner, and utterly private' and 'conversion ... that attempt[s] to remake the body and its person' focused on physical exteriority (Katznelson and Rubin 2014, 9, 24). At its core, Ambedkar's mass conversion to Buddhism is a change in mind, the psychic, where the embrace of different principles and *an alteration of how one sees the world* enables the fulfillment of democratic promise. Ambedkar's account is markedly interior, not only with respect to his emphasis on Buddhism's mental revolution in contrast with Marxist bloody revolution (mind over body) but also with his emphasis on nativity and nationalism, with an affinity for an ancient past, rather than foreignness and internationalism, as the place of democratic fulfillment. In contrast, the core of EVR's mass conversion to Islam is a change of body, the somatic, where the embrace of different practices and an *alteration of how one is seen in the world* enables the fulfillment of democratic promise. EVR's account is markedly exterior, not only with respect to his emphasis on physical appearance but also with his fusion between Islam and Marxism, where embodied practices are prioritized over mental principles, and

---

[5] For example, see Karthikeyan and Gorringe (2012) and Jeffrey, Jeffery, and Jeffery (2008).

subsequently foreignness, the international, and a dramatic future are privileged over nativity and a national past. Such seeing is not the Foucauldian 'gaze' of power's surveillance, nor is such being-seen the Debordian 'spectacle' of obfuscating visuality, but rather both are distinct efforts to coordinate the relationship between 'outward behavior' and 'interiority['s] ... realiz[ation]' (Mahmood 2001, 56). Moreover, such seeing/being-seen bears on how systematic injustices suffered at home can make a 'foreignness of belonging' (Roberts 2016) appealing, perhaps inviting the interrogation of 'self-rule' itself. In short, within this chapter's evidentiary bounds, there appear to be alternative genealogies of anti-caste ideas and actions, where Meenakshipuram draws attention to how Ambedkar's and EVR's shared emphasis on mass religious conversion led to different ways of starting democratic time.

Prefatory Problematics

Before turning to the two concepts of conversion themselves, one should note that the questions they raise engage broader democratic problematics. The following discussion's backdrop is a worry that Ambedkar's salience in recent decades is irrevocably bound up with a certain politics of availability, where Ambedkar's familiar academic training and accessible English materials eclipse the 'vernacular' production of regional activists,[6] like the far less formally educated merchant EVR, when pushing beyond claims alleging some 'poverty of political theory in India' to explore how subcontinental hierarchy provokes Indian thought (Guru 2002). As elsewhere, perhaps political theory's tendency to privilege sophisticated literacy has provided an obstacle to, rather than opportunity for, its fuller study in South Asia. Furthermore, especially in an age of rising right-wing populisms globally, there needs to be more serious consideration of why Ambedkar, but not EVR, has been available to co-optation efforts by the BJP despite Ambedkar's absolute opposition to Hindutva and insistence that his mass conversion articulated this very opposition. If Ambedkar illustrates how 'Dalit political thought' reframes negative caste identity as State rights

---

[6] For example, Ambedkar featured in the perhaps glib remarks of Slavoj Zizek upon visiting India (Zizek 2010).

demand (Rao 2009)—or a broader 'Dalit political theory' pitting egalitarian relationships, productive labour, and oral concreteness against a reading of orthodox Hinduism's commitment to hierarchical order, manipulative profit, and textual abstraction (Ramnath 2015)[7]—then, I submit, we might see EVR as illustrating a conceptually adjacent 'non-Brahmin political theory' whose allied aim is not to remake self-rule into justice's vehicle but to critique self-rule itself as injustice's mobilization. EVR's non-Brahmin prioritized self-respect (*cuya-mariyatai*) over self-rule, grounded in the belief that self-rule's conjuring of political sovereignty was not freedom's image against Brahmanism but rather was itself Brahmanical unfreedom.[8] That is to say, if 'Dalit' marks an effort to produce representation out of exclusion, illustrated in Ambedkar's psychic conversion as an alternative nationalism available to co-optation, 'non-Brahmin' may challenge the very aim of representability, illustrated in EVR's somatic conversion as an internationalist alternative refusing such co-optation. The following prefatory problematics regarding freedom's typology, subaltern representation, and religious mass anticipate the subsequent discussion of Ambedkar and EVR.

My chapter's title is a riff on Isaiah Berlin's essay 'Two Concepts of Liberty'. As is well known, Berlin distinguishes between negative liberty, as 'freedom from' interference, and positive liberty, as 'freedom to' self-direct (Berlin 1969, 160).[9] He claims that 'the great contrast between the two concepts of negative and positive liberty' consists in the 'logical distinct[ion]' between the former's questions 'How far does government interfere with me?' or 'What am I free to do or be?' and the latter's questions 'Who governs me?' or 'Who is to say what I am, and what I am not, to be or do?' (Berlin 1969, 130). Berlin insists these are not 'two different interpretations of a single concept, but two profoundly ... irreconcilable attitudes to the ends of life' (Berlin 1969, 166). I suggest there is something theoretically generative about coupling, though not equating, negative liberty with EVR's somatic conversion (Islam) and positive liberty with Ambedkar's psychic conversion (Buddhism).

[7] See also Ilaiah (2005).

[8] Of course, 'Dalit' has always denied self-rule's *sufficiency*, engaging oppressed identities elsewhere to fortify itself (Clifford 2007).

[9] I am bracketing his 'hybrid form of freedom'.

Somatic conversion fits negative liberty's compatibility with self-rule's absence—'[f]reedom in this sense is not ... logically ... connected with ... self-government' (Berlin 1969, 129–30)—and insistence on the 'empirical self' that is otherwise dismissed as saturated by 'irrational impulse, uncontrolled desires, my "lower" nature, the pursuit of immediate pleasures, my "empirical" or "heteronomous" self' (Berlin 1969, 132). Psychic conversion fits positive liberty's demand for self-rule— 'deriv[ing] from the wish ... to be his own master ... to be the instrument of my own, not of other men's, acts of will ... which affect me, as it were, from outside'—and insistence on the 'ideal self' arising out of the 'metaphor of self-mastery' and a 'dominant self ... identified with reason, with my "higher nature" ... with ... my self "at its best"' as commensurable with 'something wider than the individual ... as a social "whole" ... a race, a church, a state, the great society' (Berlin 1969, 131–2). Accordingly, our two concepts of conversion share Berlin's concern over 'splitting ... personality into two' and 'distinguishing between two selves': EVR's somatic conversion shares in Berlin's negative-liberty worry over an '"empirical" or "heteronomous" self' marked by 'desires' being 'dominat[ed]' by an 'ideal, or "autonomous' self"' marked by 'transcenden[ce]' (Berlin 1969, 134, 132); Ambedkar's psychic conversion shares in Berlin's positive-liberty project of creating a better 'ideal, or "autonomous" self' of self-rule. Though both ultimately rely on an opposition between reason–freedom and superstition–unfreedom, EVR's somatic conversion does not rely on the 'autonomous, original, "authentic" behavior' at the heart of anticolonial nationalist demands for self-determination as Ambedkar's psychic conversion does (Berlin 1969, 157–60).[10]

But we will see at least three productive limitations to this coupling. First, vis-à-vis economics, EVR's somatic, not Ambedkar's psychic, appeals to the communism Berlin associates with positive liberty. Second, vis-à-vis coercion, Ambedkar's psychic, not EVR's somatic, demands the non-violence Berlin associates with negative liberty. And third, Berlin's suggestion that '[m]ere incapacity to attain a goal is not lack of political freedom' (Berlin 1969, 122) would strike both EVR and Ambedkar as obscene, since both saw legitimate politics as enabling a fuller sense of human

---

[10] EVR subsequently complicates equations between self-determination and freedom of the sort in Baum and Nichols (2013).

capacity.¹¹ Perhaps these cross-valenced liberties arose because of the shared marginalized position of both EVR and Ambedkar when confronted with the colonial/national binary exhausted by British-imperialist/Brahmin-nationalist positions, subsequently needing to articulate various third-way theorizations. If so, especially given our South Asian context, this invites reflection on a set of concerns associated with the 'subaltern' as the name of such marginalization, defined by Ranajit Guha as 'the demographic difference between the total Indian population' and 'dominant groups, foreign as well as indigenous' (Guha 1982, 44).

It is no coincidence that the year 1981 is home not just to Meenakshipuram's event but also to Guha's preface to volume 1 of *Subaltern Studies*, declaring the importance of 'the material and spiritual ... condition' of 'subordination' against 'dominance'; a right populism evident in BJP's response to the conversion and the Left historiography of *Subaltern Studies* insisting on 'the politics of the people' were simultaneously prompted by India's democratic crisis in the Emergency. Recent years have witnessed a rising interest in the translatable equivalence of 'subaltern/Dalit' and subsequent comparisons between Antonio Gramsci and Ambedkar, where 'the generic name "subaltern" obtains a geographical, historical, and social specificity in the name "Dalit"' by sharing programmes of 'counter-hegemony' (Zene 2013, xviii, 12, 10). Yet, related subcontinental political mobilizations, such as 'non-Brahmin', were no less counter-hegemonic. This claim is literal: EVR repeatedly challenged 'the system of hegemon and coolie [*ejaman kuli murai*]' and resulting 'individual agreements [*tanippatta cammantankal*]' (*Kuti Aracu* 1930, 11) during the 1920s and 1930s, suggesting that converging long distance inter-war experiences led like-minded activists to mobilize shared etymological roots (here, the shared Indo-European roots producing *ejaman* [in Tamil, from Sanskrit] and *hegemon* [in English, from Greek]) into the service of 'subaltern' critique. All this invites the question:

---

¹¹ It may be productive to see how Arendtian investments in spaces of appearance and non-sovereign freedom may variously resonate with these concepts of conversion. But Arendt's concern that the state's commitment to socioeconomic equality encouraged totalitarianism rather than democracy would have been wildly out of line with both Ambedkar's and EVR's political visions (Arendt, 1958). See also Markell (2006).

what is the relationship between non-Brahmin and Dalit with respect to the 'subaltern' and the cross-valenced liberties of our two concepts of conversion?

At the risk of sounding overly structural, both Ambedkar's Dalit and EVR's non-Brahmin occupy an excluded subaltern 'outside' to a hegemonic self/other binary exhausted by indigenous-Brahmin-nationalist and foreign-British-imperialist. How does this outside relate to thought and action? Is the outside a place from which to launch efforts at inclusion, not as subordinate but through representing oneself as coherent opposition, such as with an alternative nationalism? Or is the outside a passage for moving even further away, not as resignation but through mobilizations of dislocated possibilities unrepresentable in the here and now, such as with an internationalist alternative? Gayatri Chakravorty Spivak's classic essay 'Can the Subaltern Speak?' may serve as a guide here. She shares our tri-positional structure of outside:self/other where the outside is named 'subaltern' whose 'identity is its difference', and the self/other identities are named 'Brahmanic-hegemonic India' and 'colonial British' (Spivak 1988, 285, 282, 297). However, for Spivak, it is neither Dalit nor non-Brahmin but the 'figure' of 'the third-world woman' who is paradigmatically subaltern, so far outside as to be illegible, since 'both ... colonialist historiography and ... [anticolonial] insurgency ... keeps the male dominant. If ... the subaltern has no history and cannot speak, the subaltern as female is even more deeply in shadow' (Spivak 1988, 307, 287). For Spivak, if one looks 'on the other side of the international division of labor' whose capitalist present extends the 'patriarchal social relations' of imperialism's past, the third-world 'woman is doubly in shadow', an outside beyond representation (Spivak 1988, 288).

Spivak's concern is over first-world academics claiming to speak for third-world peasants, concluding with the aporia of the subaltern woman inevitably muted.[12] Our concern, however, is not aporetic but analytic, if not programmatic: how to further distinguish and unfold our two concepts of conversion. If we read Spivak's essay not as about first-world representations of third-world movements but instead as an exploration of how representation's deployment can be used to achieve political change, I suggest that—with respect to conversion as the time of Indian democracy—the non-Brahmin,

---

[12] The essays in Morris (2010) focus largely on such aporetic concerns.

not the Dalit, best illustrates the characteristics central to Spivak's subaltern in at least three ways.

First, the non-Brahmin is defined by international difference, favoured by Spivak, while the Dalit is defined by a national identity. This goes beyond any facile prefixed equation of 'non-' with difference ('non-Brahmin') and beyond the absence of 'non-' with identity ('Dalit'). Islam's appeal for EVR is its globality rather than its regionality; it is dissociated from a particular people and thus a universal markedly different from historical identity, at times seguing into Marxism as the mark of foreignness while attending to economic issues of labour in the wide world. Who they are *is not* what they were. In contrast, Buddhism's appeal to Ambedkar is its regionality, a local past with global possibilities but local nonetheless, marking a people with distinct ways of being native to enable political representation in local institutions. Who they are *is* what they *really* were.

Second, the non-Brahmin, not the Dalit, involves the representation Spivak endorses. Spivak famously reads Marx to distinguish between two senses of representation (*vertreten* and *darstellen*), the first in 'the political context' and the second in 'the economic context' (Spivak 1988, 278). The former is a speaking-for that worries Spivak, especially when involving first world on behalf of third world, while the second is an acting-with that Spivak endorses, claiming that 'confront[ing] [subsistence farmers, unorganized peasant labor, etc.] is not to represent (*vertreten*) them but to learn to represent (*darstellen*) ourselves' (Spivak 1988, 288–9). Ambedkar's Buddhism pursues representation in Spivak's worrying sense, enabling an assertive political speaking-for required within the workings of national institutions. EVR's Islam pursues representation in Spivak's endorsed sense, as a transformational economic acting-with demanded across the workings of international labour.

Third, these two senses of representation map our two concepts of conversion onto radically different understandings of the subject. Spivak dismisses political representation as presuming a 'sovereign subject' in the form of "heroes', paternal proxies, agents of power' invested in 'invocations of ... authenticity' drawing upon 'nostalgias for lost origins ... as ground for counterhegemonic ideological production' (Spivak 1988, 272, 279, 294, 307). Ambedkar's conversion—as an articulation of a mixed-valence positive liberty—courts such sovereign mastery and origin recovery to oppose

Brahmin hegemony. Instead, Spivak favours economic representation acknowledging a 'divided and dislocated subject whose parts are not continuous or coherent', requiring foremost a situational 'staging of the world' to understand the relationship between self and society (Spivak 1988, 276, 279). EVR's conversion—as an articulation of a mixed-valence negative liberty—embraces such situational staging within a social context to understand individual dislocation in Brahmanism.

In short, read through Spivak's subaltern as illuminating representation's dual possibilities rather than doubly shadowed impossibility, Ambedkar's psychic conversion prefigures the outside as a place to launch *inclusive projects* through a speaking-for sovereign subject of political representation—that is, an internal alternative nationalism. In contrast, EVR's somatic conversion prefigures the outside as a passage for moving even *further away* through an acting-with dislocated subject of economic representation—that is, an external internationalist alternative.

Our question, however, must involve two terms markedly absent in both Spivak and Berlin above but generally considered central to the study of 'subaltern' movements: religion and mass. As Guha asks, must scholars 'conceptualize insurgent mentality ... in terms of an unadulterated secularism' where leaders have a 'worldly consciousness' that dupes 'other-worldly' following masses, or can scholars 'grasp religiosity as the central modality of ... consciousness' and 'resultant contradictions' (Guha 1983, 37)? In order to further engage and distinguish our two concepts of conversion, we can see the limits of a this-worldly-leader/other-worldly-masses split being pressed in Talal Asad's influential dismissal of Clifford Geertz's definition of religion in 'Religion as a Cultural System'. Asad criticizes Geertz's definition of religion as set 'primarily in terms of consciousness' and thus 'isolated from social practices and discourses', worried that Geertz's otherworldly religion misses how 'the religious world is ... affected by experience in the common-sense world' (Asad 1983, 239, 250). However, Asad's eagerness to find in Geertz's religion a Marxist target ('a mode of consciousness which is other than consciousness of reality') that unwittingly projects the Christian experience upon the world—where religion changed from a 'pre-condition for normal social life' to a 'privatised' individualism prioritizing 'belief as a state of mind' after the scientific revolution—leads Asad to overlook the importance of the 'mass' in Geertz, where religious experience is in fact produced from common-sense worldly relationships (Asad 1983, 237, 247, 244, 249). Whereas Asad models his concern with religion's this-worldly 'authorising process' on the 'medieval Church['s]' clerical power over congregants (Asad 1983, 244, 246), Geertz at times locates religion's this-worldly authorising process within the shared experience of collective action, turning to Balinese 'mass trance, spreading like a panic', which 'projects the individual ... out of the common-place world ... into that most uncommonplace one', crossing 'a threshold into another order of existence' involving 'frenzied activities ... on the brink of a mass amok' requiring 'physical restraint' (Geertz 1993, 116–17).

Religion as a product of Geertz's mass movement resists Asad's critique: Asad presumes an institutional/individual dyad when finding Geertz's religion 'essentially cognitive', whereas Geertz's mass illustrates a religious experience acknowledging the 'historical conditions necessary' in a markedly physical 'common-sense world' to create a 'religious world' (Asad 1983, 252, 250). Geertz's 'mass' is not, for example, Walter Benjamin's, where technological changes create the 'masses' through a reorganization and re-evaluation of 'human sense perception' away from 'concentration', the 'optical', and sancrosanct 'uniqueness' and towards 'distraction', the 'tactile', and the 'habit' of everyday 'transitoriness' potentially 'gratified' by reactionary fascist war but equally 'receptive' to progressive socialist reform (Benjamin 1968, esp. 222–3). Geertz's mass movement is instead enabled by a new social relationality that tends towards frenzied concentration. This new social relationality of 'a mass amok' retains the 'individual' of 'the common-place world' through its projection into the 'most uncommonplace one', a 'threshold' perspective that could enable the very critical consciousness of social relations that Asad believes Geertz's religion undermines. That is, the 'materialist' critique Asad lodges against Geertz's religious 'consciousness' might short-circuit a path to the very consciousness of relationality that would enable such a materialist critique. On this front, we might see the physical considerations at the core of EVR's concept of conversion, rather than the cognitive ones of Ambedkar's, as fundamental for Geertz's threshold-crossing masses.

Regardless, it is the critical consciousness authorized and enabled through the collective actions of religious mass movement, available to Geertz's approach but foregone by Asad's, that is central to both EVR's and Ambedkar's concepts of conversion: both EVR and Ambedkar believe that current configurations of power are subject to critique through mass conversion. The subsequent shared questions of EVR and Ambedkar are: How can mass conversion provide the means to critique and change conditions of subordination? Is physical or psychological change the first step of mass conversion, and thus the first step towards the subsequent critical consciousness that mass conversion grounds, as the time of Indian democracy? The following discussion of Ambedkar's and EVR's concepts of conversion engages the above-mentioned problematics of freedom's typology (with crisscrossing positive and negative valences), subaltern representation (parsing efforts to speak-for sovereign national subjects as a place or to act-with dislocated international subjects as a passage), and religious mass (where collective experience exceeds institutional/individual models to produce critical consciousness) when wrestling with the theoretical frame for Meenakshipuram's event.

Ambedkar

Ambedkar's Buddhism claims that conversion fulfills democracy's promise through interiorities, prioritizing individual mind and collective nation as democracy's domains. Framed by Ambedkar's Buddhism, Meenakshipuram suggests an alternative nationalism, reconceived through cognitive changes and retrieving a different indigeneity. Ambedkar articulates his psychic understanding of conversion across three theses echoing Indian nationalism.

First, religion precedes politics. By 'religion' Ambedkar means 'the rules imposed for the maintenance of society'; 'religious revolution' entails a move toward 'individual welfare and progress' (Ambedkar 2003, 122 ['What Way Emancipation?']). The precedence of such religion over politics is 'a thesis which ... cannot be controverted' based on 'history', where 'political revolutions have always been preceded by social and religious revolutions' (Ambedkar 2014, 410). Ambedkar believes his focus on such religion as rules is novel, emphasizing his 'functioning of moral order in society' for democracy as distinct from 'political scientists' focusing simply on government (Ambedkar 2003, 483 ['Conditions

Precedent for the Successful Working of Democracy']). Given the Untouchable experience of a dysfunctional moral order, Ambedkar believes that 'conversion is [as] necessary to the Untouchables as self Government is necessary to India'; that is, there needs to be an 'en masse conversion' dramatically changing religion to ensure a meaningful 'self-government' involving the people (Ambedkar 2003, 140, 146 ['What Way Emancipation?']).

Second, mind is prioritized over body. Ambedkar's religious conversion involves mental change, adopting a 'new doctrinal basis ... in consonance with liberty, equality, and fraternity; in short, with democracy' (Ambedkar 2014, 539). This extends from Ambedkar's concern with 'mental slavery', with Hindu caste discrimination 'deeply rooted in our minds', and thus religious conversion offers 'the only antidote' because it provides 'freedom of the mind ... the real freedom' and creates an 'awakened consciousness' linked to individual, rational mastery against superstitious subordination—'a man who is his own master, him alone, I consider a free man' (Ambedkar 2003, 128 ['What Way Emancipation?']). His focus on individual mastery through 'mental attitudes' leads Ambedkar to his 1956 mass Buddhist conversion as markedly cognitive, involving oaths and beliefs that 'should be accepted ... with comprehension', as a 'conscious' act, and where 'books' are appropriate vehicles to 'remove ... doubts and suspicions' and achieve 'full knowledge' (Ambedkar 2003, 536, 544 ['The Buddha Dhamma Will Be the Savior of the World']). Though Ambedkar certainly claims that the emancipatory project of conversion is 'material as well as spiritual' (Ambedkar 2003, 117 ['What Way Emancipation?']), the spiritual has precedence, since 'the secular system cannot last very long' without 'the sanction of ... religion' (Ambedkar 2003, 515–16 ['Why I Like Buddhism']). Ambedkar subsequently positions conversion as distinct from the material: 'Self-respect is dearer to human beings [than] material gain' (Ambedkar 2003, 535 ['The Buddha Dhamma Will Be the Savior of the World']), and therefore '[m]y conversion is not for any material gain' but based on '[n]othing but spirituality' (Ambedkar 2003, 144 ['What Way Emancipation?']).

Third, democracy's location is native, not foreign. In the 1930s, Ambedkar is clear that the *outside* is the source of democracy's promise—'unless you join some other religion, you cannot get the strength from outside', evident in the 'equal treatment' of Muslims and Christians by 'Hindu society' (Ambedkar 2003, 121,

137 ['What Way Emancipation?']). But by the 1950s, Islam and Christianity seemed too outside; the Muslim 'invasion of India' destroyed Buddhism through 'violence', while Christianity's missionary activity threatens indigeneity (Ambedkar 2003, 506–12 ['Buddhist Movement in India']). Buddhism appealed because, despite being 'over powered ... by Brahmins' (Ambedkar 2003, 510 ['Buddhist Movement in India']), it 'survived ... for 2000 years in India' and thus is not 'new' nor 'borrowed from anywhere. This path is ... purely Indian' (Ambedkar 2003, 541–42 ['The Buddha Dhamma Will Be the Savior of the World']) and 'not ... alien' (Ambedkar 2003, 507 ['Buddhist Movement in India']), so '[l]et no one ... say that I have borrowed my philosophy ... from the French Revolution. ... My philosophy has roots in religion and not in political science ... [a religion] derived ... from the teachings of ... the Buddha' (quoted in Keer 1995, 459). The Buddha's indigeneity is foremost among the 'grounds' for Buddhism's preference, a native 'rational religion ... [without] room for superstition'. And by the 1940s Buddhism's Indian homeland, for Ambedkar, should be a nation state, a native region requiring regionalized 'Parliamentary Government' administration (Ambedkar 2003, 422–8 ['Failure of Parliamentary Democracy Will Result in Rebellion, Anarchy, and Communism']).

Given his investments in a parliamentary nation state, native principles, and a sense that religion or spirituality, as rules of social order, precede political revolution and are distinct from material gain, Ambedkar distinguishes the Buddha from Marx, moral principles from bodily concerns. Both world views focus on what 'man wants for ... life on earth', not 'with God and Soul and life after death', but Buddhism's this-worldly reforms entail 'bloodless mental revolution' and a 'change of mind' rather than Marxism's physical 'bloody revolution' and bodily 'violence' (Ambedkar 2003, 515–16 ['Why I Like Buddhism']). Ambedkar's 1950s worry, amid a looming Soviet threat to Asian sovereignty (Ambedkar 2003, 428 ['Failure of Parliamentary Democracy Will Result in Rebellion, Anarchy, and Communism']), that Marxist 'philosophy' is crudely material—about 'full meals, sound sleep, and see[ing] movies' (Ambedkar 2003, 537 ['The Buddha Dhamma Will Be the Savior of the World'])—extends from his 1930s dismissal of socialism as insufficiently 'grappl[ing] with the problems created by the prejudices which make Indian people observe the distinctions of high and low, clean and unclean' (Ambedkar 2014, 422). Marxism is inattentive to the differences that mark 'any given time or ... any given society', and Indian difference is marked by caste's unique 'division of labour accompanied by ... gradation of labourers' that exists foremost in the mind, requiring Buddhist conversion (Ambedkar 2014, 417, 424).

These features of Ambedkar's Buddhism inform a markedly interior understanding of religious mass conversion: where religion precedes politics, and therefore principles could be free from power; where mind is prioritized over body, suggesting a capacity for disinterested action; where freedom's location is native, not foreign, favouring a shared past over an alien future; and, therefore, pitting a Buddhist mental revolution against a Marxist bloody revolution, demanding force's absence rather than its presence. If used to frame Meenakshipuram, Ambedkar's marked *interiority* suggests conversion is primarily psychic, a change of mind over body. This framing, I argue, differs dramatically from how religious mass conversion to Islam is discussed by EVR, whose sensibility is far more *exterior*, emphasizing a somatic change, body over mind.

EVR

At least one concrete citation supplements the ambient references to EVR around Meenakshipuram mentioned earlier. A 1981 Tamil booklet titled *Meenakshipuram Thoughts* (*Minatcipura Cintanaikal*), published by a Muslim press, reproduced writings and speeches from figures across the Indian political spectrum, past and present, to situate Meenakshipuram historically and theoretically. Eight pages are set aside for 'Periyar's Thoughts' (*Periyarin Cintanaikal*). Aside from a few of these pages providing remarks from EVR around the time of Independence, the rest are devoted to the republication of a speech EVR delivered in October 1929 at the Truth Seeker's Meeting in Erode, EVR's hometown and his Self-Respect Movement's headquarters (Pilal 1981, 41–6).[13] This speech's immediate occasion resembles Meenakshipuram's: a small village's Untouchable mass conversion to Islam that inspired Untouchable conversions elsewhere to 'protect...their self-respect [*cuya-mariyatai*]' (*Kaivalyam* 1929, 6). This speech, I argue, raises a

---

[13] The original speech is: EVR (1929a).

tension between seeing and being seen while coupling mass movement with both Untouchable Islamic conversion and proletarianized global labour to challenge nation-based articulations of political power.

Though unfortunately unremarked in *Meenakshipuram Thoughts*, the year 1929 is very significant—it begins EVR's participation at *Mawlid*, the celebration of the birth of the Prophet Mohammed during the month of *Rabi' al-awwal*, which was in the month of August in 1929. I argue that EVR's *Mawlid* speeches from 1929 to 1931 insist on the tension between seeing and being seen while aggressively dismissing any understanding of religion or Islam as mental or spiritual, positioning Islam within a world-historical frame of progressive social reforms ultimately fulfilled by Marxism, embracing foreignness while refusing nativity, and inviting an understanding of politics unavoidably saturated by force. In short, EVR's understanding of what is democratically effective in mass conversion is very different from Ambedkar's.

The late 1920s are significant too. Non-Brahmins in south India then began understanding conversion not as evidence of political failure but as a demand for political fulfillment. In the mid-1920s, non-Brahmins echoed Gandhian concerns, worried that 'Christian Missionaries and Muslim Maulvies' are like 'hawk[s]' luring vulnerable communities to 'a foreign [*ayal*] religion', disrupting the balance of religious populations and bringing 'great ruin' to 'us and our precious Hindu religion [*matam*]' (Virappapillai 1925, 10). Decisively breaking with Gandhi in 1927 because of his insistence on a separate-but-equal logic of caste, non-Brahmins subsequently saw great virtue in Christianity and Islam as neither a 'sect' of nor having any 'relationship with the Hindu religion' (Kaivalyam 1929, parts 2, 3), turning to conversion to religions whose origins were perceived as non-Indian to achieve democratic aspirations against the failed democratic posturing of native elite Brahmins (Kaivalyam 1929, parts 1, 3). In this raw moment of non-Brahmin reversal, reframing mass conversion to 'foreign religion' as freedom's achievement rather than unfreedom's evidence, EVR delivered the October 1929 speech cited in Meenakshipuram's wake.

In this speech, Islamic conversions appealed to EVR as a way of achieving democracy's promise in two modes: first, as a way of being seen differently rather than simply seeing differently, prioritizing bodily appearance over mental principles; second, as global mass mobilization with a labour-inflected challenge to regionalized governmental authority. This argument is evident by attending to the original October 1929 speech as a whole rather than its partial 1981 republication, which contained only the first of the speech's three thematic segments: a discussion of conversion to Islam (which was republished), followed by a lengthy dismissal of Hindu ceremonies and a reflection on global powers of unfreedom (which were not).

The October 1929 speech's first segment makes the traditional, radical materialist move in Indian epistemology: an emphasis on *pratyaksa* [*pirattiyatcam*], or direct observation, as the sole way of knowing, excluding other cognitive means (*pramana*) such as inference or testimony (Dasgupta 1922, 294).[14] EVR invokes *pratyaksa* to claim religion as consisting solely of principles that help humans live collectively 'for mankind's this-worldly life [*ivvulakam valkkai*]', and not 'for the sake of experience in "the higher world" [*mel lokam*] or "the lower world" [*kil lokam*] or after death with a "subtle" [*cutcum*] body' (EVR 1929a, 7). But *pratyaksa* in the speech seems helpful only for identifying the *obstacles* to Untouchables' achieving what non-Brahmins call 'self-respect'—economics, education, political representation, social degradation, and so on. To *positively* achieve self-respect, and to fulfil democratic promise, EVR focuses not on seeing but on being seen. He claims: 'Some have written to me that the Mohammadean religion creates a rough nature [*murattu cupavam*]. If that is true, I think it indeed is a good idea to recommend the Mohammadean religion' (EVR 1929a, 8). Though he tactfully rephrases this to 'courageous [*tairiya*] nature', EVR's point is that being seen differently is required to inculcate an 'unrestrained refusal of desire to agree with degradation and humiliation' (EVR 1929a, 8). After all, for such a 'rough nature' to be meaningful to EVR's epistemology and evident to those who have written him, it must be available to the direct observation of *pratyaksa*—that is, a change in how one is seen. Moreover, it is not only Islamic conversion that provides the appearance necessary to achieve self-respect but rather a conversion of a particular sort: 'until real [*unmai*] equality–unity in Hindu society, there is no other way except for Untouchables to become Mohammadeans *en masse* [*kumpal kumpalay*]' (EVR 1929a, 8).

[14] See also Mohanty (2000, 11–40).

The 1981 republication of EVR's October 1929 speech ends here, maintaining a tension in the means of achieving self-respect between an individual's seeing-differently through the clarity of *pratyaksa* and collectively being-seen-differently with a particular appearance through mass conversion to Islam. The speech's unrepublished second thematic segment includes EVR's concluding remarks regarding Islamic conversion, where he dismissed female purdah (*kosha*) as a culturally dispensable rather than essential practice, gesturing to Islamic advances in women's 'rights [*urimai*]' evident in Turkey and Afghanistan to 'thunderous applause' (EVR 1929a, 8). This second segment, which is the bulk of the speech as a whole, goes on to repeat EVR's criticisms of Hinduism and temples for which EVR is well known; the south Indian temple was a centre of political authority, social honour, and economic redistribution and thus a major concern to non-Brahmin efforts to cultivate self-respect (Appadurai and Breckenridge 1976).

The shorter final third of EVR's October 1929 speech is more striking, for here the speech's only other mention of the 'mass' occurs, suggesting a productive engagement with the earlier 'mass' of Untouchable Islamic conversion. Worried that India is a 'poor' and 'destitute nation ... frequently visited by famine' and consumed with expensive ceremonies that only bring about 'shame and degradation' to the vulnerable, EVR describes India as 'a nation that boards a ship for the sake of wage-labor [*kuli*] to a foreign country ... with crumpled wage-laborers [*kulikkararkal*] lying starved *en masse* without labor [*tolil*], without work [*velai*]' (EVR 1929a, 14). This doubled appearance of the mass in the speech's first and third segments invites a link between Untouchable Muslim converts and proletarianized global labour, thereby suggesting that regional obstacles to the masses' self-respect may require international remedies beyond national horizons. That is, the vulnerable masses are not simply Untouchables converting in India, they are labourers starving on ships seeking employment, thereby inviting reforms extending beyond regional self-rule if not questioning altogether the capacity of self-rule's regionalized administration of State power to address mass suffering.

Accordingly, EVR segues in the speech's third and final segment from global labouring masses to the rejection of governments with nation-state horizons, describing a 'world history' where two agents collude to form the 'stratagem' of all governments:

'Those who are people-of-atrocity and people-of-cunning are those-of-high caste [*jati*] called the Priests and those-of-theft and those-of-arrogance are the Kings' (EVR 1929a, 14). As agents who 'deceive the people [*janankal*]' and 'need to invent a method to administer power [*atikkam*]', these two agents of regional government administration, everywhere in the world, turn to 'making the people feel low through [reducing] knowledge and wealth', for '[i]f a man is one-of-knowledge then a Priest cannot deceive [him], if one-of-wealth then a King cannot make [him] afraid'. In other words, the broader context of EVR's concern with the labouring masses seeking global employment—a concern redeploying the masses from his earlier discussion of Untouchables converting to Islam seeking self-respect—is one in which 'Brahmins who are the priests and Kings who are the rulers', that is, knowledge and power, are *universally* coupled in regionalized administrations of authority. Through his two uses of the word 'mass', EVR thereby invites reflection on the relationship between Islamic conversion and global labour, between eradicating particular Indian Untouchability and challenging regionalized government in the world.

Just a few months earlier, in August 1929, EVR began speaking at *Mawlid*. His six *Mawlid* speeches from 1929 to 1931 echo the broader claims of EVR's October 1929 speech regarding just *how* mass religious conversion to Islam was effective by emphasizing physical externality rather than mental internality, maintaining a tension between seeing and being seen, and coupling issues of Untouchable conversion with global labour (EVR 1929b; EVR 1930a; EVR 1930b; EVR 1931a; EVR 1931b; EVR 1931c.).[15] Though sharing Ambedkar's emphasis on liberty, equality, and fraternity, EVR's *Mawlid* speeches illustrate marked differences with Ambedkar's concept of conversion, including a focus on progressive historical reform, where the recent overcomes the ancient, and an understanding of religious propagation that cannot be disassociated from violence.

EVR and other Self-Respecters speaking at *Mawlid* often started by acknowledging what may be surprising: Muslims inviting atheists to speak at birthday celebrations of the Prophet Mohammed.

---

[15] The dates suggest EVR spoke at both Sunni and Shi'a celebrations of *Mawlid*.

As EVR claims, 'For you, who practice the Islam path with what is said to be greater religious devotion ['bhakti'] than the people of any other religion, to invite such a person as me is a great wonder [*aticayam*]' (EVR 1931a, 10). But EVR's *Mawlid* speeches reveal that such invitations were not merely expressions of strategic political alliance or the appeal of Islamic egalitarian doctrine,[16] though these were certainly at play, but also an opportunity to reveal shared understandings of the transformation required to achieve self-respect.[17]

Like Ambedkar's Buddhism, EVR's Islam emphasizes this-worldly principles—'all religions are principles brought about by learned-ones of each age intended for the benefit of the people's this-worldly life ... and for the experience of pleasure [*inpam anupvam*]', not 'an instrument for the meaning of the soul' nor 'some path for a stage above this-worldly life' (EVR 1929b, 7). This includes 'fraternity', as sharing the same eating leaf regardless of another's homeland; 'equality', the absence of 'high low'; and liberty [*cutantiram*]. EVR is particularly interested in the 'many liberties of women and Untouchables' in Islam in contrast with Hinduism (EVR 1930b, 11), evident again in Turkey and the 'Afghan nation', including how 'women have right [*urimai*]' with respect to 'property', 'widow remarriage', 'liberty to study', and 'the liberty to leave if a husband and wife do not go together'.[18]

But unlike the academic Ambedkar, the less formally educated EVR is not at all interested in words: he is not interested in books, oaths, and doctrines. EVR repeatedly claims never 'to say a single [thing] about what was written in each religions' foundational texts', such as the 'Hindu Veda' and 'Koran', 'because I am not one who has read all those', dismissing religious 'books' as without 'a single benefit [*palan*] for us; by writing sugar in a letter will it be sweet to the tongue?' (EVR 1929b, 8). EVR emphasizes not only that he has not 'tried to read' such texts but that he is not 'worthy to do that' (EVR 1931b, 7), dismissing 'research of textual foundations'

---

[16] This contrasts sharply with More (1993).

[17] Islam here is not about 'attaining personal salvation through righteous behaviors' (Donner 2010, xii) but rather 'the supreme value in the Islamic ... message is ... social justice' (Rahman 1970, 5).

[18] 'Wedding *rattu*' as 'divorce', from the Arabic word for refusal (EVR 1929b, 8; EVR 1931a, 15).

as for a 'student exam' (EVR 1931a, 10), not meaningful for assessing the 'comparative-value [*taratammiyam*]' of religions (EVR 1929b, 8; EVR 1931a, 10).

EVR's basis for religious evaluation is instead, again, the radical epistemology of direct perception: 'Because one may make a "philosophical meaning [*tattuvarttam*]" however one may want' through textual interpretation, 'I will be discussing the matters which we see in *pratyaksa*', assessing Hinduism and Islam through 'results experienced' (EVR 1929b, 8). EVR believes that 'the instrument [*karuvi*] [by] which [one] measures the greatness of religion' includes questions like: 'In each and every religion, how do people behave themselves? How are people treated? Therefore what result has that society attained?' Real philosophy is articulated through 'action [*kariyam*]', not 'the pages of a book' (EVR 1931a, 10), demanding a certain synesthesia, where philosophy can be heard only through the seeing of direct perception: 'The Islam religion says in *pratyaksa* 'help ... the lame, the crippled, the hunch-backed, and the blind'. The principle of the Hindus says in *pratyaksa* 'help the lazy-bones ... who rejoice eating up the hard-work of those-of-the-town' (EVR 1931a, 15).

As we saw in October 1929, such *pratyaksa* is not sufficient for achieving self-respect but requires a more embodied disposition: it is not simply how one sees but how one is seen that is important.

On the one hand, EVR claims that '[w]e need to clear [*paricuttam*] our own eyes and try to examine', by 'wearing glasses', correcting 'cataracts' or being 'nearsighted', and being 'cleared of any sort of color' so as not to tint the world 'red' or 'yellow' (EVR 1931b, 8). These clear eyes and corrective lenses cut through mere 'guise' [*vesham*]. Such 'deceptive guise [*veli vesham*] in the name of religion' (EVR 1929b, 9) is a 'stumbling block' not only for 'Hindu Muslim unity' (EVR 1930a, 7) in India but for world-historical unity, preventing a universal 'moralit[y] ... suitable for the good of humanity' (EVR 1929b, 7), the achievement of 'the true human *dharma*', and 'unity and peace for the world's people' (EVR 1930a, 7).

On the other hand, Islam's appeal is *precisely* its guise. When discussing the need to see the world through corrective, untinted lenses, EVR claims that 'one should see everything with confident reason and with a mind of clear impartiality [*natunilaimai*] ... confidently explain[ing] in public [*veliyil*] the seen truth [*unmai*]' (EVR 1931b, 8). Yet confidence, and related values like valour and daring, are supplemental to *pratyaksa*, found in Islam as 'a religion which gives manliness [*anmai*] and valor. How?—[Muslims] are more daring than others. If others see them the others are afraid but [Muslims] are not afraid of anyone' (EVR 1929b, 8). EVR does not embrace Islam *to see through* mere appearances, which we might associate more with Ambedkar's cognitive emphasis on world views, but to *be seen in* a particular appearance, thereby focusing on the physical 'guise', not the doctrine, of Islam as transformative.

EVR not only differs from Ambedkar in his understanding of mass conversion's core transformative basis, stemming from embodied, not cognitive, changes, but also with respect to the *time* of democratic fulfillment. Whereas Ambedkar favoured Buddhism as ancient, EVR favours Islam as recent. For EVR, the Prophet Mohammed was the 'highest' of the 'Great-Ones [*periyar*]' among 'religious leaders' and 'generally' should be followed by 'all people' because His 'religion (principle) [*sic*] ... was later and is more recent than all other religions. Therefore ... it removed all errors and faults among other religions and is [thus] that which has an [appropriate] amount of reform' (EVR 1929b, 7). Historical progress explains why Hindu principles are opposed to Islamic ones, an opposition between 'old-religion and new-religion' (EVR 1930a, 7), where Hinduism is 'the condition of the world's people from the very beginning' and thus regressive (EVR 1930b, 12). In ancient times, 'everywhere in the world Hindu religious principles ... had spread' (EVR 1929b, 7) and all 'were uncivilized and ignorant in the same way' (EVR 1930b, 11). For EVR, Mohammed faced this very universal uncivilized ignorance in Arabia.

Islam's world-historical fulfillment of progressive social reform makes it suitable for the world itself: 'Because it is a religion of contemporary reform ... [Islam] is the [most] excellent religion among all the religions in the world' (EVR 1929b, 8), one whose 'philosophy' is 'suitable for all of the world's people' (EVR 1930a, 7). To support this progressive history, EVR invokes 'Darwin's Theory Evolution Theory' [*sic*] to establish the claim that 'change is progress', though survival's fitness here was determined not by hierarchical competition but cooperative equality (EVR 1390b, 11). Furthermore, Mohammed's recency means that he was the world-historical overcoming of previous figures like Christ and the Buddha, despite their equally being 'slandered as atheists and given great suffering' by their contemporaries because of their social reform efforts (EVR 1929b, 7). The foreign Christ's half-human nature was an improvement upon other-worldly divinities, but Christianity's post-Reformation factionalism and claim about a second coming made him inferior to Mohammed, a fully human 'messenger of god' who demonstrated 'reason' by saying 'hereafter in the world, no more prophets will appear' (EVR 1930b, 11). And while the native Buddha shared with Mohammad a fully human nature, 'a child born of a mother and father' through 'union [*kuti*]' 9 EVR 1931a, 10), and while his rejection of divinity was certainly attractive, EVR finds that the Buddha has simply become 'imagined [by the] common people [*janankal*] as [an] avatar' folded within the Hindu pantheon and thus 'without the slightest benefit' to society (EVR 1930b, 11). Therefore, in terms of 'justice, rules, orders, self-respect, advancement, liberty, and the development of man's society' (EVR 1931a, 10) 'the new principles need to borrow from the Prophet' (EVR 1930b, 11).

Not only did Islam overcome Buddhism world-historically, but the next step in world-historical fulfillment is the very thing Ambedkar contrasts with Buddhism: Marxism. Though EVR's progressive history demands that the world 'consent to the Islam principle' since 'the world is a slave to reform' (EVR 1931a, 16) and 'reason'—which means that everyone, not just Muslims, should observe *Mawlid* and pay 'respect' to the Prophet Mohammed, including non-Brahmin Self-Respecters—Marxism is the next step: 'If one wants to classify a principle beyond the Islamic religious principles, it must today be the Russian religion. Other than that, [Islam] has given to the people freely as much liberty, fraternity, and heroism as possible' (EVR 1930b, 11). EVR's *Mawlid* speeches could even be read as prefatory to the Self-Respect Movement's translation of *The Communist Manifesto* published in October 1931. The *Manifesto's* translation of 'communism' was *samadharma*, or 'equal dharma' (Baxter 2016),[19] and EVR's immediately preceding *Mawlid* speeches of 1931 claim that atheistic reforms, which he believed to constitute the core of Islam, were necessary for *samadharma* to 'spread': 'God feeling is an obstacle for world progress, the

---

[19] More broadly, I would suggest that EVR's position on Islam invites engagements with praxis-driven projects of emancipatory coupling between religion and Marxism, such as in Guttierez (1973), rather than some focus on allegedly shared autocratic tendencies, as in Lewis (1954).

growth of knowledge, equality, and *samadharma'* (EVR 1931c, 7). Presumably, like Islam, Marxism will 'dare ... even to change itself, making reform in the way fitting the contemporary condition and time-nation-occurrence'—in stark contrast with Ambedkar's concern over Marxism's contextual inattentiveness.

The compatibility EVR sees between Islam and Marxism reveals two deeper theoretical points of contrast with Ambedkar.

First, rather than the national and native, which grounded the Buddha's appeal for Ambedkar, EVR favours the international and foreign. Islam, like Communism, opposes nationality, eliminating 'war of nation against nation', and EVR is concerned that 'saying "Your Nation, My Nation" maintains narrow aims and class disgust [*vakuppu tuvesham*]' (EVR 1931c, 7).[20] For EVR, Islam, like Marxism, refuses particularities of 'nation, religion, caste, color, and class [*vakuppu*]' (EVR 1931c, 7), which link birth and origins to life and ends, out of an investment in 'reason' declaring 'no difference in birth among people' nor 'from place to place' (EVR 1931b, 8). EVR goes further, celebrating the ways in which Tamils and Muslims are both allegedly foreign, equally categorized by Sanskritized upper castes as *mleccha*. For EVR, the internationalism animating both Islam and Marxism does not 'praise the difference between their own society and a foreign society' but perhaps even invites one to imagine oneself as foreign (EVR 1931c, 14).[21]

The second departure from Ambedkar's Buddhism deals with the relationship between religious propagation and violence: Ambedkar believes that force should not be involved, favouring Buddhism's bloodless mental revolution, while EVR claims instead that 'all religions are violently propagated' (EVR 1930b, 11). EVR questions the concern that 'Muslims are those who use force [*palatkaram*] to grow [their] society' (EVR 1931c, 14) with 'the sword in one hand and the Koran in the other' (EVR 1930b, 12) by asking, 'Is there anyone who can say that Hindus also do not use force?' (EVR 1931c, 14). After reflecting on the hypocrisy

---

[20] The relationship between *vesham* and *tuvesham*, 'disguise and disgust' as it were, may prove fruitful for future explorations of subcontinental political theory more broadly and non-Brahmin political thought in particular.

[21] For a discussion of the relationship between strangers and the public that productively engages EVR's investments in the foreign, see Warner (2002).

of Hindus 'saying "Love! Love! [*anpu*] Compassion-for-all-living-things [*jivakarunyam*]!!!"' evident in the vegetarian demand 'Don't eat goat and chicken' (EVR 1931a, 15), EVR attends to the slaughter in Hindu history and myth, the gruesome Vedic punishments for dissidents, the threatening 'letters that come to me daily, the many speeches spoken about me', and the 'propaganda [*piraccaram*]' by 'Saivites-Vaishnavites ... opposing my principles' to conclude that 'the sword propagation said to be done by the Mohammadeans pales in comparison' (EVR 1930b, 12). Since there is no distinction between coerced religion and authentic religion, the difference between Hinduism and Islam cannot be force's presence but force's effect. To establish how Hindu force has resulted in a 'completely empty-direction [*cunyaticai*] ... a wasted-direction [*kshinaticai*]' of divisiveness and hierarchy (EVR 1931c, 14) in contrast to the unity, valour, and daring associated not with Islamic religious principle but with Muslim 'guise', EVR claims that, unlike the dramatic Muslim response to a similar situation, the Hindu response to a fellow Hindu beaten by a Muslim is to say, '"whoever beat him, what concern is it to us" and simply leave' (EVR 1931a, 15). Hindu non-violence is called 'love [*anpu*]' though really is 'the absence of valor and solidarity', while Muslim violence is called 'roughness [*murattuttanam*]' though really it is an articulation of fraternal equality (EVR 1931b, 7–8).

What we see in EVR's speeches from 1929 to 1931, a period referenced in reactions to Meenakshipuram in 1981, is a point-by-point opposition to Ambedkar's understanding of how mass conversion results in democratic transformation: in EVR's view it is not texts but actions, not ideas but bodies, not force's absence but force's presence, not native/nationalism but foreign/internationalism, not past but future, not Marxism's opposition but its embrace—in short, it is not an internal psychic change of world view but an external somatic change in how one is viewed in the world that marks Islamic mass conversion's appeal for EVR and thus the time of democracy.

There is not space here to discuss Islam's role in the changed political landscape of Tamil-speaking south India after the 1937 sweep of Gandhi's Congress Party in the elections provided for in the Government of India Act of 1935—a bill that further made political representation turn on communal reservations defined by religion and caste and an election that saturated the political horizon with *swaraj*, both of which altered conversion's effects. But we can briefly note some changes and continuities. For example, in a June 1943 speech reflecting on this earlier Mawlid period, EVR discusses Islamic conversion as an individual tactic, which could involve reconversion, to achieve political and economic benefits within a national space marked by liberal diversity—a far cry from his earlier mass movement fulfilling world-historical progress and achieving definitive transformation. Moreover, this speech reveals how EVR dramatically turned away from his earlier international aspirations by the 1940s, now claiming that '[w]e [*nam*] (Dravidians or Tamils) have a border which could become a nation [*neshan*]', defining this 'we' in terms of 'mother-language' and 'race [*inam*]'[22] and in opposition to a variety of features related to 'the foreigner' (EVR 1943, 3). Yet, despite these profound reversals that too often go unremarked, EVR continued to insist on Islam's conversion because it changes how one is seen. Alongside emphasizing the importance of seeing directly through religion as mere 'guise' [*vesham*], this guise remains the very thing that constitutes Islam's transformative power: 'putting on the Turkish skullcap and tying the red lungi' creates 'valor, dignity, and daring of life for society', the 'appearance' of which generates 'hesitation from the Government to the Brahmin, according to a fire growing a bit in the mind'.[23]

* * *

In 2005, I spent several months around Meenakshipuram to better understand its memory. Though most of Meenakshipuram's residents denied my naive hunch when directly asked about EVR's influence, even as most insisted that those with direct experience

[22] These remarks resonate with the short extracts from EVR in 1947–8 pitting a 'Dravidian race' against 'Aryan power [*ariyar atikkam*]', republished in Pilal (1981), 47–8. Such remarks radically depart from EVR's claims circa 1930, as discussed in the present chapter.

[23] EVR 1943, 3. More broadly, EVR's often overlooked focus on guise and conversion, as discussed in the present chapter, may provide opportunities to engage recent LGBTQ mobilizations of EVR's idiom of 'self-respect' in Tamil Nadu. For example, how might EVR's guise and conversion relate to the 'appearance–reality contrast' discussed in Bettcher (2014)?

of the event had left or passed on, two claims repeatedly arose. First, the conversion took place in the name of *cuya-mariyatai*, 'self-respect'; though EVR was not mentioned by name, his central term of concern was. Second, the conversion responded to a brutally caste-ridden condition of *arajakam*, 'anarchy'; conversion to an international religion was a response to the nation state's failure to provide local law and order. Evidence of such international possibilities revolved around a place called 'Dubai', the origin of the toys of the local imam's daughter and the location of husbands and sons sending remittances home to the area. My visit followed the short-lived Tamil Nadu Prohibition of Forcible Conversion of Religion Ordinance, later Act, passed in 2002 during the 1998–2004 period of the BJP-led central government. The ordinance prompted the media to feature headlines such as 'Meenakshipuram Redux'[24] and scholars to reflect on Ambedkar as 'burst[ing] the ideological premises' of religious conversion's politicization, defying pat tensions between spiritual conviction and material coercion by showing how spiritual reform was not distinct from but preceded political independence and how individual empowerment was not set in contrast to but in fact required mass movement, providing 'new metaphors and models of conversion' (Jenkins 2007, 463; and Kent 2007, 384). Yet, this chapter has suggested that, as a matter of historical fact, Meenakshipuram invites an engagement with EVR just as much as with Ambedkar—if not more. Moreover, as a matter of political theory, where 'conversion [is] the time of ... democracy', Meenakshipuram provides a rubric for reading EVR, one rooted in a decisive context around 1929, and another for reading Ambedkar, one rooted in a decisive context around 1956, generating contrasting conceptions of how religious mass conversion makes a political difference—either in EVR's external somatic changes in appearance or in Ambedkar's internal psychic changes of principle—in order to challenge Brahmanism's hierarchy and achieve liberty, equality, and fraternity.

One may argue that the bright-line distinctions I have drawn here between Ambedkar and EVR are not only unnecessary but incorrect. For example, Ambedkar certainly discusses somatic concerns with clothing's role in personal presentation while underscoring the relationships between labour and caste; likewise, EVR

[24] *Outlook* (2002).

is unquestionably concerned with psychic issues of ideology's role in the self's construction while furious over the lack of caste representation in government posts. Moreover, Ambedkar *in 1929* and EVR *in 1956* undoubtedly converge to an extent: Marxism appealed in the wake of global capitalism's collapse in the Great Depression just as Marxism repelled at the Cold War's dawn on the eve of the Vietnam War in Buddhist Southeast Asia; Islam appealed in the years before its aggressive nationalist mobilizations just as Buddhism appealed to a newly independent Indian nation scrambling to imagine its own secular heritage. Furthermore, the Dravidian identity that eclipsed non-Brahmin difference by the 1940s in defining the politics of EVR's thought and movement could suggest subsequent confrontation, rather than transparent alliance, with the Dalit.[25] In fact, Meenakshipuram could be read as a dramatic staging of this very development: Dravidian Thevars oppressing Dalit Pallars who turned to EVR's earlier non-Brahmin concept of conversion. All this being true does not mitigate the possibility that mass religious conversion, as the time of Indian democracy, invited both EVR and Ambedkar to elaborate on just what the core change was in conversion that would lead to political difference. I hope my chapter's framing does not irredeemably fix a mind–body dualism as much as point to how, as a matter of practical sequence, EVR and Ambedkar acknowledged beginning with one or the other. As a rubric for reading their work, Meenakshipuram invites an understanding of Ambedkar's and EVR's shared effort to challenge Brahmanical hierarchy and liberate subjugated communities as one involving contrasting conceptions of conversion's core change.

These concepts of conversion relate to the time of democracy, in India if not elsewhere, by engaging problematics of freedom's typology, subaltern representation, and religious mass. They transcend Berlin's negative/positive valences of freedom: Ambedkar's concept involves the positive liberty of autonomy,

---

[25] Along with many others, Ravikumar has argued that EVR's Dravidian excluded Dalits. See, for example, Ravikumar (2004). Though I hope the present chapter invites a more textured reconsideration of such arguments pitting EVR against the Dalit, the alleged 'vacuum' in contemporary Tamil Nadu's politics following the recent deaths of the two major Dravidian parties' leaders does raise important concerns over 'the Dravidian's' future and, subsequently, the time of Indian democracy.

but non-violent; EVR's concept involves the negative liberty of heteronomy, but communist; and given the non-hegemonic 'subaltern' position of Ambedkar's Dalit and EVR's non-Brahmin, both concepts insist that socioeconomic incapacity *is* political freedom's lack. Positioned within a structural outside distinct from a hegemonic British-imperialist/Brahmin-nationalist binary, both concepts deploy, rather than are muted by, Spivak's dual subaltern representations: Ambedkar's conversion attempts to recover a native Buddhist identity to leave this outside place and represent politically, whereas EVR's conversion suggests a transformative difference as foreign Muslim, which, as if not outside enough, is a passage toward Communism's economic representation. Such collective action in the name of religion is not necessarily bound within an institution/individual framework, of concern to someone like Asad worried about privileging spiritual consciousness over a commonsense world, but rather authorized by the threshold-crossing of Geertz's mass that projects the individual from the commonplace world through shared actions that could create a critical consciousness unavoidably connected to social relationships.

In short, in light of our two concepts of conversion, the February 1981 mass conversion of 180 Dalit families to Islam in the small village of Meenakshipuram provides an opportunity for reflecting on subcontinental political theory as wrestling with seeing through alternative nationalisms and being seen in internationalist alternatives, beyond 'self-rule', as the core of mass conversion's relationship to the time of democracy. Such issues are not unimportant given the rise of right-wing populisms globally today, inviting renewed attention to figures such as EVR, who have resisted such populist co-optation, and to events like Meenakshipuram, which unwittingly played a role in such populism's Indian rise.

References

Ambedkar, B.R. 2003. *Dr. Babasaheb Ambedkar, Writings and Speeches*, vol. 17, part 3. Bombay: Education Department, Government of Maharashtra.

———. 2014. *Annihilation of Caste*. London: Verso.

Appadurai, Arjun, and Carol Breckenridge. 1976. 'The South Indian Temple: Authority, Honour, and Redistribution'. *Contributions to Indian Sociology* 10, no. 2: 187–211.

Arendt, Hannah. 1958. *The Human Condition*. Chicago: University of Chicago Press.
Asad, Talal. 1983. 'Anthropological Conceptions of Religion: Reflections on Geertz'. *Man* 18, no. 2: 237–59.
Baum, Bruce, and Robert Nichols, eds. 2013. *Isaiah Berlin and the Politics of Freedom: 'Two Concepts of Liberty' Fifty Years Later*. New York: Routledge.
Baxter, Matthew H. 2016. '*Bhutams* of Marx and the Movement of Self-Respecters'. *History of Political Thought* 37, no. 2: 336–59.
Benjamin, Walter. 1968. 'The Work of Art in the Age of Mechanical Reproduction'. In *Illuminations*, edited by Hannah Arendt, translated by Harry Zohn, 217–51. New York: Schocken.
Berlin, Isaiah. 1969. 'Two Concepts of Liberty'. In *Four Essays on Liberty*, 118–72. London: Oxford University Press.
Bettcher, Talia Mae. 2014. 'Trapped in the Wrong Theory: Rethinking Trans Oppression and Resistance'. *Signs* 39, no. 2: 383–406.
Clifford, Bob. 2007. '"Dalit Rights Are Human Rights": Caste Discrimination, International Activism, and the Construction of a New Human Rights Issue'. *Human Rights Quarterly* 29, no. 1: 167–93.
Dallmayr, Fred. 1996. *Beyond Orientalism: Essays on Cross-Cultural Encounter*. Albany: State University of New York Press.
Dasgupta, Surendranath. 1922. *A History of Indian Philosophy*, vol. 1. Cambridge: Cambridge University Press.
Donner, Fred M. 2010. *Muhammad and the Believers*. Cambridge, MA: Harvard University Press.
EVR. 1929a. 'Erotu Unmainatuvor Cankam: E.Ve. Ramacamiyar Upanniyacam: Matam Marutal; Carasvati Pujai' ('Erode Truth-Seekers Society: EV Ramacami's Address: Religious Change; Saraswati Puja'). *Kuti Aracu* (20 October): 7–9, 14.
———. 1929b. 'Tiru. Makamatu Napi Piranta Nal Kontattam: Cattiyamankalattil Tiru. E.Ve. Ramacamiyarin Corpolivu' ('Birthday Celebration of Mr. Mohammad the Prophet: Mr. E.V. Ramacami's Lecture in Cattiyamankalam'). *Kuti Aracu* (25 August): 7–9.
———. 1930a. 'Cattiyamankalattil Tiru Napi Piranta Nal: Ramacami Talaimaiyil Natantatu' ('Mr. Prophet's Birthday in Cattiyamankalam: Conducted with Ramacami as Chair'). *Kuti Aracu* (24 August): 7, 14.
———. 1930b. 'Erotu Napikal Pirantanal Kontattam: Janap Ke. Katar Cayapu Talamai Vakittar: E.Ve. Iramacamiyin Piracankam' ('Erode Celebration of The Prophet's Birthday: Janap K. Katar Sahib Serves as Chair: E.V. Ramacami's Oration'). *Kuti Aracu* (24 August): 11–13.
———. 1931a. 'Cattankulattil Iramacami Upanyacam' ('Ramacami's Address in Cattankulam'). *Kuti Aracu* (2 August): 10, 15–16.
———. 1931b. 'Erottil Tiru. Mukamatu Napi Pirantanal Kontattam: E.Ve. Iramacami Talaivar: Velur Maulvi Sharputin Cayapu Upanyacam'

('Celebration of Mr. Mohammad the Prophet's Birthday in Erode: E.V. Ramacami as Chair: Velur Maulvi Sharbudin Sahib Address'). *Kuti Aracu* (9 August): 7–8, 17.

———. 1931c. 'Kovaiyil Napikal Nayakam Piranta Nal Vaipavam: Tivanpakatur C.S. Irattinacapapati Mutaliyar Em. Es. Ci. Talaivar: Maulvi Nainar Mukamatu Cayapu, Ravcakip Ci. Em. Iramaccantirañ Cettiyar, E.Ve. Iramacami Upanyacarkal' ('The Prophet Messenger of-Allah's Birthday Celebration in Coimbatore: Divan Baktur C.S. Rattinacapapati Mudaliyar MSC as Chair: Addresses by Maulvi Naynar Mohammad Sahib, Ravsahib C.M. Ramachandran Chettiar, and E.V. Ramacami'). *Kudi Aracu* (23 August): 7, 14.

———. 1943. 'Ninkal Muslimkal Akavittal: 2000 Cuyarajyam Vantum Payanillai: Tolar Em. Ci. Raja Macota Ennayirru? Unkalukku Ulaikka Alunta? Ulaittalum Palanpera Mutiyuma? Cennaiyil Periyar Corpolivu' ('If You Become Muslims: No Benefi t even if Two Thousand Swaraj[es] Come: Whatever Happened to Comrade M.C. Raja's Bill? Is There a Man to Struggle for You? Even If There Was Struggle, Would There Be Any Benefit? Periyar's Oration in Chennai'). *Vitutalai* (28 July): 3.

Geertz, Clifford. 1993. 'Religion as a Cultural System'. In *The Interpretation of Cultures: Selected Essays*, 87–125. Waukegan, IL: Fontana.

Gopalan, T.N. 1981. 'Converts Quote EVR'. *Indian Express*, 19 August.

Guha, Ranajit. 1982. 'On Some Aspects of the Historiography of Colonial India'. In *Subaltern Studies*, vol. 1, 1–8. New Delhi: Oxford University Press.

———. 1983. 'The Prose of Counter Insurgency'. In *Subaltern Studies*, vol. 2, 1–40. New Delhi: Oxford University Press.

Guru, Gopal. 2002. 'How Egalitarian Are the Social Sciences in India?' *Economic and Political Weekly* 37, no. 50: 5003–9.

Guttiérez, Gustavo. 1973. *A Theology of Liberation: History, Politics, and Salvation*. Maryknoll, NY: Orbis Books.

Hindu. 1981. 'One Hundred Sixty Harijans Embrace Buddhism'. 7 December.

Ilaiah, Kancha. 2005 [1996]. *Why I Am Not a Hindu: A Sudra Critique of Hindutva Philosophy, Culture, and Political Economy*. Calcutta: Samya.

Indian Express. 1981a. 'Avadi a Far Cry from Meenakshipuram'. 28 November.

———. 1981b. 'Police-Thevar Onslaught Drove Harijans to Islam'. 10 November.

India Today. 1981. 'Islam's New Children'. 16–30 July.

Jaffrelot, Christophe. 1996. *The Hindu Nationalist Movement in India*. New York: Columbia University Press.

Jeffrey, Craig, Patricia Jeffery, and Roger Jeffery. 2008. 'Dalit Revolution? New Politicians in Uttar Pradesh, India'. *Journal of Asian Studies* 67, no. 4: 1365–96.

Jenkins, Laura Dudley. 2007. 'True Believers? Agency and Sincerity in Representations of 'Mass Movement' Converts in 1930s India'. In *Converting Cultures : Religion, Ideology, and Transformations of Modernity*, edited by Dennis Washburn and A. Kevin Reinhart, 435–64. Leiden: Brill.

Kaivalyam. 1929. 'Matamarrattin Karana Vilakkamum Araycciyum' ('Reasons of Religious Conversion Explanation and Research'), parts 1 and 2. *Kuti Aracu* (27 October, 3 November): 3, 18.

Kalam, Mohammed A. 1990. 'Religious Conversions in Tamil Nadu: Can These Be Viewed as Protest Movements?' *Indian Anthropologist* 20, nos 1/2: 39–48.

Karthikeyan, D., and Hugo Gorringe. 2012. 'Rescuing Ambedkar'. *Frontline* (5 October).

Katznelson, Ira, and Miri Rubin, eds. 2014. *Religious Conversion: History, Experience, and Meaning*. Burlington, VT: Ashgate.

Keer, Dhananjay. 1995 [1954]. *Dr. Ambedkar: Life and Mission*. Mumbai: Popular Prakashan.

Kent, Eliza F. 2007. '"Mass Movements" in South India, 1877–1936'. In *Converting Cultures: Religion, Ideology, and Transformations of Modernity*, edited by Dennis Washburn and A. Kevin Reinhart, 367–94. Leiden: Brill.

Khan, Mumtaz Ali. 1983. *Mass-Conversions of Meenakshipuram: A Sociological Enquiry*. Madras: Christian Literature Society.

Kuti Aracu. 1929. 'Mata Marankal: Tiruvannamalaiyil: Cumar 200 Atitiravita Kutumpankal Makamatiyarakat Tayar' ('Religious Conversions: In Tiruvannamalai: About Two Hundred Adi-Dravida Families Ready to Become Mohammadeans') (27 October): 6.

——. 1930. '*Vipacaram*' ('Adultery') (26 October): 11.

Laine, James W. 2007. 'The Body as the Locus of Religious Identity'. In *Converting Cultures: Religion, Ideology, and Transformations of Modernity*, edited by Dennis Washburn and A. Kevin Reinhart, 325–44. Leiden: Brill.

Lewis, Bernard. 1954. 'Communism and Islam'. *International Affairs* 30, no. 2: 1–12.

Mahmood, Saba. 2001. 'Feminist Theory, Embodiment, and the Docile Agent: Some Reflections on the Egyptian Islamic Revival'. *Cultural Anthropology* 16, no. 2: 202–36.

Markell, Patchen. 2006. 'The Rule of the People: Arendt, *Arche*, and Democracy'. *American Political Science Review* 100, no. 1: 1–14.

Mohanty, J.N. 2000. *Classical Indian Philosophy*. Lanham, MD: Rowman and Littlefield.
More, J.B.P. 1993. 'Tamil Muslims and Non-Brahmin Atheists, 1925–1940'. *Contributions to Indian Sociology* 27, no. 1: 83–104.
Morris, Rosalind, ed. 2010. *Can the Subaltern Speak? Reflections on the History of an Idea*. New York: Columbia University Press.
Mujahid, Abdul Malik. 1989. *Conversion to Islam: Untouchables' Strategy for Protest in India*. Chambersburg, PA: Anima.
Outlook. 2002. 'Do Conversions Guarantee a Better Life? No Longer a Hindu: Case Studies from All over India'. Special issue, 28 November 28.
Pandey, Gyanendra. 1991. 'In Defence of the Fragment: Writing about Hindu–Muslim Riots in India Today'. *Economic and Political Weekly* 26, nos 11/12: 559–72.
———. 2006. 'The Time of the Dalit Conversion'. *Economic and Political Weekly* 41, no. 18: 1779–88.
Pilal, Tancai. 1981. *Minatcipura Cintanaikal* (Meenakshipuram Thoughts). Iravanceri: Ikpal.
Puniyani, Ram, ed. 2005. *Religion, Power, and Violence: Expression of Politics in Contemporary Times*. New Delhi: Sage.
Rahman, Fazlur. 1970. 'Islam and Social Justice'. *Pakistan Forum*, no. 1: 4–9.
Ramnath, Maia. 2015. 'No Gods, No Masters, No Brahmins: An Anarchist Inquiry on Caste, Race, and Indigeneity in India'. In *No Gods, No Masters, No Peripheries: Global Anarchisms*, edited by Barry Maxwell and Raymond Craib, 44–79. Oakland, CA: PM Press.
Rao, Anupama. 2009. *The Caste Question: Dalits and the Politics of Modern India*. Berkeley: University of California Press.
Ravikumar. 2004. 'Periyar's Hindutva'. *Outlook*, 10 September.
Roberts, Nathaniel. 2016. *To Be Cared For: The Power of Conversion and Foreignness of Belonging in an Indian Slum*. Berkeley: University of California Press.
Seshadri, H.V. 1981. *Warning of Meenakshi Puram*. Bangalore: Jagarana Prakashana.
Singh, S. Nihal. 1981. 'Lessons of Meenakshipuram'. *Indian Express*, 14 July.
Spivak, Gayatri Chakravorty. 1988. 'Can the Subaltern Speak?' In *Marxism and the Interpretation of Culture*, edited by Cary Nelson and Lawrence Grossberg, 271–313. Basingstoke, UK: Macmillan.
Sunday. 1982. 'The Meenakshipuram Report'. 13–19 November, 17–26.
Verghese, B.G. 1981. 'Confusing Cause with Effect'. *India Today*, 16–30 September.
Viramani, Ki. 2003 [1981]. *Minatcipurattil Matam Marram En?* (Why Religious Conversion at Meenakshipuram?). Chennai: Unmai Vilakkam Patippakam.

Virappapillai, Karuvali Shriman Pa. 1925. 'Piramatam Pukutalum Tintamaiyum' ('The Entering of Other-Religion and Untouchability'). *Kuti Aracu*, 20 September, 9–10.

Viswanathan, Gauri. 1998. *Outside the Fold: Conversion, Modernity, and Belief*. Princeton, NJ: Princeton University Press.

Warner, Michael. 2002. 'Publics and Counterpublics'. *Public Culture* 14, no. 1: 49–90.

Zene, Cosimo. 2013. *The Political Philosophies of Antonio Gramsci and B. R. Ambedkar: Itineraries of Dalits and Subalterns*. New York: Routledge.

Zizek, Slavoj. 2010. 'First They Called Me a Joker, Now I Am a Dangerous Thinker'. *Times of India*, 10 January.

Part Two

Cultural Justice

7

Marginality, Suffering, Justice*
Questions of Dalit Dignity in Cultural Texts

PRAMOD K. NAYAR

This chapter assumes that representations of marginality, suffering, and social injustice in cultural texts dealing with Dalit lives in contemporary India raise questions of dignity. Thus, while they do address concerns of social inequality, historical wrongs, and the failure of the juridical apparatus, they also examine the idea of Dalit dignity.

Etymologically the word 'dignity' comes from the Latin word for 'worthiness'. Obviously, the idea implies a dual meaning: worthiness in one's own eyes, and a social evaluation of worthiness. The second meaning is linked to another etymological origin of 'dignity': 'worthy, proper, fitting' and 'to accept'. This is our cue to examine the question of dignity and cultural discourses around it.

My thesis is two-fold. First, Dalit dignity is organized around caste-determined labour that fits them into hierarchies of social dignity but which, in savage irony, renders them undignified *as* humans through social death. Thus, the Dalit can only acquire dignity through acts of non-agential, undignified labour over which they had no choice, and for which their bodies are only to be used

---

* An earlier, shorter version of this essay was presented at the 'Reclaiming Social Justice: Revisiting Ambedkar', International Conference, Bengaluru, 21–3 July 2017. It was subsequently published in eSocial Sciences in October 2017 (reprinted here with permission).

by others in order to safeguard the interests of others. Second, the self-conscious, agential *narrative enactment* of life-as-death and the performance of death enables the Dalit text to establish the dignity of the Dalit body.

Before addressing the texts themselves, I set out to frame the question of dalit dignity via other readings.

Between Immanent and Civic Dignity

It is inexplicable that the word and the concept, so central to the theories of human rights, have been so undertheorized. There appears in many twentieth century texts an implicit or explicit link between rights and dignity. For instance, in the German Constitution (1945), Article 1 has the declaration: 'human dignity is inviolable'. In Article 2 it adds: 'The German people *therefore* acknowledge inviolable and inalienable human rights as the basis of every community, of peace and of justice in the world.' The Helsinki Accords (1975) claim that human rights 'derive from the inherent dignity of the human person'. And, of course, the Preamble to the Universal Declaration of Human Rights (UDHR) (1948) says in its opening line:

> Whereas recognition of the inherent dignity and of the equal and inalienable rights of all members of the human family is the foundation of freedom, justice and peace in the world.

Later this declaration would add:

> Whereas the peoples of the United Nations have in the Charter reaffirmed their faith in fundamental human rights, in the dignity and worth of the human person and in the equal rights of men and women and have determined to promote social progress and better standards of life in larger freedom.

The Preamble to the Indian Constitution speaks of 'fraternity, assuring the dignity of the individual' but does not examine the idea of dignity in any sustained manner. Upendra Baxi, however, believes that 'the Indian constitutional combination of fraternity and dignity wages a war against the indignity of caste-based apartheid' (2014, 431).

In terms of the philosophical foundations that seek normative modes of defining human dignity, Marcus Düwell writes:

> The scope of ascription of human dignity is *universal* in the sense that it applies to all human beings, it is *egalitarian* insofar as each human being is equal with regard to his dignity and references to human dignity are justifying *duties towards others* that have the form of *categorical* obligations. (2014, 27, emphasis in original)

Josiah Ober attempting to theorize dignity writes:

> Dignity can be defined as *non-humiliation* and *non-infantilization*. We suffer indignity—humiliation and/or infantilization—when our public presence goes unacknowledged, when we cringe before the powerful, when we are unduly subjected to the paternalistic will of others and when we are denied the opportunity to employ our reason and voice in making choices that affect us. (2014, 53–4, emphasis in original)

Like Ober, other commentators such as Sanjay Palshikar have defined humiliation as 'an unwelcome assault on human dignity' (2009, 79). Humiliation, says Upendra Baxi, is the 'Other of dignity' (2014, 429). Gopal Guru posits a 'set of concepts that form into a logical class comprising humiliation, shame, insult, indignity, and misrecognition, as also the opposite set of values, that is, respect, dignity, and recognition' (Baxi 2014, 2).

It thus seems safe to say that dignity is linked to questions of recognition (hence respect from the others, or the world) and a sense of self-worth. The denial of dignity, leading to humiliation, may also, therefore, be read in terms of the erosion of a sense of self due to social contexts. (I am not, at this point, examining the right to die with dignity and other bioethical, biomedical issues. Arguments in this domain draw upon, among others, principles laid out by the Council of Europe's Convention on Bioethics (1997) and by UNESCO's Universal Declaration on Bioethics and Human Rights (2005). It is linked to injustice, marginalization, and suffering, in other words.

Critics studying the discourses around human rights have addressed the 'foundational fiction' of human dignity (as Nobel Laureate J.M. Coetzee termed it). For instance, Elizabeth Anker in her *Fictions of Dignity: Embodying Human Rights in World*

Literature writes: 'liberal human rights discourses and norms ... are ... underwritten by the dual fictions of human dignity and bodily integrity' (2). There is, scholars note, a link between suffering and dignity. Cultural critic Lata Mani writes:

> First, that suffering leads to a loss of dignity; second, the absence of choice leads to suffering and indignity; and third, control over self and circumstance facilitates freedom from suffering and in so doing, preserves dignity. Deducible here is an ideal of mastery over self and context or at least, the ability to set limits on how one is impinged upon by social forces and more broadly, by the conditions of life. (2011, 24)

Dalit texts that document atrocities, violence, denial, repression, and outright erasure of Dalit lives are, in effect, documenting the denial of civic dignity even when they speak of individual violations. Civic dignity, as Josiah Ober defines it, is neither meritocratic (by rank/lineage) nor immanent (all humans as possessing dignity). Ober writes:

> Meritocratic dignity, as we have seen, is predicated on intensely personalized relationships. Human dignity, as an inherent attribute of the individual, rests neither on personal nor on political relationships among people. Civic dignity stands in between these poles: it is predicated on a shared status of political equality among a body of citizens—a defined set of people who are jointly committed to the preservation of a public domain (Greek: *politeia*; Latin: *res publica*), but who are not social peers and who may have no personal ties with one another. Civic dignity is available to and protected by free citizens who have an equal opportunity to participate in a public domain of decision and action. Because civic dignity is grounded in *political* and not in personal relations, it cannot be reduced, conceptually, to meritocratic or to universal human dignity. (2014, 55)

Reading Dalit cultural texts, one is struck by the oscillation between dignity as immanent and dignity as a civic condition, emerging from interactions across communities and castes, and reliant upon a social order. Ambedkar in his writings was aware that ascribing dignity to *all* humans was pointless unless there was a political mechanism to ensure equal access to the public domain.

Ambedkar's first use of the term 'dignity' in his classic *Annihilation of Caste* is in connection with the perceived slight to the upper castes. Ambedkar writes: 'The Hindus looked upon the use of metal pots by untouchables as an affront to their dignity, and assaulted the untouchable women for their impudence' (2014: vol. 1, 40). And again: 'The Hindus of Chakwara thought otherwise, and in righteous indignation avenged themselves for the wrong done to them by the Untouchables, who insulted them by treating ghee as an item of their food—which they ought to have known could not be theirs, consistently with the dignity of the Hindus' (2014: vol. 1, 40–1).

Elsewhere, in his 'Note to The Indian Franchise Committee (Lothian Committee) On the Depressed Classes, submitted on 1 May 1932', Ambedkar would reiterate:

> Why will not a Hindu touch an untouchable? Why will not a Hindu allow an untouchable to enter the temple or use the village well? Why will not a Hindu admit an untouchable in the inn? The answer to each one of these questions is the same. It is that the untouchable is an unclean person not fit for social intercourse. Again, why will not a Brahmin priest officiate at religious ceremonies performed by an untouchable? Why will not a barber serve an untouchable? In these cases also the answer is the same. It is that it is below dignity to do so. (2014: vol. 2, 492)

In his *Philosophy of Hinduism* Ambedkar explicates the Manu penal code that was designed, in Ambedkar's interpretation, to protect the dignity of the Hindus. Ambedkar writes:

> The most striking feature of Manu's Penal Code which stands out in all its nakedness is the inequality of punishment for the same offence. Inequality designed not merely to punish the offender but to protect also the dignity and to maintain the baseness of the parties coming to a Court of Law to seek justice in other words to maintain the social inequality on which his whole scheme is founded. (2014: vol. 3, 31)

In his 'Safeguards for the Scheduled Castes' in *Constitution of the United States of India*, Ambedkar would write: 'The Hindu has a Code of life, which is part of his religion. This Code of life gives him many privileges and heaps upon the Untouchable many indignities which are incompatible with the dignity and sanctity of human life' (2014: vol. 1, 426).

Ambedkar aligns the caste system, then, with the *perceived* loss—and threat of loss—of dignity to the Hindus, implying that the oppressive caste system becomes a way of preserving *their* dignity against intrusions by the so-called lower castes. This is where Ambedkar's discourse crosses domains with UDHR and the moral-philosophical discourse of the 'inherent' dignity of all human beings while being alert to the necessity of political mechanisms to ensure this dignity for all. What Ambedkar points to is a simple enough historical development in Indian polity: the 'upper-caste' Hindus were extremely conscious of their dignity, and any perceived slight to this was to be thwarted. That is, the caste system as an oppressive social mechanism was a weapon employed to defend the dignity of the Hindus, suggesting that the Hindus—or at least a section—were imbued with the sense of their own individual and collective worth. Dignity is inextricable from their collective identity *qua* Hindus, and the defence of one was the defence of the other. In other words, human rights could be denied, claimed, or defended once dignity had been differentially ordered and allotted.

Dignity, in Ambedkar's reading of Manu and Hindu history, is self-recognition that demands the other's recognition. If dignity is 'an elevated status in a status-ranking' (Hartogh 2014, 201), then it follows that the denial of this status from other ranks in the hierarchy may be read as an affront to dignity. Dignity, therefore, is not only about identity but about a social position, in this reading: it is primarily civic dignity. When Ambedkar points to the Hindu anger over supposed affronts, he is referring to not merely the idea of inherent dignity but also to social hierarchies with their attached notions of dignity.

Ambedkar's emphasis is on the precise construction of selective inalienable dignity as a human being which precedes the selectivity of the human rights regime in the form of the caste system. In other words, it is ontological dignity born of a moral imperative that *precedes* any legal doctrine or political theory of rights. When ontological dignity is reified along specific lines such as caste then, as a consequence, many fall outside the legal frame of rights.

Indeed, the loss of dignity has become a major theme in cultural psychology and human rights discourses even as studies have focused on everyday contexts. For instance, the Humiliation Inventory of Evelin Gerda Linder (2001) developed a scale of humiliation (see www.humiliationstudies.org/documents/hartling/HartlingAssessingHumiliation.pdf), all of which focus on everyday life. Questions of dignity and humiliation, then, constitute the *moral-philosophical* underpinnings of legal discourses of human rights, equality, justice, and emancipation. When we assume dignity is inherent rather than earned, then we have an entirely different perspective on the question of rights because, as Düwell, Braarvig, and Brownsword note, the concept 'does not, and probably cannot, exist in a society without laws to protect the *rights* that flow from it rather than the principle itself' (2014, xix).

The postcolonial state of exception and postcolonial necropolitics is founded on policing the borders of dignity. The denial of a productive life with the fulfilment of its potential is the denial—it is *not* the violation of dignity, because violation implies the existence of something open to being violated—of Dalit dignity.

In his book *Radical Inequality*, a study of Gandhi and Ambedkar, Aishwary Kumar suggests that for the Phules and later B.R. Ambedkar,

> [the] conception of freedom foregrounded those everyday prohibitions—indignity, segregation, untouchability—that seemed too mundane, too constrained by an obsession with the ethics of social life, especially on the scale of a nationalism concerned with grander projects of spiritual well-being. (2015, 20)

Kumar's emphasis is on the structures of social inequality that work at the level of the *everyday*, and hence are ignored in favour of larger nationalist themes and issues. Marginalization and exploitation manifest as everyday indignities, suggests Kumar. In each case, one notes, there is a tension between dignity as a universal condition accruing from being human, and dignity as a civic condition framed within socio-political processes.

Cultural Representations and Dalit Dignity

To return briefly to Elizabeth Anker's work, the dignified body, she argues, is a coherent, autonomous and agential body: 'the dignified individual in possession of rights is imagined to inhabit an always already fully integrated and inviolable body: a body that is whole, autonomous and self-enclosed' (2012, 3–4). Corporeality, she writes, is 'a baseline condition that precedes the ascription of dignity and rights to an individual' (2012, 4).

Elsewhere, I have examined dehumanization, infantilization, and infrahumanization as processes that violate the autonomous human body (Nayar 2016). I do not wish to revisit that line of argument here. Instead I focus on three specific modes of asserting dignity that one can discern in Dalit cultural texts today: spatiality, labour, and the performance of life and death.

Spatiality

In response to Gandhi's idealization of the Indian village, Ambedkar was categorical that the village was 'a sink of localism, a den of ignorance, [and] narrow-mindedness' in his 'Speech Delivered in the Constituent Assembly on 4 November 1948' (2010, 176). Later in his 1948 *The Untouchables* Ambedkar would explicitly refer to the question of space:

> social separation ... was a case of territorial segregation and of a cordon sanitaire putting the impure people inside a barbed wire, into a sort of cage. Every Hindu village has a ghetto. The Hindus live in the village and the Untouchables in the ghetto. (2014: vol. 7, 266)

Elsewhere in *Untouchables or the Children of India's Ghetto*, in a chapter appropriately spatial in its title, 'The Indian Ghetto—The Centre Of Untouchability—Outside the Fold', Ambedkar would note

> The Indian village is not a single social unit. It consists of castes. But for our purposes, it is enough to say—
> I. The population in the village is divided into two sections—
> (i) Touchables and (ii) Untouchables.
> II. The Touchables form the major community and the Untouchables a minor community.
> III. The Touchables live inside the village and the Untouchables live outside the village in separate quarters.
> IV. Economically, the Touchables form a strong and powerful community, while the Untouchables are a poor and a dependent community.
> V. Socially, the Touchables occupy the position of a ruling race, while the Untouchables occupy the position of a subject race of hereditary bondsmen. (2014: vol. 5, 20–1)

And in *States and Minorities* he would say: 'It is the close knit association of the Untouchables with the Hindus living in the same villages which marks them out as Untouchables and which enables the Hindus to identify them as being Untouchables' (2014: vol. 1, 425).

Ambedkar would note that the prohibitions from using public facilities such as wells, temples, or from riding on a horse or a palanquin through main roads were constitutive of the practice where sections of society were left to the indignity of begging for water (Ambedkar would document his experiences at school when he was disallowed the use of the school water supply) or using side roads. As Cháirez-Garza has argued, Ambedkar was alert to the social construction of space and saw social relations, especially untouchability, as a mode of organizing the spaces of the village. By emphasizing the proximate lives of 'upper' and 'lower' caste Hindus, Ambedkar is able to propose that it is this proximity that drives the upper castes to introduce social segregation. The result is the indignity of being a part of the public and yet not.

In one sense, the Dalit movements to gain access to temples and public spaces anticipate 'Occupy' because it is the attempt in fact to assert themselves *as* the Indian public. Dalit texts such as Bama's *Karukku* and Valmiki's *Joothan* often spend a considerable amount of time describing the Dalit ghettos and the social organization of their space by the upper castes, the squalor inside the ghettos and the norms of usage of public spaces. To participate in public spaces of their own volition without recourse to fear or opprobrium is to be a part of the public. Spatial and social boycotts, therefore, are modes of violating the dignity of the Dalit precisely because these 'bodies' are limited to specific modes of civic presences.

Labouring Bodies and Dignity

The policing of dignity as social reification was diagnosed early by Ambedkar. In his chapter 'The Revolt of the Untouchables' of his book *Untouchables or the Children Of India's Ghetto*, Ambedkar would write:

> The Hindu Social Order is based upon a division of labour which reserves for the Hindus clean and respectable jobs and assigns to the Untouchables dirty and mean jobs and thereby clothes the Hindus with dignity and heaps ignominy upon the Untouchables. (2014: vol. 5, 258)

When Ambedkar famously critiqued the caste system as a division of labourer and labour, he was pointing to the intrinsic link between identity reification and the larger issue of dignity. Gisa Lindemann, also examining dignity as a social creation, writes:

> The more advanced the division of labour is, the more a society is dependent on individuals being capable of performing different kinds of labour in different sub-groups. It is the individual that has to handle diverse role expectations in an individual manner. Therefore, the notion of the individual person becomes a structural necessity for modern society. In this way, the individual human being comes to hold dignity. (2014, 193)

Lindemann elaborates:

> It is not the individual as a biological nor as a rational being who has dignity, but rather the individual as an emergent normative structural necessity of a functionally differentiated society. The concrete biological, individual human being has dignity as long as she/he obeys the basic normative necessities of functional differentiation. (2014, 193)

The division of labour that Ambedkar spoke of is effectively the social organization of Hindu society by earmarking certain bodies as destined only for certain kinds of labour. A naturalization of the association between certain bodies and certain forms of labour is effected in the social organization of a village, as almost every Dalit memoir and autobiography documents. A Dalit who uncomplainingly performs his assigned labour, is then, in traditional definitions of 'dignity', dignified. That is, the Dalit who sticks to his pre-destined role alone, performing undignified work with no choice of abandoning it, alone is granted dignity. There is no scope, clearly, for the *acquisition* of dignity for the Dalit, in the traditional caste-determined model.

Following from this reading: when individuals refuse to fit into the functionally differentiated order, with their 'assigned' places in life, for example, through social and professional mobility, then it is deemed that they have lost their dignity. The battle for equality is then a battle for fluidity across the differentiation. If a person refuses to accept the normative conditions of functional differentiation s/he loses dignity, or more accurately, may have her/his dignity taken away. But this is precisely the point: for the historically disenfranchised, Ambedkar's questioning of the pre-existing functional differentiation is a call to define dignity as the *resistance* to such a differentiation. Dignity, if it hinges upon mobility and a *lack*-of-fit into existing differentiation, is then an assertion of agential dignity. This could be at the individual or collective-communitarian level.

I shall have reasons to return to this question of labour later, but it is worth noting that Ambedkar, like Lindemann, is speaking of civic dignity. Civic dignity for the Dalit body is possible only when s/he performs undignified labour. Any resistance to this socially ascribed dignity linked to certain kinds of work would result in beatings and dehumanization.

Corpsing and Dignity

I propose that Dalit cultural texts adopt a singular strategy to speak of their violated dignity, as both individuals and as a collective. Following the work of David Marriott (2016) on African Americans, I shall term this 'corpsing'.

The word 'corpsing' (verb) signifies a blunder occurring when, in the performance of a role, an actor is 'put out' of his part. A role that is corpsed is one that exposes the limits of performance and, depending on the metaphor, denotes the 'death' of theatre *as* theatre. A role that is corpsed, which is something contrary to the usual performance of a part, is one that evidently does away with an actor's mastery (of illusion) and no more clearly than when the disjoint between persona and part is exposed. Corpsing is also evident outside theatre; we see it when people fail to live up to or grasp their social roles (Marriott 2016, 32).

The question Marriott asks is, 'What if one's role is to be socially that of failure or if one is ordered and commanded to perform a role through one's corpse-like obliteration, would this not mean that corpsing can only occur when one refuses that spur and its contagious pleasure? Would this not be an example of a "death" of death'? (2016, 34). African Americans, Marriott argues, 'live under the command of death (as citizens, parents, siblings, and subjects); consequently those who obey this rule are said to live under a law of symbolic death and are regarded as subjects who are already dead. Social death has to do with how rules of life are connected to the symbolically dead' (2016, 34).

For Dalit lives to go beyond the tradition that relies on what Marriott terms the 'symbolic representation-as-disfiguration' (2016, 38), its cultural texts must change the understanding of what it means to be Dalit and *living*. Roles that enact social death—whether in the form of indignities, beatings or forced labours of the *safai karamcharis* (a person engaged in or employed for sanitation work), a whole new conception of living, 'beyond the common wretchedness, neuroses, and social dishonor' (Marriott 2016, 61) will be needed.

Performing Life

It is the indignity of life enacted *as* death that is documented in *Karukku*, *Outcaste* (by Narendra Jadhav), *Akkarmashi* (Sharankumar Limbale), and the poetry of Dhassal. The point is: these texts do not deal with extreme cultures of violence. They demonstrate how indignity is not the indignity of death but the indignity of living *as though* they are corpses without agency.

In Valmiki's *Joothan*, when he has to deal with the carcass, he proves he is alive because he uses his body but he uses it *without* agency. Proving he is alive as a Dalit is to demonstrate his social death. In the earlier Shankarrao Kharat's 'Corpse in the Well' (in Dangle's *Poisoned Bread*), when the boy asks his father who is guarding the corpse as to when he would eat, the father responds, 'Who cares if a Mahar lives or dies?' Later, when the constable questions him, Anna, the father, says, 'The Mahar's village duty is only to guard the corpse. How can we touch it? What would the heirs of this corpse have to say?' So the constable wishes to know what the family members of the dead man would have to say, and Anna responds: 'The heirs of the corpse will say, "were we dead that you touched our kinsman's corpse?"'

Reflecting upon the state of the nation, Sikhamani in his poem 'Pardon' (2013) writes:

> To appreciate the real picture of this nation
> I need another life.

This is an extraordinary image. Sikhamani could be saying he needs to be born again to appreciate India's true picture. But it is also possible that he is deploring the fact that when leading a Dalit's life he cannot understand the true picture of India. Sikhamani is suggesting a disconnect between forms of life and forms of signification. The real picture of the country is irretrievable, or beyond understanding, because its signifiers are not available to the Dalit's life, whose signifiers are primarily about the loss of choice of meaning, except those *assigned* to them. It is the end of signification that Sikhamani mourns, and consequently the end of living itself.

I have four key points to make in cultural constructions of Dalit life.

First, enacting life in Dalit texts draws attention to the social death they experience. The language of living matter conveys this social death. Thus, the insults and abuse, including physical beatings, torture, and chronic hunger, that constitute the bulk of the Dalit autobiographical narrative may be read as the enactment of life *as* death. Then, enacting essential 'Dalitness' through symbolic representations is to be complicit with the very processes of essentializing that brought about social death, and so the Dalit texts refrain, often, from portraying essentialisms. Instead Bama, Valmiki, Jadhav, and others even when speaking of their community's rituals or belief systems also speak of their resistance to these. For instance, Bama and Limbale speak with some derision about the superstitions of their community. Rather than lapse into nativist valourization of their practices, the Dalit text, recognizing that such a self-essentializing discourse, would also open them to essentializing by the upper castes and thereby condemn the Dalits to the same identities they have been fighting to escape from. Third, the slave uses his body, but does not perform work or labour. The Dalit labour is not human but allows others, specifically the upper-caste landlord or factory-owner capitalist, to *be* human (I adapt here Agamben 2016). In other words, the Dalit labouring body does not possess agential control over his/her body or labour. It is deemed non-productive except when it serves the interest of the upper-caste in an inverted biopolitical regime. Finally, life and living is about the *form* of life and its possibilities. 'Form-of-life' is the set of facts but also the potential and possibilities of living (Agamben 2016). When the form-of-life is denied a Limbale, a 'Baba' (in Jadhav's *Outcaste*), Bakha, or a Velutha, all possibilities of dignified living, are denied them as well.

The role of 'being Dalit' means the death of the actor/actant. It means enacting the social death ordained for the Dalit, although they may be ignorant of this 'corpsed' role. Thus, when they obliterate/erase themselves because it is *expected* of them (obliteration is the social role assigned to the Dalit), then they are deemed to be alive: their enactment of their social death is proof that they are truly Dalit lives. Accepting social death, willingly or out of ignorance (and this might be generational), is to be alive. Dalitness murders itself when it feels most alive because then it performs what it is expected to perform, as a *Dalit body*: it is the social ordering of 'Dalit life' or 'Dalit death' which, if the Dalit takes on, results in the murder of himself *as* Dalit.

When sources, origins, and teleologies are emphasized (for example, in claiming a pre-Hindu origin), it traps the Dalitness within the same rhetorical and symbolic structures that enabled their essentializing. That is, when the Dalit undertakes to prove s/he is alive as Dalit, it is self-essentializing that is the obverse of the essentializing used historically to outcast them. Essentializing Dalit lives is to accept the socially ordained lives, which itself is death-like.

Enacting social and symbolic death in life to prove they are alive is to be complicit with the racist inhumanizing language that killed them. The Dalit is not seen, even by Dalits themselves, beyond the symbolism of being a body, or a corpse. Dalit life sustains itself as already dead. As Toral Gajarawala puts it, it is not cataclysmic and massive events of death that such cultural texts around Dalit lives document. Rather it is 'the mundane relationship to death experienced on a daily basis by the Chamar' (2013, 182). That is, in the process of living up to what is expected of them *as* Dalits, they die socially, denied their dignity in the civic set-up.

Performing Death

When Valmiki in *Joothan* speaks about his labours, he presents it as akin to dying. He thus closes off life as a Dalit because it is akin to (social) death. When skinning the carcass of the dead animal, he describes his emotions as 'drowning in a swamp', 'the blood inside me was congealing' (2007, 35). Bama links humanness with dignity when she poses a series of questions: 'Are Dalits not human beings? ... Are they without wisdom, beauty, dignity?' (2012, 27). She even wishes, she writes, 'that it would be better to be dead and gone rather than carry on living like this' (2012, 78). In the very opening pages of Jadhav's *Outcaste*, Damu requests the villagers to inform his family that he would be home late because he was set the duty of guarding a corpse, the constable retorts: 'Do you think we were born as messengers for you lowly outcastes? Your woman is not going to die if she does not eat one night. And if she does, who cares?' (2003, 4)

Later, Damu speculates: 'What did they care if a Mahar lived or starved, or even died? All they were concerned about were the high-born' (2003, 6).

In each of these cases, the Dalit text enacts death as a way of affirming life itself, because to claim life is to enact social death at the hands of the caste system.

I suggest that Dalits employ the language, complete with tropes and figural turns, of corpsing.

They do so by enacting and performing death through the language of corpsing, which is to expose the theatre of death. They reference a void (both social and interior) *as* Dalitness (and vice versa) which then prevents their absorption into a narrative of historical wrongs or teleologies of (casteist, patronizing) emancipation, and its romanticization. Third, enacting death and void is to stay contingent and flexible, open-ended, and plural. Finally, Dalit language is about not essentializing 'Dalitness'—because this essentialising is precisely what casteist and racist language does. Dalitness is about denying essentialisms through ambiguity, open-endedness of, and refusal of teleologies and fixity of meanings. When we say a Dalit text is singular it means that its opacity must be maintained, so should its resistance to established meaning, or perhaps even translation. Dalit texts might need to reject the quest for origins, because it is in origins that the essentializing tropes begin.

Dalitness goes beyond a traditional mode of speaking of interiority and substance (or secret and ultimate meaning), which would be a romanticization of Dalit lives. Fragmented interiorities in Bama or Jadhav are instances of this refusal to subject themselves to the norms of the standard autobiographical modes. Dalit writing demonstrates how Dalit lives are constantly rendered, or play 'dead' within the signifiers of law, history, and social codes available to them. When the Dalit author claims an emptiness inside, it is a marker of the failure of signification, or rather, of the signification assigned to them which would reiterate their exclusion.

This performance of death suggests that existing signifiers are corpsing signifiers, but there is no 'beyond' such a signification. It is by drawing attention to corpsing as a socially accepted signifying system that the Dalit asserts Dalitness: demonstrating an awareness of the conventions that render them dead. Dalitness is about *performing* a corpse-like remnant, which reveals the corpsing qualities of language, social structures—consciously drawing attention to the *performance of death* and not life. (To perform Dalit life is to perform its social death, since this is what is ordained for it).

Dalitness must itself be deemed as a void whose emptiness is irretrievable whether in the form of historical allegory or romanticism. The enactment of the void is the enactment of neither historical reduction (Dalits perceived and portrayed as empty) nor romanticism (void as actually possessing substance). It lies beyond retrieval because processes of retrieval are themselves complicit with the structures that 'voided' the Dalits. Also, the assumption of retrieval assumes a plenitude *before* the 'voiding' by the social order.

* * *

It is, of course, as Laura Brueck warns us, absurd to 'characterize all Dalit writing … as occupying a singular oppositional idiom' (2014, 4). Nevertheless, seeing significant patterns and developing frames for reading the aesthetics of these texts ensure that they are not consigned to the ghetto, or idiom, of social documents alone. Hence, this paper's insistence on the narrative enactments.

In the case of the caste-driven biopolitical regime, the Dalit in fact represents a not properly human life that renders possible for others the *bios politikos*, that is to say, the truly human life, to adapt Giorgio Agamben (2016, 21).

The enactment of life-as-death and the performance of death enables the Dalit text to establish the dignity of the Dalit body. Marginality, suffering, and justice are enacted symbolically and materially around Dalit bodies, and their representations in textual form demands new strategies, of which this paper has outlined two: the enactment of life and the performance of death.

If the photographic image, as Roland Barthes argued, is aligned with death, then what is the valency of the photograph of a corpse? Is it the living image of a dead thing? As Peter Schwenger argues, 'When a real corpse is subject to this figurative corpsing, then, certain issues of the photographic image are raised in their most extreme form' (2000, 396).

Adriana Cavarero in her work on horrorism has argued that destruction of the 'ontological dignity of the human figure' is true horror (2011, 9). However, in these texts and discourses, playing at this loss, or enacting this loss, is a means of surviving the strategies of horror imposed by the social order. To survive, argues Didier Fassin, 'is to be still fully alive *and to live beyond death*' (2010, 83, emphasis in original). To survive, as the Dalit does in all these texts, is to live beyond the horror to which their living has condemned them. To survive is agential, and the marker of dignity.

To survive is also to remain recognizably human after all the horror. As Francois Debrix puts it,

> Even in horror, even when the body, life, and the human have been frozen and left in place to be dismantled and reduced to dust, something will live on. Yet, ultimately, this something that lives on can and perhaps must be seen as a someone, as a *human* body or life that has been transferred to or transmuted into things, objects, words, and all their traces. (2017, 91, emphasis in original)

The sense of worth—dignity—is what the text enacts in the process of enacting the death of the Dalit, while being alive. The humiliation of life-as-death is subsumed by emphasizing the performance of death. What is fitting, to return to the etymology of dignity, is to not *accept* the traces of the history of humiliation, but to be *aware* of the traces so as to make different, and informed, choices for the future.

These choices cannot be asserted purely in an autonomous manner, even by humans. Certain ecologies need to be in place for human beings to lead productive lives. When Dalit texts describe the poverty, squalour, disease, and unliveable conditions of their existence, even putatively, choices are foreclosed to them. We cannot, then, interpret the dignity of the individual independent of the dignity of the collective—which entails the creation of ecologies that enable the community as a whole to not only survive but also thrive.

References

Agamben, Giorgio. 2016. *The Uses of Bodies. Homo Sacer IV.2*, translated by Adam Kotsko. California: Stanford University Press.

Ambedkar, B.R. 2010. 'Speech Delivered in the Constituent Assembly on 4 November 1948'. In *Thus Spoke Ambedkar*, edited by Bhagwan Das, 160–86. New Delhi: Navayana.

———. 2014. *B.R. Ambedkar: Writings and Speeches*, vols 1, 2, 3, 5, and 7, edited by Hari Narake. New Delhi: Dr Ambedkar Foundation, Ministry of Social Justice and Empowerment, 2nd edition. Available at http://drambedkarwritings.gov.in/content/. Last accessed on 6 December 2019.

Anker, Elizabeth S. 2012. *Fictions of Dignity: Embodying Human Rights in World Literature*. Ithaca and London: Cornell University Press.

Bama. 2012. *Karukku*, translated by Lakshmi Holmström, 2nd edition. New Delhi: Oxford University Press.

Baxi, Upender. 2014. 'The place of dignity in the Indian Constitution'. In *The Cambridge Handbook of Human Dignity: Interdisciplinary Perspectives*, edited by Marcus Düwell et al., 429–36. Cambridge: Cambridge University Press.

Brueck, Laura R. 2014. *Writing Resistance: The Rhetorical Imagination of Hindi Dalit Literature*. New York: Columbia University Press.

Cavarero, Adriana. 2011. *Horrorism: Naming Contemporary Violence*, translated by William McCuaig. New York: Columbia University Press.

Cháirez-Garza, Jesús Francisco. 2014. 'Touching Space: Ambedkar on the Spatial Features of Untouchability'. *Contemporary South Asia* 22, no. 1: 37–50.

Debrix, François. 2017. 'Horror beyond Death: Geopolitics and the Pulverisation of the Human'. *New Formations* 89–90: 85–100.

Düwell, Marcus. 2014. 'Human Dignity: Concepts, Discussions, Philosophical Perspectives'. In *The Cambridge Handbook of Human Dignity: Interdisciplinary Perspectives*, edited by Marcus Düwell et al. Cambridge: Cambridge University Press.

Düwell, Marcus, Jens Braarvig, and Roger Brownsword. 2014. 'Why a Handbook on Human Dignity?' In *The Cambridge Handbook of Human Dignity: Interdisciplinary Perspectives*, edited by Marcus Düwell. Cambridge: Cambridge University Press.

Fassin, Didier. 2010. 'Ethics of Survival: A Democratic Approach to the Politics of Life'. *Humanity* 1, no. 1: 81–95.

Gajarawala, Toral Jatin. 2013. *Untouchable Fictions: Literary Realism and the Crisis of Caste*. Fordham University Press.

Guru, Gopal. 2009. 'Introduction: Theorizing Humiliation'. In *Humiliation: Claims and Context*, edited by Gopal Guru, 1–19. Oxford University Press.

Hartogh, Govert Den. 2014. 'Is Human Dignity the Ground of Human Rights?' In *The Cambridge Handbook of Human Dignity: Interdisciplinary Perspectives*, edited by Marcus Düwell et al. Cambridge: Cambridge University Press.

Jadhav, Narendra. 2003. *Outcaste: A Memoir*. New Delhi: Viking.

Kumar, Aishwary. 2015. *Radical Inequality: Gandhi, Ambedkar and the Risk of Democracy*. Stanford: Stanford University Press.

Lindemann, Gisa. 2014. 'Social and Cultural Presuppositions for the Use of the Concept of Human Dignity'. In *The Cambridge Handbook of Human Dignity: Interdisciplinary Perspectives*, edited by Marcus Düwell et al. Cambridge: Cambridge University Press.

Mani, Lata. 2011. 'Human Dignity and Suffering: Some Considerations'. *Economic and Political Weekly* 46, no. 36.

Marriott, David. 2016. 'Corpsing; Or, the Matter of Black Life'. *Cultural Critique* 94: 32–64.

Nayar, Pramod K. 2016. *Human Rights and Literature: Writing Rights*. London: Palgrave-Macmillan.

Ober, Josiah. 2014. 'Meritocratic and Civic Dignity in Greco-Roman Antiquity'. In *The Cambridge Handbook of Human Dignity: Interdisciplinary Perspectives*, edited by Marcus Düwell et al., 53–63. Cambridge: Cambridge University Press.

Palshikar, Sanjay. 2009. 'Understanding Humiliation'. In *Humiliation: Claims and Context*, edited by Gopal Guru, 79–92. Oxford University Press.

Schwenger, Peter. 2000. 'Corpsing the Image'. *Critical Inquiry* 26: 395–414.

Sikhamani. 2013. 'Pardon'. In *From those Stubs, Steel Nibs are Sprouting. New Dalit Writing from South India: Dossier II: Kannada and Telugu*, edited by K. Satyanarayana and Susie Tharu. New Delhi: HarperCollins.

Valmiki, Omprakash. 2007. *Joothan: A Dalit's Life*, translated by Arun Prabha Mukherjee. Kolkata: Samya.

8

Asura
Myth into Cultural Reality

Y. SRINIVASA RAO

Civilized and barbarous, cultured and uncultured, pure and polluted, approachable and unapproachable, touchable and untouchable, and beautiful and ugly are some of the parameters through which we measure the status, value, and the graded positions of individuals and social groups in India. The caste Hindus or the upper caste, who invented the caste system and who are also the custodians of Hindu culture, held the right to create a graded society. They conspired to keep the hard-working agricultural community away from knowledge, resources, and respect, and called them Untouchables. These supposedly superior races, castes, and ethnic and social groups labelled the people belonging to agricultural communities as 'others' to place them on a lower level as part of a larger conspiracy.

In the evolution of human societies, every society goes through certain transitions as a result of which value and social positions allocated to humans and social groups are either challenged by the 'others' or are further entrenched. A transition set in motion by historical forces in the nineteenth and twentieth centuries presented those oppressed with a congenial environment to initiate the process of contestation. Asian and African academia began emphasizing anti-Eurocentrism from the second half of the nineteenth century, Dalit subaltern anti-caste movements emerged towards the last quarter of the nineteenth century, and African Americans countered racism and white supremacy in the United States of America in the second half of the twentieth century. All these antimetanarratives have emanated from rights movements as forms of counter narratives. It took a long time for the oppressed to realize the conspiracy. They needed a congenial environment to be created through their relentless struggles or through support extended by sympathetic external agencies. This provided them with the opportunity to speak up, react, respond, and rebuild.

In a phase-wise contestation, the oppressed first ask for natural rights; second, for equal and special rights; and then, eventually, initiate the process of cultural separation in order to rebuild a historical identity as the ultimate response to the continuous cultural and social humiliation. The last phase is quite aggressive and it is in this phase that the subaltern gives clarity on their assertion. Since it is history that provided superior status and identity to their socially privileged counterpart—such as the upper caste in India—the subaltern or the suppressed, too, use it as a tool for identity building through cultural reconstruction, which provides the needed respect, courage, and equality. Their history and culture need to be liberated from the clutches of the mainstream history and culture within which they are either located at the margins or mythicized and demonized, and thereafter reconstructed.

From the assertion of natural rights to the departure from mainstream majoritarian culture, we could see how it played out over the past two centuries for the subalterns. It has been a slow and steady process. During the nineteenth century, most of the lower caste intellectuals were involved in building the theoretical base for contestation. In the twentieth century, they improved the theory further and translated it into praxis (activism-based actual movements) of equal and special rights. In fact, theory and activism have reciprocated each other's progress. In the twenty-first century, the subaltern have acquired the capacity to construct counter-narratives to build a culture of their own as a counter to the dominant culture, and, to point out, in the process, the social criminality involved in constructing the subaltern as less social, cultureless, and ahistorical.

Therefore, creating a counterculture is a conscious effort of castes and communities placed on a lower level in the caste hierarchy. After acquiring the ability to rescue their culture from dominant narratives and images, employing literary criticism, the subalterns build new narratives, histories, and images for social and cultural respect and historical equality.

However, during this process, they might fall into the trap of justifying the ahistorical as historical (figures and stories), as rescuing their culture, which provides historicity, might not be easy. The very idea that the historical subaltern can get trapped in the ahistorical dominant narrative and that the culture of the subaltern has to be rescued from this narrative leads to natural suspicion that such a historicization is nothing but the justification of the 'ahistorical'. Historicization of the ahistorical is an exercise that has been successfully carried out by the majoritarian religious and communal and upper caste forces for a long time.

In the three simultaneously carried out academic exercises—re-read, rescue, and rewrite—they discover their narratives, which got entangled in the dominant narratives; separate theirs from it, providing historicity by subjecting these narratives and forms to rational scrutiny; and release them from the prison of the dominant myths and epics by highlighting the significance of history and culture, removing the cultural and social negativity attached to them, and providing newness and freshness. These exercises release the subaltern from the mental cultural enslavement of the majority and liberate them. Thus connected by a common ideological or social interest and objective, which might change with changes in time and context, the subaltern could form a sociocultural alliance through which they not only build a new and fresh subaltern culture but also transform the social alliance into a formidable political alliance. This should become the prime objective, eventually.

If this is the objective, then the major questions that needs to be answered is the following: Will such a counterculture lead to the disintegration of the nation? Is divisiveness inherent in it? Though the subaltern needs to consider these questions, one could argue that the creation of a counterculture would only lead to the building of new social identities and the strengthening of existing ones by the historicization of the supposedly ahistorical. The aim of creating a counterculture is to fight for historical and cultural equality while staying within the larger frame of the social/cultural/religious identity of the nation. Yes, the subaltern tries to examine the possibility of disassociating from the universal narrative (such as, in India, the so called 'national'/Hindu narrative) within which they are placed at the margins. This proposed disconnection does not mean that they are being divisive. After fighting for cultural equality for a long time, the existence of inequality in various forms forces them into such a separation.

In India, this disconnection is located within the larger narrative of Hinduism as well as nationalism. However, the counterculture intentionally distinguishes between itself and mainstream Hinduism to gain cultural authenticity. It either supports or subscribes to any form of cultural nationalism or any idea of nation based on its culture. After all, India is a multicultural society, a counterculture created by the subalterns, by any logic, would not lead to division. This Gandhian paranoia,[1] if it exists, needs to be seen as an intentional obstruction of cultural freedom. Moreover, a social minority naturally would not possess the power to build social identities that might acquire characters of caste nationalism. It is the social or cultural majority that uses its majority status to build national identities based on history or ahistory. A subaltern rejects some of the characters of Hinduism, not because those are from Hinduism, but because those are inhumane, illogical, unscientific, and inappropriate for the time and context. Therefore, counterculture can be seen either as a serious reform measure that challenges the irrational/illogical foundations of the Hindu way of life, or as a process that creates a distance between a way of life that is still being governed by religious/social orthodoxy and one that would be governed by humanism, realism, rationalism, and progressivism. In fact, though it is a huge claim to make, if subalterns build a new way of life, as opposed to being victims of suffering and oppression, they would consciously eliminate all the cultural/social/ritualistic negativity that still rules the roost in mainstream culture—they would create a new culture with a fresh history, which would be aided by humanism and scientific rationality.

---

[1] Gandhian Paranoia is a fear of Dalits breaking away from Hinduism, causing damage to it and eventually posing a challenge to the foundational tenets of Hinduism, since they suffered under it for generations altogether. Such a challenge is a threat to the very survival of Hinduism. But in actuality, it never happens. Even if Hindu Dalits as well as those who converted to other religions join together, their numerical strength would not be enough to challenge Hinduism.

The sufferers should not become the oppressors at any level of the social ladder. Therefore, the counterculture would need to be completely new and one that rejects all cultural and social forms that are based on internal inequality. This process would also provide the rational/scientific/intellectual subalterns a chance to scrutinize their own culture, which would give them historical/cultural/social authenticity as a social group. This authenticity is intentionally denied them in classical texts. If subalterns do not create a counterculture, they will forever be at the margins as ahistorical social groups.

The next question that arises is this: Is counterculture anti-modern? Before we answer this, we need to understand modernity in two ways: modernity as anti-tradition and modernity as a force of rationalization. Modernity as rationalist philosophy is not free from manipulation, control, and misuse. It is allocated with functions that are either inbuilt or inherent and thus assumes the freedom to perform them. It can be stripped of its positive function that would have transformed the subalterns suffering from religious and social orthodoxy in many ways. In the hands of the custodians of the classical culture, modernity was not only used as a tool to save the social and religious absurdities from scientific scrutiny but also employed in such a way that it could rationalize and normalize these absurdities.

While producers of the classical culture of the pre-modern times—authors of texts—have decided the cultural and social position of the subalterns, the custodians of the same culture, in the process of countering the onslaught of Western modernity on these religious/social absurdities, used modern arguments to devise layers of epistemological justification and save most of the majoritarian culture from being dismissed as absurd, inhuman, unethical, immoral, and unsuitable for the time and context. Hence, the counterculture is not against modernity. It performs two functions: it uses modernity to scrutinize and purify the obscurantism and absurdities and it questions the hypocritical application of modernity by reformers—leaders and academia who belong to the upper caste. Subalterns cannot dismiss modernity. However, given the context in which the counterculture is being constructed, the subaltern is also not averse to the criticism of modernity as they belong, perhaps, to one of the communities that are getting affected by the large-scale scientific and technological projects. They form part of the anti-science and technology movements. However, scientific rationality and science and technology are not the same. Though both seem problematic to them, they still see scientific rationalism as an unfinished project in India. Since, the upper caste declared that modernity is no more viable, the subaltern took charge of it for the purpose of self-reform.

Historical Proof for the Counter

Societies at the global, national, regional, and local levels are multicultural (on racial, religious, ethnic, caste, and linguistic lines). However, not a single society consists of equally distributed communities demographically. Which factors (in some cases single and in some cases multiple) provide identity to the majority and minority vary from one society to the other. It is not the demographic constituency alone that decides majority and minority status. It is the culture built on histories or ahistories that provides the requisit strength to the majority or weakness to the minority. Therefore, multicultural societies, such as India, mostly seem to require history and culture in order to build communal/caste identities. For the subalterns, such essential history needed to be freshly written. They had to work hard to find the historical proof needed to provide authenticity, validity, and value to their historical identity. This does not mean that the subalterns do not have history; they lacked the privilege and opportunity to produce historical evidence and proof.

Sanskrit and other regional languages in ancient India; Urdu and Arabic in the medieval period; and English along with other European languages in the modern period were the textual languages used by the upper caste and class to produce, document, propagate, and disseminate classical and modern knowledge. To a large extent, subalterns would not have had access to education as their native language would have been either subsumed within these alien languages or destroyed by them. Therefore, historical proof in the form of religious, semi-religious, rational, secular, and fictional texts was quite less. Hindu classical religious myths, epics, and Puranas contain the history of the subalterns but in the form of ahistory. It is either enough for the dominant narrative to document the history of the subalterns or to dismiss them as ahistorical by presenting their culture as ahistorical with the intention of dehistoricizing the subalterns. This makes them ahistorical communities with no historical, cultural, and social identity. Therefore, historicizing the supposed a history of the subalterns and writing fresh histories are two important functions of the subaltern historiography. This combined effort would enable us to build counter-historical narratives.

D.D. Kosambi and Irfan Habib have evolved an interdisciplinary approach that focuses on non-textual evidence such as archaeological, anthropological, and ethnographical proof to write on material culture in ancient India. Marxist historiography might provide the proof needed to construct the history of the subalterns. Dalits can borrow the methodology of the Marxists and conduct their own investigation into ancient history from the Dalit perspective. The textual criticism could liberate the historical asuras.

This is the first step towards producing historical proof of the indigenous Dalits. However, when counter-images are produced and narratives are reconstructed, the Dalit historian should not fall into the trap of repeating the images of the aboriginals originally produced by the upper caste. Those images and the narratives were the outcome of the ideology of the racial majority in ancient times. These images are ugly, negatively supernatural, superhuman, and cannibalistic.

Since the intellectual and educated Dalit will not be interested in adopting as a forefather the mythical asura as they were depicted in classical religious texts, there are two possible ways of reimaging the asuras in contemporary times. One, since many subalterns (backward castes, Dalits, and Adivasis) have been worshipping the mythical asura as they were and drawing inspiration from them, in the initial phase of creating the counterculture, they could be allowed to continue worshipping the mythical asura in the same form till the reimaged figures gain prominence. Second, since finding historical proof about the mythical asuras is not easy, a logical first step for providing historicity is foregrounding it on the nativity.

This is what the Dalit and subaltern reformers and intelligentsia, including Jotirao Phuley, B.R. Ambedkar, and E.V. Ramasamy Naicker (popularly known as Periyar) did and laid the ideological foundations in the nineteenth and twentieth centuries in their literary and academic works. Unlike D.D. Kosambi and Irfan Habib, these intellectuals were targeting texts. They selected religious scriptures and texts that sanctified the humiliating narratives, descriptions, and images of the local rulers and their people. Ambedkar called the local race the Nagas and Dravidas, Phuley called them the Kshatriyas, and Periyar called them the Dravidians. When the Aryans invaded the Indian subcontinent between 2000 and 1500 BC, they had already faced the local Naga race before. In the face of stiff resistance, mythicization and demonization were employed as the best strategy to justify the massacre of the native race by the advanced Aryan race. *Alberuni's India* (Sachau 2003), clearly exposes this. Most of the texts Alberuni refers to talk of Hindu places in the North as belonging to gods and non-Hindu places in the South as belonging to demons.

Abu Raihan Muhammad Ibn Ahamad Alberuni, contemporary of the Mahammad of Ghazna (1007–1025 AD) and his successor Masud (1030–33 AD), and possessing mastery over Arabic, Persian, and Sanskrit, and knowledge of astronomy, astrology, philosophy, religion, and traditions of India and other countries, has provided vivid accounts of India and noted that there is no consistency in the meanings and positions of asuras in the Hindu religious texts. To point out this inconsistency, Alberuni refers to the text *Samkhya* that mentions three created beings: the spiritual ones being the highest, men being in the middle, and animals being the lowest (Sachua 2003, 57). There were eight spiritual beings: Brahaman, Indra, Prajapathi, Saumya, Gandharva, Yaksha, Rakshasa, and Pisaca. Contrast this with the Bhagvad Gita in which Vasudeva, who talks about three forces,[2] claims that the second force causes development of stupidity, leads to fatigue, and induces actions in Yaksha and Rakshasa. While the *Samkhya* places asuras in the category of spiritual beings, Vasudeva placed them in the non-believers category, which included those who neither believe in god nor attend to his commandments. He feared that such forces

---

[2] If the first of the three primary forces prevails, it causes development of intellect, purification of the senses, and production of action for the angels. If the second force prevails, it causes development of stupidity. It causes fatigue and induces action in Yaksha and Rakshasa. If the third force prevails, it causes development of ignorance and makes people easily beguiled by their own wishes. It finally produces weakness, carelessness, laziness, procrastination in fulfilling duties, and prolonged sleep (Sachau 2003, 57–8).

(asuras) would make the world godless and would be occupied with things that were harmful in the world and beyond (Sachau 2003, 57–8). After coming across this confusing order of names, Alberuni came up with eight classes of spiritual beings most popular among Hindus: devas or angels belong to the Hindus of the North; *daithya*s and *danava*s were demons of the South who opposed the Hindu religion, persecuted cows, and, despite being near Hindu devas, continued to fight with them; *gandharva*s make music for the devas; *yaksha*s, the treasurers and guardians of the devas; *rakshasa*s, ugly and deformed demons; *kinnara*s, those having a human body but with a horse's head; nagas, beings in the shape of serpents; and *vidhayadara*s, demon sorcerers who perform a certain kind of witchcraft. Alberuni also refers to the Matsya Purana, which has allotted colours to the four directions and *varna*s (castes): the East is white like Brahmins, the north is red like Kshatriyas, the south is yellow like Vaishyas, and the west is black like Sudras (Sachau 2003, 184). In the scheme of racially segregated habitation, the Matsya Purana allocates different areas to living beings based on their social status and functions. It locates all living beings in Mount Meru, the mountains of the earth, also known as Purusaparvatha. Other great mountains around Mount Meru were allocated to the rest. The Himavant Mountain, which was covered with snow, was where rakshasas, pisacas, and yakshas were residing; the nagas resided on Nishada.[3] Here, the nagas and the rakshasas are not in the same area and their shapes are not the same. Thus, Alberuni's references to these texts not only help us understand the existing confusion in the names and their order but also expose the existing disconnect between the historical nagas/Dravidians and the mythical asuras, which were otherwise clubbed together to demonize the native race.

Phuley, Ambedkar, and Periyar have made serious attempts to release the asuras from the mythical narratives, tried to demystify

---

[3] In the rest of the areas such as Hemakuta resided gandhravas and apsaras; Nila was inhabited by brahamarshis and anchorites; Svela was inhabited by daityas and danavas; and Sringaravat was inhabited by pitras, the fathers and grandfathers of devas. The centre of all this was Havrita, the highest of all. The whole is called Purusaparvatha. The area between Himavant and Sringavant is called Kailasa, the playground of rakshasas and apsaras.

their characters, and provide historicity. For the construction of the counterculture, these three, and Alberuni, of course, have built the foundational textual criticism without which the anti-caste movements would have been impossible. The objective of the three was the same. However, Ambedkar's attempt was a bit more sophisticated in building the line of counter-arguments, but not in the rejection of classical narratives. Phuley and Periyar used rational and radical language to ridicule the inbuilt absurdity in the idea of an unchallengeable cultural norm. Their language, though it appears to be that of lay humans, is the language of natural rationalism, which was essential to counter the illogical foundations of the classical Aryan narratives. However, simultaneously, as pointed out earlier, the subalterns that were contesting the negativity ascribed to subaltern historical figures, such as Mahabali, Narakasura, Mahishasura, and Ravana, could adopt these figures as they were or with modifications as a first step or as a primary claim. Since their status as mythical, demonic, and ahistorical was Aryan ascribed, subalterns did not need to wait till their historicity was proved.

When there has been consistent effort to present mythical/ahistorical characters such as Vamana as historical, it should also be countered immediately. Proving both, that Vamana is ahistorical and that Mahabali is historical, is essential. From *Alberuni's India*, it is clear that *sura*s and asuras are imagined characters. Perhaps, here, both the historical native rulers and the Aryans were mythicized for a defined purpose. In this, the Aryan was depicted as god and good and the native as bad and evil, which is an Aryan conspiracy. Of this conspiracy, all three intellectuals trace the origins to religious texts: Ambedkar examined the Rig Veda, the Taittireyi Brahamana, and the Satpata Brahamana; Phuley and Periyar examined the Matsya Purana and the Bhagawatam, and the Ramayana, respectively. They adopted textual criticism, natural rationalism, and humanism as tools to counter Aryan narratives. From the Phuley, Ambedkar, and Periyar re-readings, it is quite clear that they were not reading the *sura*s and asuras as mythical beings. For them, the *sura*s and asuras were synonyms for Aryans and native rulers.

Jotirao Phuley, in order to counter the Aryan narratives (Vipras and Upadhyas—localized names for Brahmins as authors of texts as well as race), focused on the *Bhaghawatam*. In his *Slavery*, Phuley (2008) uses the word Kshatriya to refer to the native rulers (not the ones from Manu's four varnas). He has deciphered the meaning of words such as *matsya*, the fastest canoes on the sea, and *kurma* (or *kachcha*), a boat bigger in size but that travelled slowly, by which Iraniyan Aryans travelled across the western sea and landed on the west coast of India. The leader of those Aryans who came in canoes attacked the Shankhasura (the first confrontation/conflict between Aryans and native rulers). Phuley highlighted the absurdity of various avatars including that of Matsya (fish), Kurma (tortoise), Varaha (boar), Narasimha (lion head and human body), and Vamana (dwarf Brahmin boy). While animal and semi-human (half human and half animal) avatars were a dominant feature among Aryan *suras*, among asuras, only Mahishasura is given a semi-human form (buffalo–human). This is evened out by Narakasura, Ravana, and Mahabali being portrayed with demonic characteristics. He juxtaposes all these avatars to elucidate the conflict between the Aryans and the native Kshatriyas: Matsya vs Shankhasura, Kachcha or Kurma vs Kashyapa, Varaha and Narasimha vs Hiranyakashyapu, and Vamana vs Bali Raja and Banasura (son of Bali Raja).

From Matsya to Varaha, the conflicts seem to be political but, from Nursimha (the corrupted form of which is Narasimha), the Aryans seem to adopt different strategies. Narasimha, the treacherous, deceitful, scheming, brutal, and ruthless man conspired against Hiranyakashyapu, the native ruler, by influencing Hiranyakashyapu's son, Prahalada, through the son's teacher. After being indoctrinated into the religion of the Aryans, Prahalada, under the influence of Narasimha, turned against his father and rejected his religion. Prahalada is a case in point where a native, Hiranyakashyapu, was trying to save his son from the influences of the alien Aryan religion (Phuley 2008, 28). Narasimha was using his religion as a tool to corrupt the young innocent prince to usurp the kingdom of Hiranykashyapu. Before Hiranyakasyapu's assassination, the reason for conflict between the *suras* and asuras was territorial expansion, but this episode points to conflict between the religions of the natives and the aliens. The alien religion was being imposed systematically in order to make it universal. Phuley traced the lineage of Mahabali to Hiranyakashyapu, who was his great grandfather. Prahalada realized the conspiracy against his father but did not take revenge. His son, Virochana, strengthened the kingdom that was thereafter inherited by Mahabali (Phuley 2008, 29).

Though Phuley did not elaborate on who expanded Bali's kingdom, by the time Bali inherited it, it seems that the geographical extent of the kingdom of Bali Raja consisted several islands of Simhaladweepa (he refers to an island called Bali as proof), the Konkan region to the south of Kolhapur, and parts of the Mawal region. These were divided into nine parts and there was a tenth division near Ayodhya in the Kashi region. This, according to Phuley, was bigger than Ajapal's and Dasharath's kingdoms. Among his ten divisions, seven paid taxes, which earned him the name 'Protector of the Seven'. Today, Mahabali (Maveli in Malayalam) is worshipped in Kerala and some parts of Maharashtra. Perhaps Kerala was part of the Konkan region under his rule.

In his scheme of the kingdom, Phuley infers, there was a federal structure, revenue collecting and justice-dispensing mechanisms, as well as patronage for the arts. These are part of the real historical kingdom. In substantiating the existence of the federal administration, he refers to the *khand*s (divisions) of the Bali kingdom that were administered by a *khandoba*, with a *mahasubha*[4] as a revenue collection officer and a *nau khanodancha nyayi* as the officer for justice dispensation. There were two assistants, known as *mallukhan*s, whose number could be determined by the status of the *khandoba*s. One such officer of Jejuri was entrusted with quelling the rebellion of the wrestlers in the neighbouring chieftains land and thus came to be known as Malla Ari (the enemy of the wrestlers).[5] Bali's revenue system was adopted by Muslims and studied by Egyptians. Phuley also attributes two ragas—Malhar and Bhairav—to two different officials from Bali's kingdom. The raga Malhar was created by Malla Ari, who was also called Marthanda. He was a connoisseur of music. The raga Bhairav was created by Kalbhairi, who was also called Kotwal in the Kashi region. Contemporary Muslim musicians seem to have engaged with these two ragas. While engagement with the first raga by a Muslim singer, Miyan, resulted in the creation of the raga Miyan Malhar, Tansen, who

---

[4] *Mahasubha*, in due course, perhaps, became *mahsoba*—one who is worshipped in Maharashtra. In it, a stone is kept in a corner of the field. Once the stone is worshipped, work commences in the field.

[5] Mallukhan is an interesting combination and it makes one wonder how such a combination emerged. What is the meaning of 'mallu' in Mallukhan. The word 'Khan' is used as a suffix by Muslims. Malla Ari also seems to be connected to the traditional martial art. The meanings of both are not the same though.

engaged with the second raga, seems to have found it difficult to master. Phuley even says that the *daur*, a musical instrument created by Kalbhairi, was better than the tabla and the mridangam, the dominant instruments in classical music.

With these elaborate references to Bali and his kingdom with all its essential features, Phuley locates Bali in a proper historical frame, sans any mythic quality. Cultural practices (such as picking up the thali/tray)[6] that were in existence during this time in Maharashtra as well as popular sayings, chants (war cries such as *Harahara Mahadeva* [O great lord Shiva, save us from the ocean of birth and death], *Jotibacha Chang Bhala* [flourish/shine well], hail the rise of Sadananda, and hail Mallukhan the Proud), slogans, and proverbs have been used to place Bali in history. Phuley quite often mentions that Bali was a worshipper of Shiva, the cultural and religious connection of which could be seen by him in the fact that Sunday is considered a holiday of lord Shiva's and Marathas such as the Mangs, Mahars, Kunbi, Mali, and others did not consume food or water till they bathed the idol and worshipped it (Phuley 2008, 32). 'Gold of Shilangna' is another expression that refers to the Vamana plundering the capitals (*angans*) of Bali after his death and his son failing to stop him (Phuley 2008, 31).

Phuley locates both Dussera and Diwali in the conflicts between Bali, Vamana, and Banasura. This bears no similarity, whatsoever, to the conflicts of Devimahatyam or Mahishasuramarthanam, in which Durgadevi slays Mahishasura; Bhagawatam, where Krishna's wife, Satyabhama, slays Narakasura; or the Ramayana, in which Rama kills Ravana. Even at present, there is no pan-Indian myth as to why Dussera and Diwali are celebrated. There are both religious and secular explanation for them. However, most of northern India celebrates Diwali to welcome Rama's homecoming and Ravana's death, and Dussera gets mingled with Durga slaying Mahishasura. There is also a secular reason as to why these festivals are celebrated. This secularization of Diwali and Dussera as festivals of

---

[6] Whenever Bali assigns important task to one of his noble men, who has guts to complete that task then that noble who did have the grit would come forward chanting the war cry Harhara Mahadev and picks up beetle leaves with the coconut, then bowing, he would apply the turmeric on his forehead and raising the contents of the tray in his pallu.

peace and prosperity could be attributed to liberal Hindus trying to eliminate plurality and to provide a pan-Indian universality. Later, the neo-capitalism, which sees the large-scale culture of majority as a potential tool for promoting consumerism, extended its support to secularization, commericialization, and modernization (the way it is celebrated using electric illumination and so on). However, the Hindu classical narrative of Diwali and Dussera, as celebrations of *suras* killing asuras not only continued to grow in popularity within major Hindu constituencies, but also grew as cultural superstructures, and these festivals acquired the status of national festivals. This automatically forces the people of other cultures to join in the celebration in the name of being secular. However, in actuality, the minority is being forced to submit to the power of the majority's cultural superstructures.

Rather than providing only the more popular myths behind Dussera and Diwali, Phuley presents both the Aryan version and the Kshatriya version of Dussera. While the Aryan version of Dussera gained pan-Indian recognition, the Kshatriya (Dravidian) version was suppressed for political gain. According to Phuley, while the Aryan version celebrated the death of Mahabali, the Kshatriya version celebrated the coming of Banasura from the battlefield where he had fought with Vamana after the death of his father. The ritual of Vijayadasami or Dussera for Brahmin families, according to Phuley (2008, 33), is based on the following:

> When Vamana reached home, his wife kept an idol of Bali made from flour on the threshold [and] jokingly said 'Lo and behold; there is Bali come again to fight you'. Later, Brahamans brought changes in the ritual. While kicking, the Brahaman man first places his left foot on the left side of the image of Bali and then pricks his stomach (potbelly) with a twig of the Apta tree and then putting his foot over his image, enters the house.

Phuley also provides the contrasting Kshatriya version of Dussera. In it, the reasons as well as the rituals and expectations were different. It celebrated the return of Banasura and his men. After fighting Vamana for nine days, on the tenth night of Ashwin, Banasura men reached their houses. The women made *bali* (flour and rice idol) and kept it on the threshold with lamps in trays with which they moved around their men folk as a ritual of welcoming them. Later, the ritual changed a little bit. The women of Kshatriya danced around their husbands with earthen lamps in their hands (Phuley 2008, 33).

Interestingly, in both versions Bali was praised by the women of both races. Both the Vipra women welcoming the Vamana and his men and the Kshatriya women welcoming Banasura and his men on the tenth day of the Aswini made *bali* and prophesized that 'Bali will come and establish the kingdom of the God on earth again' (Phuley 2008, 33).

The counter-narrative of Diwali offered by Phuley is a celebration of the Kshatriya Banasura over Vamana. After regaining the needed strength to fight Vamana, Banasura made advances on Vamana and defeated him by driving him and his people towards the Himalayas and depriving them of food. Thus, Vamana starved to death and that was his end. It was this success, argued Phuley, that gave the Kshatriyas happiness and resulted in celebrations. After the victory, Banasura gave a great banquette to his army men, distributed the wealth among his nobles, and sent them to their respective regions. The women celebrated the victory by making festive food for their brethren, feeding them to their heart's content, and waving the auspicious earthen lamps around their faces on the second day of the bright fortnight of Karthika, believing that Bali would come and bless them on the Bhaubeej Day of the Diwali festival (Phuley 2008, 34).[7] This ritual is performed by Kshatriya women but not their Brahmin counterparts. Alberuni's description of 'Dibali' too has close connection with Bali though the reason is not the same. According to him, it is celebrated on the first day of Karthika when the sun marches to Libra. It celebrated Lakshmi, wife of Vasudeva, liberating Bali who was a prisoner in the seventh earth (*patala*) and allowing him to go into the world. Hence, it was called Baligajya or the principality of Bali (Sachau 2003, 465).

Ambedkar's textual criticism was much more academic and informed. His focus was on using aspects of race, nation, and

---

[7] The second day of the bright fortnight of Kartika; on on this day, women of all age groups were so happy that they cooked festive food for their brothers, fed them to their hearts' content, and then waved the auspicious earthen lamps around their faces and reminded them of the prophecy of the coming of Bali by saying, 'May all evil disappear from here and may Bali's kingdom descend.' This is known as the Bhaubeej Day.

langue to historicize the subaltern. Most of the texts were riddled with inconsistencies and concocted narratives. In the *Rig Veda*, there were references to the idea of an Indo-Aryan nation made of five tribes that got assimilated into one common people (Ambedkar 2013, 30). However, he could not find consistency in the opinions from different texts as to the identity of these tribes. Yaska, in his *Nirukta*, says that it denotes the Gandharvas, Pitris, devas, asuras, and *rakshasa*s. The *Aupamanyava* says that it denotes the four varnas and the Nishadas. Ambedkar found these absurd because the *Rig Veda* said that glory would be brought on the five and that they would be inseparable like heaven. If such is the case, argues Ambedkar, then the *rakshasa*s would not have been part of the tribe (Ambedkar 2013, 30). The *Taittireyi Brahamana* says that while the Brahmin caste sprang up from the gods, the Sudras came from asuras. The same text also says that Sudras had sprung from non-existence (Ambedkar 2014c, 30). In the same text, on the origin of the universe, there were two contradictory references regarding asuras. Prajapathi, after taking shape and form, and taking earth as base, created asuras from his abdomen and milked out food in an earthen dish for them (Ambedkar 2014a, 90). After that, Prajapathi created living beings. It is between the creation of this real, living, local race and of the imagined demonic asuras that the authors of the religious texts confuse the general society, equating the mythical demonic asuras with the native kings and the mythical *suras* with the Aryan kings. Stanley Rice's two invasions theory on the origin of untouchability argues that the outcastes were the aboriginals, first invaded by the Dravidians, and the Dravidians were later invaded by the Aryans. He further said that, after the Dravidian invasion, the outcastes as survivors became, as caste tended to coincide with occupation, the drum-beating, leather-working, and farm-labouring classes—as serfs, they had been relegated to this from early times. In disproving Rice's theory, Ambedkar called it too mechanical as the Aryans were not homogenous and it is not clear whether the Aryans, Dravidians, Dasas, and Nagas refer to people of different races or are different names for people belonging to the same race (Ambedkar 2014b, 290). He also argues that historians wrongly assumed that Dasas were a separate race. The Nagas and Dasas were the same and the Nagas were neither uncivilized nor aboriginals, but they were non-Aryans. Similarly, the Nagas and Dravidians, from Cape Cameron to Kashmir, were not different races. For Ambedkar, references to the Nagas and Aryan rulers in Vedic literature reveal a spirit of conflict and dualism, and a race for superiority between two distinct types of culture and thought (Ambedkar 2014b, 293). The *Rig Veda* contains the first reference to the snake-god, Ahi Vitra, the enemy of the Aryan god, Indra. The Aryan tribe was not worshiping Ahi Vitra, who was an enemy with considerable powers and needed to be eliminated. It is this demonized Naga whom Ambedkar locates in the wide range of intermarriage relations with royal families throughout the country.

Ambedkar believed that a proposition that the southern Dravidians and northern Nagas are one and the same might face questions regarding the fact that they speak different languages. But he was confident that it is explicable. For this, he looked into three aspects: (*i*) question on the language of the asuras, (*ii*) the origin of the word Dravida, and (*iii*) the pan-Indian nature of the Tamil language. Quoting the work of Oldham, Ambedkar argues that there were separate vernacular languages of tribes that were, apparently, descendants of the asura tribes. The *Sahahasa Chandrika* says that the *paisachi* language was spoken in the paisaca countries of Pandya, Kekaya, Vahlika, Sahya, Nepala, Kuntala, Sudesha, Bhota, Gandhara, Haiva, and Kanoj. Among all the vernacular dialects, the *paisachi* language was said to have lesser infusion of Sanskrit (Ambedkar 2013b, 298). He quotes the work of Professor Muir, who quoted from the *Rig Veda* about the word *mridavach*, the language of asuras. The word *mridavach* translates as injudiciously speaking, which is further explained by Sayana as one whose organs of speech have been destroyed. It was in the *Satpata Brahamana* that the asura deprived of language was undone by crying 'He lava'. People who spoke in such an unintelligible language were called Mlechas. Such a language was banned for the Brahmins and Manu called those tribes outside of the four varnas that spoke such languages Mlechas, or even Arayas and Dasyus. However, he did not believe that all the asura vernacular languages were degenerated, despite their being subjected to the onslaught of Sanskrit. Miur refers to the grammarian Rama Tarkavasiga who used the phrase 'those who speak like Nagas' in the later period to point out that some of them protected their language, religion, and customs. He cites the Dravidian Pandhyas as one such tribe that spoke the paisacha language. All this evidence proves that the Dravidians of southern India are of the same stock as the asuras or Nagas of northern India.

By dwelling on the word Dravida, Ambedkar tried to prove the pan-Indian nature of the pre-Aryan Nagas. According to him, the word Dravida came from the original Tamil word *damitta*. When it was imported into Sanskrit it became *damilla* and, eventually, it became Dravida. Therefore, the word Dravida, the language of the people, does not denote the race of the people (Ambedkar 2014b, 300). The races that spoke this language were not limited to the South, a fact that is in direct opposition to what has been projected in Vedic literature. It was the language of India from Kashmir to Cape Cameron. It was due to the contact between the Aryans and Nagas and the impact of Sanskrit that the Nagas of the North gave up Tamil as their mother tongue and adopted Sanskrit in its place. But the Nagas of the south adhered to their mother tongue Tamil (Dravida language) and, therefore, they are called Dravidians. Hence, for Ambedkar, while the Nagas of the North were the racial and cultural category, the Dravidians of the South are a linguistic category. This proves that there were only two races—the Aryans and the Nagas—and there was no Dravidian invasion.

Periyar, perhaps the greatest radical rationalist the country has ever seen in the twentieth century, was not as academic like Ambedkar. He was revolutionary but not a reformer. Therefore, Periyar completely dismissed the accepted popular Vedic narratives of both Aryan *suras* and Dravidian asuras. He thought that radical rejection in the public gaze was the best method for questioning the inbuilt irrationality in the construction of mythological suras or gods and their power. Of course, Amebedkar's act of burning the *Manusmriti* and Periyar's act of breaking the idols of the Pullayar (Vinayaka or Ganapathi) were equally radical. Yet, Periyar's confrontational radicalism is simple and down to earth. His use of the common man's language seems to invoke the sleeping non-Brahmin. Perhaps, he saw langue, the methods of rejection, and attacks which were seen as 'derogatory' and 'insulting' to Hindus as being necessary tools in pointing out the humiliation and maltreatment that had resulted from the demonization of the Dravidian ancestors and their culture. Therefore, his criticism targets the very foundations of the Aryan conspiracy. The purpose of his essay 'Ramayan: A True Reading', as the title suggests, is to counter the Valmiki's narrative in order to provide historicity to Ravana. Thus, he argues that when the Aryans invaded the Dravidas, they maltreated and dishonoured the latter and wrote a false and coloured history. It is this that they call the Ramayana, wherein Rama and his accomplices are styled as Aryans; Ravana as a *rakshasa* (Dravidian); and Hanuman, Sugriva, Vali, and others as monkeys. Contrary to the holiness and divinity ascribed to Vishnu, of whom Rama is an avatar, Periyar sees moral decadence in Vishu who, as Tirumala, was involved in immoral acts such as killing the wife of Biruhu Muni and resorting to deception to impair the chastity of the wife of Jalandrasuran. From Valmiki's *Ramayana* it is evident that Rama is depicted as wicked in thought and deed, and an embodiment of lies, treachery, artifice, cunningness, hard-heartedness, and so on. Yet, it was the ability of the Aryans and their mastery over the language in which myths, Puranas, Brahamanas, and other such Vedic texts were produced that enabled them to camouflage their racial arrogance and crimes committed on native tribes with self-ascription of divinity and godliness. This mythicization of the actual massacres of tribes into good and evil binaries not only placed the Aryans on a higher pedestal as a race and as a social as well as cultural group, but also guaranteed them a continuous safe haven despite their committing crimes on other tribes. This also allowed them to demonize the native tribes so that their political persecution could be located in the scheme of god punishing the evil. It was neither mythical nor cultural; it was a political conspiracy to hide the crimes committed by Aryans on Dravidians eternally. Therefore, mythical texts, such as epics and Puranas, were the literary tools used cleverly to camouflage the atrocities of the Aryans in the process of the Aryanization of the subcontinent.

It is against this narrative that Periyar presents Ravana as an honest, kind-hearted, and duty-bound king and shows that he was responding to the domination of Vedic rituals, which were causing serious damage to the environment and animals. If Ravana was objecting to Dasaratha's Putrakamesti Yajgnam, he was doing so because it involved the sacrificing of viviparous and oviparous creatures. Therefore, as a sovereign ruler, it was his duty to oppose the cruelty against animals. Though he was a scholar and a powerful king, his demonization in the Ramayana has become his defining character—kidnapper of an other man's wife.

In the Making

Organized religions such as Christianity, Islam, and Hinduism have emerged as unchallengeable religions with their demographic strength in a congenial political environment and vice versa. All through the times, they have followed the policy of absorbing not only smaller religious denominations, particularly those that might possess close or distant similarities to their initial phases, but also distinctly different religions, which have emerged as a response to the domination of these organized religions in their latter phases of development. If there was any resistance to such an absorption, they were forced to submit or face persecution. Hinduism, as an organized religion is no exception. It has been following the same policy since Vedic times.

In its long process of absorbing the similar and prosecuting the different, Hinduism has not left a single religious denomination untouched. Yet, there are certain regional cultures that are similar to the larger extent but still have been able to maintain a certain amount of distinctness based on cultural, social, and regional differences. This desire to be different, in fact, is not cultural alone but also emotional, sentimental, and political. Their regional distinction built with locally available cultural forms becomes their regional identity, which is essential for meeting the aspirations of the religion. Even those similar cultures, which have submitted or surrendered themselves to the process of Hinduization long back, are still maintaining their distinct nature in one way or the other. Total submission is impossible. Even the absorber would not expect a total elimination of differences or total submission. But it expects the similar culture to, at least, subscribe to the commonality of the larger culture and it also expects such an acceptance to be publicly displayed in a manner such as adopting certain ritualistic forms and norms and performing the same publicly in order to declare that such an adoption has been carried out. If not, the organized religions develop and invent strategies to impose the commonality on the similar religions.

In the last decade or so, there has been a visible effort by the subaltern intelligentsia and educated to build a counterculture that would maintain its distinct nature from Hinduism. They have been translating their ideology on the alternative or the counterculture into reality. Since, they are in constant engagement with the theory of assertion, they are also involved in inventing methods for reclaiming lost history. This can be achieved by responding to the unacceptable continuity of the caste Hindu cultural domination that curtails the genuine growth of subaltern intelligentsia and its rigorous desire to attain the capacity to theorize. These capabilities lead to the production of counter-sociological and -historical theories that can compete with already existing theories, which for long provided caste Hindus unchallengeable authority over the subalterns and curtailed the available space for the upper caste intelligentsia to theorize on subalterns. There is nothing wrong in caste Hindu intelligentsia theorizing the subaltern experience. However, the truth is that the subaltern acquiring the capacity to do so may not gel well with the superstructure. Acquiring the ability to theorize is quite natural but it is seen as dangerous as it could lead to a situation where the long-standing discriminative/illogical social and cultural narratives are made to come under scientific scrutiny. What irritates the authors and custodians of the caste Hindu narratives is that they are being challenged by those who should not even be talking about them. Thus, both the subaltern's acquisition of the ability to theorize and the transformation of theories proposed by their earlier reformers and theorists into workable culture by present day conscious subalterns would pose a serious challenge to not only the caste Hindu intelligentsia but also the caste Hindus as an unchallengeable social agency. As expected, the responsibility of the entire work, as it must, seems to have fallen on the shoulders of the subalterns in the universities and colleges in metropolitan cities. However, there is also a visible contribution to the theorization from the peripheries—the subaltern cultural assertions are not taking place in the metropolis alone. It is happening in small towns, villages, and in Adivasi hamlets. This simultaneity is due to the fact that the subaltern in the metropolis is also a subaltern at the peripheries. Therefore, they act as a bridge between the metropolis and the peripheries. As per my understanding, such connectivity between the subaltern at the periphery and the subaltern at the metropolis is essential for both theorizing the experience of the subaltern and for translating the counterculture theories into reality. Apart from this, the subalterns at the periphery would need the subalterns in the metropolis as a guiding force in their continuous struggle for assertion and in their fight for justice. The subaltern in the metropolis in their capacity as bureaucrats, teachers, lawyers, students, or activists could provide support to the subaltern at the periphery. It is a must, as in the process of translating theories of counterculture into reality, that the subaltern at the periphery face serious threats from caste Hindus at the periphery. Apart from this, metropolitan and peripheral reciprocity, and cooperation of lower caste social groups is essential for the construction of the counterculture because the force they are challenging by building the counterculture is not an easy opponent to deal with. In fact, using its inbuilt power, its internal mechanisms immediately get activated to dismiss the counterculture as antinational and divisive.

Though the counterculture is not new, it made a conscious declaration of its arrival in 2011. The subaltern at the periphery has been engaging with the counterculture but has not come in conflict with the mainstream much. The subaltern counterculture acquired a radical nature when subalterns in universities and towns began to challenge the mainstream narratives of the so-called homogeneous national culture, in which subaltern ancestors were portrayed as evil demons and villians. The year 2011 saw a wave of Ravana pujas all over India in celebration of Ravana as a counter to the homecoming celebration for Rama for Diwali. On 9 October 2011, clashes erupted in Jawaharlal Nehru University (JNU), New Delhi, over the celebration of Mahishasura Martyrdom Day, when students of All India Backward Students Forum (AIBSF), JNU, celebrated the day in a hostel mess hall (Ranjan 2016). When the subalterns celebrated the festival in JNU, it angered the radical Hindu student groups. As a university, JNU is a space where mature minds are involved in the cultivation of reason; the idea of India and the Constitution of India both mandate universities to be secular. It is ironic that in such a place the Hindu majority's rituals are performed and festivals are conducted. It is equally ironic that administrative agencies never find fault with public educational institutions where Hindu rituals are performed unabatedly. In such a space, where it does not matter whether it is dominated by a caste or religious majority, the counter to the majority culture is seen as a problem. This is not something new. However, it took some time for the subaltern to build a narrative that would address the question of humiliation as well as the essentiality of de-mythicizing the pre-Aryan native race and its rulers to provide historicity. Such a task would perform multiple functions, which would bring positive changes in the lives of the subalterns. It establishes historical equality, provides cultural independence, promotes economic discipline and rational thought, and offers political power. It is with such intentions that the subalterns in the metropolis and at the periphery together saw countering the mainstream in the democratic sphere as being relatively easy if not unproblematic.

However, when the subaltern embarks upon building a counterculture that could be a historical reality, they are confronted by how the worship of asuras in the peripheries (Dalits and *bahujan*s in rural areas and Adivasi hamlets in hilly areas) and in a few towns as they are described or depicted in the Puranas, epics, and mythologies is dissimilar to the historical narratives produced by the subaltern intellectuals. As mentioned ealier, Ambedkar, Phuley, and Periyar opposed the demonization of native rulers in one tone. This means that these three would have wanted the Dalit–*bahujan*s and Adivasis to respect or admire, if not worship, the historical figures they described in their works. Since their ideas could not reach the subalterns at the periphery, these uneducated masses adopted ahistorical mythical asuras as heroes, if not gods. Therefore, over time, the puranic mythological asuras will have to be replaced with the historical figures of native rulers. For subalterns in the metropolis, understanding the historical asura might be easy, but it might not be so for the subaltern at the periphery. It is through a conscious campaign that the latter will be convinced and will agree to replace the Dashanan (10-headed) with the historical Ravana. Here, the subaltern in the metropolis might face difficulty. However, recently, Kerala showed the way. It has made a serious attempt to reimagine one of the characters that was understood to be an asura. For long, Malayalis have accepted the image of Mahabali as a mythical figure and worshipped him. Now, the new figure of Mahabali, redrawn by the Kerala Devasam Board, fits the description of the ruler and has also liberated him from the humiliating association with him as a potbellied ruler. The same could be adapted to all the 'asura' figures.

Unlike Ravana, Mahishasura, and Narakasura, Mahabali is fortunate enough to be located in a defined writing of regional culture and identity. Among these native rulers, he is the only one worshipped for being a benevolent ruler. His welfare state, perhaps, had no match in ancient India. Despite Kerala being a Hindu-dominated state, a Dravidian king has become the sole identity of Malayalis, which has facilitated the Kerala government's refashioning of his image.

Onam is celebrated mainly in honour of the worthy and benevolent king, Mahabali, who is welcomed by all sorts of people during the Onam season. Onam is probably the only ancient festival in India that is not attached to any caste, religion, or God. Unlike Diwali, Christmas, and Eid, Onam is truly secular and is tagged as a festival for 'Malayalees' and not for Hindus alone (Varghese 2016). Kerala, somehow, in terms of religious festivals, at least, does not give the impression that it is part of a pan-Hindu culture. However, the Hindu population in the state is as orthodox as the Hindu population in the North. This section follows practices such as *theendamai*, a more severe form of untouchability. Festivals such as Deepavali, Ayutha Pooja, Vinayaka Chathurthi, Holi, and Rakhi, which were specific to northern India have now achieved pan-India status, and yet they are not part of Kerala's festive culture. This does not mean that Kerala is away from Hinduism. But, rather, it consciously maintains a balance between the regional secular identity and the larger Hindu communal identity.

There are various versions of Onam. The far-right Hindus of the Rashtriya Swayamsevak Sangh (RSS) see Vamana, the avatar of Vishnu, as the liberator of Kerala from the ruler Mahabali. Hence, Onam for them is a celebration of the birthday of the liberator. In 2016, Amit Shah, national president of the Bharatiya Janata Party (BJP), used his social media account on Twitter to wish people for Vaman Jayanthin, sharing a picture of the Brahmin boy pushing Bahubali to the nether world. According to the Puranas, Hindu gods were threatened by the popularity of the charismatic leadership of Mahabali. The Brahmanical narratives consider Mahabali an impure asura and the rustic 'other' of pure Hindu divinities (Arafath 2017).

The intention of the BJP, with its present political strength, is to invent new meaning by negating already existing narratives, which present Vamana as a villain who cheated Mahabali in a conspiracy to end the golden rule that made even the gods feel envious. This insignificant place allotted to Vamana in the entire festival dissatisfies the Hindus who wish to use religious festivals as a potential tool for re-engineering and thus generating communal political capital. By presenting Onam as the harvest festival and by integrating Mahabali's visit in it, secularists in Kerala were successful in eliminating its religious, pan-Hindu link and in rebuilding the regional, historical identity of Malayalis. Subalterns and Dalits totally disagree with both, the secular narrative and the right-wing reinterpretation of Vamana as a liberator. They call Vamana a murderer of the asura king Mahabali and also argued that the secularization of Onam by caste Hindus was an attempt to deprive them of their history. They believe that Mahabali was killed by the *savarna* conspiracy.[8] The subaltern narrative did not find popularity because it challenged the domination of the upper caste and questioned the foundational irrationality of caste itself. However, the secular narrative created with the aspiration to promote Kerala as having a unique cultural identity did succeed. It is this narrative which found 'acceptance' across castes and religious communities. Under these circumstances, the Kerala model of liberating the native ruler from the Vedic narratives to provide historicity might be adopted.

The fact that asuras are worshipped across India, at present, substantiates Ambedkar's theory that the Nagas were present across India. The influence of the Hindu religion, Vedic rituals, myths, epics, and festivals is pan-Indian, which seems to be the determining factor for the pan-Indian presence of the asuras. Apart from Mahabali, who is worshipped or revered in Kerala alone, Narakasura, Mahishasura, and Ravana are recognized as such across India. Mahabali, in Kerala, is welcomed from the nether land and is worshipped once a year on Onam. The rest of India celebrates the death of Narakasura, Mahishasura, and Ravana as demons killed by gods/goddesses—Satyabhama, Durgadevi, and Rama, respectively. In performing rituals of the counterculture, the subalterns consciously resist being part of the dominant narrative. Abstaining from participating in the rituals of the dominant culture is the first step and asserting the rituals of the counterculture, in the form of worshipping the so-called evils of Hindu mythologies, is a second step. For instance, Ravana, Kumbhakaran, and Meghnada, the asura brothers from Lanka, the enemies of Rama, are considered evil by caste Hindus. For this reason, their effigies are burned on Dussera. On the other hand, in Mandasur, on the boarder between Madhya Pradesh and Rajastan, the asura brothers from the Ramayana are worshipped. However, no effigy of Rama is burned. To burn an effigy

---

[8] *Savarna* is communities with caste or touchable caste-Hindu communities. Even the Sudras could be accommodated into it. But it could also mean upper caste. Here, *savarna* conspiracy refers to a method employed by the upper caste to justify the elimination of Dravidian asuras. Since they possessed the ability of producing narratives, demonization of asuras become possible.

of Rama in a Hindu-dominated country, the vulnerable subaltern would need courage. Subalterns in Tamil Nadu have been showing that courage. The anti-Brahmin movement from the beginning of the twentieth century has resulted in the creation of a strong conscious and radical subaltern constituency. They have been displaying how it is radical to reject the mainstream narrative by adopting the ritual of burning effigies of Rama and Sita and performing Ravanaleela as a counter to Ramleela, a ritual in Delhi where a grand effigy of Ravana is burnt in which the president, prime minister, opposition leaders, and other such government officials participate. In 1970, under the leadership of Maniyammai, wife of Periyar, Ravanaleela was conducted for the first time in Madras. On 12 October 2011, in response to the Mahishasur Movement in North India, some Periyarite anger resurfaced. At a well-publicized event in Chennai, activists of the Thanthai Periyar Dravidar Kazhagam (TPDK—Elder Periyar Dravidian Group) burned the effigy of Rama and Sita (Stephen 2016). This reaction to the movement was limited to only Tamil Nadu in the South because of its legacy of non-Brahmin movements.

The Mahishasur Movement, which started in JNU, stirred up new movements in North India. North Indian subalterns woke up to claim their history by conducting parallel festivals to celebrate Narakasura, Mandasura, Mahishasura, and Ravana. These festivals presented them with an opportunity to highlight their culture (counterculture) that had been in existence for long. As their culture was different from the mainstream but remained in the periphery, it offered them a chance to assert their right to question the manipulation and misuse of their history and it allowed them to design a subaltern culture that in many ways distinguishes itself from the mainstream culture. They have been trying their best to lay the foundations of their culture on non-religious, non-ritualistic, rational humanism. They are divorcing this counterculture from the Vedic and puranic *sura*s and adopting historical native rulers by consciously replacing rituals with lectures and discussions on their historical ancestors. They even assert worshipping asuras as a constitutional right and argue that the burning of effigies by caste Hindus is not only inflicting wounds on their community but is also an act of treason. In accordance with Article 244 under Part X of the Indian Constitution, Adivasis have been guaranteed special rights under the Fifth Schedule. In Scheduled Areas,

Adivasis worship Ravana, Kumbhakaran, and Mahishasura who are referred to as *rakshasa*s by other caste groups. Further, it would lead to action under provisions of the Scheduled Castes and Tribes (Prevention of Atrocities) Act, 1989, and Section 124A of the Indian Penal Code. There are even provisions to terminate officials who support such crimes. Based on these provisions subalterns in the North oppose the burning of effigies by caste Hindus and warn them of legal consequences as well. Along with all these constitutional measures, this movement has given much needed courage to subalterns who were suffering under psychological and cultural fear. The domination of Hinduism has resulted in subalterns, especially Dalits and Adivasis, being deprived of spirituality. The very juxtaposition of asuras against Hindu gods worked as an invisible or undeclared restriction on the worship of asuras by Dalits and Adivasis. This movement has certainly provided psychological strength to subalterns and helped liberate them from fear. In Rokda village, Janjgir-Champa Disctrict, there is a Mahishasura (Bhaisasur) shrine worshipped by Adivasis and Dalits. There have been many concerns that they do not express openly out of fear. They fear that if they are identified as followers of asura *parampara* (tradition) and *sanskruti* (culture), the community will have to face repercussions at the hands of the dominant caste Hindu community. The fear that State institutions would view them as *rakshasa*s (demons or criminals in modern terms), look down on them, and target and corner them has kept them from using mainstream means of expressing their history and culture. However, subaltern activist leaders from the subaltern, who are much more aggressive than academics from the subaltern, have been providing the necessary confidence and guidance to the subaltern masses to celebrate their ancestral heroes in a historical and scientific way. Digree Prasad Chauhan, leader of the Dalit Mukti Morcha, has argued that the 'cultural imperialism of Hindutva has blinded subalterns. Therefore, breaking away from its shackles of slavery by worshipping the real heroes and rejecting the killers (Aryan *suras*) is essential and moolnivasis [first inhabitants of the land] have to be affirmative about what their true history is' (George 2017).

Thus, through different ways and means, subalterns have reached a stage where they can openly declare that they can worship their heroes (if not gods) who are certainly not demons. This resonated throughout northern India. The folk songs of the Santhal tribes of Jharkhand are about Mahishasura. In Purulia (West Bengal), a big fair is organized to mark the worship of Mahishasura (George 2017). The slaying of asuras by *suras* might be an 'ancient truth' that the *savarna*s have conveniently propagated, but it is being rejected here. 'During Durga Pooja, the Asur tribe in Jharkhand, lock themselves up in their houses during the day and come out at night to mourn the death of their king, Mahishasura. They fear that if they come out during the day, *devas* would slay them' (George 2017).

After the movement, North-Indian Dalits and Adivasis started tracing genealogical connections to their ancestors and achieved the confidence to worship supposedly demonic asuras without fear and according to their beliefs. The Bisrakhs of Uttar Pradesh believe that their name was derived from the sage Vishrava, father of Ravana, and their village was the birth place of Ravana and the place where Vishrava discovered Swayambhu Shiva Linga. They worship father and son during Navaratri. In Gadchiroli, Maharastra, the Gond tribes worship Dashanan during the tribal festival Falgun and believe that it was Tulasidas's Ramayana that demonized Ravana, not Valmiki's. Periyar, too, believes that Valimki was appreciative of the character of Ravana (Periyar 2005, 637).[9] In Mandya and Kolar, Karnataka, Shiva and Ravana are worshipped in temples during the harvest festival. In Kakinada there lives a fishing community that perhaps worships Ravana. It is home to the only temple in Andhra Pradesh that is dedicated to Ravana. In Vidisha, Madhya Pradesh, he is worshipped as a symbol of prosperity by the Kanyakubja Brahmins, a sub-sect of the Brahmins who believe that Ravana belongs to their sect. There is also a village called Ravangram. In Mandsaur district, Madhya Pradesh, which shares it border with Rajasthan, Ravana is hailed as a son-in-law by the Namdeo Vaishnav Samaj, a sect that believes that Ravana's wife, Mandodari, hailed from their town.

---

[9] Periyar mentions 10 merits of Ravana: a great learned man, a great saint, a master of scriptures (Sastras and Vedas), a merciful protector of his subjects and relatives, a brave man, a very strong man, a chivalrous soldier, a very pious man, a beloved son of God, and a recipient of many boons. He wrote that these merits are mentioned by Valmiki and praised Ravana on several occasions.

In Kanpur, the Dashanan Mandir located outside the Chhinnamasta Temple at Shivala seems to have been built by a king, Guru Prasad Shukl, in 1890. Once a year, on the morning of Vijayadashami, this temple is opened for worship of Ravana. Perhaps, as Shiva is worshipped there regularly, Ravana, as a devotee of Shiva, is prayed to on Vijayadashami, though not as a deity or god. They believe that Ravana had mastery over all 10 *mahavidya*s (great wisdoms) or the Dasha Mahavidyas and that people who worship Ravana on this day will get wisdom. In Indore, the Valmikis, like the Namdev community in Mandsaur and the Kanyakubja Brahmins of Vidisha, believe that Ravana was an intellectual and knowledgeable person who learnt all the Vedas and pleased Shiva with his devotion. Members of the Valmiki Samaj at Pardeshipura in Indore worship Ravana as a god on Dussera. Their devotion can be gauged from the fact that they avoid looking at the Ravana Dahan (the burning of Ravana's effigy). In Bengal, Asuras observe a period of mourning during Navaratri. Similarly, Ravana worshippers in Haryana also mourn during this period. For them, it is a period of sorrow and sadness when the world celebrates the assassination of their god. In Bundelkhand (Madhya Pradesh and Uttar Pradesh), Dalits pray to Mahishasura to rescue them from calamities such as drought, bad yields, epidemics, and so forth. Similar belief systems exist in parts of Haryana, Telangana, Jharkhand, Bengal, Maharashtra, Andhra Pradesh, Karnataka, and Tamil Nadu.

Like Bali in Kerala and Maharashtra, Mahishasura is popular in north-western India. Commonly portrayed as a demon in Hindu mythology, Mahishasura is a central figure in the counterculture movement (Ranjan 2016). He is worshipped by tribal communities such as the Asur, Santhal, Bhil, and Koruku tribes, and subaltern castes such as the Yadav, Kushwaha, and Kumhar castes. The name of Mysuru in Karnataka is said to be derived from 'Mahishasura *ooru*' (Mahishasura's country).

The legend of Mahishasura, his description and image, is a bit different from that of other asuras—he is half animal and half human (his body is of a buffalo and his head is of a human). But like Mahabali, he was powerful. So powerful, in fact, that, in order to defeat him, Brahma, Vishnu, and Shiva had to come together as one force in the form of Durga. They transformed themselves into women to deceive Mahishasura and kill him.

The counterculture is gaining momentum in places where asuras are worshipped. The JNU tussles and the harsh responses of the caste Hindus have enabled the subalterns at the periphery to come out into the open to celebrate their ancestors and declare their intentions. Though they have also raised concerns within the state, the subalterns at the periphery have taken the opportunity to declare their independence and celebrate their culture, which the mainstream considered absurd and bizarre. A few months after the JNU episode, in Bhawanpur, near Patna, Bihar, Mahishasura was celebrated in an alternative celebration on Dussera that they called Amar Shaheed Mahishassur (Immoratal Martyr Mahishasur; Pramod 2016). Interest in such events has snowballed ever since. In West Bengal alone, Charian Mahto said, there were 24 functions in 2013, 74 in 2014, and 182 in 2015. A function that Mahto held last year, the organiser said, drew a crowd of 20,000 (Ranjan 2016). The festival was not a ritual but a social/educational festival of discussions, debates, and the dissemination of knowledge on the legacy of their ancestors. Interestingly, the subaltern at the periphery that is part of the intelligentsia uses these festivals to educate, to remove religious dogmas, and declare independence from superstitions, beliefs, and priests. These meetings also include songs on anti-caste heroes such as B.R. Ambedkar and Jotirao Phuley. Community organizations and social organizations have intense discussions on questions such as the following: Who is Mahishasura? Who is Ravana? Why are their deaths celebrated every year? The youth, in particular, have started raising these questions with community elders, leaders, researchers, and other persons with knowledge of community aspects. These young men and women from the community went on to read more about their own history as retold from a non-Brahmanical perspective. Reading in groups and sharing what they learnt from these different sources, the young who were educated in these subaltern communities are now seeing these historical figures as freedom fighters against Aryans.

★ ★ ★

Thus, it is quite visible that the subalterns in the metropolis that are part of the intelligentsia have been making efforts to historicize the mythical asuras by reading and re-reading ideologues from the nineteenth and twentieth centuries who have already laid the foundation for such an exercise. In the process of constructing the counterculture, the subalterns in the metropolis and at the periphery have consistently been calling back their heroes of ancient times (native rulers as historical figures) and masters of colonial times (foundational fathers of their identity). The intensity of resistance by the subalterns at the periphery coupled with the rewriting of history by the subalterns in the metropolis seems necessary and, thus, the processes were simultaneously carried out. For building a stronger counterculture that can counter the mainstream, one has to rely on the aggressive historicization of the mythical asuras and on giving shape and form to the new subaltern culture that distinguishes itself from the mainstream by eliminating the inbuilt absurdities and supernaturalism. This, subalterns are quite consciously doing, not only in the process of historicizing but also in understanding and revering. This seems to be the main difference between the mainstream culture and the counterculture. Despite being mostly uneducated or kept out of education, the subaltern masses are developing into a rational society that respects the historical more than the mythical. In fact, the subaltern masses are building an exemplary culture that automatically eliminates the irrational or mythical elements. This counterculture will be appropriate for the rational societies of the twenty-first century.

References

Ambedkar, B.R. 2013a. 'Aryans against Aryans'. In *Writings and Speeches of Dr. Babasaheb Ambedkar*, vol. 7. Bombay: Dr. Babasaheb Ambedkar Source Material Publication Committee, 86–101.

———. 2013b. 'Racial Difference as the Theory of Untouchability'. In *Writings and Speeches of Dr. Babasaheb Ambedkar*, vol. 7. Bombay: Dr. Babasaheb Ambedkar Source Material Publication Committee.

———. 2013d. 'The Riddle of the Shudras'. In *Writings and Speeches of Dr. Babasaheb Ambedkar*, vol. 7. Bombay: Dr. Babasaheb Ambedkar Source Material Publication Committee, 21–37.

Arafath, P.K. Yasser. 2017. 'Onam, Mahabali and the Narrow Imaginations of the Right'. *The Wire*, 4 September.

George, Godly M. 2017. 'Adivasis Dance Today: The First Ever FIR Filed Against Durga Puja'. *Countercurrents.org*, 29 September.

Neelakantan, Anand. 2015. *Asura: Tales of the Vanquished: The Story of Ravana and His People*. Mumbai: Platinum Press.

Periyar, E.V. Ramasamy. 2005. 'Ramayan: A True Reading'. In *Collected Works of Periyar E.V.R.*, 603–660. Chennai: The Periyar Self-Respect Propaganda Institution.

Phuley, Jotirao. 2008. *Slavery*. New Delhi: Critical Quest.

Ranjan, Pramod. 2016. 'Facing Demons: The Reclamation of Mahishasura as a Heroic Figure', *The Caravan*, 1 March.

Sachau, Edward C., ed. 2003. *Alberuni's India*, vols I and II. New Delhi: Indialog Publications.

Stephen, Cynthia. 2016. 'Mahishasur in the North and Ravan Leela in the South'. *Forward Press*, 13 October.

Varghese P.J. 2016. 'India: Controversy Over Kerala Onam and Vamana Jayanti'. *Mainstream*, vol. 54, no. 44, 22 October.

9

Cultural Rights in the Context of Ambedkarite Social Justice

JOHN CLAMMER

Dr B.R. Ambedkar's life work is, and rightly so, closely associated with his tireless work towards uplifting the Dalit community, his work as an economist, and his major role in the drafting of the Constitution of independent India. Consequently, he is seen as largely political in nature. However, there are, in fact, many other dimensions to his activities, writings, and speeches. A careful reading of his collected works shows how his thoughts ranged all these issues, but it also provides evidence of his deep concern with questions of religion and culture. When discussing the liberation of excluded communities (in the Indian context, largely Dalits and tribal people), the question of culture is often missed out as it belongs to broader fields of study such as development studies. But reading Ambedkar's works, it is evident that although this was, apparently, not a central issue for him, it is implicit in many of his statements and in the form of the Constitution itself. In other words, the fight against the exclusion, marginalization, and denigration of the Dalit community, in particular, involved for Ambedkar issues of dignity, identity, recognition of cultural equality, and empowerment, in all senses of the word. Reading 'between the lines', as it were, of Ambedkar's thoughts, the questions of cultural recognition and dignity loom large. This essay however is not mainly an exposition of Ambedkar's comments on culture, but, rather, it uses them as a point of departure to show how such issues are integral to any comprehensive understanding of human rights and social justice, and how they derive, in a direct way, from Ambedkar's writing and speeches. His core concern, it seems to me, was precisely that India could never fully be a democracy, fully free or fully equal (despite the provisions of the Constitution), without a holistic conception and practise of full inclusion and respect for all the constituent cultures, castes, religions, and ethnic groups that make up the immensely complex Indian society. It is important then to draw on these ideas and consider how they can be developed. I would certainly argue that there can be no greater legacy for Dr Ambedkar than to see the influence of his ideas continuing to profoundly shape the present debates about rights and their implementation.

Framing Ambedkar: Human Rights and Cultural Rights

The notion of human rights is, of course, familiar. The Universal Declaration of Human Rights (UDHR), promulgated by the United Nations (UN) in 1948 in the aftermath of the horrors of the Second World War, is rightly seen as one of the most important documents of the post-war international legal framework. The UN itself was then only three years old, and while the UDHR is unfortunately often honoured for stepping into the breach, the UDHR is only highly significant in that, in principle, it binds signatory governments to a body of rules that ensure fundamental rights to all social categories. Thus, it provides a document against which one can measure the actual performance of governments in the field of rights and also one which enables activists, minorities of various kinds, those wronged, and those concerned with the true implementation of international treaties to hold governments and other public and private agencies to account (and India is, of course, a signatory). But the UDHR, written in the aftermath of war and its consequent atrocities (by a UN that was much smaller and less geographically and culturally representative than it is at present), pays little direct attention to cultural rights—these are only implied in the provisions relating to the rights to self-determination, free expression, and freedom of religion. This lack was soon evident and the gap has been, to some extent, filled by the subsequent International Covenant on Civil and Political Rights and the

International Covenant on Economic, Social, and Cultural Rights. However, while these have all moved in the right direction and while it has become increasingly obvious that neither development nor sustainability are adequately fulfilled without close attention to rights, the notion of cultural rights is still left vague in international legal instruments.

As a result, some additional attempts have been made to expand the notion of cultural rights, particularly in the covenants generated by the United Nations Educational, Scientific, and Cultural Organization (UNESCO), the UN body specifically concerned with culture. This expansion has been embodied in a number of UNESCO declarations including, most significantly, the 2001 Universal Declaration on Cultural Diversity and its successor, the 2005 UNESCO Convention on the Protection and Promotion of the Diversity of Cultural Expressions. Preceding and between these there were promulgated a number of more specific declarations relating to culture, including those relating to world heritage protection, illicit transport and export of cultural property, and underwater heritage, as well as broader declarations such as the Declaration of Principles on Tolerance (1995) and the Declaration on the Responsibility of the Present Generations Towards Future Generations (1997). While UNESCO's promulgation of principles of cultural toleration and preservation, and promotion of cultural diversity is laudable, problems remain, such as its inability to actually enforce or police any of these declarations, its use of vague and rather essentialist definitions of culture, and its weak assumption that governments will indeed actively put into practice the commitments that they have formally agreed to by signing various UNESCO and UN declarations. In other words, the extension of human rights into the realm of cultural rights remains weak. But here, drawing from Ambedkar's works, I would argue that cultural rights are essential to ensure the dignity and recognition of diverse cultural expressions, and that social justice requires political and economic access and equality, possibility of free cultural expression, encouragement of creativity and imagination, and access to cultural resources across all social groups. This implies the notion of cultural rights, a concept that I will now try to unpack in more detail, as it has evolved post-Ambedkar.

Yvonne Donders defines cultural rights as the following: 'Cultural rights can be broadly defined as human rights that directly promote and protect cultural interests of individuals and communities and that are meant to advance their capacity to preserve, develop and change their cultural identity' (Donders 2015, 117). In fact, in the title of her essay, she does not refer to cultural rights, but to what she terms 'cultural human rights'. The concern of UNESCO regarding the preservation of cultural diversity is very understandable given that local cultures around the world, for various reasons, are indeed threatened by censorship, suppression, exclusion from mainstream discourses (such as art history), and erosion. Additionally, they face the impact of globalization and the spread of almost universally accessible monocultures, such as Hollywood, and forms of mass culture and popular culture propagated by the mainstream media. An important step, then, is the recognition of cultural rights as an important aspect of human rights.

There are many reasons that can be advanced to support this position. For example, in development studies, the realization has grown that a purely instrumentalist approach to culture, insofar as culture is discussed at all, while significant up to a point, is severely limited. Naturally, any wise development policy needs to be compatible with the culture into which it is to be introduced,. However, even in areas such as healthcare and agriculture, to limit culture to such a subordinate role as to simply see it as a mechanism for inserting pre-determined development policies is to profoundly underestimate its significance. For culture is not something that is simply 'added on' to other more economic approaches of development, it is the 'water' in which human beings swim—it determines our use of language, our patterns of eating and sleeping, our consumer choices, our attitudes to nature, our sports and leisure pursuits, the nature of our preferred housing, our costumes and hairstyles, art, music, theatre, and many other aspects of daily life. Indeed, it essentially constitutes daily life. Even economics is rooted in culture, for example, in terms of what we value and how we express that sense of value in material and immaterial labour. This not only points to a much richer concept of culture than acknowledged in development studies, but also suggests that it is both a source of pride, identity, and dignity. As UNESCO and the United Nations Development Agency (UNDP) have begun to recognize, a significant aspect of livelihood and, in many cases a route out of poverty, is encapsulated in the notion of the 'creative economy' (UNESCO and UNDP 2013), an insight that points not only to 'culture and development', but equally to the 'development of culture'.

Such an approach, recognizing that culture is an essential part of the human enterprise, has yet further implications. Any viable concept of sustainability, particularly one that pushes for a future of fulfilment and civilization rather than simple survival, must include thought on cultural futures. Indeed, the argument can be made that it is our culture that has got us into our current planetary crisis and, therefore, we must create a more sustainable, just, and ecologically responsible one if we as a species are to have a future at all (Clammer 2016). Any social future must include our cultural activities, expressive arts, architecture, games, music, and fashions. It has long been perceived in the older 'human needs' approach to development that human life requires not only food, shelter, and clothing, but that it also has aesthetic, cultural, and leisure needs, requires contact with nature, and desires opportunities to express creativity in whatever manner was appropriate to a particular time and space. This implies need for a holistic approach to social policy that includes all these dimensions, and which recognizes that cultural diversity and vitality is as significant for human futures as is biodiversity. For much the same reasons, monocultures of any kind are fragile, diversity creates strength, and embedded in human cultures and their languages is a huge body of knowledge and experience, which, like species in nature, once lost cannot be recovered.

Cultural Rights and Cultural Activism

The notion of activism is often associated with overtly political activity. But in practice, the concept can have much wider application. If we can agree that cultural rights are an integral part of human rights in their broadest sense (and that without them, humans would certainly be condemned to a sterile and one-dimensional lifestyle), then it becomes our duty to promote them, especially as these rights pertain to the ignored or undervalued cultures of excluded groups. There is, in other words, a need for cultural activism, which can take many forms. These can include the active promotion of indigenous cultural production and its incorporation into wider cultural discourses. For example, tribal art was long neglected in India until its recent 'discovery', its documentation in books and monographs, and its promotion and sale in commercial galleries. Most conventional histories of art ignore tribal art completely or relegate it to the category of 'craft'. Much the same can be said of Australian aboriginal art, which is now regarded as extraordinary in its aesthetic qualities but was likewise marginalized until it was again 'discovered' in the relatively recent past. Its discovery has had the effect of stimulating artistic production to the point that now such art is considered valuable and collectable and has begun to appear in galleries and museums around the world, not just in ethnographic ones. Such activities not only promote 'creative industries' (which face the ever-present danger of their products simply becoming more commodities), but can also stimulate imagination in unexpected and fresh ways. The Kolkata-based artist, Amitava Bhattacharya, and his sculptress wife, Anita, have worked among tribal and poor communities in West Bengal, Koraput (Orissa), and Madhya Pradesh, with tribal women and children and displace Tibetan craftsmen in particular. They have found that exposure to art with the possibility of producing it (including jewellery) and the exploration of new designs has not only had positive economic effects, but has also triggered imagination and undiscovered talents of multiple kinds—cultural practice is leading to liberation (Bhattacharya 2012). Other measures include extending legal and copyright protections to indigenous cultural products and resisting illegitimate cultural appropriation, pressuring governments to actually and actively meet their obligations under the various UN and UNESCO declarations and covenants to which they have put their signatures, ensuring that human rights are balanced by the corresponding responsibilities, and working to ensure that a broad concept and practice of human rights is adhered to in a comprehensive way.

There are very concrete outcomes to such cultural activism. The right to, and practice of, authentic cultural expression has a positive feedback loop to the ideals and reality of dignity, creativity (which once unleashed can take many forms), and social imagination as well as the endogenous development of the culture in question. Such qualities are the basis for empowerment, which again may take political forms as well as strengthen senses of identity and self-worth, and ones ability to imagine changing the world. But at this point it is necessary to reflect on the concept of culture. In a sense, all cultures are equal: Aboriginal culture combines material simplicity with remarkable development of complex kinship patterns, art, mythology, and geographical and ecological knowledge. Its lower levels of technology do not make it 'primitive'. But, at the same time, any given culture may contain elements that are dysfunctional to a harmonious social environment or personal freedom—slavery, cannibalism, female genital mutilation. But they also evolve. As Michel Foucault has documented, punishment in the West has evolved over the last few centuries from brutal public executions, torture, and mutilation to a regime of incarceration, rehabilitation, and 'care for the soul'. No culture is totally static, and in the context of globalization, almost all cultures come into contact with one another. One important aspect of cultural activism is the nurturing of minority or excluded cultures, not only with the aim of representing them on a larger stage ('giving voice' as it were), but also to persuade the members of those cultures of the real value of their cultural expressions, whether those be visual, performative, or literary, or take some unusual form that falls between the categories of conventional cultural analysis (tattooing, pottery, weaving, house-painting, the arts of the handicapped, or 'art brut' or 'outsider art'—produced by the inmates of prisons or asylums). Many societies without caste systems have their own 'Dalits'—groups excluded socially, such as the Burakumin of Japan, or psychologically, such as the handicapped who are denied a full place within society and its institutions, opportunities for work, and possibilities of expression.

Amartya Sen and Martha Nussbaum have argued persuasively for what they term a 'capabilities' approach to development and related social issues. By this they mean an approach that identifies and nurtures the possibilities, resources, and talents to be found in virtually any community (Nussbaum 2011; Sen 2009). Although Nussbaum speaks of 'creating capabilities', I prefer to think of it as discovering them, lending them dignity, and helping to provide outlets for the capacities not unleashed and the latent energies and abilities. These abilities have been crushed by neglect; social and caste oppression and non-recognition; historical forces of colonialism; slavery or forced migration; and invisibility in the eyes of the mainstream media, cultural critics, and cultural historians. Nussbaum has taken the argument even further, suggesting that the encouragement of an active and accessible culture is a prerequisite for democracy (Nussbaum 2012). This certainly accords with

Ambedkar's position that formal democracy is hollow unless filled with the reality of autonomy, equal access to resources, and 'the recognition of rights' and 'voice' not occurring just once every four or five years, without which 'democracy' simply becomes the tyranny of be the majority, or worse, the power vehicle of an influential minority within that majority (Ambedkar 1987).

History has shown that many social movements (feminism, the environmental movement, peace movements, and so forth) are rooted in culture. Their ability to mobilize people to action goes far beyond their capacity to mobilize political resources, as vital as those may be. Rather, to touch the wellsprings of motivation, they have found it necessary to find the deep cultural levels—values, attitudes to life, and conceptions of the future—that impel people to action and rouse them from passive acceptance of their current lot. Similarly, many cultural movements prove to be also and equally social movements. In the European context, the Situationist International movement combined art, utopian ideas about urban reform, radical ideas about economics, and fresh ideas about individual and collective freedoms and lifestyle possibilities into a new configuration (Wark 2011). It is not surprising that most revolutionary movements (in China, the Soviet Union, and Cuba, for example) have utilized the arts—visual art (especially poster art and murals), theatre, dance, poetry, opera, and music—to propagate their goals. Few people are emotionally moved by propaganda, but many are by performance. As the world falls further into the grip of globalization, new forms of cultural activism become necessary to combat its negative side, and it is often though cultural means that such opposition is most effective (Starr 2000). Globalization, and the cultural homogeny that it tends to produce, is often opposed by the rise of localism—the revitalization of local cultures, economies, and forms of life. Many minority groups have discovered that a dialectic can be created between the universalism of human rights and local identities. An example of this are the Ainu people of northern Japan who have successfully struggled to have their identity as a national minority recognized by the State and for their cultural expressions (art, carving, dance, language, ritual, and religion) to be recognized as distinctive and a valuable component of what is actually a multi-ethnic state, despite Japanese imaginings of homogeneity.

There is an anthropological tendency to see cultures as 'pure', and hence beyond criticism, especially by outsiders. But such a position cannot be maintained in the face of obvious social injustice. Where a group is excluded and its cultural expressions denigrated or ignored, it is clearly the role of the cultural activist to protest to draw attention to this process of marginalization and to help the community formulate good arguments about why the culture should be recognized and respected. As suggested above, all cultures are dynamic. They change with the evolution of their internal processes and creativity, and through contact with other cultures and larger forces of globalization. To encourage existing cultures to move towards embodying rights, responsibilities, and social justice is now a goal. While this may not have been possible in the past, it is now a priority if a sustainable and desirable future is to be created for all humanity and for other creatures that share the same biosphere as we do.

Cultural Rights and Social Justice: Re-discovering Ambedkar

The multidimensional nature of social exclusion requires equally holistic remedies. These must include the struggle for cultural rights, cultural freedom, and recognition. Tragically, widespread social exclusion persists in the world despite decades of 'development'. In fact, this 'development' has led to new forms of social exclusion, such as the advent of the welfare state in many countries, and new categories of the oppressed being generated by globalization, and soon if not already, by climate change (Bauman 2004). Against these tendencies, a number of bulwarks must be built: the non-negotiable nature of human and cultural rights and the obligation of governments who are signatories to the various rights conventions to absolutely uphold them. This encourages moves towards a 'maximal' not minimal understanding of sustainability—one that looks to the future enrichment of human life and the biosphere, not merely its maintenance; the development of culture, not only as a means to other ends, but as an end in itself; the recognition that there are many forms of aesthetics, and that the standards of taste of one culture are not necessarily those of another. Culture is a site of struggle since it defines the parameters of world views and with them attitudes to nature, to gender, to equality, to social roles, and to legitimate modes of expression. While it defines what is, it also points to the future—what may be, and what human imagination can envisage and hopefully bring about when those cultural futures are humane, creative, and equal.

When one turns back to the collected works of Ambedkar one finds the seeds of all these themes: his concern with caste, with the Muslim population of India, with women, and his huge, if ultimately unsuccessful, efforts to have the Hindu code bills passed by Parliament. This would ensure the enshrining of basic rights in the Indian Constitution, and as Gail Omvedt aptly puts it 'the creation of social equality and cultural integration in a society held enslaved for so long by the unique tyrannies of caste and varna ideology' (Omvedt 2004, xiv). Caste itself has cultural roots rather than economic ones (although its effects on its victims and beneficiaries may well be economic). The routes that Ambedkar pursued in his search for these outcomes were many:

(a) he felt deep concern over education and the creation of educational opportunities for the underprivileged (something he had himself experienced);
(b) he focused on identification and eradication of social evils (what contemporary social scientists are now calling 'social suffering' [Kleinman, Das, and Lock 1997]);
(c) he felt concern over religion (and hence, eventually, over religious conversion) as the source of many social evils (in particular untouchability) as well as a source of relief from such evils and a source of human rights;
(d) he was committed to democracy, rationality, and the threefold values of the French revolution—liberty, equality, and fraternity;
(e) he contemplated over the use of poetry as well as propaganda in struggles against casteism and class and the role of such radically egalitarian figures as Kabir (Omvedt 2004, 75; Hess 2016); and
(f) he theorized about the idea of the nation as a project and not yet as an accomplished fact (something that it could not be while it harboured deep inequalities and mechanisms of exclusion in its practice and ideologies).

All these issues are as topical today as they were in Ambedkar's time, not only in India, but wherever social exclusion, cultural denigration, and inequalities on the basis of gender, race, or religion existed. The message is, unfortunately, timeless, since the *conditions* that generated Ambedkar's thought and practice still persist, and his teachings will remain relevant until they disappear. Among the many levels of struggle to make this happen is the cultural: the pursuit of dignity, identity, expression, creativity, and sustainability, which together must form the basis of any future society worth living in.

But if the *conditions* still exist, so do the aspects of Ambedkar's writings and practice that touch upon the issues of exclusion and social injustice. His writings, like those of his great 'rival', Gandhi's, were rarely theoretical writings. They arose out of the very real struggles that Ambedkar actively involved himself in for the whole of his adult life. His well-known points of contention with Gandhi—over Congress policies towards separate electorates for Dalits as well as for Muslims and Scheduled Tribes, over industrialization as opposed to the promotion of the 'village republics' favoured by Gandhi, and, of course, over the major issue of whether 'harijans' were part of Hinduism (Gandhi's position) or not (Ambedkar's position)—help us see the larger philosophy behind the particular points of difference (Masselos 1987). Ambedkar was, of course, a highly educated individual, a professionally trained economist with higher degrees from Columbia University and the London School of Economics and Political Science (LSE), as well as a training in law. I have often thought it symbolically interesting that the LSE is in a gloomy side street just off the major thoroughfare of the Strand in London, on which are situated the Inns of Court, just around the corner from the School. Ambedkar and Gandhi must certainly have walked the same London pavements in pursuit of not-dissimilar goals, whatever their later differences. But the divergences tell us much about Ambedkar's thinking. And while the Ambedkar–Gandhi disputes are a well-documented subject in scholarship on and in India, less attention has been paid to Ambedkar's thinking on culture, and it is to this that I will now turn.

As we have noted, Ambedkar was a highly trained and sophisticated economist. Although, despite his intense interest in highly practical matters—such as water and irrigation—late in his career (Thorat 1998), he is mostly associated with his directly political work and of course with his major role in the framing of the Indian Constitution. There is little evidence (perhaps unfortunately for later history) that Ambedkar had any professional relations or discussions with the leading Gandhian economist J.C. Kumarappa, a neglected but, in my view, important figure who today might be seen as one of the pioneers of sustainability as reflected in his concept of 'the economy of permanence'. While Gandhi himself did not systematically pursue the economic implications of his thought, it was essentially Kumarappa who took up those ideas and developed them into a philosophy and practice, one very much concerned with economic justice as its motivation and goal (for a recent study, see Govindu and Malghan 2016). It is, of course, pure speculation, but one wonders what new directions of thought and possible alternative futures might have arisen for India if these two seminal thinkers had met and exchanged ideas.

There are also important parallels between Ambedkar's thinking and that emerging in the black liberation movements gaining strength in the post–Second World War period in the United States of America (USA). In 1959, three years after Ambedkar's death, Martin Luther King visited India for a month at the invitation of Nehru and the Gandhi Smarak Nidhi, and with the support of the Quakers in India and the USA (for a detailed study of his itinerary, see Bryant 2018). Of course, it cannot be said whether King and Ambedkar would have met had the latter still been alive. King was evidently aware of caste and its parallels with the excluded position of blacks in the USA because on 12 February he gave a talk at Ramjas College of the University of Delhi on the subject. But a story is also told of his visit to a school for Dalit children in Trivandrum on 22 February where the head teacher introduced him as a 'fellow untouchable from the USA', a designation that, at the time, affronted King. It was only later, after his return to the USA, that he admitted in one of his sermons that indeed Untouchable was a good designation for equally excluded and denigrated black people in that country. It is quite possible that King knew of Ambedkar's name and work, not only because the latter had lived and studied in the USA and had corresponded with W.E.B. Du Bois, the leading black American thinker and activist of the time, but also because his 1945 book, which was highly critical of Gandhi and the Congress, had been published in the USA under the title *People at Bay*, a title modified from its Indian original *What Gandhi and Congress Have Done to the Untouchables* (available now as Ambedkar 1990: vol. 9). That book is a bitter attack on Gandhi and the Congress, and had King known of it, it may have dissuaded him from meeting its author, since the main purpose of his visit was to pay his respect to Gandhi who he saw as not only the prophet of non-violence, but also as the leader of a massive and finally successful movement of civil disobedience against colonial rule. But one important link between Ambedkar and King was that both saw organized industrial labour as a major tool of liberation for Dalits and blacks respectively. The felt it would not only draw them into urban and more technologically advanced forms of work, but also giving them collective bargaining power, something hard to achieve on the basis of trying to raise caste or race consciousness alone—important, but not in itself enough to trigger transformative social movements. Economic liberation was then, for both men, a condition for cultural, social, and political liberation.

The basis of Ambedkar's work, its constant theme, was his struggle against social evils, not simply, or even mainly, against liberation from colonial rule. The reason for this is that, despite his, in many ways, economic radicalism, Ambedkar saw rightly that it would be social and cultural causes that would promote true transformation: roads, bridges, canals and the like were certainly of immense value, but they in themselves would not create the 'revolution'—the abolition of caste, legalization of intermarriage, changes in family and inheritance laws, and the valuation of local and minority cultures—these were the necessary preconditions for genuine change (Ambedkar 1989: vol. 6, 233–4). So it is important to remember that while Ambedkar was a 'developmentalist and believer in progress' (Omvedt 2004, 15), a champion of educational reform, and an opponent of the idea that rural India was the repository of the best values. This thinking had a sociocultural base, something enshrined not only in his seminal contributions to the formulation of the Constitution, but expressed in many other ways, such as his (ultimately unsuccessful) attempts to get the Hindu code bills passed, a law that would have revolutionized the traditional Hindu family laws of succession, inheritance, and women's rights. His arguments for this show clearly his unyielding stance on principles of equality, rights, and fraternity (Ambedkar 1995: vol. 14, 14). His rejection of the earlier Congress doctrine of political reform before social reform shows clearly his stand on these issues, which is not surprising perhaps given his own experiences of discrimination and poverty that had marked his early years and the period when he was trying, despite his very advanced educational qualifications, to establish himself professionally in Bombay and beyond.

It is in this context that Ambedkar's views on religion can be fruitfully examined. I have asked myself whether his conversion to Buddhism was merely a strategic move or one motivated by genuine admiration for the religion. I think, without doubt, the latter. His struggles with Hinduism and his rhetorical question—'the Hindu religion is ours or not?'—his flirtation with Sikhism, and his final decision in favour of Buddhism were all very considered moves, accompanied by extensive reading, and, in the case of Buddhism, a trip to Burma to seek advice and support there. Ambedkar himself wrote on Buddhism and it is clear that in seeking a new religious identity outside the casteism of Hinduism, he was seeking one that embodied his ideals of equality and fraternity (Jondhale and Beltz 1998). In an address given in 1956 on Marxism and Buddhism to the World Buddhist Congress, he suggested that while many of the propositions of Marxism were still valid, the Marxist system as a whole had failed to address the fundamental existential issues of human life, and that it was only in Buddhism that the ideals of the French Revolution—the famous triad of liberty, equality, and fraternity—could be realized (Ambedkar 1987). Insofar as Hinduism was, in his view, the origin and maintaining force of the inequality and exclusion faced by the Dalit community, it was not only necessary to seek a new, non-Hindu religious identity, but specifically one that identified with the fundamental social and cultural values that he espoused. Democracy for Ambedkar was not simply a matter of voting, or even of the fair distribution of seats and protection of weaker sections of the electorate from political colonization and domination by the more powerful sectors. It was one that might be called a 'holistic' notion—one permeating all strata of life and cultural expression. This was expressed in his views on access to basic civil rights for Untouchables, such as free access to water tanks and wells, to public spaces and public transport, and to education and to employment and social contact, such that caste Hindus would eat with and admit to their homes, as guests as well as servants, members of the hitherto Untouchable community. These views were further reinforced by his own detailed researches into the origins of caste—work that, even with his intensive work as minister of labour at the time, resulted in two books published in 1947 and 1948 (now reprinted together in Ambedkar 1990: vol. 7).

Two major illustrations of this philosophy can be found in Ambedkar's struggle for the Hindu code bills, which would have greatly extended liberties to Indian women, and of course his role in the framing of the Constitution. Here again there is an interesting parallel with Martin Luther King, since both saw their respective constitutions as enshrining absolutely basic rights and liberties that were universal and beyond negotiation. It is not insignificant that he named the last political party that he formed the 'Republican Party', inspired by its north American counterpart. His struggles in both cases illustrate his fear that, in his famous phrase, Independent India would be 'building a castle on a dung heap'. That noxious heap could only be removed by adhering in practice to the principles of equality, access, and dignity enshrined in the Constitution, foremost among which was the removal of the scandal of untouchability. The foundation could not possibly be the shifting and decaying dung heap, but the observation of basic rights, the human rights embodied in the UDHR, and the cultural right to recognition and respect for all the communities of India, tribal, Dalit, Christian, Muslim, or whatever. For culture is a site of struggle, not only for recognition, but because it points to what can be as well as what is. It is the source of social imagination—the ability to imagine alternative futures and the routes through which they can be realized. Whatever his practical achievements and failures, Bhimrao Ramji Ambedkar stands as one of the great social imaginaries, not only for India, but for every situation in which freedoms are denied, dignity withheld, and inequality justified, and for the great values of the French Revolution for which he stood throughout his career undermined and distorted—liberty, equality, and perhaps above all, genuine fraternity.

References

Ambedkar, B.R. 1979–2003. *Dr. Babasaheb Ambedkar: Writings and Speeches*, edited by Vasant Moon. 17 Volumes. Mumbai: Education Department, Government of Maharashtra.

Bauman, Zygmunt. 2004. *Wasted Lives: Modernity and Its Outcasts*. Cambridge: Polity Press.

Bhattacharya, Amitava. 2012. *A Diary of an Art Master*. With an Introduction by John Clammer. Kolkata: Privately Printed.

Bryant, Aaron. 2018. 'Democracy beyond the Borders: Martin Luther King, Jr. and his Tour of India, 1959'. In *Visual Histories of South Asia*, edited by Annamaria Motrescu-Mayes and Marcus Banks. New Delhi: Primus Books.

Clammer, John. 2016. *Cultures of Transition and Sustainability*. Basingstoke and New York: Palgrave Macmillan.

Donders, Yvonne. 2015. 'Cultural Human Rights and the UNESCO Convention: More than Meets the Eye?' In *Globalization, Culture and Development: The UNESCO Convention on Cultural Diversity*, edited by Christiaan De Beukalaer, MiikkaPyykkonen, and J.P. Singh. Basingstoke and New York: Palgrave Macmillan, 117–31.

Govindu, Venu Madhav, and Deepak Malghan. 2016. *The Web of Freedom: J.C. Kumarappa and Gandhi's Struggle for Economic Justice*. New Delhi: Oxford University Press.

Hess, Linda. 2016. *Bodies of Song: Kabir Oral Traditions and Performative Worlds in North India*. New Delhi: Permanent Black.

Jondhale, Surendra, and Johannes Beltz, eds. 1992. *Reconstructing the World: Dr. Ambedkar's Understanding of Buddhism*. New Delhi: Oxford University Press.

Kleinman, Arthur, Veena Das, and Margaret Lock, ed. 1997. *Social Suffering*. Berkeley and London: University of California Press.

Masselos, Jim, ed. 1987. *Struggling and Ruling: The Indian National Congress 1885–1985*. Bangalore: Sterling Publishers.

Nussbaum, Martha. 2011. *Creating Capabilities: The Human Development Approach*. Cambridge, MA: Belknap Press of Harvard University Press.

———. 2012. *Not for Profit: Why Democracy Needs the Humanities*. Princeton and London: Princeton University Press.

Omvedt, Gail. 2004. *Ambedkar: Towards an Enlightened India*. Gurgaon: Penguin Books India.

Sen, Amartya. 2009. *The Idea of Justice*. Cambridge, MA: Belknap Press.

Starr, Amory. 2000. *Naming the Enemy: Anti-Corporate Movements Confront Globalization*. London and New York: Zed Books.

Thorat, Sukhadeo. 1998. *Ambedkar's Role in Economic Planning and Water Policy*. New Delhi: Shipra Publications.

UNESCO and UNDP. 2013. *Creative Economy Report 2013*. New York: UNDP; and Paris: UNESCO.

Wark, McKenzie. 2011. *The Beach beneath the Street: The Everyday Life and Glorious Times of the Situationist International*. London and New York: Verso.

10

Education in a Hierarchical Culture

RAJU SAKTHIVEL

India is one of the leading players in the information technology (IT) field. It is claimed that India's scientific and IT manpower is a source of envy in the international arena. India is also acclaimed as the largest democracy with socialistic leanings. However, India also has many dubious distinctions which are hardly noticed and problematized. One of the painful distinctions of India is that it has the largest number of children who do not have access to elementary or primary education (minimum eight years of schooling). According to the mid-term appraisal report of the 10th Five-Year Plan, 28.5 per cent of children (that is, 42 million) up to the age of 14 were out of school during the year 2001 (Planning Commission 2002a). India also has one of the largest numbers of child labourers in the world: 125 million (Bajpai and Goyal 2004, 11). Almost all of these children belong to the discriminated castes of India. As these children grow, they will add to the illiterate adult population of India. Unsurprisingly, the already existing adult illiterate population of India by international standards is disturbingly high. As most illiterate parents do not have political and social power, the likelihood of their children missing out on literacy is near certain. Moreover, if children are not sent to a proper school, we find them in a number of improper places such as involved in beggary, child labour, compelled to enter brothels, and so on.[1] India,

---

[1] See Weiner (1991) for details.

once the land of enlightenment, seems to be caught in the vicious vortex of illiteracy.

The denial of free and compulsory schooling to children amounts to robbing them of the charms of their childhood and the hope for a meaningful future. In a modern society, 'literacy is no longer a specialism, but a pre-condition of all the specialisms' (Gellner 1983, 142), to acquire membership of the productive roles and resources of social life and to safeguard oneself from the scourges of exploitation or ill-treatment. From an economic perspective, today's children are the future 'human capital' as they contribute to the economic growth of the country. Education creates new occupations and permits mobility across occupations. Industry demands constant upgradation of existing and, often, production of skilled manpower. The defence and security interest of a nation will be undermined if the most powerful weapons of a country are dumb and illiterate. Education makes communication possible between social groups. Communication in turn produces social intercourse leading to the development of a sense of belonging among various social groups, thereby binding them into a cohesive society. It is essential to both individual and social efficiency (Dewey [1916] 1997). The cultivation of a national spirit and the construction of a nation cannot be achieved if education is kept away from the reach of the vast majority of the people. As modern democracy calls for citizens' rights and participation, education has a vital role in making the working of the democracy meaningful. Choice of profession, a key feature of democracy, is determined by education. Yet, education is determined by the existing power structures in society. Power exerts itself in many forms. Traditional beliefs constitute the bastions of power, and thus discriminations. Apart from representation in and share of direct political power, discriminations based on gender, race, and caste can be dissolved to a greater extent by socialization of the investment in human capital, for the investment will break the occupational rigidity and privileges—the control mechanism of traditional powers. But the investment in this form of human capital is meagre. Schultz observed that 'there are many hindrances to the free choice of professions. Racial and religious discriminations are still widespread. ... Such purposeful interference keeps the investment in this form of human capital substantially below its optimum' (Schultz 1961, 13–14).

Many industrialized countries did, however, adhere to the need for universal literacy of the members of the political community called the nation state and have achieved compulsory primary education. Newly developing economies have also taken primary education seriously to overcome traditional barriers, for its negligence has great implications both for the society and the State. Unfortunately, the performance of India in the field of primary education is quite disappointing when compared with the other developing countries. A study of the United Nations Organization (UNO) reveals,

> Many countries—including Chile, China, Cuba, the Republic of Korea, Singapore, the Slovak Republic, Sri Lanka, Tunisia, and Uruguay—have built education systems in which primary completion is universal, and many have made progress in improving learning. Most of these countries are middle-income countries today, but many achieved universal primary completion when they were at the same stage of development as today's poorer countries. (UNO 2006, 46)

On the other hand, it is quite revealing to note that China, which had started with almost same level of primary school enrolment in the late 1940s, has over the decades 'far outperformed India in terms of school enrolment ratios and on indices of the efficiency of primary education' (Rao, Cheng, and Narain 2003, 153). Despite this dismal performance in primary education, India has focused its energies on developing higher education, though a mere 6 per cent of its population of the age of 18–23 is in higher educational institutions.[2]

As a corollary of this policy negligence, the fiscal intervention of the State in terms of allocation of resources to primary education has been meagre. The Education Policy of 1968 envisaged that public expenditure on education as a proportion of GDP would increase to 6 per cent over time. By 2002, even after 34 years of the policy pronouncement and despite the achievement of six-fold increase of GDP, the

> public expenditure on education increased from 1.68% to only 4.02% by 2002. During the 1990s, after the economic reform policies were

---

[2] See Thorat (2006) for the disparities relating to the access to higher education. The aforementioned study reveals that the access for SCs/STs and OBCs is very less when compared to their population. This is the pioneering study recognizing the inter-caste disparities in higher education. The report is crucial for it comes from the University Grants Commission, the apex body governing higher education in India.

introduced, public expenditure on education declined from above 4% in 1990–91 to about 3.95% in 1998–99. Thus, raising public expenditure on education to a level of 6% of GDP has remained a national commitment [sic] for nearly forty years. (Planning Commission 2002b)

Many studies have found that primary education has received less fiscal support than higher education (Rao, Cheng, and Narain 2003). This is all the more intriguing given the fact that investment in primary education gives higher social rate of returns than higher education (Gounden 1967).[3]

In other words, in contrast to other developing countries, the Indian state has intervened more in favour of higher education and invested more fiscal resources in higher education than in primary education. To put it symbolically, India has invested more in 'silicon slates' than on 'blackboards' ever since its Independence. This queer situation raises certain questions, such as what informs the policy priority of India; why has India been performing poorly in the field of primary education compared to similar poor countries; why a country such as China, which is comparable to India in size and cultural and linguistic complexities, could move ahead of India; and finally, why has India invested in a thin slice of its population for higher education and not in the vast majority of its children.

This apparent contradiction has been studied. Rao, Cheng, and Narain (2003) attributed the socio-contextual factors in the role of the State in causing cross-country differences in primary schooling. Dreze and Sen (2002, 137) have attributed the State's neglect of primary education to 'the lack of political clout from the illiterate masses'. Further, they observed that not only government authorities but social and political movements as well have neglected the social value of basic education. On the other hand, in a seminal study of the issue of child labour, Weiner (1991) noted that in other countries governing elites were often at the forefront of making primary education compulsory (even where common people opposed it). He also found that the belief systems of State officials and those influential outside the government, and their notions of social order and education as the means of maintaining social differences, were the fundamental reason for the lack of State intervention in the field of primary education.

---

[3] See also Public Report on Basic Education (PROBE) Team (1999).

Weiner's study of the issue is thorough and sincere when compared to many other studies in the field. However, his attention was not on the historical roots of the belief system that still holds sway in the Indian mind. The educational policies of independent India are an extension of the colonial policy, which accommodated the pre-colonial social order. And the castes that inherited power from the British pursued the ideology of Hinduism despite socialist and secular claims. Therefore, as education is the key to social mobility, a sure means to get out of the rut of traditional occupational rigidities, India's caste elites viewed its spread to the masses as a threat to their positions of privilege and power, and felt the need to consolidate their hold by making use of the State resources and power. These ideological fears and anxieties were manifested in fiscal policy as well: the negligence (or denial) of primary education to the masses and concentration on higher education to the dominant castes. Making use of colonial documents and the suppressed or deliberately ignored contemporary voices of the nationalist era, we trace the link between the caste system and education and its repercussions on society, of which child illiteracy is an unmistakable manifestation.

Belief Systems, Education, and Social Structure in India

Indian society is characterized by much diversity in terms of the number of languages spoken, ethnic communities, and various faiths such as Islam, Christianity, and Buddhism. The Constitution of India recognizes equality of all, irrespective of caste, creed, sex, and religion. However, what is so peculiar about the Indian social system is that the social identity of an individual is ascertained by 'caste'—the rank or status under Hinduism accorded to individuals based on the group to which they belong. Even though Islam and Christianity do not recognize the caste system of Hinduism, despite their converts coming from the Hindu social fold, the overtones of caste differentiations get manifested in these religions too. Today, India, thus, has two constitutions. One is the de jure Constitution of India which was promulgated in the wake of the transfer of power from the British. The other is the *Manusmitriti* (Laws of

Manu),[4] the de facto constitution whose cardinal faith is the inexorable inequality of men based on birth.

Chatur Varna: The Hindu Social Order

The caste system is the basis of Indian social relations. It is essentially a feudal, pre-industrial system of governance and hierarchical organization of society based on occupations assigned in advance. It emphasizes the differences between various social groups and is a static, stratified, and immobile system.[5] Bhimrao Ambedkar (1891–1956), the founding father of sociological studies in India, defined caste as 'not merely a division of labor but also a division of laborers. ... It is a hierarchy in which the division of laborers are graded one above the other. ... This division of labor is not spontaneous; it is not based on natural aptitudes'. Further, he observed, 'The division of labor brought about by the caste system is not a division based on choice. Individual sentiment, individual preference has no place in it. It is based on the dogma of predestination' (Ambedkar 1979: vol. 1, 48–9). Under this system, education and the pursuit of business are assigned to certain castes exclusively, to the disadvantage of many. Gandhi, the nationalist leader of Indian National Congress, defended the virtues of hereditary occupations, stating that

> the law of varna [rank of a caste in the Hindu system] teaches us that we have each one of us to earn our bread by following the

---

[4] It should be noted here that the *Manusmriti* was accorded tremendous legal authority and value. It was used as the main source of 'Hindu law' in the courts of law of the East India Company until the famous Indian Penal Code of India was drafted by Lord Macaulay.

[5] See Gellner (1983: Chapter 2 and Figure 1) for a schematic description of social organization in an agrarian society. This has much in common with Manyavur Kanshiram's diagram, though both are independent analyses. The caste/estate system in India came into existence only after the fall of the Buddhist empire (as during the Mauryan, Harsha, and Kanishka Empires which espoused Buddhism as their state religion). In the Buddhist empire the emphasis on education for both men and women was fundamental. The monopoly of education by the clerisy, as in the case of Hinduism, is foreign to Buddhism. (I thank Professor Gyana Aloysius, a pioneering scholar in the field of Buddhism in the British Era, for introducing me to this fascination study of Gellner.) See also Aloysius (1997). (I am also thankful to Ravi Kumar, A. Marx, P. Velsamy, and Kavithasaranam.)

ancestral calling. It defines not our rights but our duties. ... The calling of a Brahman—the spiritual teacher—and a scavenger are equal and their due performance carries equal merit before god. (Omvedt 2004, 71)

Thus foreclosing any role for human agency and progress, Gandhi idealized a static stratified system.

The caste system draws its chief justification from the religious injunctions laid down by Manu, the founder of Hinduism (Bühler 1886). The Hindu religion divides society into four occupational groups based on birth. These are called the *Chatur Varna*—Brahmin, Kshatriya, Vaishya, and Shudra. The first occupational group, the Brahmin, is entitled to education and posts of power and administration in the offices of the rulers. The second occupational group, the Kshatriya, is entitled to bear arms. The third occupational group, the Vaishya, can alone carry on the professions of profit and business. The last occupational group, the Shudra, is meant to perform all menial jobs. Hinduism is, thus, a compulsory collection and compartmentalization of castes into hereditary occupational endogamous groups with differing status in the society. This arbitrary ranking of men as 'high' and 'low' is called 'graded inequality'—'an ascending scale of hatred and a downward scale of contempt [which] indeed could be a perpetual source of conflict' (Jaffrelot 2000, 19).[6] Those who rebelled against this ideology were called *avarna*s (non-believers) and were rendered 'Untouchable'. The Untouchables, also called Dalits (broken or oppressed), are victimized by caste and subjected to all sorts of impediments. The phenomenon of untouchability is a vicious form of social isolation and a most effective control mechanism of the Hindus to perpetuate and protect the caste system. Untouchability is an anti-educational and anti-social project whose political programme is de-schooling, disarmament, dispossession, and disembodiment of the autochthonous Buddhist communities.

[6] See also Ambedkar, *Annihilation of Caste* (1936), reprinted in *Dr. Babasaheb Ambedkar: Writings and Speeches* (Bombay: Government of Maharastra, 1979). For details about the life and work of Ambedkar, see Zelliot (1992); Jaffrelot (2000); Kadam (1991); Omvedt (2004, 2011) to name a few. See Sukhadeo Thorat (1998) and Chellam (2018) for the contributions of Ambedkar in the field of economics and national planning and Constitution making.

Castes in Modern India

Today, the three traditionally dominant castes are interchangeably called 'others' or 'forward castes' and constitute 15 per cent of the population. All the other castes and groups are together called 'Backward Classes' in the Constitution of India. The Shudras are classified as Other Backward Classes (OBC) and make up 54 per cent of the population. The Untouchables are called the Scheduled Castes (SCs), comprising 22.5 per cent, and the Tribal people are known as Scheduled Tribes (STs), 7.5 per cent of the population. According to the report of the Mandal Commission (constituted under the authority of Article 340 of the Constitution of India), submitted to the Parliament of India in 1980, these classes together constitute 85 per cent of the total population of India (Mandal 1980).[7] The SCs constitute the single largest caste, with a population of 220 million. The Backward Classes are backward in educational and social aspects because they are ritually and religiously ineligible for rights to education, freedom of occupation, and pursuit of happiness. They do not have any right to liberty and protection to life. This system of social relations even today underlies the norms that regulate access to resources and the position of the individual and collectives in the society. The International Labour Organization (ILO) observed,

> Caste-based discriminations confine Dalits to occupations associated with their caste ... such as 'manual scavenging'[8] or removal of dead animals. ... Dalits are generally not accepted for any work involving contact for water and food for non-Dalits or entering a non-Dalit residence. ... They are excluded from a wide range of work opportunities in the area of production, processing or sale of food items, domestic work and the provision of certain services in the private and public

---

[7] The Mandal Commission recognized caste-based inequalities as the chief reason for the social and educational backwardness of the majority communities and necessity of introducing affirmative action for their improvement. The recommendation was made to the Government of India in 1980, but was not implemented until 1990.

[8] Manual scavenging is the removal of night soil of the dominant castes, by hand, by the victims of caste system. Eighty per cent of the manual scavengers are women. This practice is imposed and rampant in Rajasthan and other states in India. See the documentary *The Lesser Human Beings* by Dhristy.

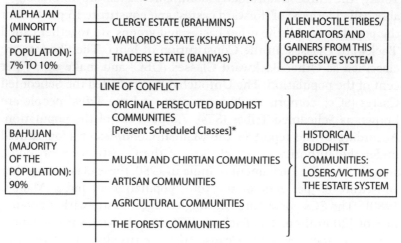

*These communities, the founding pillars of Buddhist civilization, consisted of kings, shramanas (religious teachers of Buddhism), and Bahujan people of various walks of life

Figure 10.1 Hindu Social System

Source: Author.

sectors ... limited access to education, training and resource such as land or credit further impair their equal opportunity for access to the non-caste–based discrimination occupations and decent work'. (ILO 2007: part II, para. 3, 36)[9]

This iniquitous social system has been depicted in Figure 10.1.[10]

Though this iniquitous system has not been critically subjected to economic analysis, Nobel Prize–winning economist Joseph Stiglitz did not fail to notice that while some 250 million people's life is

---

[9] See also Dalit Solidarity Network for the report, available at idsn.org › portfolio-items › idsn-annual-report-2007, last accessed on 22 March 2020.

[10] I am thankful to Boopalan from Chennai, a senior officer in the department of the auditor general, and Gopinathan from Bangalore, a deputy collector turned social engineer leading a popular educational movement in India, for providing me with this framework of Manyavur Kanshiram. See Mane (2006), Kumar (2003). I thank Ashok and Pramod Kureel of the Jawaharlal Nehru University, New Delhi, and Gautama Book Depot, New Delhi.

shining, 'for the other 800 million people of India, the economy has not shone bright at all' (Stiglitz 2006, 26). However, the evil effects of caste system and low equilibrium trap that it engenders has been studied by another Nobel Prize–winning economist, George Akerlof (1976, 599–617). Unfortunately, since Ambedkar (the first economist who studied the national dividend of India and the pernicious impact of caste system on national wealth) the problem of caste has been a matter of eloquently studied silence among the argumentative developmental economists and sociologists of India for reasons best known to them; reasons which need not detain us, however.

Myths of Origin Are Not Innocent

That the majority of the population has no access to resources and are condemned to be the 'servile castes' and that only 15 per cent of the population has become the 'governing castes' is no mere historical accident, nor is it a product of mythicization. The theories of divine origin of caste are later inventions. The myth goes that from the divine body (Purusha Suktam of the Rig Veda) the four varnas have originated. In order of ranking, from the mouth the Brahmin, from the shoulder the Kshatriya, from the stomach the Vaishya, and finally from the legs—the lowest part of the god—the lowly Shudra were born. Such mythologies do not seem to be innocent, given their social function. Walton R. Johnson observes, 'Myths are intimately related to ideology. The social function of ideology is "legitimization of the existing social order, the post-hoc justification of political policies and action, and rationalization of sectional interests"' (Johnson 1982, 234n11).[11] The beneficiaries of caste system, therefore, brush the socio-economic and political realities aside and theorize on the divine origins of caste system. They legitimize caste inequality and the attendant inhuman treatment of the Bahujan (The Great Majority) as 'natural'[12]

---

[11] I gratefully acknowledge my teacher in Chennai, Professor A. Marx, for introducing and sharpening my understanding on the ideological aspects of social, political, and religious systems.

[12] The typical case in point is Mohandas Karamchand Gandhi. He, without any remorse, justified the varna system and was dogmatic that the caste system is perfect and each should follow their ancestors' callings. Further, Gandhi justified that as each part of the body does its duty for the

and insist on endogamous practice so as to ensure the operation of hereditary law of occupations assigned to the different castes.

As opposed to this, Ambedkar argued that the theories of castes have taken 'caste very lightly as though a breath has made it. ... It is true that caste rests on belief, but before belief comes to be the foundation of an institution, the institution itself needs to be perpetuated and fortified' (Ambedkar 1979: 1, 22). An inquiry into the conditions of the institutions and the mechanism by which these institutions came to be perpetuated and fortified is crucial to demystify the belief system of castes. In a similar vein, C. Linblom, as cited by Martin Smith, has argued that 'we fall into a bad habit of simply taking for granted that people in society will think alike, as though agreement was a natural phenomena that requires no explanations. Even natural phenomena require explanation. ... Agreement on political fundamentals cries for an explanation' (Smith 2006, 29).

The explanation for the re-emergence of Hinduism lies in its antagonism towards Buddhism in India. The religion of Buddhism was a great intellectual and moral revolution in ancient India. Its egalitarian and universalistic principles had led to mass enlightenment. The great Buddhist empires, such as the Mauryan Empire, established renowned universities; opened mass schools; and enrolled children without any discrimination on the basis of gender and status. Naturally, this revolution posed a great challenge to the Brahmanical religion (Davids 1903), and a counter-revolution was staged by the conservative elements. The counter-revolution established the feudal system by ruining the first pan-Indian Buddhist Empire of the Mauryas. Hinduism emerged as the cultural and religious logic of feudalism by laying down the stratified, rigid social order. Thus, the issue of caste, the under grid of feudalism,[13] was devised and religiously justified

---

harmony of the organism, so also each caste/varna has to carry out its own 'dharm' (religiously sanctioned duty) for the harmony of the body social, that is, the social organism. This 'organistic' view of society and its justification of the inequality of men based on the sole criterion of birth, however, were not acceptable to the victims of the system.

[13] See Ohno (2006) for a comparative view of the treatment of Buddhism in India and Japan. Here, I thank Professor Ohno for his discussions about the Shogan-imposed rigid, stratified, bureaucratic social class system in Japan, which once and for all wiped out my haunting doubts about the religious explanations of caste system in India. But with that the similarity ends. The point that myths conceal reality is crucial. The story

by Brahmanism, the chief element of Hinduism. Regarding the fundamental differences in the world view, social norms, and moral and conceptual universe of Buddhism and Brahmanism, Patanjali described 'the hostility between Buddhism and Brahmanism ... as innate as is that between the snake and mongoose' (Thapar 1989, 211). The literature is replete with references to mass persecutions

of India takes a different turn. The word 'hindu' was first used by Mughals to denote the geographical region of the river Sindu. It came very late in history, the twelfth century. Before that the land of India was known as Jambudipa, the land of elephants, symbolizing both Buddha and the fact that India has a lot of elephants. Even Chinese chronicles call India a 'country of elephants'. The Jataka tale of the Buddha as an elephant is well known. Moreover, since the Arabs could not pronounce the word 'Sindu' properly, its corrupted form 'Al Hind' came into use, and hence the word Hinduism. Thus, Hindu originally implied geographic and regional characteristics rather than religion. However, this word was used by the British to denote all non-Muslims. Nonetheless, Hinduism's strict adherence to the caste system was created in the medieval period. The caste system, the logic of feudalism, was imposed after the successful staging of the counter-revolution, the military coup by the Brahmins, Kshatriyas, and Banias (Vaishyas) against the Buddhist Empire. The Buddhist emperor was assassinated in the coup, the first political assassination in India. The coup established the feudal order called Hinduism against the Buddhist polity and society. The rise to dominance of this oligarchy meant the imposition of perpetual slavery and untouchability on the defeated Buddhist communities. The educated Buddhist society was forced to forget its philosophy, literature, and the art of reading and writing. Reading, writing, and listening to philosophical tenets of Buddhism were declared punishable crimes; tongues were cut and molten lead was poured in the ears. Thus, the laws of Hinduism as outlined in the *Manusmiriti* came to be implemented. In this sense, the feudalism of Tokugawa, Japan, is different from that of India. In the Tokugawa era, education was not denied. The Terakoya system ensured universal literacy. In India, Hinduism in the form of feudalism re-emerged by destroying the educational and intellectual civilization and culture of Buddhism. Thus, both feudalisms are fundamentally opposed in their characteristics and consequences. Tokugawa encouraged any intelligent person to be a teacher; boys and girls were admitted into schools without any discrimination. On the contrary, Buddhist communities in India were forced to forget their learning, culture, and schools and universities; libraries were burnt and destroyed; scholars and laity were persecuted, speared, and embargoed. The techniques of embargo or freezing the development of educated communities of Buddhists took the notorious forms of untouchability, unseeability, and unapproachability.

executed by Brahmanical forces against the Buddhists. The burning of the libraries of Nalanda University, which was the first international university in the world; the razing of Buddhist temples and universities by Brahmanical feudal lords; and the eventual execution of the policy of social ostracization and religious persecution of Buddhists in the form of untouchability has been well documented.[14] This historical background is necessary for understanding the Hindu religious injunctions against reading and writing and the compulsory denial of education to the majority in order to perpetuate the caste system. Why and how education was denied and what its link is with occupational rigidity are matters that are central to the stability of caste system.

Denial of Education: The Root Cause of Reproduction and Stability of the Caste System

The system of caste could not have been perpetuated for so long and reproduced so successfully without the systematic and effective denial of the 'right to education' to a majority of members of the society. According to Ambedkar, to accomplish this subjugation of the masses, the Brahmins, the chief architects of caste system, used six techniques of oppression:

> 1) graded inequality between different classes; 2) complete disarmament of the shudras and the untouchables; 3) complete ban on education of the shudras and untouchables; 4) total exclusion of the shudras and untouchables from places of power and authority; 5) complete prohibition against the shudras and the untouchables for acquiring property; and 6) complete subjugation of women. (Ambedkar 1991: 9, 215)

The strategy of disarmament and economic sanctions against the right to bear arms and pursue a business of profit were employed

---

[14] See the books of B.R. Ambedkar: *Who are the Untouchables?*; *Revolution and Counter Revolution in India*; *Buddha and His Dhamma*; *Who are the Shudras? And How They Became the Fourth Varna?*; and *The Riddles of Hinduism*, collected in Ambedkar (1989), for a detailed history of the mortal conflict between Brahmanism and Buddhism. I am thankful to Dr A. Rammaiyya, Dr. J. Mohan, and Dr. Umanathan, Tata Institute of Social Sciences, Mumbai, for details.

to pre-empt any rebellion against the system and economic independence and self-development of the majority. A well-integrated, interlocked, mutually reinforcing, closed system of castes was brought into existence, making the escape from the system a near impossibility. A total ban on education of the masses could not have been enforced by singing hymns and breathlessly reciting the Vedas. Rather the denial of access to education has to be carried out by means of force and fraud. The Brahmins were, in fact, very apprehensive of the prospect of an armed rebellion of the majority against the system. Therefore, they promulgated the disarmament of the Shudras and the Untouchables as a rule of law. 'Indeed, so strongly did the Brahmins believe in the disarmament of the Shudras and the Untouchables that when they revised the law to enable the Brahmins to arm themselves for the protection of their own privileges, they maintained the ban on the Shudras and the Untouchables as it was without lessening its rigour' (Ambedkar 1991: 9, 215). The myths and the application of force are the techniques of 'blow hot and cool'. They are intended to perpetuate the system. Thus, the system obtains its endurance by excommunicating the rebels and co-opting the conformists (Akerlof 1976).

Restricting access to education further ensures the reproduction of privileges reserved by occupational rigidity. Ambedkar notes this as follows.

> Brahmins, the chief and the leading element in the governing class, acquired their political power not by force of intellect—intellect is nobody's monopoly—but by sheer communalism. According to the laws of *Manusmriti* the post of the Purohit, King's Chaplain and Lord Chancellor, the posts of the Chief Justice and Judges of the High Court and the posts of Ministers to the Crown were all reserved for the brahmins. Even for the post of the Commander-in-Chief, the Brahmin was recommended as a fit and a proper person though it was not in terms reserved for him. All the strategic posts having been reserved for the Brahmins it goes without saying that all ministerial posts came to be reserved for the brahmins. This is not all. The Brahmin was not content with reserving places of profit and power for his class. He knew that mere reservation will not do. He must prevent rivals shooting up from other non-Brahmin communities equally qualified to hold the posts and agitate and blow up the system of reservations. In addition to reserving all executive posts in the State for Brahmins a law was made whereby education was made the monopoly and privilege of Brahmins. (Ambedkar 1991: 9, 231)

Challenges to the Caste System

The system of caste did not go unchallenged. In fact, modifying the thesis of Marx, one can say that after the defeat, not disappearance, of Buddhism, the history of India is a history of struggle against the caste system. A million mutinies occurred which went unrecorded in the annals of history. The struggles against the caste system, however, took a decisive leap with the emergence of Satya Shodak Samaj (Truth Seekers Society) established by Mahatma Jothiba Phule (1829–1890) in Maharashtra in 1873. He revolted against the Brahmanical monopoly and superstitions against the education of the Shudras and the Untouchables. He articulated the consequences of the deprivation of education: 'Without education knowledge is lost; without knowledge development is lost; without development wealth is lost; without wealth Shudras [the majority] are ruined.' (Omvedt 2004, 1)[15]

Mahatma Jyotiba Phule was the first to start schools for the masses, and his wife Mahatma Savitribai Phule was the first female teacher in India. Both of them struggled to dispel the ignorance caused by the centuries-long ban on education imposed by the Hindu social order. In the south, Mahathero Venerable Punditha Iyothee Thass (1845–1914) (Geetha and Rajadurai 1998),[16] with the support and patronage of Olcott and Mahathero Anagarika Dharampala, had initiated mass schools and educational institutions for the mass spread of education among the majority. Maharaja of Kolhapur Chhatrapathi Sahuji on 21 July 1902 issued the royal order granting 'reservation' (affirmative action) in employment in the principality of Kolhapur to the Bahujan for their upliftment through education and employment in society. Similarly, Maharaja Krishna Raj Wudiyar of Mysore issued a royal decree sanctioning 'reservation' to the educationally and socially backward masses, the Shudras and the Untouchables. In Madras, the Justice Party and the Self-Respect Movements spearheaded by E.V. Ramaswamy and the Sri Narayanguru Dharmaparipalana Shaba in Kerala, under the guidance of Rajarishi Narayana Guru, carried forward the struggle against the caste system. In their struggle against this inhuman

---

[15] I am thankful to Mr Shivaghanam, Viddiyal Patthipagam, Coimbatore, for introducing me to Jothirao Phule's works).

[16] See Suresh Mane (2006) and Illiya (2005) to name a few.

system, the social revolutionaries found some sympathetic supporters in the British Empire as well. For example, Charles E. Trevelyan (1807–1886), the then Madras governor, took bold steps to pass some of the most progressive pieces of social legislation in the history of India. But while anti-caste struggles were taking shape, influenced by the Western ideas of liberty and freedom of man, traditional forces were in the process of finding a new source for reviving and revitalizing their hold on the masses.

Education as a Site of Ideology: The Empire and Cultural Brokers

During the British Raj the system of monopoly of education and the caste system, religiously sanctioned by Hinduism, became legalized and institutionalized. This happened as the Brahmins wilfully supported the entrenchment of the British Raj in India. In the intervening Mughal period, though a significant segment of them managed to be bureaucrats, the overall cultural hegemony of these classes was down and lifeless. Hinduism as a religion has no internal strength to call upon the support of the masses at times of crisis. Hinduism can survive only by anchoring itself and drawing its succour from the powers that be as it has no mass base. The Bengali Hindus were, in fact, waiting for a source on which they can subsist and rise. The British just proved to be that exact source. The interaction of the British and the Bengali Hindus, especially the Brahmins, took various forms that had far-reaching implications on the entire people of India, particularly in the field of education.

The Orientalist Position

The ascendancy of the British Empire in India was different from that of other empires. Rather than 'outright conquest that resulted in the imposition of new institutions and traditions, the British Raj was characterized in its founding period by shrewd adaptations to, and skilful manipulation of, existing political institutions, social customs and cultural symbols' (Zatoupil and Moir 1999, 1). The British Empire was quick enough to learn that its survival and consolidation of power lay in enlisting the support of the traditional literati caste, its traditional learning, and the literature of the Sanskrit language. This policy of availing the service of the culture for empire building found ready support from the native influential caste.

The necessity to 'incorporate' local elites in the administrative apparatus of the Company, both for the interest of the empire and to reward and buy the loyalty of these elites, got formally expressed in the policies of Warren Hastings, the first governor general of India (1773–85). Lynn Zastoupil and Martin Moir note that Hastings was instrumental in forging an imperial vision of 'the British [securing] their power by trying to act like Indian rulers', a policy that came to be called 'Orientalism' (Zatoupil and Moir 1999, 2). Hastings's polices were 'reconciliatory' to the traditional culture of Sanskritic learning and the interests of its guardians. This policy of Hastings was vigorously followed by his successors. Jonathan Duncan, Benares resident in 1792, while proposing rules for an Institution of Hindoo College ('an academy for the preservation and Cultivation of the Laws, Literature and Religion of that nation'), 'reserved' posts for Brahmins in strict obedience to the laws of Manu. He especially noted that 'it would be better that all except the Physician should be the Brahmins' and that 'Brahmin Teachers ... have a preference over Strangers in Succeeding to the Headship and the Students in succeeding to the professorships'.[17]

Even John Stuart Mill, who was mainly responsible for the formulation of drafts of the East India Company's dispatches about Indian education, frowned upon the policy of educating the masses in India, contrary to his position in Britain where he advocated for the compulsory education of all children. Mill opined, 'The class to whom alone we can look for instruments in bringing home English ideas to Oriental comprehension, upon whom alone we can rely as our 'interpreters', is the learned classes: men of letters by birth and profession'. Indeed, Mill feared that any disengagement of the British from these learned classes would 'convert [them] into enemies of our schemes of education, if not enemies of our rule'.[18]

---

[17] 'Part of a letter from Jonathan Duncan, Resident at Benares, to Earl Cornwallis, governor-general in council of Fort William in Bengal, dated 1 January 1792', in Zatoupil and Moir (1999, 79).

[18] 'First draft of a Court of Directors' Public Department dispatch to India (Previous Communication 1828) prepared by John Stuart Mill, assistant to

Thus, all Orientalists, starting from Hastings, Duncan, and J.S. Mill, were uncritical supporters and admirers of the Brahmanical monopoly of education and viewed the caste elites as their natural alleys to further their interest.

Anglicists and Their Downward Filtration Theory

Contrary to the Orientalist view, the other imperial vision that arose in the early 1830s proposed an altogether different educational policy for India. Since, the empire was no longer in need of the service of the local power brokers, it radically viewed that its duty was to enlighten the Indian natives. This policy had its roots in the writings of Charles Grant (1746–1823), an evangelist and an employee of the East India Company who became a member of the Court of Directors. He deplored the superstitious lives of the natives of India and argued as early as 1792 for the dispelling of the darkness by 'introducing the light'[19] of Western science and literature: useful knowledge and skills to the masses. However, it was in 1835, during the tenure of Lord Macaulay (1800–1860), the law member of the governor general's council, that the validity of the Sanskritizing policy and its utility came under attack. The policy of 'Angilicization' was most fervently argued for by Macaulay to uplift India from 'a language ... barren of useful knowledge ... fruitful of monstrous superstitions ... false history, false astronomy, false medicine, [and] false religion'.[20]

Macaulay's policy of introducing Western education, and thus 'useful knowledge', reflected the grand evangelist concerns of Charles Grant. It had the lofty ideal of creating a 'class' of persons who are English in intellect and morals and thus 'fit vehicles' to

---

the examiner of Indian correspondence, with marginal comments by the president of the Board of Control, Sir John Cam Hobhouse, c. July–December 1836', in Zatoupil and Moir (1999, 234).

[19] 'Part of chapter IV of Charles Grant's Observations on the state of society among the Asiatic Subjects of Great Britain, Particularly with Respect to Morals. Written Chiefly in 1792', in Zatoupil and Moir (1999, 83).

[20] 'Minute recorded in the General Department by Thomas Babington Macaulay, law member of the governor-general's council, dated 2, February 1835', in Zatoupil and Moir (1999, 170).

spread the enlightened knowledge of the West to the vast masses of India. Pragmatically, a direct policy of educating the masses would mean fiscal expenditure. Therefore, Lord Macaulay observed:

> It is impossible for us, with all our limited means, to attempt to educate the body of the people. We must at present do our best to form a class who may be interpreters between us and the millions whom we govern; a class of persons Indian in blood and color but English in tastes, in opinions, in morals, and in intellect. To that class we may leave it to refine the vernacular dialects of the country; to enrich those dialects with the terms of science borrowed from the Western nomenclatures and to render them by degrees fit vehicles for carrying knowledge to the great mass of the population.[21]

Unfortunately, the dream of Macaulay of producing 'honorary English men' in India became a farce. The men who were expected to become 'fit vehicles for carrying knowledge to the great mass of the population' were themselves the traditional barriers to the acquisition of knowledge by the great masses. As Lynn Zastoupil and Martin Moir note, the vanguards of English education in Bengal were culturally very conservative and the introduction of English did not signal 'cultural subjugation. ... Even more compelling evidence [is] that Indians had their own agenda in promoting western education' (1999, 15). Contrary to Macaulay's intentions, the need for adapting Hinduism to changing circumstances was felt by the early Hindu revivalist Rajaram Mohan Roy. A Brahmin himself, Roy rejected the sacredness of Sanskrit language and petitioned to the British seeking the introduction of Western knowledge for the traditional learned castes of Hindus. The caste elites clearly foresaw the power of the English language and thus took possession of it in their hands as a tool to consolidate their traditional hold of power over the masses. Thus, English education ended up modernizing tradition, rather than breaking it, and introducing modernity. Unfortunately the Angilicist policy discounted the power of that 'artificial institution' called caste and failed to take into consideration its strategic use in the hands of the caste elites.

---

[21] Minute recorded in the General Department by Thomas Babington Macaulay, law member of the governor-general's council, dated 2, February 1835', in Zatoupil and Moir (1999, 170).

Vernacularists: Lonely Adam!

The fact that both Orientalists and Anglicists, in spite of their differences, focused on the native high castes led to the policy outcome of educating the 'higher classes' at the cost of elementary education of the masses. Thus, 'higher education' of the 'higher classes' attracted the vision and finance of the foreign rulers. However, 'primary education' suffered an ideological failure in the absence of articulate interests to back it up despite the valuable study and advocacy of William Adam (1796–1881), who insisted and called for vernacular-based elementary instruction. Adam's voice was in the minority and never received due policy attention. Only in the south, Madras officials focused on reinvigorating elementary education at the village level. But such an effort got aborted, as in 1839 the new governor insisted on introducing in Madras the General Committee for Public Instruction (GCPI), with its focus on higher education.

The GCPI of Bengal also rejected William Adam's suggestion that the government should concentrate on elementary education. The committee reiterated the doctrine of downward filtration, arguing that it was best to concentrate on the education of select groups who would serve as conduits for the diffusion of Western learning among the people of India. The British emphasized higher education that could provide well-trained clerks, judges, and civil servants for the British government (Zatoupil and Moir 1999, 31). Thus, in the proceedings, the issue of elementary education or mass education got sidetracked as it was in the interest of neither the empire nor the traditional castes. The neglect of primary education was supported by two assumptions: that knowledge would 'filter downward' and that on account of 'limited' fiscal resources the government could not afford to undertake such a huge responsibility of educating the great body of India.

Position of the 'Higher Classes' towards Elementary Education

The Brahmins and the other dominant-caste Hindus did not evince any interest in spreading literacy among the masses. J.A. Baines (1847–1925), the census commissioner in 1891, noted that the antagonistic influence against the more general spread of literacy was

> the long continued existence of a hereditary class whose object it has been to maintain their own monopoly of all book-learning as the chief buttress of their social supremacy. ... The opposition of the Brahmin to the rise of the writer castes ... and the repugnance of both, in the present day, to the diffusion of learning amongst the masses can only be appreciated after long experience. (Quoted in Ambedkar 1991: 9, 468)

Regarding the attitude of the native higher classes towards the education of the masses, even 64 years after the introduction of English education in 1835, Baines further observed:

> It is true that the recognition by the British Government of the virtue and necessity of primary education has met with some response on the part of the literate castes, but it is chiefly in the direction of academic utterances, which cannot, in the circumstances, be well avoided. ... The real interest of the castes in question is centred on secondary education, of which they almost exclusively are in a position to reap the advantage. (Quoted in Ambedkar 1991: 9, 468)

These sentiments subsequently characterize almost all policy pronouncements of independent India in the field of social amelioration, especially with regard to primary education. The fact that these classes had come to be the 'governing class' of independent India meant that higher education was to receive the utmost attention and fiscal support.

The Stand of Nationalist Elites on Education for the Masses

To be sure, the established castes have reasons to oppose change of the status quo; however, that need not reflect the opinions of the governing elites. In fact every society has its own elites. The elites guide, influence, and channel the energy and imagination of the nation or people towards a charter or vision. They make the economic and political systems to which the majority conforms as a matter of habit or trust. Except for crisis and revolutions, the business of governance is not seriously looked into by the people. Even the revolt or rebellion against an oppressive system is theorized and spearheaded by elites. The elites can be religious or spiritual leaders, political leaders, intellectuals, businessmen, or military. Education from the national point of view can be a great political tool in the hands of the governing elites. Apart from being used as a means of maintaining social inequality, it can also be used as a social equalizer, allowing the aspirations of the masses to be realized. Therefore, the ideas of governing elites deserve serious attention.

Gandhi, Caste, and Education of the Masses

The most prominent nationalist in India was M.K. 'Mahatma' Gandhi, whose grip over the Indian National Congress was complete. Gandhi was fundamentally attached to the traditional Hindu social order. He stressed that 'the four divisions are alone to be fundamental, natural and essential. ... I am certainly against any attempt at destroying the fundamental divisions' (Jaffrelot 2005, 61). Similarly, the rejection of heredity in caste was unimaginable to him. Gandhi held it close to his heart that 'the law of heredity is an eternal law and any attempt to alter that law must lead us, as it has before led, [sic] to utter confusion. I can see very great use in considering a Brahmin to be always a Brahmin through out his life' (Jaffrelot 2005, 61). This was the attitude and belief of the 'Mahatma'—the great soul—of the Indian National Congress towards the issue of caste and hereditary privileges and punishments. If 'heredity of caste' is eternal, there is no way to break it. If education is allowed, the eternal law of hereditary caste, with its traditional occupations, will be interrupted, leading to confusion. In any case, the four-fold division is 'natural and essential and fundamental', so there is no question of allowing education to the castes who are by 'heredity' not entitled to education. The choice is clear: No education for the masses, that is, children of the dominated castes. In fact, Gandhi devised the 'Warda Plan' of basic education which recommended that each child should learn their traditional caste occupation for half a day in school, for it will help him to 'earn' to 'learn', whilst the Brahmin and other allied-caste children were encouraged to 'learn' to 'earn'! Gandhi desired education to be allowed only to the extent of putting the child back in his traditional occupation. In fact, learning the 'traditional' occupation was called 'education'. Gandhi declared: 'Literacy is not even the beginning of education' (Weiner 1991, 105).

Nehru on Affirmative Action

Of all the disciples of Gandhi, Jawaharlal Nehru deserves the first and foremost place of pride for no one was as near and dear and had such complete blessings of Gandhi. Unlike Gandhi, Nehru had shown himself as a moderate in religious approach—modern, secular, and forward looking. Therefore, one could have expected something different from Nehru. However, the annals of history do not absolve him. Reputed for his secularism, Nehru showed no qualms in shedding it when the calling of his religion was to be obeyed. The official Congress historian, Dr Pattabhi Sitaramayya, recorded that Nehru was 'very conscious of the fact that he is a Brahmin'.[22]

It can be argued that each individual is entitled to hold the highest opinion about himself. However, what that individual does as a public authority is important. Caste pride, insofar as it does not come in the way of the efficient and impartial discharge of duty, need not be open to scrutiny. Unfortunately, Nehru's public life and policy action not only failed him but also brought to light facts which cannot be defended. His caste consciousness and the desire to preserve the educational and administrative powers for men of his own caste came to the fore in the question of OBC reservations. The Kelkher Commission, appointed to study the question of social and economic backwardness and to propose measures to improve the lot of this large segment of the Indian population (more than 60 per cent at the time), made a rather conservative recommendation in 1956. The report grudgingly admitted the relevance and necessity

---

[22] For example, he performed the funeral rituals of his father through the hands of the Brahmins as per the orthodox prescriptions of Hinduism. It was not only was Nehru who was conscious about his so-called superiority of caste identity; his sister, Mrs Vijaya Laxmi Pundit, was as well. When the question of not declaring one's caste in the census return was discussed in the All-India Women's Conference held in Delhi in December 1940, 'Mrs. Pandit disapproved of the idea and said that she did not see any reason why she should not be proud of her Brahmin blood and declare herself as a Brahmin at the Census' (Ambedkar 1991: 9, 209).

of adopting the reservation principle to ensure the upliftment of the backward classes. However, it was not even tabled in the Parliament. Nehru's government unanimously decided that there was no need to reserve positions for the backward classes. Nehru himself came out heavily against the principle of reservation—a measure of social justice—and officially made it clear in his dispatches to the chief ministers of the states (Jaffrelot 2003, 227–8). In a letter addressed to all chief ministers on 27 June 1961, Nehru said:

> I have referred above to efficiency and to our getting out of our traditional ruts. This necessitates our getting out of the old habit of reservations and particular privileges being given to this caste or that group. ... I dislike any kind of reservation, more particularly in services. I react strongly against anything which leads to inefficiency and second-rate standards. ... If we go in for reservations on communal and caste basis, we swamp the bright and able people and remain second-rate or third-rate. I want my country to be a first class country in everything. The moment we encourage the second-rate, we are lost. I am grieved to learn how far this business of reservation has gone based on communal considerations. ... This way lies not only folly but disaster. (Jaffrelot 2003, 228)

The ahistorical perspective of his analysis is quite perplexing, given the fact that Nehru showed a lot of interest in history. Nehru was not unaware of the historical injustices inflicted on the majority by the Hindu system of castes and would certainly have understood the point of providing affirmative support in the form of reservation of seats in government jobs and educational institutions as a means of improving the masses.

State, Caste, and Education in Independent India: Stability and Growth

The Congress was not only the first party to inherit power from the British but also remained in power for five long decades in postcolonial India. The State that was inherited at the time of transfer of power was retained almost in all aspects, except for the erection of new institutions that were needed to consolidate its power. The Sanskritist/Orientalist attitude became the official ideology with the strategic retention of English for the conduct of business of the

State and commerce. The Congress hardly created or established anything new for the integration and unity of the nation because it was never a party of the masses but of the 'notables' and elites. Indeed, all political parties, including the Communist parties and the saffron variants, are led by caste elites, except the political parties of the oppressed classes.

The Governing Castes of India

Ambedkar diagnosed the issue of governing elites (before Vilfredo Pareto [1935] and C.W. Mill [1956]) and their strategic alliances:

> It is of course impossible for the Brahmins to maintain their supremacy as a governing class without an ally to help them on account of their being numerically very small. Consequently, as history shows, the Brahmins have always had other classes as their allies to whom they were ready to accord the status of a governing class provided they were prepared to work with them in subordinate co-operation. In ancient and mediaeval times they made such an alliance with the Kshatriyas or the warrior class and the two not merely ruled the masses, but ground them down to atoms, pulverised them so to say—the Brahmin with his pen and the Kshatriya with his sword. At present, Brahmins have made an alliance with the Vaishya class called Banias. The shifting of this alliance from the Kshatriya to the Bania is in the changed circumstances quite inevitable. In these days of commerce money is more important than sword. That is one reason for this change in party alignment. The second reason is the need for money to run the political machine. Money can come only from and is in fact coming from the Bania. (Ambedkar 1991: 9, 452)

The Kshatriya castes have not disappeared, however. As controllers of land, they have been transformed into the zamindari (landlords) or business classes. The three dominant castes don the roles of landlords, bureaucrats, and business classes in India today. The Congress party is simply an oligarchical association of these traditional castes and their modern incarnations. Therefore, as beneficiaries of Hinduism, they do not want to undertake any action that will break the sacred system of caste enjoined by Manu.

Christophe Jaffrelot, a critical political scientist, has observed in his detailed study of the Congress regime that

> after [I]ndependence, the party leaders, including Nehru, recruited even more influential local personalities to serve its electoral interests,

developing an interlocking network of 'vote banks' whose incumbents joined the nationalist intelligentsia in the party machine. Thus it was that in the two decades after independence congress established the supremacy of the upper castes in the political system of North India. While it was almost a dominant party, the over-representation of the upper castes among its MLAs [members of legislative assemblies of the provinces] and MPs is striking. (Jaffrelot 2003, 84–5)[23]

This is the natural corollary of the fact that the Congress, since its inception, was dominated by Brahmins (40 per cent) and upper castes (49.5 per cent) (Jaffrelot 2003, 49). Jaffrelot noted how the institution of

> democracy offered them all a flexible set of bargaining procedures which allowed for the division of spoils, while resisting popular pressure. ... It also offers an explanation for [the Indian state's] social defects. The bargaining form of collaboration between elite groups was congenial to political democracy but drastically limited the chances of success of a genuine policy of social distribution. India was bound to have political democracy without social democracy. (Jafferlot 2003, 86)

Such a democracy does not require literacy. Rajiv Gandhi, the grandson of Nehru, theorized the link between democracy and literacy in an address delivered at Harvard University, USA, in October 1987. Asked whether it was not a blot on Indian democracy that so many people were illiterate even so many years after Independence, Rajiv Gandhi explained: 'I do not think literacy is the key to democracy. ... Wisdom is much more important. We have seen—and I am not now limiting myself to India, I am going beyond to other countries—literacy sometimes narrows the vision, does not broaden it' (Weiner 1991, 101). That Rajiv Gandhi made such a statement belied the purported policy of his own government. Just a year earlier, the National Education Policy (1986) 'committed' India to promote progress in primary education and its extension to hitherto disadvantaged groups such as girls and the SCs and STs.

---

[23] How Nehru institutionalized this vote bank politics by co-opting former maharajas and by nominating them in constituencies where they had a good chance of winning also can be seen on Jaffrelot (2003, 143).

Bureaucracy and the Command Economy

The negligence of primary education by the independent State thus did not merely have its roots in the British Raj. It is a direct fallout of the traditional policy of the caste system. Even the policies pursued by the postcolonial State contributed towards the consolidation of the world view of the caste system as, in essence, these policies did not vary much from the objectives of the caste system. The caste elites, who had a head start because of the British policy of creating a class of Honorary Englishmen, used the inherited fiscal resources of the State to consolidate their hold in independent India. During the British era, these caste elites were appointed in the colonial bureaucracy. They occupied the entire State apparatus. Therefore, the need for manpower tremendously increased. Further, manning the State at the top echelons and other strategic posts and positions was the surest way to ensure control over State and society. The caste elites already had a vast network of private schools through which their children were educated. Subsequently, successive planning commissions valued higher education as the top priority to create a minuscule affluent middle class and the intelligentsia/ideologues of postcolonial India to take up bureaucratic posts, manage the private and public sectors, and man the media and other agencies of the public sphere so as to 'manufacture consent' among the masses.

Unlike inheriting elites of other countries who immediately embarked on the universalization of primary education, the caste elites were guided mainly by considerations of consolidating power. There was a clearly discernible pattern of sharing and using of State power among the three castes: the Brahmins to man the bureaucracy, public sector, judiciary, and press and media; the Bania (Vaishya) to take control over industry and business; the Kshatriyas to accumulate land and dominate the vast majority (85 per cent) of the population, illiterate and dependent on agriculture at the time of Independence. However, these oligarchical castes don different roles to further their interests, which requires a three-pronged strategy for the use of the State apparatus and resources: investment in higher education; promotion and protection of 'infant industries' from foreign competition; and avoidance of land reforms. The appropriation of State resources thus came to be directed toward the establishment of higher education institutions (the 'modern temples'), the heavy industrialization strategy, the 'command economy', and the 'Green Revolution'. This strategic use of the State has produced the diasporic intelligentsia of the Brahmins, the business empires of the Banias, and the bullock cart capitalists of rural India. In this world view, the masses need no land, no literacy, and no democratic role in the national life of India.

The universalization of primary education would have led to the migration of literate rural masses to urban centres in search of jobs and to meet the requirements of industrial demands. Unlike Japan, where the parallel development of indigenous industries was encouraged (Ohno 2006)[24] along with the modernization of industries, the Indian state, despite its romantic claims of a self-sufficient village economy, invested mostly in the heavy industries whose capacity to absorb skilled rural migrants was limited. Further, in the absence of education, rural youth remained as bonded labour under the ruthless control of the Kshatriyas, the landlord castes. As a consequence of the compulsory denial of education, the agricultural sector suffers from the Lewisan classical problem of unlimited supply of labour with zero marginal productivity. However, the structural logic of caste power requires the perpetuation of farm slavery and fettering of productive talent in the rural areas.

The Brahmins who man the State bureaucracy provide the steel frame protection to the landlord castes from any armed rebellion and peasant protests. In his study of the Indian state, Herring asked: 'How can fundamental structural change be effected through the very institutions that service and reproduce the existing society and reflect the existing distribution of power and privilege?' He found that the bureaucracy is very much embedded in traditional sources of power and privileges instead of being a mechanism to uphold constitutional values. Bureaucrats, a relatively advantaged lot, are landowners themselves or seek to obtain the privilege, status, and security provided by landownership. This pits their structural position as landowners against their official task of carrying out land reform. That this dilemma is easily resolved in favour of their personal interests can be traced to the nature of 'ordinary administration' (Gupta 1989, 794). The Brahmins were traditionally feared not for their intellectual power or religious beliefs of purity, superiority of birth, and ritual, but for their power as bureaucrats,

---

[24] I am grateful to Professor Ohno for imparting an insiders' yet critical view of the Japanese economy.

even in the Mughal period. The Brahmin devoid of bureaucratic power is simply a non-entity; the institutions of post-Independence India were designed to perpetuate the dominance of Brahmins in the bureaucracy.

Bureaucracy is a product of higher education and also the instrument through which fiscal resources can be allocated to protect the interests of the Brahmins and their two allies. Therefore, the caste elites are naturally concentrated in higher education. The system of higher education in India by the end of the 1980s, according to Tilak and Verghese, became 'one of the largest systems in the world, with about 10 million students enrolled in 188 universities ... [and an investment of] 0.9% of GNP ... [which is] nearly one-third of the total education budget' (1985, 83). On the other hand, given the texture of the caste state, financing elementary education was considered too big a burden to be borne by the central government. Therefore, the states were asked to provide primary education while the centre financed institutions of national importance. The report of Sir John Sargent, the advisor in the Central Advisory Board of Education (CABE) in 1944, recommended compulsory provision of primary education by 1960 and clearly rejected 'the plan of Gandhi that elementary school education could pay for itself through the sale of articles produced by the pupil' (Weiner 1991, 106). However, the Zahir Hussain committee on education was strongly in favour of Gandhi's plan. The 'lack of resources' argument became the official doctrine. Unanimously then, 'by the early 1950s officials within the government of India concluded that the financial resources for the establishment of universal compulsory education by 1960 were not available as a consequence of the government's decision to undertake large development projects' (Weiner 1991, 107). Their view that primary education has to be a self-financing system was another way of stating their desire for the status quo.

Elementary education's share of the national budget has declined with every successive Five Year Plan. The Ministry of Education's review stated that 'from 56% in the first five year plan ... by the sixth five year plan (1980–85), it was down by 36%' (cited in Weiner 1991, 91). Further, the review stated:

> While in 1950–51, 43 percent of the educational budget was for primary education, by 1976 the expenditure on primary education has declined to 27 percent. ... Total expenditure per student per year by

the centre and the states has declined in real terms. Very little money is available for science equipment, kits, posters, and charts, or books, even black boards. (Cited in Weiner 1991, 94–5)

Tilak and Vergese, who studied how higher education is financed 'in a developing country like India where universalization of elementary education still eludes, and mass illiteracy is dominant', found that 'during the three decades ending in 1980, the share of the government in total expenditure on higher education increased from 49% in 1950–51 to 78% in 1979–80' (Weiner 1991, 83–4). However, the beneficiaries of the system are 'about one-twentieth of the total student population in the country'. They also noted that 'the student composition of the professional courses is mostly skewed in favour of better socioeconomic groups of population' (Tilak and Varghese 1985). Yet they are heavily subsidized. The PROBE survey (1999, 17) suggests that north-Indian parents spend about INR 318 per year (more than USD 6) (on fees, books, slates, clothes, et cetera), on average, to send a child to a government primary school. This is a major financial burden, especially for poor families with several children of school-going age. The truth of Weiner's observation is unmistakable:

> Rhetoric notwithstanding, India's policy makers have not regarded mass education as essential to India's modernization. They have instead put resources into elite government schools, state aided private schools, and higher education in an effort to create an educated class that is equal to educated classes in the west and that is capable of creating and managing a modern enclave economy. (PROBE Team 1999, 5)

This was to continue despite the recital in each Five Year Plan that education is an 'investment in human resources' and essential to economic growth. Money flows through the canals of ideology. The fiscal is ideological.

The Rhetoric of Trickle Down

The focus on higher education was justified by invoking the idea of 'trickle down', which was the central and all-pervasive logic of the planning era. The development plans were premised on the assumption that once the pie grew, everyone's share would be bigger. Accordingly, the vast majority of the population of the country was told to sacrifice present consumption for a joyful bounty of the future. 'Trickle down' was also expected to work in the field of education. That is, it was assumed that the social classes with the exclusive privilege of State-sponsored access to higher education would, in turn, contribute to the literacy and educational attainment of the masses.

However, the crucial assumption of the 'trickle down' analogy is that there is social porosity that can permit this percolation. The fact is that the society was not a porous medium. Rather it was watertight, a compartmentalized society based on the hierarchical notions of caste system. The system of caste was, in fact, sustained by excluding the rest of the society from access to education. Those who were in control of the resources simply closed the door. Therefore, it will amount to missing the point if the analogy of 'trickle down' is taken for granted as a metaphor, since such an analogy functions as a powerful mask to legitimize the exclusive monopoly of the educational and other resources by the traditional elites.

Governing Elites and Stability Concerns

Weiner's vital study brought back the issue of caste in the limelight without invoking any discourse of social justice or political movements led by the victims of the caste system. Weiner presumably did not make any reference to such social and cultural movements in order to avoid the prejudice of the Indian mind that he was joining hands with the majority (the Untouchables and Shudras). His concern was very clear—to make comprehensible the reason why primary education was made neither compulsory nor free in India. He advanced his thesis in clear-cut terms:

> The central proposition of this study is that India's low per capita income and economic situation is less relevant as an explanation than the belief systems of the state bureaucracy, a set of beliefs that are widely shared by educators, social activists, trade unionists, academic researchers, and more broadly, by members of the Indian middle class. These beliefs are held by those outside as well as those within the government, by observant Hindus and those who regard themselves as secular, and by leftists as well as by centrists and rightists. At the core of these beliefs is the Indian view of the social order, notions concerning the respective roles of upper and lower social strata, the role of education as a means of maintaining

differentiations among social classes, and concerns that 'excessive' and 'inappropriate' education for the poor would disrupt the existing social arrangements. (PROBE Team 1999, 5)

The fear that education would break the caste system, that is, 'disrupt the existing social arrangement', is at the heart of the argument of the members of the Indian middle class—those who are inside the government and those who are influential and outside the government. It should also be emphasized that the term 'middle class' is not equivalent to 'backward castes'. Rather, it refers to the dominant castes—the Brahmins and the allied castes. Christophe Jaffrelot in another context brought to light the fact that 'upper castes', such as the Brahmins, are 'unfortunately' being described as 'middle classes' (Jaffrelot 2003, 49).[25] Therefore, the State, under the siege of these upper castes, deliberately ignored the imperative of compulsory primary education. While it gave higher education to men of its own caste, it clothed its bias with the discourse of 'merit' (that there was no suitable candidate available from the SCs, STs, and OBCs) and created numerous islands of excellence and institutions of national importance that they stated were above considerations of caste and creed. Meanwhile, they advised the masses to put 'duties [caste occupations] before rights [education, and so on]'.

Caste, Child Labour, and Education

By perpetuating the caste system, the educational policy of independent India is fundamentally a violence perpetrated on its chil-

---

[25] The term 'intelligentsia', as defined by Gellener (1983) and cited in Jaffrelot (2000), is a class that became alienated from the masses through education. Jaffrelot's chief concern is to examine whether the Congress Party is a party of 'intelligentsia' or 'notables' (local power elites). Our comment here is that even Gellener's definition of 'intelligentsia' is not an appropriate term for describing the 'Indian middle classes', for these castes appropriate education for the consolidation of their traditional hold over the masses, and they consciously deny education to 'alienate' the masses from decision-making and democratic processes of national life. That is, the alienated are not the 'middle classes' here, but the mass of the Indian majority. Therefore, the middle classes are simply the ideological arms, the 'traditional intellectuals' in the Gramscian sense, of the 'notables' for sharing the spoils of resources of the majority.

dren who in no way are a source of conflict or cause of prejudice. In his important study, Weiner notes that though the system of stratification is by no means unique to India,

> what is distinctive is a particular kind of social mobility, the mobility of groups rather than individuals. While there is considerable group mobility in India, powerful forces of both institutions and beliefs resist changes in group status. Even those who profess to be secular and who reject the caste system are imbued with values of status that are deeply imbedded in Indian culture. (Weiner 1991, 6)

Further noting that these beliefs are fundamentally rooted in the religious notions of hierarchy and thus caste, Weiner identifies Hinduism—the religion that sanctifies caste and the belief in unalterable social hierarchy—as the main obstacle in the way of mass education. This role of Hinduism is in marked contrast with other religions.

> In much of the world, religious institutions and beliefs (including secular beliefs derived from religion) played a role in the diffusion of mass education and in state intervention, but in India Hinduism (and Islam as well) has not been a force for mass education. While in many countries theologies or secular ideologies have stood for a system of national education aimed at social equality, in India education has been largely an instrument for differentiation by separating children according to social class. For this reason those who control the education system are remarkably indifferent to the low enrolment and high dropout rate among the lower social classes. (Weiner 1991, 6)[26]

---

[26] Here, a comment on Weiner's reference to Islam is in order. While it is true that Islam imposes restriction on the education of women, it has no religiously imbedded sanctions for precluding women from acquiring knowledge, just as in the case of Hinduism. Further, Islam has no such religiously ordained division of society into different hierarchies based on occupations as is the case in Hinduism. In addition to these differences in value and belief systems, Islam has been always a source of inspiration and way out for the Untouchables and other victims of caste-Hindu system. It has been actively considered as one of the egalitarian religions where equality can be hoped for, by Ambedkar, the great leader of modern India. As a matter of fact, the largest chunk of today's Indian Muslim population is the erstwhile 'lower castes' who discarded the iniquitous Hindu social order. Moreover, the presence of Muslims in the 'government' in India is as thin as that of the SCs.

Thus, Hinduism still remains a formidable impediment in the way of universal literacy and basic education. The cultivation of the mind—education—does not exist in the world view of Hinduism. Therefore, it is not hard to see that the system of caste is fundamentally opposed to the institution and utility of education itself. Curiously, while education as a merit-certifying mechanism and legitimizer for the governing castes to sustain their dominance over the majority is recognized and ideologized, its extension to the 'servile classes' is anxiously dismissed as dangerous and disruptive to the social harmony and stability of the social order based on the traditional occupational rigidity. Thus, Hinduism is a religion of doublespeak. It is a religion of opportunism and not principles. It is a religion of power and not justice. The Brahmins, Banias, and Kshatriyas are its designers as well as audience. Hinduism, the religion of occupational rigidity, is a fetter to the mind and health of Indian society. Hinduism, the gospel of compulsory denial of education, liberty, and freedom, is what the cultural logic of feudal, anti-industrial, and anti-democratic system is based on. It has stifled the spirit and dignity of man. It cannot be redeemed; it has to be discarded. It vitiates the positive conception and imagination of a nation, the organic political community (Anderson 1991). Therefore, the issue of universalization of compulsory education is intricately related to the interlocked system of State institutions, land, and industry. Thus, it is the central aspect of the issue of the whole order and not an isolated one. Since the caste elites are in power and the State machinery is under their siege, the delivery of universal compulsory primary education calls for the delivery of the State from these caste elites in the first place. In the absence of fundamental structural changes in the entire political and economic conditions of society, the universalization of compulsory education will be a legalism, piece of rhetoric, and chimera of form over substance. The transformation of the nature of State in India calls for the democratic participation of its people who constitute the majority, the hitherto still disadvantaged lot. Democratization is not possible unless universal literacy is made available and accessible to the oppressed majority of India.

* * *

The caste system with all its oppressive mechanisms and antidemocratic ideology and practice escapes the world's attention, except as a vestigial piece of the Hindu religion. However, as Ambedkar pointed out, the mechanism of caste has a secular goal of maintaining power over the masses, and the cloak of religion is used to mask it from the rational and moral scrutiny of the world. The policy implications of this study are clear: The Government of India can continue to ignore the issue of primary education, that is, slates (the symbolic expression for universal primary education) at the cost of economic growth and security and the formation of a nation in the future. The continuance of caste-prejudiced policy will entail entropic effects for national integration and economic development despite the current celebration of India's silicon valleys. If caste can divide and disintegrate, education is the fit social cement to integrate and unite India. India can afford that social cement; it has the resources. Millions of children ask: Will it?

References

Akerlof, George. 1976. 'The Economics of Caste and of the Rat Race and Other Woeful Tales'. *The Quarterly Journal of Economics* 90, no. 4: 599–617.

Ambedkar, B.R. 1979–91. *Dr. Babasaheb Ambedkar: Writings and Speeches*, vols 1, 2, and 9. Bombay: Government of Maharashtra.

Anderson, Benedict. 1991. Imagined Communities: Reflections on the Origin and Spread of Nationalism. Revised edition, New York: Verso.

Aloysius, Gyana. 1997. *Nationalism without Nation in India*. New York: Oxford University Press.

Bajpai, Nirupam, and Sangeeta Goyal. 2004. 'Primary Education in India: Quality and Coverage Issues'. CGSD Working Paper No. 11, February. Available at academiccommons.columbia.edu › doi › download. Last accessed on 24 March 2020.

Baran, Paul A. 1957. *Political Economy of Growth*. New York: Monthly Review Press.

Becker, S. Garry. 1975. *Human Capital*. New York: National Bureau of Economic Research.

Bühler, George, trans. 1886. *The Laws of Manu*, volume 5 of *Sacred Books of the East*. Available at archive.org › stream › lawsofmanu00bh › lawsofmanu00bh_djvu. Last accessed on 24 March 2020.

Chellam, K.S. 2018. *Relevance of Ambedkarism in India*, second edition. New Delhi: Rawat Publications.

Davids, T.W. Rhys. 1903. *Buddhist India*. New York: G.P. Putnam's Sons.

Dewey, John. [1916] 1997. *Democracy and Education: An Introduction to the Philosophy of Education*. Rockland, New York: Free Press.

Dreze, Jean, and Amartya Sen. 2002. *India: Economic Development and Social Opportunity*. New York: Oxford University Press.
Fedderke, Johannes, Raphael Kadt, and John Luiz. 1999. 'Economic Growth and Social Capital: A Critical Reflection'. *Theory and Society* 28, no. 5: 709–45.
Geetha, V., and S.V. Rajadurai. 1998. *Towards a Non-Brahmin Millienium: From Iyotheethass to Periyar*. Calcutta: Samya.
Gellner, Ernest. 1983. *Nations and Nationalism*. London: Cornell University Press.
Glaeser, L. Edward, David Laibson, and Bruce Sacerdote. 2002. 'An Economic Approach to Social Capital.' *The Economic Journal* 112, no. 483: F437–F458.
Gounden, M. Nalla. 1967. 'Investment in Education in India.' *The Journal of Human Resources* 2, no. 3: 347–58.
Gupta, Akhil. 1989. 'The Political Economy of Post-Independence India-A Review Article'. *The Journal of Asian Studies* 48, no. 4: 787–97.
Illiya, Kancha. 2005. *Why I am Not a Hindu*. UK: Samya.
ILO (International Labor Organization). 2007. *Equality at Work: Tackling the Challenges*. Geneva: ILO.
Jaffrelot, Christophe. 2000 (reprint 2005). *Dr. Ambedkar and Untouchability: Analyzing and Fighting Caste*. London: Hurts and Co.
———. 2003. *India's Silent Revolution: The Rise of Lower Castes in North India*. London: Hurts and Co.
Johnson, Walton R. 1982. 'Education: Keystone of Apartheid'. *Anthropology & Education Quarterly* 13, no. 3: 214–37.
Kadam, K.N. 1991. *Dr Babasaheb Ambedkar and the Significance of his Movement: A Chronology*. Mumbai: Popular Prakashan.
Kanshiram, Manyavur, ed. 1986. *The Oppressed Indian* (February–March).
Kumar, Vivek. 2003. *Dalit Leadership in India*. New Delhi: Kalpaz Publications.
Lundberg, Shelly, and Richard Startz. 1998. 'On the Persistence of Racial Inequality'. *The Journal of Labour Economics* 16, no.2: 292–323.
Mandal, B.P. 1980. *Report of the Backward Classes Commission*. Government of India. Available at www.ncbc.nic.in › User_Panel › UserView. Last accessed on 24 March 2020.
Mane, Suresh. 2006. *Glimpses of Socio-cultural Revolts in India*. Mumbai: Samrudh Bharat Publications.
Mills, C. Wright. 1956. *The Power Elite*. Oxford: Oxford University Press.
Ohno, Kenichi. 2006. *The Economic Development of Japan: The Path Travelled by Japan as a Developing Country*. Tokyo: GRIPS.
Omvedt, Gail. 2004. *Ambedkar: Towards an Enlightened India*. New Delhi: Penguin Books India.
———. 2011 [1976]. *Cultural Revolt in a Colonial Society: The Non-Brahman Movement in Western India*. New Delhi: Manohar.

Pareto, Vilfredo. 1935 [1916]. *The Mind and Society: A Treatise on General Sociology*. English translation edited by Arthur Livingston. New York: Dover.

Planning Commission. 1951. 'First Five Year Plan'. Ministry of Finance, Government of India.

———. 2002a. Report of the Working Group for the Xth Plan. Ministry of Finance, Government of India. Available at http//*planningcommission*. nic.in/plans/planrel/fiveyr/welcome.html. Last accessed on 23 March 2020.

———. 2002b. 'The Mid-term Appraisal of Xth Plan (2002–7).' Ministry of Finance, Government of India. Available at http// *planningcommission*. nic.in/plans/planrel/fiveyr/welcome.html. Last accessed on 23 March 2020.

PROBE Team. 1999. *PROBE (Public Report on Basic Education)*. USA: Oxford University Press.

Rao, Nirmala, Kai-Ming Cheng, and Kirti Narain. 2003. 'Primary Schooling in China and India: Understanding How Socio-Contextual Factors Moderate the Role of the State'. *International Review of Education* 49, no. 1/2 (March): 153–76.

Schultz, W. Theodore. 1961. 'Investment in Human Capital'. *The American Economic Review* 51, no. 1: 1–17.

Scott, James C. 1998. *Seeing Like a State: How Certain Schemes to Improve the Human Condition Have Failed*. New Haven: Yale University Press.

Smith, Martin. 2006. 'Pluralism'. In *The State: Theories and Issues*, edited by Colin Hay, Michael Lister, and David Marsh. New York: Palgrave Macmillan.

Stiglitz, Joseph E. 2006. *Making Globalization Work: The Next Steps to Global Justice*. Allen Lane: Penguin.

Thapar, Romila. 1989. 'Imagined Religious Communities? Ancient History and the Modern Search for Hindu Identity'. *Modern Asian Studies* 23, no. 2: 209–31.

Thorat, Sukhadeo. 1998. *Ambedkar's Role in Economic Planning and Water Policy*. Delhi: Shipra Publications.

———. 2006. 'Higher Education in India: Emerging Issues Related to Access, Inclusiveness, and Quality.' Lecture delivered in Bombay University as part of Nehru Memorial Lecture, University of Mumbai, 24 November. Available at www.ugc.ac.in › oldpdf › chair_sdt › chairman_nehru_lecture. Last accessed on 23 March 2020.

Tilak, J.B.G. 1989. 'Centre-State Relations in Financing Education in India'. *Comparative Education Review* 33, no. 4: 450–80.

Tilak, J.B.G., and N.V. Vergese. 1985. 'Discriminatory Pricing in Education'. *Occasional Paper* No. 8. New Delhi: National Institute of Educational Planning and Administration.

Weiner, Myron. 1991. *The Child and the State: Child Labor and Education Policy in Comparative Perspective*. Princeton, NJ: Princeton University Press.

UNO (United Nations Organization), Task Force on Education and Gender Equity. 2006. *Towards Universal Primary Education: Investment, Incentives and Institutions*. Available at www.ungei.org › millenniumproj_univprimaryeducation05. Last accessed on 23 March 2020.

Zatoupil, Lynn, and Martin Moir. 1999. 'Introduction'. In *The Great Indian Education Debate: Documents Relating to the Orientalist-Anglicist Controversy, 1781–1843*. Surrey: Curzon Press.

Zelliot, Eleanor. 1992. *From Untouchable to Dalit: Essays on the Ambedkar Movement*. New Delhi: Manohar.

11

Ambedkar in/and Academic Space*

JADUMANI MAHANAND

Marxism and liberalism have been the dominating discourses in the domains of social sciences and humanities. Liberal and Marxist philosophies are said to be radical, critical, progressive, democratic, and secular. These theories have universal justification. The question is: How do Indian Marxist or liberal scholars interpret the social and material conditions of Indian society? Generally, I contend that Brahmanism as a system of thought is reflected as an influence in their writings and teachings. Whether this is because of their academic persuasion/interests or their caste privilege or simply bad faith is a question that needs to be addressed.

Academic space is more or less synonymous with the university, where knowledge is produced. It is a free space where one can learn, research, investigate, interrogate, search for truth, and develop a certain scientific attitude and critical thinking skills in order to formulate normative ideals for the society, the polity, and the academic institutions themselves. All shades of ideas are supposedly discussed and debated. And yet, Upendra Baxi was compelled to remark a couple of decades ago that Ambedkar had been completely disregarded, forgotten, and neglected by the entirety of the Indian academia (Baxi 2000). Similarly, Christopher S. Queen and Perry

---

* This chapter was developed after the death of Rohith Vemula, which triggered a pan-Indian Ambedkarite student movement and exposed the brutality of caste discrimination in Indian universities. I would like to thank Muktamayee Kumbhar for her encouragement.

Anderson have each written that Dr Ambedkar is virtually unknown outside of India, whereas M.K. Gandhi is well known throughout the world (see Anderson 2012; see also Queen 2008).

Why is it that Ambedkar—a thinker par excellence—is rarely taught in the social sciences or humanities disciplines in Indian universities? By contrast, Ambedkar has become a political banner for the political right, left, and centre to rally around. Does this imply that the academic space is contested and that there are at play deeper power relations of a different character than those within the public political sphere? If no purely academic justifications are available for the academic curricula to exclude thinkers such as Ambedkar and other anti-caste and Adivasi thinkers from the core academic syllabus, this exclusion would have to be regarded as an unethical academic conspiracy.

In what follows, I try to problematize the idea of the university as an academic space. In so doing, I first ask why Ambedkar is not routinely taught in compulsory courses in Indian curricula. Second, I ask in what ways Ambedkar is made present in Indian academic discourse—as a producer of knowledge, as a purveyor of ideas, or as an identity. Finally, I conclude with remarks serving to summarize what it is that Ambedkar seems to mean to the Indian academic space and how he and his work is preponderantly perceived by academic institutions.

Problematizing Academic Space in India

Since the death of Rohith Vemula, the existence of caste discrimination on the campuses of Indian universities has become common knowledge. The Thorat committee report of AIIMS revealed the different forms of caste discrimination that exists in subtle ways. This is crucial evidence that speaks volumes regarding the nature of the academic space in India—in a way, such practices spell out the hidden sociocultural positions attached to professors, staff, students, and even high-ranking officials in educational institutions. The university is not outside of society, it is a part of society; social and cultural practices are often reflected in the behaviour of the university community. N. Sukumar aptly writes of universities as modern *agrahara*s (N. Sukumar 2016), an *agrahara* being an area where Brahmins live. Today, one may witness upper castes exercising the rights traditionally ascribed to them. Since Independence, academic discourse has been—in terms of knowledge production and domination—controlled by Brahmins and upper castes who are at the top of the caste hierarchy (that is, twice born). One may also witness the top twice born (TTB) migrating to foreign universities and, thereby, playing a strong role in the production of knowledge worldwide.[1] Traditionally, education/knowledge as a source of power is ascribed and assigned to Brahmins according to the *Varnashramadhrama* (Santosh and Abraham 2010).

The university as a public academic space in India has been hegemonized by the TTB. The TTB maintain the purity of knowledge in universities by controlling their courses, syllabi, and curricula, thereby also reserving the highest positions for themselves. This is visible in the statistics on high-ranking administrative positions in universities: out of a total of 496 vice chancellors, 6 are SC, 6 are ST, and 36 OBC.[2] In this context, how should we understand academic space in India? How do Indian academics understand the questions raised by Ambedkar in his intellectual, social, and political discourses?

Pedagogy and Intellectual Practice

The National Council of Educational Research and Training (NCERT) prepares the syllabi for intermediate– to high school–level education. Among the various textbooks prepared by the NCERT for social sciences, Ambedkar can only be found in political science textbooks, that too not as a thinker/theorist of the social sciences but as a Dalit leader. Ambedkar's introduction in the second edition of the NCERT history textbook is little more than a symbolic gesture, as his name appears in a discussion on the Poona Pact of 1932. This appearance of Ambedkar is less than a page long, and is primarily for the purpose of highlighting his confrontation with Gandhi. In the textbooks of subjects such as sociology and economics, Ambedkar's name does not even make an appearance. By way of comparison, one may consider M.N. Srinivas and G.S. Ghurye's writings on caste, which are included as core studies in the syllabi of sociology, as they are considered to be scholarly. Ambedkar's

---

[1] South Asian Studies/Centre in Western universities, where majority of professors belong to upper castes and are Brahmins.

[2] The data has been collected through RTI from the UGC, dated 1 January 2018.

writings on caste and gender are unknown even to the sociologists and anthropologists who prepare the syllabus.

The worst offenders are the philosophy and economics textbooks in which Ambedkar is nowhere to be found from intermediate level all the way up to MA programmes. This is in spite of Ambedkar's doctorate in the discipline of economics and his numerous path-breaking writings in the field. Vivek Kumar argues that Ambedkar is not considered to be a sociologist in India (V. Kumar 2016, 18). Aakash Singh Rathore writes, 'Despite the number of university buildings and centres named after B. R. Ambedkar in India, there are disproportionately few of Ambedkar's texts on the syllabi of any of the serious research departments in the country' (Rathore and Verma 2011). The Ambedkar chairs in some of the universities exist without any Ambedkar course on the curriculum, and most of the chairs are non-functional. There are no MPhil, PhD, or Post-doctoral programmes offered by Ambedkar centres and chairs in India. The centres and chairs exist merely to celebrate Ambedkar Jayanti or conduct uninspiring conferences on routine themes in a ritualistic manner.

A decade ago, Gopal Guru wrote 'How egalitarian are the social sciences in India?' (Guru 2002). The article lighted a spark amongst the TTB academics as they attempted to respond to Guru's critique. This question is still prevalent in discussions on university campuses, but is only raised by Dalit students. In another context, Johannes Beltzs remarks that the sociology community has so far largely ignored Ambedkar, which is surprising because his analysis of Indian culture, the caste system, authority and religious power, and the religious foundation of the Hindu social order are significant contributions to contemporary debates in sociology. Similarly, Vivek Kumar writes, '[P]ossibly, Ambedkar was the first Indian trained in sociology and anthropology from a foreign university, who also published his article in a foreign journal. Yet he was not included in the list of founders of anthropology and sociology in India' (V. Kumar 2016). Aakash Singh Rathore writes:

> In the field of postcolonial studies, Ambedkar has been all but ignored. Postcolonial theory is another field of study dominated by high-caste intelligentsia, but insofar as this group is generally radical and leftist, it is difficult to attribute their exclusion of Ambedkar to class or caste bias. (Rathore and Verma 2011, xxii)

Taking a cue from Guru, knowledge is historically controlled and monopolized by the TTB. In other words, intellectual activities maintain the hierarchization of knowledge. Knowledge becomes a criterion for exclusion, particularly when we look at the syllabus, curriculum, and methodology used in the production/distribution of knowledge.

The general perception of Ambedkar amongst Indian academics is that his thought is limited to caste and untouchability, and that his writings, speeches, and politics are cynical and derogatory towards Hinduism. This characterization is subtly to be found everywhere. Political theorist Rajeev Bhargava writes, '[the] great Dalit leader B R Ambedkar' (Bhargava 2017). Similarly, Sudipta Kaviraj writes, 'Ambedkar, undoubtedly the pre-eminent leader of the Dalits in modern India' (Kaviraj 2017). The TTBs are generally not referred to by the names of their castes. Ambedkar, on the contrary, is frequently delegated to being representative of the Dalits. At the same time, he is not recognized as a political philosopher or a sociologist, or as an economist.

In this context, Aakash Singh Rathore charges Indian political theorists with a stubborn resistance to consider Ambedkar as a serious thinker.

> I have encountered over and over again a profound resistance against introducing Ambedkar not only into the curriculum, but even across the thresholds of the doorways to philosophy departments. ... A thesis on Gandhi? Fine, carry on. Bilgrami said it's ok. A thesis on Ambedkar? The committee erupts in chorus: "but he is not even a philosopher!"[3]

Several scholars, arguing along similar lines, raise the question of why Indian academia ignores Ambedkar.[4] Thus it is well enough established that this is not a question of *if*, but of *why*.

Academic Untouchability

Indian academics seem to have failed to transgress their own social identities—their ontological position remains intertwined with their social identity. Thus, one must not be surprised to realize

---

[3] See http://www.huffingtonpost.in/aakash-singh-rathore/indian-academias-shunning-of-ambedkar-the-philosopher-reeks-of_a_22025150/. Last accessed in July 2017.

[4] Gail Omvedt, Kancha Ilaiah, Sukhadeo Thorat, Gopal Guru, Vivek Kumar, Aakash Singh Rathore, and several others.

that various sorts of untouchability are being experienced on university campuses by Dalit students. Ranging from the experiences of students in their relationships with their teachers to their experiences with other students and even those with the non-teaching staff; in each case they find themselves being treated in certain ways based on their identity, not only as a part of the hierarchy in the administrative functioning and the teacher–student relationship but also as an implicit bias against students in reserved seats who are considered to not be as worthy as students in unreserved seats. Dalit and Adivasi students, in particular, face discrimination stemming from these notions in all spheres of academic life, whether they are availing of their fellowships or in the process of writing their synopses. The casteist mentality and behaviour of students in unreserved seats, teachers, and the non-teaching staff often associate students from marginalized backgrounds with Ambedkar, thereby attaching several other connotations to them, sometimes even displaying outright contempt. For example, the Rajiv Gandhi National Fellowship (RGNF) holders of several states and central universities are often humiliated by fellow students, the office staff, and others.

The experiences of Dalit and Adivasi students, research scholars, and faculty members need to be considered in order to better understand this new form of 'academic' untouchability. To illustrate by way of some of the problems experienced by several Dalit and Adivasi students and researchers: according to them, they find it difficult to express original ideas in the classroom, while writing their synopses or their examinations, while presenting at seminars and conferences, and in writing their research papers and dissertations. They are often pigeonholed by their identity: when they raise questions and articulate their ideas or their perspectives, they are greeted with such reprimands as 'your language is unsophisticated', 'you always get sentimental when raising questions', 'Dalit and Adivasis students are weak at conceptualizing their ideas', and 'Dalit and Adivasi students and researchers employ the language of the activist, the politician, and the polemicist, but not that of the academic'. They are also greeted with such questions as, 'Why do you study here? You'd be better off doing field work.' On the occasion of a Dalit research scholar writing a dissertation that is on a par with other students, TTB examiners may be found to quip, 'It was beyond our expectation to see a well-argued thesis from you'.

If Dalits intend to do research on Ambedkar, they are generally discouraged from doing so, and it is difficult to convince a TTB supervisor otherwise, for he/she often accuses Dalit students of speaking from a purely subjective position. This is the language that is employed by the TTB academia when engaging with Dalit and Adivasi students. The same work, if conducted by non-Dalit students, is deemed scholarly and interesting.

Jawaharlal Nehru University (JNU), Hyderabad Central University (HCU), and University of Delhi (DU) are widely regarded as amongst the most progressive universities in India. However, when it comes to teaching Ambedkar in departments or centres such as history, economics, and philosophy, they remain as regressive as any other university in the country, for Ambedkar makes scant appearance in any of the numerous courses offered. In JNU, it is reported that a professor of philosophy calls Ambedkar a plagiarist, claiming that the Indian Constitution has borrowed all of its ideas from the West and that Ambedkar was instrumental in doing so. A professor of history at JNU expressed his disapproval when a Dalit student wrote 'Babasaheb' Ambedkar on his assignment. The professor ordered the student to remove the word 'Babasaheb', since such a title cannot be employed in academic writing. However, the word 'Pandit' when used as an honorific for Nehru raised no such problem.[5] Due to these sorts of prejudices being so prevalent, Dalit students frequently hesitate to answer questions about Dalits, caste, and Ambedkar during entrance examinations. Even if they can answer these questions effectively, they do not attempt to answer them for the fear of their own positions, and thus caste identities, being betrayed to the examiner by their writing, and by extension the probability of them being marked down. This has been the experience of Dalit students at JNU, HCU, and DU.

Reservation, Ambedkar, and Stigmatization

Reservation is a contentious subject in India. Some students have gone so far as to commit suicide in protest against reservations in

---

[5] See https://roundtableindia.co.in/index.php?option=com_content&view=article&id=9011:the-death-of-a-historian-in-centre-for-historical-studies-jawaharlal-nehru-university&catid=119:feature&Itemid=132, last accessed in December 2017.

higher education in India, as was witnessed during the Mandal agitation during the 1990s. Reservation in jobs and education has been a burning issue since the 1990s. Here, my focus is to look at how Ambedkar is brought into the picture in debates on reservation. It is a well-known fact that Ambedkar laid out the reservation policy as a form of social justice in Indian democracy. The SCs, STs, and OBCs are beneficiaries of this policy. In this regard, one may present a view from one of the premiere educational institutions in India: the Indian Institutes of Technology (IITs).

The situation of IITs is far worse than central and state universities in India. Dalit and Adivasi students are often referred to by their sub-caste, they face public humiliation in the form of such obscene statements as 'look at the Chamar who wants to become a doctor'. According to upper-caste students, SCs and STs do not have the same merit that students in unreserved seats possess. A professor from one of the IITs writes,

> The IITs as social space then are highly segregated, the public sphere is undemocratic, and discussions are unrepresentative of the population and their divergent aspirations. Caste intervenes to segregate, divide, and regroup in many ways: food habits in hostels, language and dialect, leisure activities, and regional and linguistic origin. The debates on reservation policies becomes occasion for casteism and SC/ST bashing, with little constraints or rebuke imposed on language and content by the institute authorities. The ideology of 'merit' so pervades the institution and its population that raising issues of social justice, and the problems and consequences of social hierarchy, become impossible, with every issue being reduced to one of individual ability. (Parthasarathy 2013, 268)

Caste determines each aspect of campus life, ranging from classroom teaching, hostel mess, and hostel room allotment to administrative work and supervisor selection. N. Sukumar succinctly portrays everyday campus life through an example. Whenever posters are written in support of Dalits and minorities, dirty and abusive remarks are scribbled on them at the hostels. He writes: 'In 2002, a Ph.D. miscreant scribbled "bastard" on Dr B.R. Ambedkar's poster in the social science building. This trend was again witnessed in 2006 when a similar incident took place in the ladies hostel' (Sukumar 2013, 216–17). Such cases may be witnessed across university campuses. Upper-caste students do not tolerate images of Ambedkar inside hostel rooms when a Dalit student puts them up. One study suggests that the entrenched caste discrimination and humiliation faced by Dalit and Adivasi students leads them to commit suicide as a form of ultimate protest (A.S. Kumar 2013).

Whenever an issue regarding reservation is raised, Ambedkar comes into the picture, being the chief architect of the reservation policy in India. In this way, Ambedkar's legacy is narrowed down to the reservation policy. Ambedkar is reservation and reservation is Ambedkar.

It is important to understand that within academic spaces, Dalit students, researchers, and faculty members study, discuss, and debate Ambedkar in order to present an Ambedkarite perspective in their research work. Of course, non-Dalit students and researchers also research and speak on Ambedkar, but there is a significant difference between the two. For Dalit students, studying Ambedkar at a university entails a liberating aspect. It makes it easier for them to articulate their experiences, to express their own views. Ambedkar becomes a vantage point from which to put forth their arguments in debates and discussions, and to form their perspective in understanding social sciences and humanities. This, of course, does not imply that Dalit students should not study other perspectives and methodologies.

Tracing an autonomous space to discuss, study, teach, and research on Ambedkar in academia is difficult. There is a general inclination amongst upper-caste scholars to conduct discourse on Ambedkar from the vantage point of Gandhi. The debate on Ambedkar and Gandhi is unending. Ambedkar is a liberal, constitutionalist, and modernist to all liberal and leftist scholars, whereas the same scholars also allege him to be an agent of the British petit-bourgeoisie whilst simultaneously seeing Marx in him. Similar ideas are to be found in the rhetoric employed by such right-wing politicians as Arun Shourie, who once alleged Ambedkar to be a 'British agent'. Without assessing Ambedkar's critical engagements with liberalism, constitutionalism, Marxism, Buddhism, and the British rule, some scholars make such procrustean judgements and express their prejudices that are now prevalent in academia. On the other hand, Western scholars find a rigorous academic robustness and an epistemic vantage point in Ambedkar's writings, speeches, and politics; however, some of them have also misunderstood Ambedkar in broader normative hermeneutical interpretations. Ambedkar's philosophical underpinnings would become much more obvious if comparative studies between Ambedkar and other

Western thinkers is performed effectively. In my recent work 'Ambedkar's Critique on Recognition', I have discussed Charles Taylor, Axel Honneth, and Nancy Fraser. Ambedkar's idea appeals to emancipatory philosophy across the society. Ambedkar has never been explored in the same way as Gandhi, as the latter's ideas are interpreted in relation to others. In other words, Ambedkar's contributions in the fields of social science, religion, philosophy, and democracy remain to be explored in terms of wider interpretations, which may not be related to the Indian Dalit context but would be treated as an academic exercise with fruits in normative philosophy, history, sociology, and so on.

Public institutions such as universities, where knowledge is produced, have a certain entrenched ethos which prevents them from properly practising research in ethical ways. Dalits in India struggle for recognition as free and equal humans with dignity (Mahanand 2020). The situation in academia is then truly pitiful since thinkers—and particularly anti-caste thinkers—are not recognized as thinkers at all but are unceremoniously pushed into the same pigeonholes as the Dalits outside of academia find themselves in.

Arguably, if Ambedkar, along with other anti-caste intellectuals, activists from different parts of India, and local Adivasi leaders could have been taught seriously from primary school to higher education, the situations in the society, politics, and education system in India would have been very different. Is the Indian education system afraid of teaching Ambedkar or is it the result of upper-caste domination of the education system? In other words, curricula are set up in such a way that teachers teach their suitable books and syllabus, without encouraging any critical engagement with the text or the tradition, and without bringing in the contexts of the content of their teaching. As such, one ought to raise the questions: What is the nature of the Indian university and academia? Is it a public space, free from the cultural, religious, and social spheres of Indian society? What is the difference between Indian educational institutions and Indian academic spaces?

The Ambedkarite Idea of the University

This section briefly tries to explore how Ambedkarites pursue Ambedkar in academic spaces. The objective of a university is to allow students to study, critically study, or debate on an issue, be it from the past, present, or future. Studying any idea or philosophy is not harmful, excluding any of them is unethical. The Ambedkarite idea of the university allows all kinds of ideas to be discussed, researched, and debated with critical engagement. Ambedkar must be studied with other thinkers in India and his writings must be studied with those of other writers. Teaching Ambedkar's writings gives scope for open engagement. Interestingly, Sharmila Rege brings the idea of Dalit-Bahujan experience into the pedagogic discourse.

> Phule and Ambedkar in different ways, by weaving together the emancipatory non-Vedic materialist traditions (Lokayata, Buddha, Kabir) and new western ideas (Thomas Paine, John Dewey, Karl Marx, for instance) had challenged the binaries of western modernity/Indian tradition, private caste-gender/public nation and sought to refashion modernity and thereby its project of education. ... Phule and Ambedkar, as may be apparent from the discussion above, seek a rational engagement with the pedagogy of culture to see how power works through the production, distribution, and consumption of knowledge within particular contexts and re-imagine a culture of pedagogy based on truth-seeking. (Rege 2010)

Over the past two decades, academic discussions on various social and political issues have been challenged by Dalit-Bahujans and feminists. The experiences of Dalit-Bahujans, Adivasis, and women are coming to be understood as part of intellectual discourse. It was difficult to talk about Ambedkar in university spaces before the 1990s; even today, many universities in India present Ambedkar either as a symbolic gesture while talking about the Poona Pact, the Constitution, the Untouchability Act, or as part of his dialogue with Gandhi. Occasionally, his writings are only superficially taught as part of the curricula in some universities. However, Dalit intellectuals are instrumental in bringing the Phule–Ambedkar discourse to academic discussion and pedagogy. There are two kinds of Ambedkarite scholars in the academic space: one is the professional kind that writes and speaks usually from an upper-caste perspective and does not take a clear stand, and the second is the sort that struggles to bring Ambedkar to teaching practice and active discussion as an intellectual exercise, and makes comparative studies with Western thinkers to find similarities and relevance.

In the University of Delhi, Ambedkar was introduced in a BA optional course after arduous efforts by the Dalit faculty. Ambedkar as a thinker and statesman offers a wide range of concepts that are of interest to scholars in social sciences and humanities. It should be noted here that the efforts of Ambedkarite scholars have been admirably articulated in their political and academic engagements. Interestingly, Ambedkar has now been introduced indirectly in a few courses—such as Dalit Politics/Studies, Social Justice and Human Rights, Dalits and the Process of Social Exclusion, Black and Dalit Literature, Ambedkar's Thought, and so on—in which his ideas are being taught as part of the course. Moreover, a few upper-caste professors and honest academicians teach Ambedkar as part of some of the optional courses, which is a recent development in academia, particularly in a few of the central universities such as JNU, DU, and HCU. Ironically, often these developments also carry a degree of stigma with them since they are initiated by Dalit faculty members in these leading universities.[6]

The Indian Institute of Dalit Studies (IIDS) was founded a decade ago, which exclusively takes up empirical work and has published a high volume of work on economic discrimination, social exclusion, and inclusive policy while keeping Ambedkar in the background. The initiative taken by the IIDS on Ambedkar's scholarship has also produced a few works on Ambedkar himself, such as *Ambedkar in Retrospect-Essay on Economics, Politics and Society* (2007), *B. R. Ambedkar: Perspectives on Social Exclusion and Inclusive Policies* (2008), *Revisiting 1956: B. R. Ambedkar and States Reorganisation* (2014), *Dr. Ambedkar and Democracy: An Anthology* (2018). Similarly, in the field of literature, the genres of Marathi and Hindi Dalit literature have appeared which critique the mainstream Brahmanical literature. Dalit literature has not received mainstream recognition, it is criticized as not having any sense of beauty or aesthetics. Dalit literature has been introduced by Dalit faculties but is yet to get recognition as part of mainstream literature. The scholars of mainstream literature claim that Dalit literature is not a form of literature because it is based on negativity and does not employ aesthetic language; whereas poets such as Namdeo Dhasal provide an immanent critique of the Indian state and society. His poetry captures the imagination and encapsulates the cultural wounds and economic exploitation of the marginalized

---

[6] UoH, DU, and JNU are the best examples. I am one who witnessed, when I opted for Dalit politics, upper castes friends their views, this course was cynical, does not have more academic rigour. Maximum students who were opted from Dalit, Adivasis, and OBC background.

communities. Similarly, Dalit autobiographical works such as *Poisoned Bread* (2010), *The Prisons We Broke* (2008), *Jhootan* (2003), or *Mrudeya* (2012) explicate the deeper social, cultural, and political experiences of Dalits in contemporary democracy so as to show how Dalits are segmented, segregated, humiliated, excluded, misrecognized, and how they face entrenched violence by the caste social order. This powerful intervention of Dalit writings is developing in the form of Dalit Experience Theory in the disciplines of social sciences and humanities (Guru and Sarukkai 2012). Dalit Experience Theory challenges certain mainstream epistemic formulations, but for now it has a long way to go.

Two years ago, a volume on Dalit studies was released that contained new writings on Dalits from different parts of India (Rawat and Satyanarayana 2016). These writings on Dalit life, politics, and history encouraged new scholarship. This volume suggested that Indian politics took a new turn with the implementation of reservation as suggested by the Mandal commission, and the consequent emergence of the Bahujan Samaj Party (BSP) has had an impact all over India. The second international conference on Human Dignity, Equality, and Democracy by Dalit Studies sought to engage in an exercise to publish a similar volume, which would again bring regional specificity with figures such as Iyothee Thass, Jogendranath Mandal, and others (this conference happened in the Centre for the Study of Developing Societies, Delhi, on 22–4 January 2018). As Dalit Studies is reaching various parts of the country, it is also bringing along with it a critical history of Dalits so as to show how they have a different conception of the idea of India. A new historiography is thus emerging.

To sum up, India is a vast country, it has a wide variety of languages, cultures, religions, cuisines, lifestyles, and schools of thought. The debate on nation, state, politics, and the nature of society with regards to inequality, unfreedom, and poverty is triggering an increased diversity of thought amongst the citizenry of the country. There are thinkers, leaders, histories, movements, architectural styles, monuments, and so forth that offer different interpretations of its ontology from various perspectives. All of this must be studied, it must be accommodated as a viable subject of study, research, and discussion: and it must be presented in a scientific way—which is how progress occurs in a society; and the contrapositive intellectual monopoly by a single idea proves regressive for the society at large. The Ambedkarite idea of the university would envisage the inclusion of all kinds of ideas to be studied for the betterment of the society as a whole.

What Lies in the Future?

From the above-mentioned observations, it is evident that the scholarship on Ambedkar is increasing now, not only within India but outside of India as well; we have as an example, the recent work on *Political Philosophy of Antonio Gramsci and B. R. Ambedkar* (2013). Other scholars such as Martin Fuchs, Scott Stroud, Lenart Skof, Martha Nussabaum, Luis Cabrera have seen theoretical potential in Ambedkar. Interestingly, Ambedkar is slowly gaining traction as he is introduced to western syllabi that seek to study India or South Asia. Of course, in India, there are contentious issues surrounding Ambedkar scholarship, particularly as posed by upper castes scholars. There is a vehement critique by Dalit movements and Ambedkarite scholars of the nature of Indian academics, and the domination of national-level politics by the upper caste-upper class elite. After 70 years of India's Independence, this is the first time that a massive project on Ambedkar's scholarship that is by congress led government. But one cannot follow this trend blindly; rather, one has to critically analyse it. In short, Indian academics of the future will be more diversified; and there will multiple questions from various regions and schools of thought, which will challenge the mainstream academic discourse.

References

Anderson, Perry. 2012. *The Indian Ideology*. New Delhi: Three Essays Collective.
Baxi, Upendra. 2000. 'Emancipation as Justice: Legacy and Vision of Dr Ambedkar'. In *From Periphery to Centre Stage: Ambedkar, Ambedkarism & Dalit Future*, edited by K.C. Yadav. New Delhi: Manohar.
Bhargava, Rajeev. 2017. 'Nehru against Nehruvians: On Religion and Secularism'. *Economic and Political Weekly* 52, no. 8 (25 February): 34–40.
Guru, Gopal. 2002. 'How Egalitarian are the Social Sciences in India?' *Economic and Political Weekly* 37, no. 50 (14 December): 5003–9.
Guru, Gopal, and Sunder Sarukkai. 2012. *The Cracked Mirror: An Indian Debate on Experience*. New Delhi: Oxford University Press.

Kaviraj, Sudipta. 2017. *Marxism in Translation: Critical Reflections on Indian Radical Thought*. Available at https://www.cambridge.org/core/books/political-judgement/marxtranslation-critical-reflections-on-indian-radical-thought/25D42DE501BC35F9DE6C5559AFDE78C4. Last accessed on 10 December 2017.

Kumar, Singh Anoop. 2013. 'Defying the Odds: The Triumphs and Tragedies of Dalit and Adivasi Students in Higher Education'. In *Beyond Inclusion: The Practice of Equal Access in Indian Higher Education*, edited by Satish Despande and Usha Zacharias. New Delhi: Routledge.

Kumar, Vivek. 2016. 'How Egalitarian is Indian Sociology'. *Economic and Political Weekly* 25, no. 18 (18 June): 33–9.

Mahanand, Jadumani. 2020. 'Ambedkar's Critique of Recognition'. *Studies in Indian Politics* 8, no. 1 (2 May). Available at https://journals.sagepub.com/doi/full/10.1177/2321023020918055. Last accessed on 30 May 2020.

Omvedt, Gail. 2004. *Ambedkar: Towards an Enlightened India*. New Delhi: Penguin.

Parthasarathy, D. 2013. 'After Reservations: Caste, Institutional Isomorphism, and Affirmative Action in the IITs'. In *Equalising Access: Affirmative Action in Higher Education in India, United States, and South Africa*, edited by Zoya Hasan and Martha C. Nussbaum. New Delhi: Oxford University Press.

Queen, Christopher S. 2008. Review of *Dr. Ambedkar and Untouchability: Fighting the Indian Caste System*. Buddhist-Christian Studies 28: 168–172. doi:10.1353/bcs.0.0018.

Rathore, Aakash Singh. 2017. *Indian Political Theory: Laying the Groundwork for Svaraj*. New Delhi: Routledge.

Rathore, Aakash Singh, and Ajay Verma. 2011. *Buddha and His Dhamma: A Critical Edition*. New Delhi: Oxford University Press.

Rawat, Ramnarayana S., and K. Satyanarayana. 2016. *Dalit Studies*. Durham, NC, and London: Duke University Press.

Rege, Sharmila. 2010. 'Education as Trutiya Ratna: Towards Phule-Ambedkarite Feminist Pedagogical Practice'. *Economic and Political Weekly* 45, no. 44 (30 October): 88–98.

Santosh, S., and Joshil K. Abraham. 2010. 'Caste Injustice in Jawaharlal Nehru University'. *Economic and Political Weekly* 45, nos 26/27 (26 June–9 July): 27–9.

Sukumar, N. 2013. 'Quota's Children: The Perils of Getting Educated'. In *Beyond Inclusion: The Practice of Equal Access in Indian Higher Education*, edited by Despande Satish and Zacharias Usha. New Delhi: Routledge.

———. 2016. 'Universities as Modern Agraharas', *Tehelka* 13, no. 5 (30 January). Available at http://www.tehelka.com/2016/01/universities-as-modern-agraharas/,Publishedin. Last accessed on 23 March 2020.

Index

academic space, in India: academic untouchability and, 260–2; Ambedkarite idea of the university, 265–69; caste discrimination and humiliation, 264; controlled by Brahmins and upper castes, 258; hegemonized by top twice born (TTB), 258–60; knowledge production and domination in, 258; National Council of Educational Research and Training (NCERT), 258; notion of, 256; pedagogy and intellectual practice, 258–60; problematizing, 257–8; reservation in education sector, 262–5; stigmatization, issue of, 262–5; study on Ambedkar, 257, 258, 262–5; Thorat committee report of AIIMS, 257; university as, 258

academic untouchability, 260–2; bias against students in reserved seats, 261; experiences of Dalit and Adivasi students, 261–2; teacher–student relationship, 261

activism-based actual movements, 171

Ad Dharm religious movement, 16

Adivasis, 176, 190, 192, 195–7, 257, 261–2, 265–6

adult illiteracy, 218

African Americans, 2; concerns over racism and white supremacy, 171; cultural and social humiliation, 171

ahimsa, 16, 45

Ahi Vitra (snake-god), 186

Akshaya Patra Foundation, 23n8; mid-day meal programme, 23n8

Alberuni, Ibn Ahamad, 177–8; description of 'Dibali', 184

Alberuni's India, 177, 179

All India Backward Students Forum (AIBSF), 191

Ambedkar, Babasaheb, 176; account of religion as *dhamma*, 33; on bond between Buddhism and the Gita, 48; as chairman of the drafting committee of Constitution, 68; conversion from Hinduism to Buddhism, 34–6, 99, 116; as founding father of sociological studies in India, 223; and journey of Moses, 7;

perception of, amongst Indian academics, 260; philosophy of religion, 91–109; project of transforming society, 35; reading of Manu and Hindu history, 156; reading of the Gita, 33–4, 37, 40–4, 58n20, 47–8; re-discovering, 210–16; Shah attributes to, 40n9; social–ethical religion, 46; social movement, 18; struggle for the Hindu code bills, 216; views on Jews and Brahmins, 107; work towards uplifting the Dalit community, 202
Ambedkar–Gandhi disputes, 212
Ambedkar Jayanti, 259
Ambedkar scholarship, 269
Anderson, Perry, 27, 106, 256–7
Annihilation of Caste, 29, 54, 55, 63, 96, 106, 108, 154, 224n6
anti-Brahaman movement, 195
anti-caste movements, 19, 23, 170, 179
anti-colonial discourse, 77
anti-colonial movement, 38
anti-Eurocentrism, 170
anti-Semitism, in USA, 9
appropriation, politics of, 107
Arthashastra, 106
Aryans, 25, 185; conflict with native rulers, 180; invasion of India, 177; spirit of conflict and dualism, 186; Vedic narratives of, 187; war against Nagas, 177
Arya Samaj, 81
ascetic brotherhood, 28
Asian sovereignty, Soviet threat to, 127
asura (demigod): Banasura, 183–4; celebrations of *suras* killing of, 183; conflict with *suras*, 180; Hiranyakashyapu, 180;
historical proof for, 175–88; indigenous Dalits as, 176; Mahabali, 180–2, 192–4; Mahishasura, 180, 182, 194, 196–9; *mridavach* (language of asuras), 186; as mythical beings, 179; Narakasura, 180, 194; positions in Hindu religious texts, 177; Prahalada, 180; Ravana, 180, 191–2, 194, 197–8; Shankhasura, 180; slaying of, 197
atmagyan, 85, 88
Aupamanyava, 185
*avarna*s (non-believers), 224
awakened consciousness, 126

Babri Masjid, destruction of, 112
Backward Classes, 225, 249; upliftment of, 241
Bahujan Samaj Party (BSP), 92, 268
Bama's *Karukku*, 159
Banasura, legend of, 183–4
Banias, 242; business empires of, 245
Basavanna (social reformer), 17
Base Christian communities, 5, 12, 190
Bauddha Darshan, 82–3
belief systems, in India, 222–3
Bhagawatam, 179, 182
Bhagwad Gita, 38, 177; Ambedkar's reading of, 33–4, 37, 40–4, 46n20, 47–8; bond with Buddhism, 48; Buddhist influence on, 45n19; Gandhi's interpretation of, 41, 46n10; psychological interpretation of, 41; Tilak's interpretation of, 41; and untouchables, 41
bhakti, ideology of, 46
Bhakti movements, 17–18, 92
Bharatiya Janata Party (BJP), 112, 120, 193

Bhikkhu Sangha, 94
birth and rebirth, cosmic scheme of, 10
birth-based hierarchy, 4
bloody revolution, 116, 127–8
Bodh Gaya, 71–3, 73n8
bodily 'violence', 127
bonded labour, 245
Brahamanical superiority, notion of, 29
Brahmanical hierarchy, 40n9, 141
Brahmanical social order, 86
Brahmanism: counter-revolution against the Buddhist revolution, 42; hostility with Buddhism, 229; reformers of, 27
Brahmins, 26, 224; devoid of bureaucratic power, 246; diasporic intelligentsia of, 245; dominance in the bureaucracy, 246; position towards elementary education, 237–8; priesthood, 16; as spiritual leader, 21
Brahmanical hypocrisy, politics of, 107
British Empire, 233–5
British-imperialist/Brahmin-nationalist binary, 120, 142
British Raj, education system under, 233, 244
Buddha and His Dhamma, 39, 55, 60, 103n13, 105
Buddhaghosha's *Visuddhimagga*, 75
Buddhahood, notion of, 67, 69, 86
Buddha, Lord: life of, 86; self-transformation in, 85; as 'the Other', 85
Buddha or Karl Marx, The, 45, 55, 100n7
Buddha's Dhamma, 53
Buddhism, 20, 92, 215; Ambedkar conversion into, 44, 99; Ambedkar's understanding of, 107–18; Bhikshu Sangha, 45; bond with Gita, 48; on brotherhood of man, 84; celebration of detachment, 45n19; challenge to the Brahminical religion, 228–9; choice of embracing, 63; coexistence, principle of, 84; democratization of, 75; destruction due to Muslim 'invasion of India', 127; Dharmapala's representation of, 71; dialectics of, 83; egalitarianism of, 37; emergence in India, 43; and European Enlightenment, 68; genealogical outline of, 70; influence on Gita via the karma theory, 45n19; *Kalama Sutta*, 103n13; *Mahapadana Sutta*, 42; *Mahaparinirvan Sutta*, 97n5; mental revolution against a Marxist bloody revolution, 128; Metta Sutta, 29; Navayana Buddhism, 44; as offshoot of the Gita or Hinduism, 42; Orientalist approaches to, 43; preservation and restoration of, 72; as relational to Hinduism, 67n1; religious conversion to, 27; restoration in India, 72; revival of, 26; Sanskrityayan's dialectics of, 81–5; social and political theory in, 84; *Tevijja Sutta*, 42; theology of liberation and, 27; value of equality in, 85
Buddhist art forms and iconography, 80
Buddhist bhikshu, 81
Buddhist communities, of India, 29, 224, 229n13
Buddhist Dialectics, 83

Buddhist Empire, 223n5; military coup against, 229n13; political assassination, 229n13
Buddhist–Marxian utopia, 82
Buddhist Movement in India, 127
Buddhist revolution, 42; counter-revolution of Brahminism against, 42
Buddhist Sangha, 37
Buddhist Suttas, 39; Ambedkar's reading of, 40–4
bullock cart capitalists, of rural India, 245
bureaucracy: colonial, 244; and the command economy, 244–7; dominance of Brahmins in, 246; and higher education, 246
burning of effigies, 195–6

campesino, dispossession of, 12
caste-based apartheid, indignity of, 152
caste-based atrocities, laws against, 10
caste discrimination, 4, 17, 23, 225; death of Rohith Vemula, 257; denial of education, 230–1; in Indian universities, 257
caste hierarchy, 258; problem of, 35; religious and social dogma of, 41
caste identity, superiority of, 240n23
caste inequality, 227; in the community of faith, 17
caste nationalism, 113, 173
caste power, structural logic of, 245
castes, definition of, 223
caste system, in India, 3, 225–7; as basis of Indian social relations, 223; beneficiaries of, 227; Brahamanical superiority in, 29; causes of reproduction and stability of, 230–1; challenges to, 232–3; eradication of, 23; governing elites and stability concerns, 248–9; Hindu notion of, 29, 96; myths of origin, 227–30; and notion of *catur-varnyam*, 23; origin of, 21; Weiner's study on, 248
Catholic Church, 4, 22
catur-varnyam, notion of, 23
child illiteracy, 222
child labour, 218, 221; and education, 249–51
Christianity, 61, 92, 106, 188, 222; of charity without truth, 11; Exodus, story of, 6–10, 13; origins of, 36; religionless, 57, 57n2; religious conversion to, 38; social gospel of Jesus, 12, 20; teachings of Jesus, 13; Ten Commandments, 12
Christian Missionaries, 129
civic dignity: definition of, 154; denial of, 152–7
civil disobedience, against colonial rule, 214
civil society, religion for, *see* religion for civil society
Cold War, 141
colonial bureaucracy, 244
command economy, 244–7
communal violence, against Muslims, 4
Communist Manifesto, The, 136
Conference of Bishops, 12, 20
Confucianism, 106
Constituent Assembly of India, 67
Constitution of India, 222, 225, 266; Ambedkar as chairman of the drafting committee of, 68; Article 244 of, 195; Article 340 of, 225; on dignity of the individual, 152; Fifth Schedule of, 195; law against caste discrimination, 4

Coomaraswamy, Ananda K., 70; construction of the 'civilizational', 77–81; *Elements of Buddhist Iconography*, 75; *Hinduism and Buddhism*, 75; *Origin of the Buddha Image, The*, 75; question of culture, 80
corpsing: performing death, 164–6; performing life, 162–4; role in human dignity, 161–6
creative economy, notion of, 205
critical hermeneutics, project of, 36n4
cultural activism, 206–10
cultural heritage, 3
cultural identity, 194, 205
cultural imperialism, of Hindutva, 196
cultural nationalism, 173
cultural property, illicit transport and export of, 204
cultural reconstruction, 171
cultural rights: Ambedkar's work towards, 203–6; and cultural activism, 206–10; and social justice, 210–16
cultural rights, definition of, 204–5
cultural separation, process of, 171
custodians of Hindu culture, 170

*daithya*s, 178
Dalit-Bahujan experience, 91, 92, 266
Dalit dignity: acquisition of, 160; caste-determined labour and, 151; cultural representations and, 157–68; idea of, 151; between immanent and civic dignity, 152–7; spatiality of, 158–9
Dalit Experience Theory, 268
Dalit literature, 267
Dalit lives, romanticization of, 165

Dalit Mukti Morcha, 196
Dalit Panther movement, 91–2
Dalits, 208; Ad Dharm religious movement, 16; agitation for human rights, 26; Ambedkar's work towards uplifting, 202; anti-caste movement, 19; breaking away from Hinduism, 173n1; political theory, 118; religious conversion to Buddhism, 27, 28n10; untouchability, stigma of, 4; *see also asura* (demigod)
Dalit Solidarity Network, 226n9
*danava*s, 178
Dasha Mahavidyas, 198
Dasyus, 186
Davids, Thomas William Rhys, 25; Hibbert Lectures of 1881, 25–6
dead faith of the living, 26
Declaration of Principles on Tolerance (1995), 204
Declaration on the Responsibility of the Present Generations Towards Future Generations (1997), 204
decolonization, notion of, 49
devotee for Krishna, qualities of: *karuna* (compassion), 42; *maître* (loving kindness), 42; *mudita* (sympathizing joy), 42; *upeksha* (unconcernedness), 42
Dewey, John, 9n5, 55, 104, 108–9, 219; pragmatist approach towards religion, 108
Dhamma: *Buddha and His Dhamma*, 55; defined, 55; notion of, 54–5, 107–8
Dhammapada, 38, 45; Ambedkar's assessment of, 33–4
Dharmapala, Anagarika, 43, 70, 232; biographical details of, 71n4; Bodh Gaya Case against Hemant Giri, 72n7; creation of pan-Buddhist outlook, 71;

dual life of, 74; as Father of Modern Lanka, 71n4; as homeless defender of the faith, 72; Maha Bodhi Society, 71, 72; phases of life, 71; quest for identity, 71–4; representation of Buddhism, 71; *Return to Righteousness*, 75; visit to Bodh Gaya, 71; 'The World's Debt to Buddha' lecture, 71
dharmic law, violence of, 48
dignity, *see* human dignity
Dipavamsa, 74
discriminated castes, of India, 218
divine governance, scheme of, 101–2
division of laborers, 160, 223
division of labour, 106, 121, 159–60; and caste system in India, 223; between *glauben* (faith) and *wissen* (knowledge), 59
Diwali festival: Alberuni's description of, 184; Bhaubeej Day, 184, 184n7; Phuley's version of, 184; secularization of, 182–3
downward filtration, doctrine of, 237
Dravidar Kalakam movement, 114
Dravidas, 177, 187
Dravidian identity, 141
Dravidian Pandhyas, 186
'Dravidian race' against 'Aryan power', 139n22
Dravidians, 25, 177, 185–6; demonization of, 187; Vedic narratives of, 187
dukkha, annihilation of, 84, 86
Dussera festival: Aryan version of, 183; Kshatriya version of, 183; secularization of, 182–3
Dutch Reformed Church of South Africa, 19

East India Company, 223n4, 234, 235
economic liberation, 214
economic redistribution, 131
economic well-being, 27
economy of permanence, concept of, 213
education for the masses: English education for, 236; Gandhi, caste, and, 239–40; higher education and, 237; stand of higher classes on, 237–48; stand of nationalist elites on, 238–9; 'Warda Plan' of basic education, 239
education system, in India, 265; Anglicists and their downward filtration theory, 235–6; bias against students in reserved seats, 261; Brahminical monopoly of, 235; under British Raj, 233; caste discrimination and humiliation, 264; caste system and, 249–51; child illiteracy, 222; and child labour, 249–51; colonial policy on, 222; cross-country differences in primary schooling, 221; cultural subjugation of, 236; culture of Sanskritic learning, 224; denial of 'right to education', 230–1; for educating the 'higher classes', 237; Education Policy of 1968, 220; elementary education of the masses, 237; English education, in Bengal, 236; experiences of Dalit and Adivasi students, 261–2; Five Year Plan on, 246–7; free and compulsory schooling to children, 219; Gandhi's plan on, 246; higher education, 220, 237; ideology of Hinduism and, 234; ideology of Hinduism and, 222; in independent India, 241–2; Macaulay's policy of introducing Western education, 235–6;

for the masses, *see* education for the masses; National Education Policy (1986), 243; Orientalist position on, 233–5; policy negligence in, 220; position of the 'higher classes' towards elementary education, 237–48; primary education, 220, 222, 237–48; public expenditure on, 221; school enrolment ratios, 220; as a site of ideology, 233; teacher–student relationship, 261; universal compulsory education, 246; vernacularists and, 237; Weiner's study on, 222; Western science and literature, 235; Zahir Hussain committee on, 246
elementary education, *see* primary education, in India
English education: Angilicist policy on, 236; in Bengal, 236; power of, 236
equanimity in Buddhism: idea of, 76; value of, 85–6
Exodus, story of, 6–10, 13

farm slavery, 245
Five Year Plan, 218, 246–7
free choice in adopting religious practices, notion of, 38
freedom of religion, rights to, 38, 203
free expression, rights to, 203
Freire, Paulo, 29
French Revolution, 34, 127, 215–16

gandharvas, 177–8, 185
Gandhi, Indira, 112
Gandhi, Mahatma, 224, 227n12, 257, 264; Ambedkar's meeting with, 10; disputes with Ambedkar, 212; distinction between *varna* and *jati*, 33n1; on education of the masses, 239–40; *Harijan*, 20, 20n6; idealization of the Indian village, 158; interpretation of the Gita, 41, 46n10; objection to caste oppression, 21; plan on elementary school education, 246; 'Warda Plan' of basic education, 239
Gandhi, Rajiv, 243
Geertz, Clifford, 124–5, 142
gender discrimination, 106
General Committee for Public Instruction (GCPI), 237
genocide, 3, 7, 10
ghettos, 158–9, 166
global labour, 129, 131–2
governing castes, of India, 227, 242–3
'governing class' of independent India, 238
Government of India Act (1935), 138
graded inequality, 34n1, 106, 224, 230
Green Revolution, 245
guna-karma-vibhagasah, 23
Gutierrez, Gustavo, 19

Habermas, Juergen, 47n23; approach to post-secular society, 59
Hare Krishna movement, 22
Harijan, 20, 20n6
Hegel, G.W.F., 53, 76, 87, 92; construction of the 'Orient spirit', 87–8
heredity of caste, 239
hermeneutic project, 44–9; Habermasian model of, 47
higher classes, in India: Brahmins, 237; position towards elementary education, 237–8
higher education, in India, 220, 263; bureaucracy and, 246; disparities relating to the access to, 220n2; downward filtration,

doctrine of, 227; fiscal support to, 238; General Committee for Public Instruction (GCPI), 227; of 'higher classes', 227; inter-caste disparities in, 220n2; share of the government in total expenditure on, 247; 'trickle down' analogy, rhetoric of, 247–8
Hindu Code Bill, 211, 214, 216
Hindu communal identity, 193
Hindu culture and society, 14
Hindu family laws, of succession, 214
Hinduism, 92, 106, 188–9, 224; anti-caste leaders, 27; beneficiaries of, 242; Brahamanical superiority in, 29; Brahmin priesthood in, 16; caste system in, 96; commitment to hierarchical order, 118; cultural authenticity, 173; evolution of, 20; fundamental values of, 23; origin of caste in, 21; philosophy of, 102; Radhakrishan's view of, 61; re-emergence of 228, reformation of, 27; social disparity of, 37; structure of caste in, 16; as universal religion, 61
Hinduization, process of, 189
Hindu law, 223n4
Hindu mythological texts, 96
Hindu mythologies, evils of, 194
Hindu Nationalist Party, 28n10
Hindu social order, 38, 159, 222–3, 226
Hindu social reformers, 16
Hindu society: Brahmin, 14; division of, 24; Kshatriya, 14; Purusa Sukta, 24–5; social pyramid of, 14; Sudra, 14; Vaishya, 14; varnas (social classes), 14
Hindus of Chakwara, 155

Hindu view of life, 27
Holocaust, 3–4, 20
homo democraticus, 57
'honorary English men' in India, 236, 244
human dignity: and bodily integrity, 154; of the collective, 167; corpsing and, 161–6; Dalit dignity, *see* Dalit dignity; definition of, 153; dual fictions of, 154; foundational fiction of, 153; Humiliation Inventory, 154; of the individual, 167; labouring bodies and, 159–61; loss of, 156; notion of, 9; policing of, 159
human rights, 156; Ambedkar's work towards, 203–6; cultural human rights, 205; Universal Declaration of Human Rights (UDHR), 203
Humiliation Inventory, 156
Hyderabad Central University (HCU), 262

Indian civilization, values of, 76
Indian Institute of Dalit Studies (IIDS), 267
Indian Institutes of Technology (IITs), 263
Indian Ishathul Islam Society, 115
Indian knowledge systems, 43
Indian National Congress, 10, 223, 239; doctrine of political reform, 214
Indian Penal Code, 223n4; section 124A of, 196
Indian society, Orientalist view of, 45
Indian spiritual movements, 18
India's democratic crisis, in the Emergency, 120
indigenous-Brahmin-nationalist, 121
Indo-Aryan nation, idea of, 185

inequality: Hindu doctrine of, 93; of men based on birth, 223
inter-caste marriages, 17
International Covenant on Civil and Political Rights, 203
International Covenant on Economic, Social, and Cultural Rights, 204
International Labour Organisation (ILO), 14, 225
International Society for Krishna Consciousness (ISKCON), 22; Akshaya Patra Foundation, 23n8; on birth-based caste system, 22; on eradication of the caste system, 23; Hare Krishna movement, 22; religious leadership against caste, 23; *varnashrama* system, 23; on Vedic system of religion, 23
invisibilization, discourse of, 69
Islam, 92, 106, 188, 222; egalitarian doctrine, 133; mass conversion to, 112–13, 129

Jainism, 16, 28
Jawaharlal Nehru University (JNU), New Delhi, 191, 262; Mahishasur Movement, 195
Jews: Ambedkar's views on, 107; of Imperial Russia, 3; quotas for education, 3
John XXIII, Pope: *Pacem in Terris* (1963), 10; teachings of, 11
justice, otherness and notions of, 85–7
Justice Party, 27n9, 232

*kala suddha*s (brown sahibs), 74
Kalbhairi, 181–2
Kant, Immanuel, 92, 109; notion of universal moral principles, 108
Kanyakubja Brahmins, of Vidisha, 197–8

karma, theory of, 45n19, 47, 104
karuna (compassion), 104, 107; value of, 77
Kelkher Commission, 240
Kerala Devasam Board, 192
khandoba, 181
King, Martin Luther, Jr., 5, 22, 213
kinnaras, 178
knowledge: acquisition of, 236; production and domination, 258
Koran, 45
Kosambi, Dharmanand, 70; *Bhagvan Buddha*, 76, 76n11, 85; concern for equanimity, 75–7; contribution to Indology, 48; *Hindi Sanskriti ani ahinsa*, 77; legacy of, 84
Kshatriyas, 177, 224, 245

landlord castes, 245
Latin American theology, 6, 10, 12
liberal Protestantism: failure of, 57; humanistic theology of, 57
liberation, theology of, 5, 11, 14, 20, 136n19; Buddhism and, 27; formulations of, 16; in Latin America, 20
Lingayat faith: founding of, 17–18; protest against Hindu notions of caste, 18

Mahabharata, 96, 106
Maha Bodhi Society, 43, 71, 72
Maha Kosha tradition, 74
Mahishasura: legend of, 179–80, 182, 191–2, 194–9; Mahishasura Martyrdom Day, 191; Mahishasur Movement in North India, 195
Mandal Commission, 92, 225, 225n7, 263, 268
manual scavenging: caste-based discriminations and, 225;

definition of, 14, 225n8; and
untouchability, 14
Manusmriti (Laws of Manu),
94, 106, 175, 222–3, 223n4,
229n13, 231; Amebedkar's act of
burning, 187
marginalized groups, 3, 113
Marxian–Buddhist dialectics, 86
Marxism, 82–3, 116, 122, 127, 129,
137–8, 141, 215, 256, 264
Marxism–Leninism universalism,
48
Master Race, 3
master–slave dialectic, of the
pharaohs, 7
Matsya Purana, 178–9
Meenakshipuram, mass conversion
at: Ambedkar's Buddhism and,
125–8; conversion of Dalits
to Buddhism, 113; conversion
of Dalits to Islam, 112–13;
EVR's concepts of, 125, 128–39;
Meenakshipuram Thoughts,
128–9; as national threat, 112;
prefatory problematics of,
117–25
Meenakshipuram Redux, 140
meritocratic dignity, 154
middle class, 249, 249n26
mind–body dualism, 141
Mlechas, 186
Mohammed, Prophet, 129, 132, 135
Moral Revival Movement, 5
Moses, 6–10, 27, 29; Laws of, 10
Mount Meru (Purusaparvatha), 178
mridavach (language of asuras), 186
multi-faith democracies, 4
Muslim 'invasion of India', 127

Nagas, 177, 185–6, 194; pan-Indian
nature of the pre-Aryan Nagas,
187
Nalanda University, 81; burning of
the libraries of, 230

Namdev community, in Mandsaur,
198
Narakasura, legend of, 179–80, 182,
192, 194–5
National Education Policy (1986),
243
nationalist elites, stand on
education for the masses, 238–9
Navayana Buddhism, 44, 68–9
Nehru, Jawaharlal, 240–1
neo-capitalism, 183
non-Brahmin political theory, 118
non-Hindu religious identity, 215
non-Vedic materialist traditions,
266
non-violence, genealogy of, 41, 47,
76, 77, 119, 138, 214

Onam festival, 193–4
'Orient spirit', construction of,
87–8
Other Backward Classes (OBC), 225

paisachi language, 186
Pali language, 25
patriarchal social relations, 121
Philosophy of Hinduism, 101n9,
102, 104, 155
philosophy of religions, 78;
Ambedkar's views on, 91–9;
analyses of divine attributes,
103; multiple ontological
realities of, 105–8; philosophy
and, 102–5; religiosity and caste-
based experiences, 93–4
Phule–Ambedkar discourse,
to academic discussion and
pedagogy, 266
Phule, Jyotiba, 92, 176, 181–2;
Aryan version and the Kshatriya
version of Dussera, 183; on
celebration of Diwali festival,
184; on education of the Shudras
and the Untouchables, 232;

language Sudra and Ati-Sudra, 100; movement for empowerment of low castes, 17; revolt against the Brahminical monopoly, 232; Satya Shodak Samaj, 232; on schooling for girls, 17; on schooling for upper-caste widows, 17; *Slavery*, 179
Phule, Savitribai, 232
political conflict, religion's role in, 52, 59
political disaffection, role in weaponization of religion, 60
politicization of religion, phenomenon of, 60
Poona Pact (1932), 258, 266
poverty: in India, 4; inter-generational, 5
pratyaksa, observation of, 130, 134
primary education, in India, 220, 238; Gandhi's plan on, 246; negligence of, 222, 244; self-financing system for, 246; share of the national budget, 246; universalization of, 244–5, 247, 252
private property: ownership of, 83; Sankrityayan's writings on, 84
Prohibition of Employment as Manual Scavengers and Their Rehabilitation Act (2013), 14
public life: ethics in, 68; reconstitution of, 79
public spaces, norms of usage of, 159
purity, Hindu doctrine of, 93

quotas for education, 3

race, purity of, 3, 24
racial apartheid, in South Africa, 19
racial majority, ideology of, 176
Radhakrishnan, Sarvepalli, 25–7; view of Hinduism, 61

radical equality, 7
'radical' politics, 59–60
rakshasas, 178, 185, 188, 196
Ramasamy, E.V. (Periyar), 27n9, 92, 114, 176, 232; act of breaking the idols of the Pullayar, 187; basis for religious evaluation, 134; concern with the labouring masses, 132; confrontational radicalism, 187; criticisms of Hinduism and temples, 131; on female purdah (*kosha*) system, 131; Islamic mass conversion's appeal for, 138; LGBTQ mobilizations of, 139n23; *Mawlid* speeches, 129, 132–3; on non-Brahmin concept of conversion, 141; 'Ramayan: A True Reading', 187; remarks regarding Islamic conversion, 131; republication of October 1929 speech, 131; Self-Respect Movement, 128; on Untouchable Islamic conversion, 129; views on religious conversion, 128–39
Ramayana, 106, 179, 188; Tulasidas's *Ramayana*, 197; Valmiki's *Ramayana*, 188
Rashtriya Swayamsevak Sangh (RSS), 193
Ravana, legend of, 180, 191–2, 194, 197–8; puja, 191
religion: Ambedkar's views on, 52, 56, 108, 215; detrimental to social equality, 94; founding principles of, 95; and its necessity to human society, 94–101; multiple ontological realities of, 105–8; philosophies of, 78, 91–109; political disaffection and, 72; politicization of, 60;

pragmatic and rational sense of, 101–2; public character of, 55; racialization of, 61; resurgence of, 62; return of, 62; role in political conflict, 52, 59, 62; social construction of, 57n2; weaponization of, 60
religion for civil society: Ambedkar's vision of, 52, 53–6; Christianity as, 61; concept of, 52–64; dissonances of, 56–60; framework for, 66; resonances of, 60–4
religion of liberation, search for, 9–29
religious beliefs, 55; rationalization of, 61–2
religious conversion, 27, 28n10; Ambedkar's concept of, 132; mass conversion to 'foreign religion', 129; mass conversion to Islam, 112–13; at Meenakshipuram, 112–13; mindful conversion, 34–40; politicization of, 140; sociological study of, 38; understanding of, 128
religious identities, 15–16, 36, 53, 74, 114, 172, 215
religious radicalism, 59, 62
religious revolution, 39, 125
Republican Party of India, 92, 216
reservation policy in India: Ambedkar as chief architect of, 264; beneficiaries of, 263; as form of social justice, 263; in jobs and education, 262–3; Mandal agitation of 1990s, 263; for OBCs, 240; principle of, 241; protest against, 262
right-wing populisms, 117, 142
Rig Veda, 21, 179, 185–6, 227
Rohingyas of Myanmar, 3

Rousseau's Civil Religion, 108
rural leadership, for social change, 12

saddhamma, 104
*safai karamchari*s, 162
Sambuka (Shudra risi), killing of, 96
Samkhya, 95, 177
Sankrityayan, Rahul, 70; on annihilation of *dukkha*, 84; *Baisvinsadi*, 82; *Buddha Darshan*, 85; *dharmic vichar* (righteous views), 83; *Dharshan Digga Darshan*, 81n19, 82; dialectics of engaged Buddhism, 81–5; *Meri Jeevan Yatra*, 81n19, 82; pursuit of finding the true sources of Buddhism, 84; role in kisaan andolan, 82; views on Buddhism, 82; *Volga se Ganga*, 81n19, 82; writings on private property, 84
Sanskrit language, 186, 234, 236
Saraswati, Dayanand, 81
Satpata Brahamana, 179, 186
Savarna Hindus, 4
Scheduled Castes (SCs), 4, 97, 225
Scheduled Castes and Tribes (Prevention of Atrocities) Act (1989), 196
Scheduled Tribes (STs), 4, 225
schooling: for Dalit children, 213; for girls, 17; for upper-caste widows, 17
secularization of religion, 9; crisis of, 59; definition of, 62; modernity and, 63
self-determination, rights to, 119, 203
Self-Respect Movements, 27n9, 114, 128, 136, 232
sense of belonging, 99, 219
servile castes, 227
servile classes, 251

Shudras, 96, 224, 225; disarmament of, 231
Sikh faith, 92; founding of, 17; Guru Nanak and, 17; inter-caste marriages, 17; *karah prasad*, 17; teachings of, 17; worship service, 17
social agitation, 27
social bonds, 52–3, 61
social dignity: Dalit dignity, *see* Dalit dignity; hierarchies of, 151
social distinction, among hereditary classes, 3
social divisions by birth, determination of, 23
social divisions of caste, 10
social equality, 94, 211, 250
social–ethical religion, 46
social identity, 176, 222, 260
social inequality, 84, 151, 152, 157, 239; structures of, 157
social injustice, 151, 210, 212
social justice movement, 5, 14, 21, 27, 203, 204, 241, 248; cultural rights and, 210–16
social segregation, 159
social structure, in India, 222–3
socio-cultural alliance, 172
spiritual beings, classes of, 177–8
stigmatization, issue of, 262–5
'subaltern' movements, 120–3, 125, 141, 142, 170–6, 179, 185, 189–96, 198–200
suras, 179–80, 185, 187, 195–6

Tamil Nadu Prohibition of Forcible Conversion of Religion Ordinance (2002), 140
Thanthai Periyar Dravidar Kazhagam (TPDK), 195
Theosophical Society, 71n5
Tilak, J.B.G., 33, 42, 45, 48, 246–7; interpretation of Gita, 41

top twice born (TTB), migrating to foreign universities, 258
totalitarian regimes: barrier against the horrors of, 57; rise of, 57
'traditional' occupation, 240
Truth Seekers Society, *see* Satya Shodak Samaj; in Madras Presidency/Erode, 128

United Nations Development Agency (UNDP), 205
United Nations Educational, Scientific, and Cultural Organization (UNESCO), 204; Convention on the Protection and Promotion of the Diversity of Cultural Expressions, 204; on preservation of cultural diversity, 205; Universal Declaration on Bioethics and Human Rights (2005), 153
United Nations Organization (UNO), 220
universal compulsory education, establishment of, 246
Universal Declaration of Human Rights (UDHR, 1948), 18, 152, 156, 203, 216
Universal Declaration on Cultural Diversity, 204
universal literacy, 219, 229, 251
universal moral principles, notion of, 108
universal spirituality, 18
university: as academic space, 258; Ambedkarite idea of, 265–9; objective of, 265
University of Delhi (DU), 213, 262, 266
untouchability: academic, 260–2; concept of, 15–16; manual scavenging, 14; stigma of, 4, 10, 20n6
Untouchability Act, 266

Untouchables, 47, 155, 170, 213; *avarna*s (non-believers), 224; conversion to Islam, 112–13, 129; disarmament of, 231; occupations of, 14; prohibition from reading Sanskrit, 46; religious conversion to Buddhism, 27; *Untouchable with Dead Cow-II*, 15
upper-caste widows, schooling for, 17

Vaishyas, 224
Valmiki's *Joothan*, 159, 162, 164, 268
Vardhamana, Prince (Mahavira), 16
varnas (social classes): *chaturvarna*, 33n1, 223–4; concept of, 21; distinction with *jati*, 33n1; in Hindu society, 14, 29; law of, 21; violence of, 33
varnashrama system, 23
Vedic punishments for dissidents, 138
Vedic system of religion, 23
Vemula, Rohith, 256–7
vernacular-based elementary instructions, 237
vote banks, network of, 243, 243n24

'Warda Plan' of basic education, 239
Weber, Max, 59, 106; *Protestant Ethic and the Spirit of Capitalism, The*, 106
Western education: among the people of India, 237; Macaulay's policy of introducing, 235–6; for traditional learned castes of Hindus, 236
World Buddhist Congress, 215
World Congress of Religions (1893), Chicago, 71
world heritage, protection of, 204

zamindari (landlords) class, 242

Editor and Contributors

Editor

Aakash Singh Rathore is the author of *Ambedkar's Preamble: A Secret History of the Constitution of India* (2020) and a regular contributor to the *Indian Express* and *Outlook* magazine. Rathore has taught at Jawaharlal Nehru University (JNU), University of Delhi, and Jindal Global University, India; Rutgers University and University of Pennsylvania, USA; University of Toronto, Canada; Humboldt University of Berlin, Germany; and Libera Università Internazionale degli Studi Sociali (LUISS) Guido Carli, Italy.

His twenty previous books range in theme from political philosophy, law, and religion to literature, sports, and wine. These include *Hegel's India: A Reinterpretation, with Texts* (2017) and *B.R. Ambedkar's The Buddha and His Dhamma: A Critical Edition* (2011). He is also the author of the forthcoming book, *B.R. Ambedkar: A Biography*.

Contributors

Matthew H. Baxter is assistant professor of political science at Ashoka University, the associate editor for South Asia at *Asian Survey*, and an associated researcher in Tamil studies at the Institut Français de Pondichéry. He previously held postdoctoral positions at the Center for Cultural Analysis, Rutgers University, New Jersey, and the Mahindra Humanities Center, Harvard University, Massachusetts, and served as a visiting scholar at the South Asia Program of Cornell University, New York, USA. He is interested in questions of comparative political theory, with particular focus on Tamil-speaking south India, non-Brahmin politics, and the worldwide circulation of critical imaginaries.

John Clammer is professor of sociology at O.P. Jindal Global University. He has published widely on the issues of culture and development. His books include *Culture, Development and Social Theory: Towards an Integrated Social Development* (2012), *Art, Culture and International Development: Humanizing Social Transformation* (2015), and most recently *Cultures of Transition and Sustainability* (2016). He is currently working on a book on cultural rights.

Bansidhar Deep teaches logic and philosophy at Jawaharlal College, Patnagarh, Odisha, and is a senior research fellow at the Centre for Philosophy in Jawaharlal Nehru University, New Delhi. His areas of interest include theory of lived experiences, epistemology, philosophical methods, phenomenology, hermeneutics, sociopolitical philosophy, ethics, philosophy of social sciences, feminist philosophy, contemporary Indian philosophy, and Ambedkar.

Priyanka Jha teaches political science at the School of Undergraduate Studies at Ambedkar University, Delhi. She was a junior fellow at the Max Weber Centre of Advanced Cultural and Social Studies, University of Erfurt, Germany, as part of the long-term research project 'Religious Individualisation in Historical Perspective', where she worked on Buddhism and the making of the idea of India. Her areas of interest include the history of ideas and political thought and theory. She is presently engaging with the issue of gendered intellectual history in South Asia.

Kanchana Mahadevan is professor at the Department of Philosophy, University of Mumbai. She researches and publishes in the areas of feminist philosophy, critical theory, hermeneutics, aesthetics and political thought, and postcolonial responses to European philosophy. Her book *Between Femininity and Feminism: Colonial and Postcolonial Perspectives on Care* was published in 2014. She has been a senior fellow with Justitia Amplificata at the Centre for Advanced Studies (a collaboration between Goethe University, Frankfurt, Frei University, Berlin, and Forschungskolleg Humanwissenschaften, Bad Homburg). She is presently working on a comparison between Indian secularism and European post-secularism from a gendered point of view.

Jadumani Mahanand teaches at OP Jindal Global University, Sonepat, India. He studied political science at the University of Hyderabad and submitted his PhD thesis at the Centre for Political Studies, Jawaharlal Nehru University, New Delhi. He works within political theory, especially on B.R. Ambedkar, critical theory, caste, and recognition. He has been a DAAD (German Academic Exchange Service) research fellow at the Centre for Modern Indian Studies, University of Gottingen, Germany.

Pramod K. Nayar teaches at the Department of English, University of Hyderabad. His most recent books include *Human Rights and Literature: Writing Right* (2014). His work on subaltern memoirs, graphic texts, and poetry have appeared in *Postcolonial Text*, *Ariel*, *Indian Journal of Gender Studies*, *Studies in South Asian Film and Media*, and the *Journal of Postcolonial Writing*, among others.

Y. Srinivasa Rao teaches history at Bharathidasan University, Tiruchirapalli, Tamil Nadu. His primary areas of research include the history of science and technology of colonial and postcolonial times, focusing majorly on the impact of science and technology on subaltern communities in south India. He has published articles on electricity and regional economy and colonialism, and the development of electricity in *Economic Political Weekly* and *Science Technology & Society* respectively. He is a regular contributor to *countercurrents.org* and *roundtableindia.co.in* on issues ranging from science and technology to caste, majoritarianism, and Dalit-Bahujans.

Raju Sakthivel is a philosopher and a critical thinker. His interests vary from critical theory to constitutional jurisprudence and from Pigou to Foucault, thoroughly grounded in various schools of philosophy, including post-modernism. He has been awarded a DLit by the International Tamil University, USA, for his distinguished contributions to Tamil prose and poetry and for his mastery over Tamil literature. He is a polyglot, knowing more than eight languages, including ancient Pali, Sanskrit, and Japanese. He has researched into the socio-linguistic traces among the Sakya Kulin people of Tamil Nadu, Andhra Pradesh, and Karnataka.

Laurence R. Simon is professor of International Development at Brandeis University and director of the Center for Global Development and Sustainability. At Brandeis, he is also one of the core faculty for the South Asian Studies Program and the Latin American and Latino Studies Program. Simon is also an instructor in sustainability studies at the Harvard University Summer School. His current research focuses on social movements and the psychological and cultural barriers to social change, and he has worked in Latin America, Sub-Saharan Africa, and Asia. He earned his PhD from the Graduate School of Geography at Clark University.

Debora Spini teaches at Syracuse University, New York, USA, and New York University in Florence, Italy. Her recent research focused on religion, politics, and the public space, with a special concentration on gender issues, monotheism and violence, and the rise of xenophobic populism. Spini is the author of various essays and book chapters in English and Italian. She has authored *La società civile postnazionale* (2006) and co-edited *Civil Society and International Governance* (2010, with D. Armstrong, J. Gilson, and V. Bello), *La coscienzaprotestante* (2016, with E. Bein Ricco), and *Words, Practice and Citizenships* (2016, with M. Dantini).